T0250278

Practical Machine Learning with R

This textbook is a comprehensive guide to machine learning and artificial intelligence tailored for students in business and economics. It takes a hands-on approach to teach machine learning, emphasizing practical applications over complex mathematical concepts. Students are not required to have advanced mathematics knowledge such as matrix algebra or calculus.

The author introduces machine learning algorithms, utilizing the widely used R language for statistical analysis. Each chapter includes examples, case studies, and interactive tutorials to enhance understanding. No prior programming knowledge is needed. The book leverages the tidymodels package, an extension of R, to streamline data processing and model workflows. This package simplifies commands, making the logic of algorithms more accessible by minimizing programming syntax hurdles. The use of tidymodels ensures a unified experience across various machine learning models.

With interactive tutorials that students can download and follow along at their own pace, the book provides a practical approach to apply machine learning algorithms to real-world scenarios.

In addition to the interactive tutorials, each chapter includes a Digital Resources section, offering links to articles, videos, data, and sample R code scripts. A companion website further enriches the learning and teaching experience.

This book is not just a textbook; it is a dynamic learning experience that empowers students and instructors alike with a practical and accessible approach to machine learning in business and economics.

Key Features:

- Unlocks machine learning basics without advanced mathematics — no calculus or matrix algebra required.
- Demonstrates each concept with R code and real-world data for a deep understanding — no prior programming knowledge is needed.
- Bridges the gap between theory and real-world applications with hands-on interactive projects and tutorials in every chapter, guided with hints and solutions.
- Encourages continuous learning with chapter-specific online resources—video tutorials, R-scripts, blog posts, and an online community.
- Supports instructors through a companion website that includes customizable materials such as slides and syllabi to fit their specific course needs.

Carsten Lange is an economics professor at Cal Poly Pomona with a keen interest in making data science and machine learning more accessible. He has authored multiple refereed articles and four books, including his 2004 book on applying neural networks for economics. Carsten is passionate about teaching machine learning and artificial intelligence with a focus on practical applications and hands-on learning.

Practical Machine Learning with R

Tutorials and Case Studies

Carsten Lange

CRC Press
Taylor & Francis Group
Boca Raton London New York

CRC Press is an imprint of the
Taylor & Francis Group, an **informa** business

A CHAPMAN & HALL BOOK

First edition published 2024
by CRC Press
2385 NW Executive Center Drive, Suite 320, Boca Raton FL 33431

and by CRC Press
4 Park Square, Milton Park, Abingdon, Oxon, OX14 4RN

CRC Press is an imprint of Taylor & Francis Group, LLC

© 2024 Carsten Lange

Library of Congress Cataloging-in-Publication Data

Names: Lange, Carsten, 1960- author.
Title: Practical machine learning with R : tutorials and case studies /
Carsten Lange.
Description: First edition. | Boca Raton, FL : CRC Press, 2024. | Includes
bibliographical references and index.
Identifiers: LCCN 2023051764 (print) | LCCN 2023051765 (ebook) | ISBN
9781032434056 (hbk) | ISBN 9781032434070 (pbk) | ISBN 9781003367147
(ebk)
Subjects: LCSH: Machine learning--Textbooks. | R (Computer program
language)--Textbooks. | Social sciences--Data processing--Textbooks.
Classification: LCC Q325.5 L358 2024 (print) | LCC Q325.5 (ebook) | DDC
006.3/1--dc23/eng/20240201
LC record available at https://lccn.loc.gov/2023051764
LC ebook record available at https://lccn.loc.gov/2023051765

ISBN: 978-1-032-43405-6 (hbk)
ISBN: 978-1-032-43407-0 (pbk)
ISBN: 978-1-003-36714-7 (ebk)

DOI: 10.1201/9781003367147

Typeset in Latin Modern font
by KnowledgeWorks Global Ltd.

Publisher's note: This book has been prepared from camera-ready copy provided by the authors.

To Jian and Max

Contents

List of Figures

List of Tables

1

Introduction

With rapid advancements in recent years, machine learning and artificial intelligence (AI) have become increasingly relevant and have already started transforming many businesses. Knowledge about machine learning and AI is critical not just for STEM (science, technology, engineering, and mathematics) majors but also in many other fields, including business, economics, and other social science majors.

To better prepare students for a future with *AI*, I started teaching machine learning in 2019 to help economics students to understand and apply fundamental machine learning principles. My goal is to combine theoretical concepts with hands-on projects to equip the students with the skills to solve real-world problems. When looking for a textbook, I found some excellent books covering the foundations and mathematical theories behind machine learning. Unfortunately, unlike STEM students, many business and economics students do not have the strong mathematics and programming background required to make use of these books. On the other side of the spectrum, machine learning books that target business majors are often too focused on applications and fall short of explaining quantitative methods. Recognizing that there is a need for a machine learning textbook that implements a hands-on approach, where students can interactively work step-by-step, and that introduces the quantitative concepts in a less mathematical way gave me the idea to write this book.

This book introduces machine learning algorithms and explains the underlying concepts without using higher mathematics concepts like matrix algebra or calculus. Each chapter provides examples, case studies, and interactive tutorials. The examples and hands-on tutorials use the *R* language, which is widely used for statistical analysis and data science. *R's* relatively simple syntax makes it easy for beginners to learn the language, making *R* a good choice for teaching machine learning. No prior programming skills are required to work with this book. A designated *R* chapter introduces the *R* skills needed for the course. In addition, each chapter offers one or more interactive *R* tutorials. Students can work with real-world data and use the interactive environment to learn and experiment with *R* code in a web browser.

1.1   How the Book is Organized

The order in which machine learning algorithms are introduced in this book
does not follow the traditional order of most other machine learning textbooks.
Most machine learning books cover theoretical concepts and terminologies
upfront before applying machine learning algorithms to solve problems.

In my experience, a more effective way of teaching machine learning is to introduce the basics of an algorithm and apply the model immediately. Along the
way, we will introduce the necessary terminology and theory when they become relevant and contextual to the specific workflow that is being explained.

A good example is the *k-Nearest Neighbors* algorithm, which is usually covered
in the later part of most textbooks. Here, *k-Nearest Neighbors* is the first
algorithm covered. The reason is that *k-Nearest Neighbors* can be explained
and applied without any prior knowledge in data science. Within the *k-Nearest
Neighbors* chapter, the concept of the *confusion matrix* is explained, which can
be used to interpret the *k-Nearest Neighbors* results and is needed for some of
the subsequent chapters.

The principle of introducing essential data science concepts and terminology
on a "when-needed basis" is reflected in the chapter titles. Most chapters are
titled with the machine learning algorithm covered in the chapter — together
with a subtitle reflecting the data science concept(s) introduced in connection
with the machine learning algorithm.

1.2   Using `tidymodels` for Data Processing and Model Workflows

The `tidymodels` package (Kuhn and Wickham (2020)), an extension of R, is
used throughout the book.[1] This package unifies and limits the commands
needed to work with the various machine learning algorithms regardless of
which machine learning model is used. Only a few lines must be adjusted when
a new machine learning model is introduced. The code is more intuitive and
easy to read, which allows readers to focus on the logic of the algorithms rather
than on programming syntax. Instead of reinventing the wheel and providing
new machine learning libraries, `tidymodels` provides wrappers for the most
common machine learning models in R. This way, the code is unified, but still,

---

[1]The `tidymodels` package is the successor of the `caret` package (Kuhn (2008)). Like the
`caret` package, it simplifies data processing and model workflow management, but `tidymodels`
provides additional functionalities in a more systematic way.

the most advanced and up-to-date libraries, such as *TensorFlow* and *PyTorch* are used.

1.3 Interactive Sections and Digital Resources

Each chapter contains one or more *interactive sections* marked with the compass symbol (◎) and also contains a section called *Digital Resources*.[2]

In the *interactive sections*, readers can use a provided web link to download a file, which can be executed in *RStudio*, the interactive development environment for *R*. When the file is executed in *RStudio*, all text, formulas, and graphs from the code blocks are shown in a web browser in a format similar to the book section. In addition, readers will be able to interactively work with the *R* code by solving exercises or experimenting with the provided *R* code (modifying function parameters, etc.). This hands-on approach allows students to apply a machine learning algorithm to real-world scenarios.

In addition to the interactive sections, each chapter also contains a *Digital Resources* section. These sections provide links to short articles, videos, data, and sample *R* code scripts. The most relevant digital resources are directly available through the *Digital Resource* sections at the end of each chapter. Additional digital resources are provided on a website that is linked to the *Digital Resource* section, which is expanded and updated on an ongoing basis.

1.4 Companion Website

The book comes with a companion website that provides additional materials for students and instructors.

You can access the companion website at: https://ai.lange-analytics.com

Student resources include:

- An extended version of the *Digital Resources* for each chapter (see Section 1.3 for details about digital resources).

- A moderated forum where readers can post questions or discuss content related to the topics in the book.

---

[2]Although great efforts are made to ensure that the interactive sections and digital resources are functional, no warranty of any kind is provided.

- A blog that covers topics related to the book chapters and, in many cases, allows a *deeper dive* into the concepts covered.

- Videos that complement the chapters of the book.

- A recommendation system where readers can post ideas for the book or report errors.

Instructor resources include:

- Presentation slides for each chapter. An instructor can use these slides out of the box or adjust them to the instructor's needs.

- Not every instructor will use all chapters and sections of the book, but deciding which topics to cover can be very time-consuming. Therefore, the companion website provides several syllabus outlines depending on the length of the related course, students' backgrounds, and if the course is taught in a semester or quarter system. The recommended outlines ensure that all concepts required for a particular chapter have been covered in the previous chapters. Instructors can use a web-based application to customize the outlines. This web app will then generate the related outline, ready to be used in a syllabus.

1.5   Acknowledgments

The author wishes to thank all who helped to make this book possible. Special thanks go out to my research assistant Xavier Padilla, who reviewed all chapters, gave valuable feedback, and caught many inconsistencies and calculation errors. I would also like to thank Sebastian Chinen, who helped with indexing and editing.

My proof reader Erica Orloff caught many formatting, spelling, and punctuation errors. I greatly appreciate her thorough work.

All remaining errors are mine alone.

I am also grateful to my family, to my wife, Jian, who patiently proofread the book at various stages, and to my son Max, who tirelessly wrote Python programs for the book. These Python programs automated many tasks of the interactive and the digital resource sections, which made it possible to integrate these sections seamlessly into the book.

Last but certainly not least, I would like to thank David Grubbs, Curtis Hill, and Robin Lloyd-Starkes from Taylor and Francis. They supported me through the whole writing process and always made themselves available when I needed help or advice.

2

Basics of Machine Learning

2.1 Learning Outcomes

This section outlines what you can expect to learn in this chapter. In addition, the corresponding section number is included for each learning outcome to help you to navigate the content, especially when you return to the chapter for review.

In this chapter, you will learn:

- How Machine Learning compares to Artificial Intelligence and Deep Learning (see Section 2.2).

- How machine learning algorithms can be categorized into regression, classification, and clustering algorithms. (see Section 2.3).

- How to use important terminology correctly in machine learning (see Section 2.4).

2.2 Machine Learning, Artificial Intelligence, and Deep Learning

The terms *Artificial Intelligence*, *Machine Learning*, and *Deep Learning* are often used synonymously. However, there is a clear distinction and hierarchy related to these terms (see Figure 2.1 for an overview):

Artificial Intelligence (AI) is defined as computer algorithms that perform tasks believed to be only performed by humans. This includes rule-based algorithms (e.g., detailed instructions for a robot to assemble a car) as well as data-based algorithms (e.g., to use historical data to calibrate a prediction model). Following this definition, *AI* applications include tasks such as advanced home automation, speech recognition (*Natural Language*

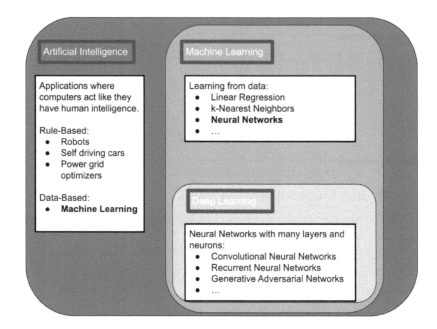

FIGURE 2.1 Artificial Intelligence, Machine Learning, and Deep Learning

Processing), Optical Character Recognition (OCR), self-driving cars, as well as systems that can produce art (see, for example, *Dall-E).*[1]

Machine Learning is a sub-field of *AI.* It is *data-based* rather than *rule-based.*

Data-based systems create the rules based on training data that are used to calibrate the machine learning model. Based on the training data, the algorithm finds the underlying rules internally.

In contrast, *rule-based* systems rely on experts to define rules that determine what to do in which situation. *Rule-based* systems are not considered *machine learning.*

Well-known machine learning algorithms include *Ordinary Least Square (OLS) Regression, Logistic Regression, k-Nearest Neighbors, Neural Networks, Random Forest,* and various cluster algorithms.

Deep Learning is a sub-field of machine learning. It uses *Neural Networks* as the core methodology.

---

[1] *Dall-E* is an *AI* system that can create realistic images and art from a description in natural language (see https://openai.com/dall-e-2/).

A *Neural Network* processes training data through layers of weighted non-linear functions (*neurons*). A learning algorithm successively updates the parameters of the *Neural Network* to improve the prediction quality (more about *Neural Networks* in Chapter 9).

If a *Neural Network* has many neurons (often millions or more) and if these neurons are organized into many layers, often with varying functionalities, the underlying algorithm is called a *Deep Learning* algorithm. Applications that usually require *Deep Learning* are *Natural Language Processing (NLP)*, advanced image recognition, and programming code completion.

Figure 2.1 shows how the above terms are related.

2.3 Machine Learning Tasks

Machine learning algorithms can be used for various purposes and can be categorized by the tasks they perform:

Regression: A regression seeks to predict a continuous variable. The prediction goal is to predict how large (or small) a specific outcome variable is — based on the fact that we know the values of other variables. Regression analysis can be linear (*OLS*). Or regression analysis can be non-linear. Examples include *Random Forest, Polynomial Regression*, and *Neural Networks*.

Classification: A classification algorithm seeks to predict a category. In many cases (including all cases covered in this book), the categories are limited to only two values, such as *Yes/No, Red Wine/White Wine*, or *True/False*. Most machine learning algorithms require the related categorical variables to be stored as an *R factor variable* (more about *factor variables* in Section 3.5.1).

Categories to be predicted can also have more than two values. These categories can be either *ordered* or *not ordered*. Examples of ordered categories include ratings such as *Good/Fair/Poor* or *Strongly Agree/Agree/Disagree/Strongly Disagree*. Examples of *unordered* categories include colors such as *Red/Blue/Green* or marital status such as *Single/Married/Widowed/Separated*.

Machine learning algorithms for *classification* include *Logistic Regression, k-Nearest Neighbors, Random Forest*, and *Neural Networks*.

Cluster Analysis: An algorithm performing *Cluster Analysis* seeks to sort observations into a given number of groups (clusters) based on variable values for each observation. The characteristics of the clusters and how many clusters are generated are often not determined before the analysis. The goal of the *Cluster Analysis* algorithm is to form clusters that are as homogeneous as possible inside each cluster and are as diverse as possible between different clusters.

Machine learning algorithms for *Cluster Analysis* include *Centroid-based Clustering* algorithms such as *k-Means*, *Hierarchical Clustering*, and *Distribution Clustering*. However, *Cluster Analysis* exceeds the scope of this book. To learn more about *Cluster Analysis* please refer to Wong (2023) for a brief overview and to Hennig et al. (2016) for a comprehensive book.

Looking at the above examples for *regression* and *classification*, you might have recognized that some algorithms can be used for both *regression* and *classification* (e.g., *Random Forest* and *Neural Networks*). In contrast, some algorithms can only be used exclusively for *regression* (e.g., *OLS Regression*) or *classification* (e.g., *Logistic Regression*).

2.4   Machine Learning Terminology

In this book, we will limit machine learning terminology to include only the essential terms. Terminology is important because when we communicate, we need to agree on the meaning of specific terms. This prevents misunderstandings and avoids defining terms over and over again.

In what follows, we define eight important machine learning terms which will be used frequently throughout the book:

Prediction: *Predicting* is to use the values of one or more known variables to estimate the value of an unknown variable (*outcome*). Predictions can be forecasts of an event in the future. For example, we might predict tomorrow's weather based on today's weather and on today's barometric change. However, Predictions are often not forecasts. For example, predicting the price of a house (today) based on its square footage (today).

Predictor vs. Outcome Variables: A predictor variable is a variable that is used to predict an outcome for an observation. The values of predictor variables are known, and they are used to predict the value of the outcome variable for the related observation. If the value of an outcome is based on a prediction, we add a *hat* ($\frown$) on top of the outcome variable. In contrast, if we know the value of the outcome variable from the data, we omit the *hat*.

Here is an example: Assume we want to predict the outcome variable $Price_i$ for a specific single-family home (this house would be our observation i), and the prediction is based on the house's square footage (predictor variable; $Sqft_i$). If the square footage of this house is $Sqft_i = 2,000$, a machine learning model might predict a price of $750,000 (outcome variable $\widehat{Price}_i = 750,000$)). Suppose we know from the data that the true value for the outcome variable is $800,000 ($Price_i = 800,000$), then we know that we underestimated the house price by $50,000 (more about prediction errors in Section 5.3).

Model: A *model* is what we use to predict the value of an outcome variable based on values of predictor variables given certain assumptions.

Suppose we try to predict home prices based on the square footage of houses using OLS regression, which assumes the relationship between the outcome price ($Price_i$) and the predictor square footage ($Sqft_i$) is linear. Then the related model could be expressed as:

$$\widehat{Price}_i = \beta_1 Sqft_i + \beta_2 \tag{2.1}$$

Equation (2.1) is our model. It models the relationship between the predictor $Sqft_i$ and the outcome $Price_i$. The model leads to a prediction of the house price ($\widehat{Price}_i$). We can use Equation (2.1) to calculate a predicted price for any value of the predictor variable $Sqft_i$, if we know the values for β_1 and β_2).

Fitted Model vs. Unfitted Model: Let us return to our model from Equation (2.1). Can we use the model to predict the price of a house if we know the house's square footage? The answer is "no" because we do not know the values for the βs (called the parameters of the model).

However, we can use a machine learning algorithm to determine the values for the parameters (the βs). Machine learning models often generate parameter values that minimize the (squared) prediction error. Using the values for the parameters (the βs) provided by the machine learning algorithm allows for predicting the outcome variable based on the value(s) of the predictor variable(s).

For example, suppose an OLS algorithm based on provided data determines that $\beta_1 = 300$ and that $\beta_2 = 150,000$ then our model would look like this:

$$\widehat{Price}_i = 300 \cdot Sqft_i + 150000 \tag{2.2}$$

A model where the parameters (the βs) have been determined by a machine learning algorithm based on training data like the one in Equation (2.2) is called a fitted model. A model where the parameters have yet to be determined and that, therefore, cannot be used for prediction (yet) is called an unfitted model (e.g., Equation (2.1)).

For instance, the *fitted model* displayed in Equation (2.2) can be used to predict the price for a house with a square footage of 2,000 sqft (predictor: $Sqft_i = 2,000$, predicted outcome: $\widehat{Price}_i = 750,000$),

Parameters: Parameters are the βs of a model. Machine learning algorithms generate the best parameter values according to a predefined goal (e.g., minimize the average squared error for all predictions for the provided training dataset).

Consequently, machine learning can be (over)simplified into the following three steps:

1. Determine the model (most models are more complex than the one in Equation (2.1)).

2. Use a machine learning algorithm to determine the optimal βs to create a *fitted model*.

3. Use the *fitted model* model to predict values for the outcome variable based on predictor variable values.

Training Data: Calibrating the parameters (the βs) of a machine learning model is a critical step in the model's calibration process. This process is called *training* a model and requires *training data*. A *training dataset* consists of the known values of the predictor variables and the corresponding known values of the outcome variable. Then, the training process calibrates the parameters to minimize the difference between the model's predictions and the actual values of the outcome variable from the training data. In other words, the training process strives to minimize the prediction error (more about training data in Chapter 6.3).

Testing Data: When using the training data to calibrate the parameters, most but not all of the observations are used. Those observations that are not used for training constitute the *testing data*. About 10% – 40% of the total observations are commonly used as *testing data*. They are usually randomly chosen from the complete dataset. *Testing data* are never used to optimize model performance in any way. Instead, they are a holdout dataset used to assess the predictive quality of a model.

Note, using *training data* to assess predictive quality is not an option! This is because we would measure how well the model can approximate the data it was trained with rather than assessing the predictive quality on new data. That is, the *testing data the model has never seen before* (more about testing data in Chapter 6.3).

2.5 Digital Resources

Below you will find a few digital resources related to this chapter such as:

- Videos
- Short articles
- Tutorials
- *R* scripts

These resources are recommended if you would like to review the chapter from a different angle or to go beyond what was covered in the chapter.

Here we show only a few of the digital resourses. At the end of the list you will find a link to additonal digital resources for this chapter that are maintained on the Internet.

You can find a complete list of digital resources for all book chapters on the companion website: https://ai.lange-analytics.com/digitalresources.html

What is AI?

A short (5 min) video by Cassie Kozyrkov, former Chief Decision Scientist at Google. Although AI is not clearly defined in the literature, Cassie Kozyrkov attempts (successfully) to provide a concise definition.

Link: https://ai.lange-analytics.com/dr?a=332

What is Machine Learning?

A short (3 min) video by Cassie Kozyrkov, former Chief Decision Scientist at Google about what is considered machine learning.

Link: https://ai.lange-analytics.com/dr?a=327

Why Use Machine Learning?

A short (3 min) video by Cassie Kozyrkov, former Chief Decision Scientist at Google. In this video, Cassie Kozyrkov explains why and how machine learning can be useful.

Link: https://ai.lange-analytics.com/dr?a=328

The Basic Idea Behind Machine Learning Algorithms

A short (5 min) video by Cassie Kozyrkov, former Chief Decision Scientist at Google. In the video, Cassie Kozyrkov gives a very basic and intuitive idea of how some machine learning algorithms work.

Link: https://ai.lange-analytics.com/dr?a=329

More Digital Resources

Only a subset of digital resources is listed in this section. The link below points to additional, concurrently updated resources for this chapter.

Link: https://ai.lange-analytics.com/dr/mlintro.html

3

Introduction to R and RStudio

R is a free programming language and environment for statistical computing (R Core Team (2022)). *R* is usually used together with the Integrated Development Environment (*IDE*) *RStudio* (RStudio Team (2022)). *RStudio* provides a graphical user interface for coding, debugging, and testing in *R*. Throughout this book, *R* is used together with *RStudio* to prepare data and to process machine learning algorithms.

This chapter aims to provide the reader with the necessary *R* knowledge. The content will cover only *R* commands and functionality essential to work with the sample *R* code used in the book in order to keep it short and simple. For a comprehensive coverage of *R*, see Wickham and Grolemund (2017) and Wickham (2019).

Every beginner or intermediate user of *R* is strongly encouraged to thoroughly work through this chapter since it describes workflows used later when working with machine learning. Advanced *R* users should at least skim through the chapter to get familiar with the workflows.

Keep in mind that there is often more than one good way to solve the same problem in *R*. For the sake of simplicity, this chapter selects the method preferred by the author. The intention here is not to claim that this method is the best, but to show examples that are adequate and clear.

At the end of this chapter you will find two interactive sections (see Sections 3.10 and 3.11). These interactive sections contain a project and exercises together with code blocks that you can load, modify, and execute in *RStudio*. To understand a programming language like *R*, it is essential that you engage in hands-on experimentation with the language.

You can find links to Digital Resources such as videos and other resources in Section 3.12. These resources will help you to improve your knowledge of *R* further.

3.1 Learning Outcomes

This section outlines what you can expect to learn in this chapter. In addition, the corresponding section number is included for each learning outcome to help you to navigate the content, especially when you return to the chapter for review.

In this chapter, you will learn:

- How to install R and RStudio (see Section 3.2).

- How to work with the standard window layout in RStudio (see Section 3.3).

- How to set up RStudio (see Section 3.3).

- How to create a project (folder) in *RStudio* (see Section 3.3).

- How to use major functionalities of RStudio (see Section 3.3).

- How to extend *R*'s functionality with R packages, and which packages you should install for this book (see Section 3.4).

- How to store different types of data in R (see Section 3.5).

- How to name R variables and objects in a systematic and easy to read way (see Section 3.6).

- How *R* displays very big and very small numerical values (see Section 3.7).

- How R commands are structured (see Section 3.8).

- How data processing and analysis can be streamlined using the tidyverse package (see Section 3.9).

- How you can create a small project to investigate the *Titanic* disaster (see the interactive Section 3.10).

- How you can apply what you have learned in this chapter in 14 short, interactive exercises (see the exercises in Section 3.11).

3.2 Install and Set Up R and RStudio

A typical setup to work with *R* consists of two components:

1. The R software which executes *R* code.

2. RStudio, where you can write, debug, and test *R* code.

These two components are two different programs. Therefore, *R* and *RStudio* need to be installed separately. It is crucial to install *R* before *RStudio*.

You can download *R* at: https://cran.r-project.org/bin/.

You can download *RStudio* at: https://www.rstudio.com/products/rstudio/download/#download.

If you have an older version of *R* or *RStudio* installed, upgrading to the latest version is strongly recommended. Use your operating system's uninstall procedure to uninstall *R* and *RStudio* before installing the latest versions. If you do not uninstall your old *R* version, the new version of *R* will be installed parallel to your old version, which is, in most cases, undesirable.

Links to detailed installation guides are provided in the Digital Resource Section 3.12 at the end of this chapter.

3.3 RStudio the Integrated Development Environment (IDE) for *R*

RStudio is a software development environment that assists in writing *R* code in a straightforward and user-friendly way. It is the most commonly used IDE for the *R* language.

3.3.1 The Window Layout in RStudio

Regardless, if *R* and *RStudio* are installed on *Windows*, *macOS*, or *Linux*, the *RStudio* windows will look similar to the ones displayed in Figure 3.1.

The lower-left window contains the R Console: Here, the user can execute *R* code directly by typing the code. For example, the user can type 1+2 and hit the Enter key (Return on *Mac*). *R* then executes the code and displays 3 as the result.

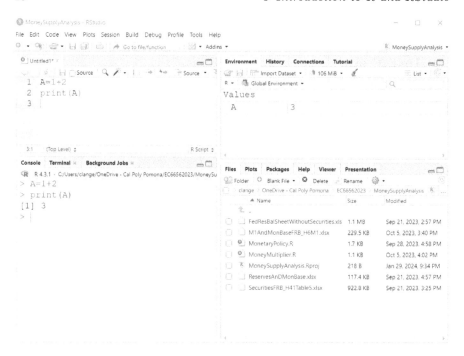

FIGURE 3.1 The RStudio Windows

Typing code directly into the *R Console* is not recommended because this workflow does not take full advantage of the *RStudio* IDE.

The upper-left window displays the code from R files: The   most commonly used files in *RStudio* are *R* script files. These files are text files and contain *R* code with one *R* command on each line. You can execute a command by placing the cursor in the respective line of the *R* script and hitting CTRL-Enter (CMD-Return on *Mac*). The command in the line is then executed, and the cursor moves to the next line (command). This allows you to execute an *R* script sequentially line-by-line by repeatedly hitting CTRL-Enter (CMD-Return on *Mac*).

When opening an *R* script file, it opens in the left-upper window in *RStudio* (see Figure 3.1). To create a new *R* script, you can use the *RStudio* menu (File -> New File -> R Script) and then use File -> Save As ... to save it in your *project folder* (more about *projects* and *project folders* below).

In the *R* script in Figure 3.1 the user typed A=1+2 and hit CTRL-Enter (CMD-Return on *Mac*) while the cursor was somewhere in the first line of the *R* script. As a result, the code line was copied to the *R Console* window and executed. 1+2 was assigned to the variable *A*. The second line of the *R* script window was executed in the same way (CTRL-Enter or CMD-Return on *Mac*) to print the value of A to the *R Console* window. This approach is better than typing directly into the *R Console* window because the code can be saved as an *R* script file (file extension .R) and is, therefore, reproducible.

The lower-right window contains the Files tab: This tab displays all files available in a project folder (see Figure 3.1). In the same window, you can choose different tabs. For example, you can display *R* plot output (tab Plots) or a list of installed packages (tab Packages).

The upper-right window contains the Environment tab: This   tab displays the content of *R* objects. Initially empty, but when a user assigns content like a number to an *R* object, the object and its content are displayed in the *Environment* tab in the upper-right window. For example, after the user assigned A=1+2 to the *R* object A, the entry A: 3 is shown in the *Environment* tab (see Figure 3.1).

When an *R* object is more complex, such as a *data frame* (more about *data frames* in Section 3.5.2), the user can click on it, and *RStudio* will open it in a separate window.

3.3.2   RStudio Configuration

Using the *RStudio* menu (Tools -> Global Options), you can configure *RStudio* in many ways. We recommend being conservative with changing options when you are not absolutely sure about the consequences.

However, it is strongly recommended to change the following settings:

- Use Tools -> Global Options, and then disable Restore .RData into workspace at startup.

- Set the option Save workspace to .RData on exit. to *Never*.

Saving the *R workspace* (the content of all *R* objects) when closing an *R* session is not necessary when working with *R* scripts because all *R* objects can be re-created with a few clicks as long as the *R* script has been saved before. Keeping *R* workspaces between *R* sessions can lead to confusion and errors. Note that setting the Global Options as described above needs only to be done once for any given *RStudio* installation.

Another good practice is to assign a specific hard drive folder to each data science project. You decide what you consider a project. Afterward, all files will always be saved into the specified **R Project Folder**.

When you work with that project, *RStudio* will save and load all files from/into this project folder by default.

You mark a folder as an *R Project Folder* by creating an **R Project** using the *RStudio* menu. Assuming the folder already exists, you can create an *R*

Project for this folder with `File -> New Project ... -> Existing Directory`.[1]
Creating an *R* project ensures that *R* will always open and save *R* scripts or
data files from and into this folder, respectively. In addition, when resuming
work on a project, one can open a recently used *R Project* with just a few clicks
(`File -> Recent Projects`). This is faster and more convenient than navigating
through the directory tree with a file explorer tool. Another advantage is that
all related files are shown in the `Files` tab in the lower-right window after the
project opens.

At the end of this chapter, in the Digital Resources section 3.12, a 5-minute
video details the procedure to create a project.

3.4   R Packages

R provides many functionalities for statistical research, including tools to organize and clean data, visualize data, and run machine learning algorithms.
If all of these commands were loaded into memory at startup, the *R* program
would require a lot of computer memory. To avoid this, *R* comes only with
minimal functionality when first installed. Then, the user can add *R* packages,
which provide additional functionality. This way, in any given *R* session, only
functionality required for the particular data science project is loaded.

To use an *R* package, two steps are required:

1. The new package has to be downloaded from the *CRAN* server
   (*Comprehensive R Archive Network*) and saved on your computer's
   hard drive. This only needs to be done once for each *R* installation. To download and install a package on your hard drive, click
   `Tools` in the menu bar and choose `Install packages ....` Then, enter
   the package name into the entry field and leave `Install Dependen-`
   `cies` checked. This way, all other packages that your new package
   depends on are also automatically downloaded and saved.

   Allthough you can also download packages from other repositories,
   packages provided through *CRAN* are authoritative because they
   are peer-reviewed and tested before being available on *CRAN*. Thus,
   the chance of downloading a low-quality or malicious package is low.

2. Before working with a package, it must be loaded into the *R* memory
   by executing the `library()` command. The `library()` command for
   each package needs to be executed only once for each *R* session.

---

[1]When choosing `New Directory`, *RStudio* will create a new directory for the project directory.

It is good coding practice to place all `library()` commands at the beginning of an *R* script.

Below is an example of how the `tidyverse`, the `rio`, the `janitor`, and the `tidymodels` packages can be loaded after they have been installed on the user's hard drive:

```
library(tidyverse)
library(rio)
library(janitor)
library(tidymodels)
```

It is good programming practice to only load those packages into an *R* script that are needed to execute the code of the script.

Frequently used *R* packages in this book are listed below:

- The `tidyverse` package (Wickham et al. (2019)) supports easy and straight-forward data processing. It is the most commonly used *R* package.

- The `rio` package (Chan et al. (2021)) allows to load various data formats with one `import()` command. Files can be loaded from the user's hard drive or the Internet.

- The `janitor` package (Firke (2023)) provides functionality for cleaning and renaming variable names to avoid spaces and special characters.

- The `tidymodels` package (Kuhn and Wickham (2020)) streamlines data engineering and machine learning tasks.

- The `kableExtra` package (Zhu (2021)) renders tables in *HTML* or *PDF* formats.

- The `learnr` package (Aden-Buie et al. (2022)) is needed together with the `shiny` package (Chang et al. (2022)) for the interactive projects and exercises in this book.

- The `shiny` package (Chang et al. (2022)) is needed together with the `learnr` (Aden-Buie et al. (2022)) package for the interactive projects and exercises in this book.

The author strongly recommends installing the packages listed above immediately. This way, when a package is used later in a specific chapter, it can be loaded into memory with `library()` without downloading it first. Installing the packages does take a while (be patient), but it only needs to be done once.

3.5   How R Stores Data

Every programming language needs containers to store and retrieve data. *R* uses *R* objects for this purpose, and it is essential to understand the concept of *R* objects to be able to use *R* with this book.

R objects are very similar to variables in algebra. Like a variable in algebra, an R object is a container that can store data such as numerical values and retrieve them when needed. However, in contrast to variables in algebra, an *R* object stores not only numerical values. It can also store letters and words (`characters`), data plots, and even the settings and results of complete machine learning models. This capacity of being able to store much more than only numerical values makes an *R* object an *object*, rather than a variable.

> ### R Objects are Containers to Store Various Content
>
> *R* objects are very similar to algebra variables. R objects are like containers that can store various types of content such as:
>
> - various Data Types,
> - plots,
> - empirical models,
> - and other more advanced content.

In the following sections, you will learn about *Data Types* that *R* supports and about *R* objects that *R* uses to store data.

Understanding both concepts is important because some of the machine learning algorithms we will cover in the following chapters will only accept specific *Data Types* and *Data Objects* as data input.

The two concepts *Data Types* and *Data Objects* can be distinguished as follows:

Data Types determine what is stored. Examples include `numerical` values, *characters*, and `logical` values (see Section 3.5.1 for more details).

Data Objects vary in the way data is stored. Examples include storing data as *single values*, as *vectors*, or as *data frames* (see Section 3.5.2 for more details).

3.5.1   R Data Types

To reiterate, *Data Types* determine which type of information is stored. In order to keep it simple, we will cover only the most commonly used R *Data Types*:[2]

- Numerical data type (num)

- Character data type (chr)

- Logic data type (logic)

- Factor data type (factor)

Numerical Data Type (num):

The numerical data type stores numerical values. Numerical values are used when performing any type of arithmetic calculation. In contrast, ZIP codes are not numerical because they are usually not used for calculations. Numerical values can be discrete (integer) or continuous (double). Note that the distinction between integer and double is not very important for this book, but you should know that integer and double values are both numerical values.

Character Data Type (chr):

In *R*, an object that provides for storing a sequence of characters, numbers, and/or symbols that sometimes form a word or even a sentence is called a character data type. Examples include first or last names, street addresses, or ZIP codes. The latter could also be stored as a numerical data type, which is bad coding practice but will not cause problems in most cases.

Note that what is called a character in *R* is often called a *string* in other programming languages.

You must surround character *Data Types* with quotation marks to distinguish them from object names. For example, if you want to assign the characters "Hello world!" to an *R* object called MyText, you must write it as shown in the *R* code block below:

```
MyText="Hello world!"
print(MyText)
```

```
## [1] "Hello world!"
```

In the example above, the print() command was used to output the object value of the MyText object to the *Console*.

---

[2]We omit *Data Types* raw and complex, which are rarely used and are not relevant for this book.

Note that the object name MyText in the R code block above is not in quotes, but the string *Hello world!* is surrounded by quotes.

Forgetting the quotes for characters is a common beginner mistake in R, but fortunately, R throws an error that points the user in the right direction when quotes are missing. You can see this in the example below where we purposely left out the quotes around *Hello*:

```
MyText=Hello
```

```
## Error: object 'Hello' not found
```

R complains by outputting the error message "Error: object 'Hello' not found" and that is correct because no object named *Hello* was ever defined. Instead, we should have assigned the character value "Hello" to the R object called MyText!

Rather than printing an R object containing a text as it was done above, we can alternatively print directly with print("Hello world!") or we can use the cat() command that allows us to print a combination of objects and text separated by comma(s):

```
MyText="Hello world!"
cat("The content of the character object is:", MyText)
```

```
## The content of the character object is: Hello world!
```

The cat() command above concatenates the character value "The content of the character object is:" with the content of the R object MyText and automatically adds a *space* character between them.

Logic Data Type (logic):

In R, a data type that stores the logic states TRUE and FALSE, is called a logic data type.[3] Different logic data type objects can be combined using "and" (&) and "or" (|). See, for example, the *Truth-Table* displayed in Table 3.1, which shows how pairs of True and False assigned to the R objects A and B are evaluated when connected with "and" (&) and "or" (|).

Internally, R stores a value of 1 for TRUE and a value of 0 for FALSE. This allows calculations on logical data, such as TRUE+FALSE+TRUE, which evaluates to 2. If this confuses you, don't worry. It will become clear when we work with R code and Logic values later in Section 3.12.

---

[3] Another term often used in mathematics for this data type is Boolean.

TABLE 3.1 Truth-Table for AND and OR

R object A	R object B	A and B	A or B
A	B	A&B	A|B
TRUE	TRUE	TRUE	TRUE
TRUE	FALSE	FALSE	TRUE
FALSE	TRUE	FALSE	TRUE
FALSE	FALSE	FALSE	FALSE

We could also store variables that are either TRUE or FALSE as numerical variables, such as 1 for TRUE and 0 for FALSE. Although this is done more often than not in data science research, it is not best practice to do so.

Factor Data Type (factor):

A factor is an *R* data type that stores categorical data in an effective way. To understand what a factor is, we must first understand what categorical data are. For instance, first or last names are not categorical data because there are a vast number of different first or last names. As explained before, they are stored as character data.

In contrast, categorical data usually have only a (very) limited amount of variations. For example, the categorical *R* object MarriageStatus can be limited to "Never Married", "Married", "Widowed", or "Divorced". Because only a limited number of categories are available (four different categories in the example), we call MarriageStatus an *R* object that stores categorical data.

Although categorical data can be stored as character data type, it is more efficient to store categorical data as a factor. *R* will internally assign 1 for "Never Married", 2 for "Married", 3 for "Widowed", and 4 for "Divorced" (1, 2, 3, and 4 are called levels in *R*). Next, *R* will internally store the coding of the level and save the actual data just as 1, 2, 3, and 4. This will save memory because "1" takes less memory than "Never Married", 2 less than "Married", and so forth. It all happens behind the scene, and the *R* user normally needs not to be bothered about it.

There are also other reasons to use the factor data type besides memory. The main reason is that a factor data type signals *R* that the *R* object stores categorical data, which often require special treatment. This will become important later when we work with classification problems in machine learning algorithms. These algorithms usually require a factor as an *outcome* variable.

3.5.2 R Object Types

Now that we know the main *Data Types* of *R*, we can start exploring how these *Data Types* are stored in various *R* objects. The list of possible *R* object types is very long because every R package developer can design their own R object type. However, throughout this book, we will use only a few different types of R objects, and we will present some of them here:

Objects that Store a Single Value:

R can store a single value of type numerical, character, or logic in an R object by assigning the value to the object. Assigning values to R objects can be done either with an "=" or the "<-"-sign. Both are equivalent in functionality, while only the latter is correct in a mathematical sense. Nevertheless, we will use the "="-sign throughout this book to assign data to R objects for simplicity.

Below are a few examples:

```
A=123.768
B=3
C="Hello World"
IsLifeGood=TRUE
```

Vector-Objects:

In R, a vector object can store a sequence of elements of the same data type such as a sequence of character, numerical, or logical values, but a mix of different *Data Types* in a single vector is not allowed.[4]

The command c() (c stands for combine) can be used to assign values to an R vector object. Below are a few examples related to the weather forecast for the next three days:

```
VecTemp=c(70, 68, 55)
VecWindSpeed=c("low","low","high")
VecIsSunny=c(TRUE,TRUE,FALSE)
```

We can use a command such as mean() to calculate the mean of a vector with numerical *Data Types* or the command length() to calculate the number of entries in a vector:

```
MeanForecTemp=mean(VecTemp)
cat("The average forecasted temperature is", MeanForecTemp)
```

```
## The average forecasted temperature is 64.33
```

---

[4]There is another more flexible R object called a list that can store a mix of Data Types in one R object and even can store other lists, but this is outside the scope of this introduction.

```
ForecDays=length(VecTemp)
cat("The forecast is for", ForecDays, "days.")
```

```
## The forecast is for 3 days.
```

Data Frame Object:

R can store a complete data table with rows and columns in an object. We refer to such a data table as a data frame object.

A data frame is very similar to an *Excel* table. The first row of a data frame defines the names of the variables that are stored in the columns — similar to a title row in *Excel*. The following rows of a data frame (starting with row two) contain the values for the observations stored in the data frame. Each row is one observation.

Each data frame column contains a named variable related to the observations. The variable's name is the first entry in the column, and the related values are stored in the following entries. These values can be of various *Data Types* such as char, numeric, or factor — you can have different Data Types for different columns. However, each column can have only one data type.

You can think of a data frame as a combination of R *vectors* arranged in the data frame's columns. In fact, you can extract a data frame column as a vector by combining the data frame name and the column name (the variable name) — separated with a "$"-sign.

Survived	Pclass	Name	Sex	Age	SiblingsSpousesAboard	ParentsChildrenAboard	FareInPounds
0	3	Mr. Owen Harris Braund	male	22	1	0	7.2500
1	3	Miss. Laina Heikkinen	female	26	0	0	7.9250
0	3	Mr. William Henry Allen	male	35	0	0	8.0500
0	3	Mr. James Moran	male	27	0	0	8.4583
1	1	Miss. Elizabeth Bonnell	female	58	0	0	26.5500

FIGURE 3.2 Screenshot of the View() Window

Let us use the famous *Titanic* dataset as an example of how to work with *data frames*: Figure 3.2 displays five observations from the data frame DataTitanic. We used the import() command from the rio package to load the *Titanic* dataset from the Internet and assigned it to *data frame* DataTitanic:[5]

```
library(rio)
DataTitanic=import("https://ai.lange-analytics.com/data/Titanic.csv")
```

---

[5]The dataset provided here was obtained using the *R* package titanic (see Hendricks (2015)).

The content of Figure 3.2 was created with `View(DataTitanic)`. The `View()` command can only be used in the *Console* of *RStudio*. It is a very useful command as it displays a complete scrollable view of a *data frame*.

Figure 3.2 reflects what you learned about *data frames*:

- The first row contains the names of the variables that are related to the observations (passengers).

  The variable *Name* is a `character` variable, *Sex* is a categorical variable (with categories *male* and *female*).[6] All other variables are numerical variables.[7]

- The observations (here: the first five passengers) are in the rows (starting with Row 2).

We can extract the *Age* variable as an *R* `vector` object and then use the `mean()` command to calculate the average age of the *Titanic* passengers:

```
VecAge=DataTitanic$Age
mean(VecAge)
```

```
## [1] 29.47
```

In the last line of the code block above, we did not assign the output of the `mean()` command to an *R* object. Output not assigned to any object will be outputted to the *Console*. As you can see, the average age of *Titanic* passengers was 29.47.

You can also find out how many passengers are considered in the data frame `DataTitanic`, as this coincides with the number of rows (observations) of `DataTitanic`. You can apply the `length()` command to any vector from the data frame `DataTitanic` to find the number of rows, as follows:

```
cat("Number of observations:", length(DataTitanic$Name))
```

```
## Number of observations: 887
```

You cannot apply the `length()` command directly to a data frame, but you can find the number of rows (the number of observations) directly from a data frame with:

---

[6]Note that *R* did assign the data type `char` and not `factor` to the variable *Sex*. This is because *R* cannot determine that *Sex* is a categorical variable. However, a user can use the command `as_factor()` from the `tidyverse` package to convert *Sex* to a `factor`.

[7]As in the original *Titanic* dataset, *Survived* is stored as a `numerical` variable with 1 for a surviving passenger and 0 otherwise. It would have been better coding practice to store *Survived* as a `logical` variable with values `TRUE` and `FALSE` (see Section 3.5.1).

```
cat("Number of observations:", nrow(DataTitanic))
```

```
## Number of observations: 887
```

In the two code blocks above, we nested the `length()` and the `nrow()` commands within the `cat()` command to generate a more informative output. In general, you are free to nest *R* commands into each other to any level you choose, but the readability of your code might suffer.

R data frames come in two varieties: i) original data frames from *base R*, which are called `data frame` and ii) a slightly more advanced version from the `tidyverse` package called a `tibble`. In older versions of *R* (before Version 4.0), there were quite a few differences between the two versions, but currently, the *base R data frame* object has been significantly improved, and both object types are almost identical. Therefore, we will treat the *base R data frame object* and the *tibble object* synonymously throughout this book.[8]

Later in this chapter, we will work with the *Titanic* dataset again. For now, it is essential to remember that data frames consist of columns representing variables (with the variable names in the first row) and rows representing the observations in the second and following rows. We can extract a variable as a vector by combining the data frame name with the variable name, separated with a "$"-sign.

When working in the *RStudio* environment, the content of a data frame can be displayed by clicking on the icon next to the data frame's name in the `environment` tab of the upper-right *RStudio* window. This opens a separate window that allows scrolling and sorting of the data frame.

Advanced Objects:

Advanced objects in *R* include *R* objects such as *plot-objects* or *model-objects*. These more complex objects typically contain instructions, data, results from statistical models, and more. We usually do not have to deal with details of these objects and leave it to the *R* program to process them appropriately. However, we will introduce commands to extract specific information from advanced objects later in Chapter 5.

Summary:

Figure 3.3 summarizes how *Data objects* can be categorized into various *R* objects such as *Single Value* objects, *Vector* objects, or *Data Frames*. Figure 3.3 also shows which *Data Types* these objects can store.[9]

---

[8]If needed, a regular *data frame* can be converted into a *tibble* with the `as_tibble()` command.

[9]For a more detailed overview of *R* objects and *Data Types* refer to Sanchez (2021), Chapter 2.5.

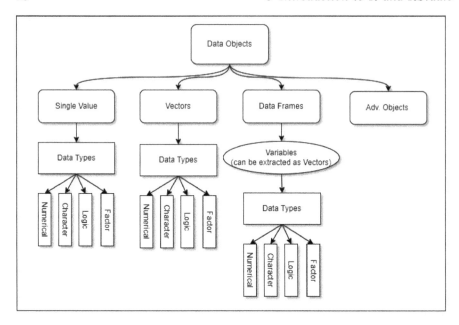

FIGURE 3.3 Data Objects and Data Types

3.6   Naming Rules for R Objects

After discussing different *R* objects, the remaining question is, are there any rules for naming these objects when writing code.

Based on your experience with high school math, you might tend to write object names with a single character, such as *X* or *Y*. You are free to do this in *R*, and in some cases it might be a good choice. However, using multiple letters for object names is recommended in most cases, as this makes your code more readable. How long your object names should be is a matter of style and taste. Too long convolutes your code; too short is not descriptive enough.

In any case, it is recommended to follow the rules that are listed below:

- An object name must start with a letter (mandatory) and no special characters such as space, "%", "$", ".", "_", or "#" should appear in object names unless required by the *R* syntax. The reason not to use special characters in object names is that some of these special characters have a distinct meaning in *R*, and some are reserved for use with specific packages.

- An object name should start with a capital letter, and the following letters are lowercase until a new word begins with a capital letter, regardless of what English grammar suggests. This type of capitalization is called *Upper-Camel*-notation. There are reasonable alternatives[10] to *UpperCamel*, but for consistency reasons, we use *UpperCamel* to name objects throughout the book. Below is an example:

```
DataPopulationGrowth=DataImpFromExcel
```

- In what follows, the first part of an *R* object name will indicate the object type such as *Data* in `DataStocks`, *Vec* in `VecLong` (for a vector), *Plot* in `PlotVarXY` (for a plot object), or *Model* in `ModelOLS` (for the results from a model). If applicable, we will also start `logic` *R* objects with the word `Is` to indicate that we are working with a condition (e.g., `IsWeatherGood=TRUE`). These rules are not required, but they make the code easier to read.

3.7 How R Displays Very Big and Very Small Numbers

Sometimes in data science projects, we work with very big numbers and also very small numbers. For example, at the writing of this book, the 2022 GDP (current dollars) of the U.S. is estimated to be $25.5 trillion or $25,500,000,000,000.

An example of a very small number is the chance of being struck by lightning: The probability of getting struck by lightning in the U.S. is about 0.00000000365 on any randomly chosen day.[11]

How should we work in *R* with such big or small numbers? Obviously, using them as they are, is not a good option. Instead, we can express numbers in scientific notation.

Let us start with the big GDP number: We could write the GDP as a number with one leading digit and state how many digits the decimal point should be moved to the right. Such as:

2.55; move decimal point 13 digits to the right

This method might be a little better than writing out a big number, but it

---

[10]Alternatives to *UpperCamel* include *lowerCamel*, or *snake_case* (see Wikipedia contributors (2023a) for details).

[11]"In the United States, a person has an estimated 1:10,000-lifetime risk of being struck by lightning"(Jensen et al. (2021)). Therefore, assuming a life span of 75 years and 365.25 days on average per year, the probability of getting struck by lightning on a random day is $\frac{1}{10,000 \cdot 365.25 \cdot 75} = 0.00000000365$.

is not well suited for calculations. However, if we consider that moving the
decimal point one decimal to the right is the same as multiplying by 10, moving
it two digits is the same as multiplying by 100, and three digits is equivalent
to a multiplication by 1000, and so on. Then we can write the GDP as:

$$GDP = 2.55 \cdot 10,000,000,000,000$$
$$\Longleftrightarrow$$
$$GDP = 2.55 \cdot 10 \cdot 10 \cdot 10 \cdot 10 \cdot 10 \cdot 10 \cdot 10 \cdot 10 \cdot 10 \cdot 10 \cdot 10 \cdot 10 \cdot 10$$
$$\Longleftrightarrow$$
$$GDP = 2.55 \cdot 10^{13}$$

The last equation writes the big GDP number in scientific notation.

We can do the same for very small numbers. For example, the probability of
getting struck by lighting. In this case, we move the decimal point to the left
because we work with a very small number. This can be done through division
by 10 for one digit, by division by 100 for two digits, and so on:

$$ProbLight = 3.65; \text{ move decimal point 9 digits to the left}$$
$$\Longleftrightarrow$$
$$ProbLight = \frac{3.65}{10 \cdot 10 \cdot 10 \cdot 10 \cdot 10 \cdot 10 \cdot 10 \cdot 10 \cdot 10}$$
$$\Longleftrightarrow$$
$$ProbLight = \frac{3.65}{10^9}$$
$$\Longleftrightarrow$$
$$ProbLight = 3.65 \cdot 10^{-9}$$

In summary, we can write both *GDP* and *ProbLight* in scientific notation as
done below:

$$GDP = 2.15 \cdot 10^{13}$$
$$ProbLight = 3.422 \cdot 10^{-9}$$

What does *R* do when we present it with these very big and very small numbers?

```
GDP=21500000000000
ProbLight=0.00000000365
cat("GDP:", GDP)
```

```
## GDP: 2.15e+13
```

```
cat("ProbLight:", ProbLight)
```

```
## ProbLight: 3.65e-09
```

R uses *almost* scientific notation except for substituting the "10 to the power of ..." with the lowercase letter *e*. This notation is not very pretty, and it is certainly not mathematically correct, but almost all statistical programs use this pseudo-scientific notation.[12]

What did you learn? When you see *R* output for very big or small numbers, you know now how to interpret the number following the letter *e*. This number tells you how many digits you have to shift the decimal point to the *right* (when the number is positive) or to the *left* (when the number is negative).

3.8   The Structure of R Commands

When working with *R* commands and especially when combining several *R* commands (piping; see Section 3.9.4), it is crucial to understand the principle structure of *R* commands.

As you have already seen, in commands like `mean()` or `sum()`, an *R* command consists of the command's name followed by a pair of parentheses. Inside the parentheses, the user can provide information for one or more arguments for the command.

In the example below, we again extract the age of the *Titanic* passengers from the data frame `DataTitanic` and store it in the *R* vector object `VecAge` (see Section 3.5.2 for more details). Then we use the `mean()` and the `median()` commands to calculate mean and median age of *Titanic* passengers:

```
library(rio)
DataTitanic=import("https://ai.lange-analytics.com/data/Titanic.csv")
VecAge=DataTitanic$Age
cat("Mean:", mean(x=VecAge))
cat("Median:", median(VecAge))
```

```
## Mean: 29.47
```

```
## Median: 28
```

---

[12]The reason for not writing out "10 to the power of ..." in the mathematically correct way stems from the time when the displays of electronic calculators could only display very simple symbols.

The two examples above already reveal some important properties regarding the structure of *R* commands:

- Each argument in a command has a name. For example, the name for the *data argument* in the mean() and median() commands is x, like in many other commands. Note that x and data are common names for the *data argument* in *R* commands. x=VecAge assigns the data from the *R* vector object VecAge explicitly to the x argument.

- *R* does not require the user to use the arguments' names as long as the values for the arguments are provided in the correct order. For example, x is the first argument for both the mean() and median() commands. Therefore, median(VecAge) is sufficient to assign VecAge to the x argument.

- Almost all *R* commands have more than one argument, each of which has a unique name. This is also true for the commands mean() and median(). However, you can see that only one argument was provided in the two examples above. This is possible because *R* uses default values if the user does not provide values for all arguments.

- As mentioned earlier, we can nest commands. In the examples above, you can see that the commands mean() and median() are nested into the command cat(). *R* allows for nesting commands to any depth. But nesting commands too deeply can make the code very difficult to read.

Let us look at the median() command in more detail. When we type ? median() in the *Console* window of *RStudio*, a help file is displayed in the *Help*-tab of *RStudio* in the lower-right window. Besides other help topics, we get information about a command's arguments, their order, and default values:

```
median(x, na.rm = FALSE, ...)
```

In this case, the command median() has two arguments: One argument called x without a default value, which means the user must assign the data to x, and a second argument named na.rm. The latter determines if missing values are removed automatically before calculating the median. The default na.rm=FALSE means that missing values are not automatically removed. However, the user can set na.rm=TRUE, for example with:

```
median(x=VecAge, na.rm=TRUE)
```

Alternatively, the user can omit the argument names as long as the values of the arguments are in the correct order:

```
median(VecAge, TRUE)
```

As a rule of thumb: In most *R* commands, the data argument is the first argument. This rule of thumb will help us later when we connect multiple *R* commands (using *piping*) in Section 3.9.4.

3.9 Data Wrangling with the tidyverse Package

Like a herd of cattle, data usually do not come as organized as we wish. As a result, we have to perform what is called data wrangling to clean and organize messy data to prepare them for analysis.

The `tidyverse` package[13] is by far the most used and powerful package in *R* for *data wrangling* and other data related tasks. The goal of the `tidyverse` package is to streamline and standardize the *R* data analysis workflow.

The `tidyverse` package is a meta package that includes about 30 other packages, including the `dplyr`, `ggplot2`, `magrittr`, and the `tibble` packages, to name a few. All these packages are installed automatically when the user installs the `tidyverse`. Likewise, when the `tidyverse` is loaded with `library(tidyverse)`, all containing packages are loaded automatically.

The following sections will focus on the `tidyverse` commands required for this book's *R* analysis. Related videos are listed in the Digital Resources section at the end of this chapter (see Section 3.12).

The reader is encouraged to study more about the `tidyverse` packages and commands. A comprehensive book by the primary author of the `tidyverse` is available as a paperback book and freely on the Internet.[14]

3.9.1 Select Data

With the `select()` command, you can select variables (columns) from a data frame. This is useful if you do not need all variables from a data frame and want to create a new data frame with less variables.

The first argument in the `select()` command is the name of the data frame you are working with. The other arguments (separated by commas) are the variables you like to select.

In the example below, we load the `tidyverse` and the `rio` packages,[15] import the complete *Titanic* dataset from the Internet, and use the `select()` command to assign a subset to a new data frame called `DataTitatinicNarrow`. The new dataset should only contain the variables (columns) *Survived*,

---

[13]See Wickham et al. (2019).
[14]See Wickham and Grolemund (2017).
[15]Note that we combine two `library()` commands in one line of code separated by a semicolon.

Pclass, *Sex*, *Age*, and the *FareInPounds*. Then, using the `head()` command, we print the first six observations of the data frame `DataTitanicNarrow` to the *Console*:

```
library(tidyverse);library(rio)
DataTitanic=import("https://ai.lange-analytics.com/data/Titanic.csv")
DataTitanicNarrow=select(DataTitanic, Survived, PasClass=Pclass,
                         Sex, Age, FareInPounds)
head(DataTitanicNarrow)
```

```
##   Survived PasClass    Sex Age FareInPounds
## 1        0        3   male  22        7.250
## 2        1        1 female  38       71.283
## 3        1        3 female  26        7.925
## 4        1        1 female  35       53.100
## 5        0        3   male  35        8.050
## 6        0        3   male  27        8.458
```

As you can see, we were successful. The data frame `DataTitanicNarrow` contains only the five selected columns.

We also *renamed* a variable. Since the variable *Pclass* in the downloaded original dataset did not comply with our *UpperCamel* standards, we used `PasClass=Pclass` to first select *Pclass* and then rename it to *PasClass*.

You can also override an existing `Dataframe` with the output of the `select()` command, as shown in the example below:

```
library(tidyverse);library(rio)
DataTitanic=import("https://ai.lange-analytics.com/data/Titanic.csv")
DataTitanic=select(DataTitanic, Survived, PasClass=Pclass,
                   Sex, Age, FareInPounds)
```

In most cases, overwriting a data frame is not advised. You can see the problem here: If, for whatever reason, the above `select()` command gets executed a second time, we would get an error message because we try to select and rename *Pclass*, but *Pclass* does not exist anymore in `DataTitanic`. It was renamed before, when we executed the `select()` command the first time.

3.9.2   Filter Data

When we used the `select()` command, we chose which variables (columns) to include in the resulting data frame. In contrast, the `filter()` command filters for observations (rows) in a data frame that fulfill specific criteria.

As with the `select()` command, the first argument of the `filter()` command is the data frame that the command processes. Then, one or more conditions specify which observations should be chosen.

In the examples below, we demonstrate a few applications of `filter()`. For this, we use the data frame `DataTitanicNarrow` that we created using the `select()` command:

Analyzing only male passengers:

If we only want to analyze the *male* passengers and then save the results in a new data frame, `DataTitanicMen`, we can use:

```
DataTitanicMen=filter(DataTitanicNarrow, Sex=="male")
head(DataTitanicMen)
```

```
##   Survived PasClass  Sex Age FareInPounds
## 1        0        3 male  22        7.250
## 2        0        3 male  35        8.050
## 3        0        3 male  27        8.458
## 4        0        1 male  54       51.862
## 5        0        3 male   2       21.075
## 6        0        3 male  20        8.050
```

In the code block above, when we filtered for male passengers, we used `Sex=="male"` as a condition. This condition could be translated to: "the variable *sex* is required to be *male*".

Please note the following two technicalities:

1. We used `==` instead of `=`. This is required in R and in most other programming languages because `==` indicates a condition rather than an assignment. Forgetting the second "="-sign in the condition is a common mistake. Fortunately, R gives a distinct error message when this happens.

2. The word "male" must be written in quotes because the condition requires that the variable *Sex* equals the char-value "male" and not the object `male`.

Analyzing only passengers with low fares:

To filter the data frame for passengers with a fare below £7 and then save the results in the new data frame, `DataTitanicLowFare`, you can use the following R code:

```
DataTitanicLowFare=filter(DataTitanicNarrow, FareInPounds<7)
head(DataTitanicLowFare)
```

```
##    Survived PasClass  Sex Age FareInPounds
## 1         0        3 male  45        6.975
## 2         0        3 male  19        6.750
## 3         0        3 male  36        0.000
## 4         0        3 male  34        6.496
## 5         0        1 male  40        0.000
## 6         1        3 male  25        0.000
```

If you look carefully at the output above, you can see that it includes fares that are 0. These are most likely observations with missing fares. Ideally, these *FareInPounds* entries should be NA (*not available*), but in this dataset, they are 0. Therefore, we can throw out these observations by adding a second condition in the filter() command and combining the two conditions with an & (and):

```
DataTitanicLowFare=filter(DataTitanicNarrow,
                  FareInPounds<7 & FareInPounds>0)
head(DataTitanicLowFare)
```

```
##    Survived PasClass  Sex Age FareInPounds
## 1         0        3 male  45        6.975
## 2         0        3 male  19        6.750
## 3         0        3 male  34        6.496
## 4         0        3 male  61        6.237
## 5         0        3 male  18        6.496
## 6         0        3 male  20        4.013
```

You can see that now the output contains no observations with 0 fare.

Analyzing only passengers 60 years and older (seniors):

To analyze only passengers with an age of 60 or greater and then save the results in the new data frame DataTitanicSeniors, we can use the following *R* code:

```
DataTitanicSeniors=filter(DataTitanicNarrow, Age>=60)
head(DataTitanicSeniors)
```

```
##    Survived PasClass  Sex  Age FareInPounds
## 1         0        2 male 66.0        10.50
## 2         0        1 male 65.0        61.98
## 3         0        1 male 64.0        27.72
## 4         0        1 male 71.0        34.65
## 5         0        3 male 70.5         7.75
## 6         0        1 male 60.0        25.93
```

Note, the output contains only passengers with age 60 and older. We used >= in the condition instead of > to accomplish this. This ensured that passengers with $Age = 60$ were included in the output.

3.9.3 Mutate (Calculate) New Variables in a Data Frame

The `mutate()` command provides something very similar to what we often do in *Excel*: We have an *Excel* table with data and want to add an extra column calculated based on one or more existing columns.

Based on a data frame, `mutate()` calculates a new variable (column) based on existing variables (columns). A command name like *calculate* rather than `mutate()` would likely better show what the command actually does, but the name is what it is — `mutate()`.

Here is an example: The *FareInPounds* in the *Titanic* dataset reflects prices of 1912 in British pounds. How much are these prices in 2023 U.S. dollars? To get an approximate value, we have to multiply the British pound prices from 1912 by 108.5[16]

Here are the detailed steps:

- We need to create a new data frame `DataTitanicNewFare` that contains a new variable (column) *FareIn2023Dollars* based on the data frame *DataTitatanicNarrow*.

- The new variable (column) *FareIn2023Dollars* is defined as: $108.5 * FareInPounds$.

- It would also be nice to delete the column *FareInPounds* afterward, as it is no longer useful.

We can accomplish all this with the `mutate()` command:

- The first argument of the `mutate()` command is (again) the data it operates on (`DataTitanicNarrow`).

- The following arguments determine how to calculate new variables and update existing variables.

- Subsequent definitions are separated by commas.

The related *R* code and the output showing the new data frame is displayed below:

---

[16]The purchasing power of a British pound from the year 1912 was about 90.4 British pounds at the beginning of 2023 (see Bank of England (2022)). Multiplying this with the exchange rate for the British pound at the beginning of 2023 ($1.2/Brit. pound) (see Federal Reserve Bank of St. Louis (2023)) gives us the multiplier of 108.5.

```
DataTitanicNewFare=mutate(DataTitanicNarrow,
                          FareIn2023Dollars=108.5*FareInPounds,
                          FareInPounds=NULL)
head(DataTitanicNewFare)
```

```
##   Survived PasClass    Sex Age FareIn2023Dollars
## 1        0        3   male  22             786.6
## 2        1        1 female  38            7734.2
## 3        1        3 female  26             859.9
## 4        1        1 female  35            5761.4
## 5        0        3   male  35             873.4
## 6        0        3   male  27             917.7
```

Note, we assign NULL to the existing variable FareInPounds, deleting it from
the data frame (the assigned value NULL makes the variable non-existent). As
you can see, mutate() also allows updating and overwriting a variable with a
new formula.

3.9.4   Linking R Commands Together with Piping

Piping is a procedure that links one or more *R* commands together. Piping pushes the output of one command as input to the following command. The *piping operator* |> connects the different *R* commands.

We will demonstrate how *piping* works with an example: Assume that based
on the data frame DataTitanic, we would like to create a new data frame
named DataFinalResult that contains:

- only the variables *Survived*, *Sex*, *Age*, and *FareInPounds*

- only female passengers, and

- the fare passengers paid should be expressed in 2023 dollars in a new variable
  FareIn2023Dollars.

As you learned already, for the first condition, you would use the select()
command to select the required variables. Next, ensuring your result contains
only female passengers, you would use filter() to filter your observations for
female passengers. And finally, to ensure the fare is expressed in 2023 dollars,
you would use mutate() to calculate the correct fare.

As explained in Section 3.8 most *R* commands have the following structure
with the data arguments as the first argument:

$$\underbrace{command}_{\text{Command Name}} \left(\overbrace{\underbrace{Arg1}_{\text{Data}}, \underbrace{Arg2, Arg3, ..., ArgN}}^{\text{More Arguments}} \right)$$

$$\underset{\text{Arguments Separated by Comma}}{}$$

This command structure will help us when *piping* the commands select(), filter(), and mutate() together.

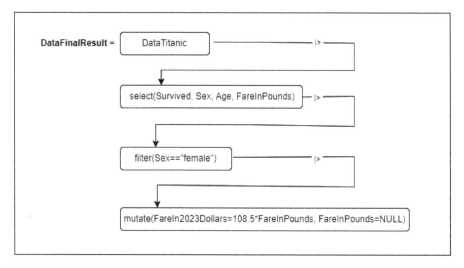

FIGURE 3.4 Piping in a Flowchart

The idea behind *piping* is displayed for our example in Figure 3.4:

i) Left of the "="-sign is the data frame that will eventually contain the result (DataFinalResults).

ii) The right of the "="-sign starts with the name of the data frame that is processed: DataTitanic.

iii) The *piping* operator |> pushes the data frame DataTitanic as the value for the first argument into the select() command. Consequently, the first argument in the select() command — the data argument — is omitted.

iv) The output of the select() command is a data frame containing only the variables *Survived*, *Sex*, *Age*, and *FareInPounds*.

v) The *piping* operator |> then pushes the output of the select() command into the filter() command as the value for its first argument (data argument). Therefore, the data argument itself is omitted in filter().

vi) The filter() command filters for female passengers and creates an all female data frame.

vii) The all-female data frame is pushed by the *piping* operator |> as the first argument into the mutate() command.

viii) The `mutate()` command finally generates the new variable `FareIn2023Dollars` and deletes `FareInPounds`.

ix) The output of the complete pipe is then assigned to the data frame `DataFinalResult`.

Following the flow chart in Figure 3.4, it is not difficult to generate the *R* code for our task:

```
library(tidyverse);library(rio)
DataTitanic=import("https://ai.lange-analytics.com/data/Titanic.csv")

DataFinalResult=DataTitanic |>
                select(Survived, Sex, Age, FareInPounds) |>
                filter(Sex=="female") |>
                mutate(FareIn2023Dollars=108.5*FareInPounds,
                       FareInPounds=NULL)
head(DataFinalResult)
```

```
##    Survived    Sex Age FareIn2023Dollars
## 1         1 female  38            7734.2
## 2         1 female  26             859.9
## 3         1 female  35            5761.4
## 4         1 female  27            1208.0
## 5         1 female  14            3262.7
## 6         1 female   4            1811.9
```

Instead of writing the pipe in one long line, we added a line break after each `|>` and indented so that the `select()`, `filter()`, and `mutate()` commands are lined up. This is not required but makes the code very easy to read. Note, *R* does not allow the *piping* operator to be at the beginning of a line!

The readability of the code is the reason that we use *piping* whenever possible for the remainder of the book. The code block below shows how much more difficult it is to read code without *piping*. Note that we do not override data frames in the code below because this can cause errors when executing a code line again or reusing a data frame.

```
library(tidyverse);library(rio)
DataTitanic=import("https://ai.lange-analytics.com/data/Titanic.csv")
DataTitanicNarrow=select(DataTitanic, Survived, Sex, Age, FareInPounds)
DataTitanicFemale=filter(DataTitanicNarrow, Sex=="female")
DataFinalResult=mutate(DataTitanicFemale,
                       FareIn2023Dollars=108.5*FareInPounds,
                       FareInPounds=NULL)
head(DataFinalResult)
```

```
##    Survived    Sex Age FareIn2023Dollars
## 1          1 female  38            7734.2
## 2          1 female  26             859.9
## 3          1 female  35            5761.4
## 4          1 female  27            1208.0
## 5          1 female  14            3262.7
## 6          1 female   4            1811.9
```

As you can see, the result is the same. However, the code above is not as easy to read as the *piping* code, and two intermediate data frames, `DataTitanicNarrow` and `DataTitanicFemale`, were created.

To generate the *piping* operator in *RStudio*, you can use the `CTRL-SHIFT-M` shortcut in *Windows* (`CMD-SHIFT-M` in *Mac*).

3.10 ◎ A Project Using the tidyverse Package

Interactive Section

In this section, you will find content together with *R* code to execute, change, and rerun in RStudio.

The best way to read and to work with this section is to open it with *RStudio*. Then you can interactively work on *R* code exercises and *R* projects within a web browser. This way you can apply what you have learned so far and extend your knowledge. You can also choose to continue reading either in the book or online, but you will not benefit from the interactive learning experience.

To work with this section in *RStudio* in an interactive environment, follow these steps:

1. Ensure that both the `learnR` and the `shiny` package are installed. If not, install them from RStudio's main menu (Tools -> Install Packages ...).

2. Download the `Rmd` file for the interactive session and save it in your `project` folder. You will find the link for the download below.

3. Open the downloaded file in RStudio and click the `Run Document` button, located in the editing window's top-middle area.

For detailed help for running the exercises including videos for Windows and Mac users we refer to: https://blog.lange-analytics.com/2024/01/interactsessions.html

Do not skip this interactive section because besides providing applications of already covered concepts, it will also extend what you have learned so far.

Below is the link to download the interactive section:

https://ai.lange-analytics.com/exc/?file=03-RAndRStudioExerc100.Rmd

3.10.1   Introduction: Was Chivalry Dead on the Titanic?

In this interactive section, you will work on a small project to determine if chivalry was dead when the *Titanic* sank in 1912[17]. The background for the project is an article written by Hannah Furness (Royal Correspondent at The Telegraph).[18] She cites a Swedish historian claiming, "It was 'not true' that women and children on board the *Titanic* survived thanks to the gallantry of men." Hannah Furness also reports anecdotal evidence about men being in the lifeboats instead of women: "Over on the starboard side, it was a different story. On the last boats to leave, the majority were men." However, Furness did not use any statistics to support her claim, although data are publicly available.

It is now your job to fill this gap. The question is:

Was the proportion of women surviving the *Titanic* disaster greater than the one of men?

If true, that would strongly indicate that the ultimate chivalry — dying to protect a woman's life — was still present when the *Titanic* sank and that Furness' claim that chivalry was dead in 1912 is likely incorrect.

3.10.2   Analyzing Titanic Survival Rates for Women and Men

You will use the same *Titanic* dataset we used before together with the tidyverse package. The *Titanic* dataset contains 887 observations about *Titanic* passengers, including variables such as a survival indicator, passenger's sex, and the class traveled in. The dataset covers about 67% of the total passengers from the *Titanic*.

Below are the first six observations from the DataTitantic data frame:

```
library(tidyverse);library(rio)
DataTitanic=import("https://ai.lange-analytics.com/data/Titanic.csv")
head(DataTitanic)
```

```
##   Survived Pclass                       Name    Sex
## 1        0      3     Mr. Owen Harris Braund    male
## 2        1      1  Mrs. John Bradley Cumings  female
## 3        1      3     Miss. Laina Heikkinen   female
## 4        1      1 Mrs. Jacques Heath Futrelle  female
## 5        0      3    Mr. William Henry Allen    male
## 6        0      3           Mr. James Moran    male
##   Age SiblingsSpousesAboard ParentsChildrenAboard
```

---

[17]The website History.com (keyword: *Titanic*) provides a comprehensive article about the *Titanic* disaster (see History.com (2023))

[18]See 2.

```
## 1   22                    1                      0
## 2   38                    1                      0
## 3   26                    0                      0
## 4   35                    1                      0
## 5   35                    0                      0
## 6   27                    0                      0
##     FareInPounds
## 1          7.250
## 2         71.283
## 3          7.925
## 4         53.100
## 5          8.050
## 6          8.458
```

Before writing *R* code, we need to develop a data analysis strategy:

Step 1: You will create a data frame, DataAnalysis, containing only the variables *Survived*, *Sex*, and *Pclass*. In addition, you will transform the variable *Survived* to a logic variable with TRUE and FALSE values, and you will rename *Pclass* to *PasClass*.

Step 2: You will divide the data frame DataAnalysis into two new data frames, DataWomen and DataMen, containing only observations for women and men, respectively.

Step 3: The data frames DataWomen and DataMen will finally be used to calculate the survival rates of women and men.

Remember, whenever you work on a data science project, develop a detailed data analysis strategy before you start coding. Otherwise, after you have spent a lot of time coding, you might need to entirely change your code because you forgot to consider an important fact.

You will now follow the steps outlined above to write the *R* code for the project. Step 1 from the data analysis strategy requires, to create a new data frame DataAnalysis that only contains the variables *Survived* (as logic data type), *Sex*, and *Pclass* (renamed to *PasClass*).

When you substitute the ... in the code below (note that the data frame DataTitanic has already been loaded in the background), the command head(DataAnalysis) will print the first six observations of the new data frame to the *Console*:

```
DataAnalysis= DataTitanic |>
              select(... ,... , ... = ...) |>
              mutate(Survived=as.logical(Survived))
head(DataAnalysis)
```

Note that in the code above, the variable *Survived* was converted from data type `numerical` to `logic` with the `mutate()` command: After `as.logical()` converted `Survived` into `logical` data type, the result was assigned to the variable `Survived` updating it with the new data type.

Step 2 from the data analysis strategy requires splitting the data frame `Data-Analysis` into two data frames:

1) `DataWomen` should only contain female passengers.
2) `DataMen` should only contain male passengers.

In the code block below you can use the `filter()` command to generate the two new data frames (note that the data frame `DataAnalysis` has been loaded already in the background):

```
DataWomen=DataAnalysis |>
        filter(... == ...)
DataMen=DataAnalysis |>
        filter(... == ...)
head(DataWomen)
head(DataMen)
```

Now that you have two different data frames that either only contain male or female passengers' observations, you are ready to calculate the related survival rates.

In the code block further below, you will calculate the female survival rate. Later, for the male survival rate, we will show you a shorter alternative.

The female survival rate ($Fem_{SurvRate}$) is defined as:

$$Fem_{SurvRate} = \frac{Fem_{Surv}}{Fem_{Total}}$$

Therefore, to calculate the female survival rate, you need to find the number of female passengers that survived (Fem_{Surv}) and the total number of female passengers Fem_{Total}. The latter is the same as the number of observations in the data frame `DataWomen` and can be calculated with `nrow(DataWomen)`.

To find the number of surviving women (Fem_{Surv}), we can use the fact that a surviving passenger was coded with `TRUE` with an internal value of 1 and a not-surviving passenger with `FALSE` with an internal value of 0. Therefore, when we extract the variable *Survived* as a `vector` object from the data frame `DataWomen` and calculate the sum from this vector, we get the number of female survivors (`sum(DataWomen$Survived)`).

With this information, you should be ready to complete the code below to calculate the rate of female survivors (note that the data frame `DataWomen` has been loaded already in the background):

```
FemSurv=...(...$...)
FemTotal=...(...)
FemSurvRate= FemSurv/FemTotal
cat("The survival rate for wommen is:",FemSurvRate)
```

You could do the same for the male passengers. However, there is a shorter alternative to calculate the male survival rate (note that the data frame `DataMen` has been loaded already in the background):

```
MaleSurvRate= mean(DataMen$Survived)
cat("The survival rate for men is",MaleSurvRate)
```

```
## The survival rate for men is 0.1902
```

Why could the `mean()` command be used to calculate the survival rate directly? It is because the mean is calculated by dividing the sum of a variable by the number of observations. This is what we did explicitly when we calculated the female survival rate.

When we use the `cat()` command to print and compare the female and male survival rates, you can see that the survival rate for female passengers is much higher than the one for male passengers:[19]

```
cat("The survival rate for women is:", FemSurvRate, "\n",
    "The survival rate for men is:", MaleSurvRate )
```

```
## The survival rate for women is: 0.742
##  The survival rate for men is: 0.1902
```

The remaining question is if the difference between the two survival rates is high enough to allow us to reject the assertion of the *Telegraph* article that *chivalry was dead in 1912*?

To answer this question, we need more analysis. *R* really shines when data are well organized, as done here — when good data engineering is performed. With the `prop.test()` command, *R* can run a test if the survival rates for women and men differ significantly. The syntax only requires the values for four arguments:

* the number of female survivors,
* the number of male survivors,

---

[19]The character value "\n" creates a line break in the *Console* output.

- the number of total female passengers, and

- the number of total male passengers.

These values have been calculated already and stored in the R Objects Women-Surv, MenSurv, WomenTotal, and MenTotal. We can provide these values to the prop.test() command grouped as two R vectors, one for the survival numbers and one for the total numbers for women and men, respectively:

```
ModelPropFemaleVsMale=prop.test(c(FemSurv, MaleSurv),
                          c(FemTotal, MaleTotal))
```

Above, we saved the output of the prop.test() command in an R object named ModelPropFemaleVsMale. We started the object name with the word Model to indicate that it stores the output of a statistical model. ModelPropFemaleVsMale is a complex object. However, when we print it with the print() command, we extract only important information from the model object:

```
print(ModelPropFemaleVsMale)
```

```
##
##   2-sample test for equality of proportions with
##   continuity correction
##
## data:  c(FemSurv, MaleSurv) out of c(FemTotal, MaleTotal)
## X-squared = 258, df = 1, p-value <2e-16
## alternative hypothesis: two.sided
## 95 percent confidence interval:
##   0.4913 0.6124
## sample estimates:
## prop 1 prop 2
## 0.7420 0.1902
```

Reading the output above backward, starting with the last line, allows us to develop the final result step-by-step. The last line from the ModelPropFemaleVsMale object shows the different survival rates for female (Prop1) and male (Prop2) passengers. The difference between these two survival rates is about 0.55. The 95%-confidence interval for the difference ranges from 0.49 to 0.61. The probability of this difference being zero (both survival rates would be the same) is expressed by the P-value in Line 6 of the output. As the P-value shows, the probability for the female and the male survival rate to be the same is almost zero.

We can summarize:

The assertion from the Telegraph that chivalry was dead in 1912 during the Titanic disaster is most likely not correct.

Now, you should be ready to pursue another small project with minimal guidance (no Hints in the code block below). How about you analyze the different survival rates depending on if passengers traveled in first, second, or third class?

First, create, based on the data frame DataAnalysis, three data frames containing only passengers in classes 1, 2, and 3, respectively. The object names followed by ... are already provided in the R code block below.

Next, substitute the ... in lines 5 – 7 with the appropriate R code to calculate the survival rates for each of the three travel classes (note that the data frame DataAnalysis has already been loaded in the background):

```
DataClass1= ...
DataClass2= ...
DataClass3= ...

Class1SurvRate= ...
Class2SurvRate= ...
Class3SurvRate= ...

cat("Survival rate in class 1:", Class1SurvRate)
cat("Survival rate in class 2:", Class2SurvRate)
cat("Survival rate in class 3:", Class3SurvRate)
```

Happy Analytics!

3.11 ◎ Exercises: Working with R

Interactive Section

In this section, you will find content together with R code to execute, change, and rerun in RStudio.

The best way to read and to work with this section is to open it with *RStudio*. Then you can interactively work on R code exercises and R projects within a web browser. This way you can apply what you have learned so far and extend your knowledge. You can also choose to continue reading either in the book or online, but you will not benefit from the interactive learning experience.

To work with this section in *RStudio* in an interactive environment, follow
these steps:

1. Ensure that both the `learnR` and the `shiny` package are installed. If not,
    install them from RStudio's main menu (Tools -> Install Packages ...).

2. Download the `Rmd` file for the interactive session and save it in your `project`
    folder. You will find the link for the download below.

3. Open the downloaded file in RStudio and click the `Run Document` button,
    located in the editing window's top-middle area.

For detailed help for running the exercises including videos for Windows and Mac users
we refer to: https://blog.lange-analytics.com/2024/01/interactsessions.html

Do not skip this interactive section because besides providing applications of
already covered concepts, it will also extend what you have learned so far.

Below is the link to download the interactive section:

https://ai.lange-analytics.com/exc/?file=03-RAndRStudioExerc200.Rmd

The following sections will allow you to review and extend what you have
learned so far. If you need help with any excises, return to the corresponding
section above.

Character Data Type

In the first set of exercises, you will work with `character` *Data Types*.

Exercise 1:

The simplest way to use `character` *Data Types* is to print them, like in the
following exercise:

```
print("This is printed text")
```

Your turn: Why don't you change the text and print again?

────────────────────────────

Exercise 2:

You can also assign characters to an *R* object, which then becomes an *R*
`character-object`, and you can print it afterward:

```
Sentence="This is text stored in an R object."
print(Sentence)
```

Your turn: Change the sentence and print it again. What happens if you forget the quotes?

Exercise 3:

Instead of using `print()` to output *R* objects to the *Console*, you can use the `cat()` command (cat stands for concatenate). This command allows combining text and *R* objects as long as they are separated by comma:

```
FirstName="Carsten"
cat("My name is", FirstName, "and I am learning R.")
```

Your turn: Assign your own first name to the *R* object `FirstName` and rerun the code.

Numerical Data Type

In the following exercises, you will assign numerical values to *R* objects and work with numerical objects and values.

We can assign a value to an *R* object using the "="-sign. Remembering to interpret the "="-sign as *"assigned to"* rather than an *"equal to"* sign like in algebra is important.

As mentioned before, an alternative to using the "=" symbol is the "<-" symbol. The latter emphasizes an assignment rather than an equality. However, throughout this book, we will use the "="-symbol for simplicity, keeping in mind that it stands for *assigned to*.

Exercise 4:

Below you find an example of how to assign a value of 23 to a variable called *A*, and then add 100 to this value:

```
A=23
A=A+100
cat("R object A contains the numeric value:", A)
```

Look carefully at Line 2 of the exercise. Given that `A=23` from Line 1, Line 2 does not mean that `A` *equals* `A+100`. Otherwise, considering Line 1: `23=23+100` — which is clearly not the case.

The correct way to interpret Line 2 is as an assignment. We assign a new value to `A`, which is 100 greater than the old value of 23.

Your turn:

- Execute the code as is and explain it.

- Assign a value 33 to A in Line 1 of the code and then use Line 2 to double the value.

Exercise 5:

We can perform algebraic calculations with numbers or numerical *R* objects. Below is an example:

```
A=2
B=4
A=500*A/10
C=A*B
cat("R object C contains the product of A and B. Therefore, C is:", C)
D=sqrt(A)
cat("The square root of ",  A, " is:", D)
```

Your turn:

- Run the code and then carefully check the calculations above.

- Explain why the value of C is 400 and not 8.

- Finally, change the value that is assigned to A in Line 1. The goal is to create an output from the cat() command in Line 7 that reads: The square root of 400 is: 20

Exercise 6:

In the code block below, you are tasked to calculate the area of a rectangle based on its length and width.

```
Length=...
Width=...
AreaRect=...
cat("The area of the rectangle is:", AreaRect)
```

Your turn: Use the two *R* objects Length and Width, assign values to these objects (e.g., 4 and 3), and then calculate the area of the related rectangle. The code is partially provided already. You just need to replace the ... with your code additions.

Logical Data Type

The following exercises cover logic *R* objects. We will assign TRUE and FALSE to different objects and combine them with & (AND) and | (OR) to see the result. We will also perform calculations with logic *R* objects. Remember that TRUE stands (internally) for 1 and FALSE for 0.

Exercise 7:

Below TRUE is assigned to two logical *R* objects. These two *R* objects are combined with an AND (&), saved into another logical *R* object, and then printed to the *Console* with the cat() command:

```
IsLifeGood=TRUE
IsMoodGood=TRUE
IsHappy=IsLifeGood & IsMoodGood
cat("Happiness:", IsHappy)
```

Run the code above, and you will see that the result for IsHappy is TRUE. This is because we require for happiness (IsHappy) that life is good and that the person is in a good mood. Both were the case; therefore, the result was TRUE for IsHappy.

Your turn: Assume that life is still good, but the person's mood changes from good to not-good. Change TRUE and FALSE accordingly. What happens to the person's happiness (IsHappy) when you execute the new code? Explain.

———————————

Exercise 8:

Here is an example for OR (|):

```
IsWeatherDry=TRUE
IsIndoor=FALSE
IsStayingDry=IsWeatherDry | IsIndoor
cat("Person stays dry:", IsStayingDry)
```

If the weather provides sunshine or a person is indoors, the person will not get wet from rain and will stay dry. Only one of the two logical objects needs to be TRUE to generate a TRUE for IsStayingDry.

Your turn:
- Run the code above and explain the result.
- Find a similar example, rename the *R* objects, change the text in the cat() command accordingly, and rerun the code.

———————————

Exercise 9:

Below is a more complex example of a person that can be exposed to dry weather (or not) and is indoors (or not) with an intact roof (or not).

```
IsWeatherDry=FALSE
IsIndoor=TRUE
IsRoofIntact=FALSE
IsStayingDry=IsWeatherDry | (IsIndoor & IsRoofIntact)
cat("Person stays dry:", IsStayingDry)
```

Your turn:
- Run the code and explain the result related to the code.
- Predict what would happen to the result if the roof was intact.
- Change the code for an intact roof, execute, and explain the result.

Vector-Objects

You already learned that a sequence of numerical, character, or logical objects is called a `vector` object.

For the following exercises, we created four related `vector` objects: `VecFirstNames` to store the first names of three persons, `VecAges` for their age, `VecIsFemale` to indicate if their sex is female (or not), and `VecNumKids` for the number of children they have. To assign values to the `vector` objects, we use the `c()` (combine) command:

```
VecFirstNames=c("Carsten", "Jose", "Jane")
VecAges=c(45,54,23)
VecIsFemale=c(FALSE,FALSE,TRUE)
VecNumKids=c(1,2,1)
```

The four `vector` objects are related because we used the same order for their values. The first value belongs to *Carsten*, the second value belongs to *Jose*, and the third to *Jane*. Therefore, we can deduce Jose is 54 years old, his sex is *male* (`FALSE` for `IsFemale`), and he has two kids.

It is a little cumbersome that we always have to track the order of elements to interpret the vector values correctly. Fortunately, this gets much easier when we use data frames in the following exercise section.

For now, we just assume the order in each of the three vectors is the same and see what we can do with the `vector-objects`.

———————————————

Exercise 10:

In this exercise, you will calculate some crucial statistics from our vectors.

Your turn: Substitute the ... in the code below and run the code:

- Calculate the number of persons in the dataset and store the result in `NumOfPersons`.
- Calculate the number of women in the dataset and store the result in `NumOfWomen`.
- Calculate the number of men in the dataset and store the result in `NumOfMen`.
- Calculate the proportion of women in the dataset and store the result in `PropWomen` in digital format.
- Calculate the proportion of men in the dataset and store the result in `PropMen` in digital format.

Note that the `vector` objects `VecFirstNames`, `VecAges`, `VecIsFemale`, and `Vec-NumKids` have already been loaded in the background.

```
AvgAge=mean(VecAges)
NumOfPersons=length(...)
NumOfWomen=...(...)
NumOfMen=NumOfPersons-...
PropWomen=...(...)
PropMen= 1 - ...

cat("We have", NumOfPersons, "persons in the dataset",
    "with an average age of", AvgAge, ".")
cat("We have", NumOfWomen, "female(s) and", NumOfMen, "male(s).")
cat(round(PropWomen,2)*100, "% are female and",
    round(PropMen, 2)*100, "% are male.")
```

Exercise 11:

In this exercise, you will perform numerical calculations on a vector. For the sake of this exercise, assume the current year is 2024. Of course, you can change this in the interactive exercise if you wish.

```
CurrentYear=2024
VecFirstNames=c("Carsten", "Jose", "Jane")
VecAges=c(45,54,23)
```

```
VecBirthYears=CurrentYear-VecAges
cat("Birth years for", VecFirstNames, "are:", VecBirthYears)
```

```
## Birth years for Carsten Jose Jane are: 1979 1970 2001
```

Run the code to estimate the birth years for *Carsten*, *Jose*, and *Jane*. The estimated birth years are calculated as the difference between the current year (the numeric value stored in the *R* object `CurrentYear`) and all three values stored in the `vector` object `VecAges`. Consequently, the result (`VecBirthYears`) contains three values and is also a `vector` object.

Your turn:

- Adjust the `CurrentYear` object to include the current year, if needed.

- Adjust the `vector` object `VecFirstNames` to include the names of three of your friends.

- Adjust the `vector` object `VecAges` to include the ages of your three friends.

- Execute the modified code to estimate the birth years of your three friends.

Data Frame Objects

In the previous exercise section, you analyzed the content of different vectors under the assumption that their elements were in the same order. It required remembering the order of elements in a vector when performing analysis, which is cumbersome and can be avoided with data frames.

You can think of a data frame as a table with variables in the columns, variable names in the first row, and related observations in all other rows — just like an *Excel* table.

The variables in the columns of a data frame are very similar to `vector` objects — except that they are part of the data frame. In fact, we will show in the following exercises that the columns of a data frame can be populated with `vector` objects and that columns of a data frame can be extracted as `vector` objects.

After a data frame object is defined, you can use commands from the `tidyverse` package to process the data. Throughout this book, we will almost exclusively work with data frames and use the `tidyverse` for data engineering.

Exercise 12:

Regardless of whether the file is on your computer or the Internet, tabular data in a file can be imported into a data frame with the `import()` command from the `rio` package.

When you run the code of the exercise below, the *Titanic* dataset will be imported to the data frame `DataFromInternet`, and with `select(Survived, Name, Sex)`, you will create a data frame that only includes the variables *Survived*, *Name*, and *Sex* from the imported *Titanic* dataset:

```
library(rio)
library(tidyverse)
DataFromInternet=
  import("https://ai.lange-analytics.com/data/Titanic.csv") |>
select(Survived, Name, Sex)
head(DataFromInternet)
```

Your turn: Another tabular dataset containing wine observations can be imported from the Internet. The dataset contains 3,198 observations about different wines and was initially developed by Cortez et al. (2009). It includes variables about wine color, several chemical properties, and an indicator for quality. The dataset is available as a tabular file at: `https://ai.lange-analytics.com/data/WineData.rds`.

- Adjust the `import()` command to assign the wine dataset to the data frame `DataFromInternet`.

- Change the `select()` command to select only the variables *wineColor* (renamed to *WineColor*), *acidity* (renamed to *Acidity*), and *alcohol* (renamed to *Alcohol*).

- Execute the modified code.

Exercise 13:

When you run the code below, you will create a data frame `DataThreeFriends` by manually using the `data.frame()` command. Since variables (columns) of a data frame are very similar to `vector` objects, you can use the `c()` command to create `vector` objects that populate the variables for the data frame.

```
library(tidyverse)
CurrentYear=2024
DataThreeFriends=data.frame(FirstName=c("Carsten", "Jose", "Jane"),
                    LastName=c("Lange","Hernandez","Doe"),
                    Age=c(45,54,23),
                    IsFemale= c(FALSE,FALSE,TRUE))
print(DataThreeFriends)
```

```
##   FirstName  LastName Age IsFemale
## 1   Carsten     Lange  45    FALSE
## 2      Jose Hernandez  54    FALSE
## 3      Jane       Doe  23     TRUE
```

Your turn:

- Change the value for `CurrentYear`, if needed.

- Enter the data of three of your friends (two male and one female).

- Use a pipe to add a `mutate()` command to the `data.frame()` command. Then use the `mutate()` command to add a variable *BirthYear* that shows the birth years for the three persons in the data frame.

- Run the code to see the results.

Exercise 14:

Commands like `sum()` or `mean()` that we used before to analyze vectors take only `vector`-objects as input. You cannot use variables from data frames directly. Therefore, to analyze variables in a data frame with commands such as `mean()` or `sum()`, you must first extract the data frame variables as vectors before these commands can process them.

Fortunately, this procedure is simple. To extract a variable from a data frame as a vector, you just need to provide the data frame's name and the variable's name, separated by a "$"-sign.

The exercise below provides an example of extracting the variables *Survived* and *Age* from the data frame `DataTitanic` as a `vector` object for further processing.

In the code block below, we use `DataTitanic$Survived` to extract the variable *Survived* as a vector and then use this `vector` object to calculate the vector's `sum()`. This sum coincides with the number of survivors in the dataset because a survivor is coded as 1 and a non-survivor is coded with 0 (note, the data frame `DataTitanic` has been loaded already in the background):[20]

```
NumOfSurv=sum(DataTitanic$Survived)
AvgAgeOfPas=...(...)
cat(NumOfSurv, "passengers survived.")
cat("The average age of the passengers was", AvgAgeOfPas, ".")
```

Your turn:

- Substitute the ... in the code block to extract the variable *Age* as a `vector` object and then calculate the average age of the passengers.

- Run the code to see the results.

----

[20]This procedure would also work if survivors were coded as TRUE and non-survivors as FALSE in a logic object because TRUE is internally coded as 1 and FALSE as 0.

3.12   Digital Resourses

Below you will find a few digital resources related to this chapter such as:

* Videos
* Short articles
* Tutorials
* *R* scripts

These resources are recommended if you would like to review the chapter from a different angle or to go beyond what was covered in the chapter.

Here we show only a few of the digital resourses. At the end of the list you will find a link to additonal digital resources for this chapter that are maintained on the Internet.

You can find a complete list of digital resources for all book chapters on the companion website: https://ai.lange-analytics.com/digitalresources.html

R and RStudio Download

Here, you will find the links to install *R* and *RStudio*. Please remember to install *R* before you install *RStudio*. Also, if you upgrade *R*, uninstall the old version first before installing the new *R* version.

Link: https://ai.lange-analytics.com/dr?a=291

How to Work with RStudio

This is a 5 min. video chapter called "RStudio Intro" from a YouTube video by Carsten Lange. The video chapter explains the basic function of *RStudio*. You might want to stop the video after the "RStudio Intro" chapter ends.

Link: https://ai.lange-analytics.com/dr?a=292

DataCamp R Course

This is a course from *DataCamp*. It introduces the basics of *R* from the start. The course is an interactive course with exercises.

Link: https://ai.lange-analytics.com/dr?a=298

More Digital Resources

Only a subset of digital resources is listed in this section. The link below points to additional, concurrently updated resources for this chapter.

Link: https://ai.lange-analytics.com/dr/randrstudio.html

4

k-Nearest Neighbors — Getting Started

In the previous chapter, you learned the basics about *R* and *RStudio*. Now, you are probably keen to apply your knowledge to create a machine learning model. Therefore, we will postpone covering key concepts of machine learning models to Chapter 5 and jump right in to create our first machine learning model.

We start with a *k-Nearest Neighbors* model in Section 4.5 predicting whether a wine is *red* or *white* based on only two chemical properties (*acidity* and *sulfur dioxide*). This model allows us to introduce the underlying idea of *k-Nearest Neighbors* and in addition some essential machine learning concepts such as:

1) Splitting the available observations into training and testing data (see Section 4.3).

2) The concept of scaling (see Section 4.6).

3) Pre-processing data and designing machine learning models with the `tidymodels` package (see Section 4.7.1).

4) Interpreting a *confusion matrix* (see Section 4.8).

The last two sections 4.9 and 4.10 are designed to be hands-on and interactive. In Section 4.9, you will write *R* code in *RStudio* to improve the model from Section 4.5 by adding additional chemical properties as predictor variables. In Section 4.10, you will work on a different project to apply *Optical Character Recognition* (*OCR*) to detect digits between 0 – 9 from handwritten notes using *k-Nearest Neighbors*.

4.1 Learning Outcomes

This section outlines what you can expect to learn in this chapter. In addition, the corresponding section number is included for each learning outcome to help you to navigate the content, especially when you return to the chapter for review.

In this chapter, you will learn:

- How to split your observations into training and testing data and why this is essential (see Section 4.3 for an introduction. The details will be covered in Chapter 6).

- What is the underlying idea of k-Nearest Neighbors (see Section 4.5).

- How similarity can be measured with Euclidean Distance (see Section 4.5).

- Why scaling predictor variables is essential for some machine learning models (see Section 4.6).

- Why the tidymodels package makes it easy to work with machine learning models (see Section 4.7.1).

- How you can define a recipe to pre-process data with the tidymodels package (see Section 4.7.1).

- How you can define a model design with the tidymodels package (see Section 4.7.1).

- How you can create a machine learning workflow with the tidymodels package (see Section 4.7.1).

- How metrics derived from a confusion matrix can be used to evaluate prediction quality (see Section 4.8).

- Why you have to be careful when interpreting *accuracy*, when working with unbalanced observations (see Section 4.8).

- How a machine learning model can process images and how *OCR* works (see the project in Section 4.10).

4.2   R Packages Required for the Chapter

This section lists the *R* packages that you need when you load and execute code in the interactive sections in *RStudio*. Please install the following packages using Tools -> Install Packages ... from the *RStudio* menu bar (you can find more information about installing and loading packages in Section 3.4):

- The rio package (Chan et al. (2021)) to enable the loading of various data formats with one import() command. Files can be loaded from the user's hard drive or the Internet.

- The janitor package (Firke (2023)) to rename variable names to *Upper-Camel* and to substitute spaces and special characters in variable names.

- The `tidymodels` package (Kuhn and Wickham (2020)) to streamline data engineering and machine learning tasks.

- The `kableExtra` (Zhu (2021)) package to support the rendering of tables.

- The `learnr` package (Aden-Buie et al. (2022)), which is needed together with the `shiny` package (Chang et al. (2022)) for the interactive exercises in this book.

- The `shiny` package (Chang et al. (2022)), which is needed together with the `learnr` package (Aden-Buie et al. (2022)) for the interactive exercises in this book.

- The `kknn` package (Schliep and Hechenbichler (2016)) to run a *k-Nearest Neighbors* model.

4.3 Preparing the Wine Dataset

Throughout this chapter, except for Section 4.10, we will work with a publicly available wine dataset that has been used widely in various machine learning competitions and tutorials. This dataset contains 3,198 observations about different wines and was initially developed by Cortez et al. (2009). It includes variables such as a wine's color, several chemical properties, and an indicator of the quality of the wine.

The goal is to develop a *k-Nearest Neighbors* model that can predict if a wine is *red* or *white* based on its chemical properties. In a first attempt, we will only use a wine's *acidity* and its total content of *sulfur dioxide* as predictor variables.

We start working with the wine dataset in the code block below:

```
library(tidyverse); library(rio); library(janitor)
DataWine=import("https://ai.lange-analytics.com/data/WineData.rds") |>
        clean_names("upper_camel") |>
        select(WineColor, Sulfur=TotalSulfurDioxide, Acidity)

head(DataWine)
```

```
##   WineColor Sulfur Acidity
## 1       red     37    10.8
## 2     white    213     6.4
## 3     white    139     9.4
## 4     white     90     8.2
## 5     white    183     6.4
```

```
## 6        red      38      6.7
```

First, we load the required packages using the `library()` commands. Then the wine dataset is downloaded from the Internet, and for better readability, variable names are changed to *UpperCamel* notation using the command `clean_names()` from the `janitor` package (see Section 3.6 for details). Next, we use the `select()` command to ensure that only the variables *WineColor*, *Sulfur* (renamed from *TotalSulfurDioxide*), and *Acidity* are included in the data frame `DataWine`.

When working with data to build and test machine learning models, we work with datasets that contain observations. We use these observations for feature engineering, building a model, optimizing the model's hyper-parameters, and assessing the predictive quality of the final model.

Can we use all of our observations for all of these purposes? The answer is "No" because we cannot use observations to optimize our model and then use the same observations to assess the model's predictive quality.

Suppose we would use the same observations to optimize the model and assess the model's predictive quality. Then the assessment would show how well the model approximates the data rather than the model's ability to predict new data.

To avoid this type of ill-designed assessment, we have to withhold some data that are never used for training or optimizing the model. In other words, we set aside some data the model will never see during development. These data are called testing data, while the data used for training and optimizing the model are called training data.

Kuhn and Silge (2022) use the concept of "spending" observations to explain the concept of training and testing data: Just like you can *spend* the same dollar bill only once, you can *spend* (use) an observation from a dataset only once. You can either *spend* (use) an observation for optimizing a model (the observation becomes part of the training data) or for assessing the final model (the observation becomes part of the testing data) but not for both. Assigning observations to either the training or the testing dataset is usually done randomly.[1]

---

[1] An exception are time series data, where the most up-to-date data are assigned to the *testing* dataset.

Training and Testing Data

When working with data to build machine learning models and evaluate their predictive quality, we split the observations into two different datasets.

Training data are used to optimize a machine learning model, which includes finding the parameters and *hyper-parameters* that provide the best promise for a well-performing model.

Testing data constitute a holdout dataset exclusively used to assess the predictive quality of a machine learning model.

Never use testing data for any kind of optimization!

Why we must follow the above rule strictly will be covered in detail in Chapter 6.

The decision of which proportion should be used for training and which proportion should be withheld for assessment is difficult. As a rule of thumb, about 60% – 85% of the observations should be used for training and the remaining observations for testing. In any case, we have to ensure that the training dataset contains sufficient observations to optimize the model parameters.

Writing R code to randomly assign observations to either the *training* or *testing* dataset can be tedious. Fortunately, with the R tidymodels package, randomly splitting a dataset into *training* and *testing* data is straightforward.

In the R code block below, we load the tidymodels package and then use initial_split() to define the splitting criteria to assign observations to either the training or the testing dataset. The command intial_split() performs the split, and the results are saved in the R object Split7030. With the commands training(Split7030) and testing(Split7030) in the following two lines, we extract the training and testing data and assign them to the data frames DataTrain and DataTest, respectively:

```
library(tidymodels);
set.seed(876)
Split7030=initial_split(DataWine,  prop=0.7,  strata=WineColor)

DataTrain=training(Split7030)
DataTest=testing(Split7030)
```

The set.seed() command in the second line initializes R's random number generator. This is recommended because we want to avoid creating a setup where we must deal with different training and testing data every time we execute the code. Consequently, we initialize the random number generator using an integer number. This way, every time the intial_split() command is executed (and initialized with "876"), it generates the same random outcome. You can choose the integer in set.seed() as you wish. The argument `strata=WineColor` ensures that red and white wines in the training and testing data are similarly distributed.

4.4   Visualizing the Training Data

Exploring data visually before running a machine learning model is always a good idea. Figure 4.1 shows a scatter plot of the training data with *Sulfur* (total sulfur dioxide; measured in mg/liter) at the horizontal axis and *Acidity* (measured as tartaric acid in g/liter) at the vertical axis. The colors of the wines are encoded with *red* and *yellow* to mark *red* and *white* wines, respectively. We also added a *blue* point representing a wine with an unknown color.

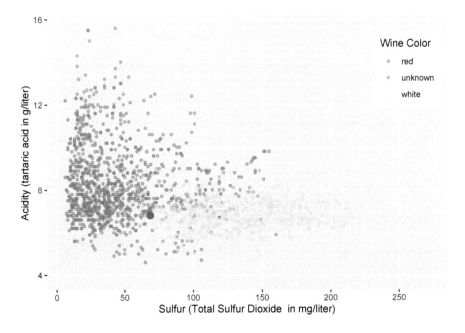

FIGURE 4.1 Acidity and Total Sulfur Dioxide Related to Wine Color

From the plot in Figure 4.1, you can already develop some intuitive approaches for classifying *red* and *white* wines before we implement *k-Nearest Neighbors*.

Before reading on, look at Figure 4.1 and try to develop one or more rules for classifying the wines into "red" and "white".

In a first attempt, we try to separate the *red* and *white* wines exclusively by *Acidity* leading to a horizontal decision boundary like in Figure 4.2. A decision value of *Acidity* = 8 looks reasonable. Wines with an acidity less than 8 would be considered *white*, while all others would be regarded as *red*. Following that rule, the wine with an unknown wine color (*blue* point) would be classified as *white* (we do not know if this prediction is correct).

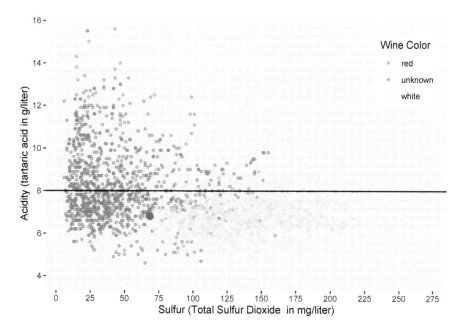

FIGURE 4.2 Horizontal Decision Boundary for Acidity and Total Sulfur Dioxide Related to Wine Color

As Figure 4.2 shows, such a decision boundary would classify most white wines correctly. This is because most white wines have an *Acidity* < 8 (below the decision boundary) and are therefore correctly classified as *white*. About half of the red wines have an *Acidity* > 8 (above the decision boundary) and would also be classified correctly as *red*. However, the other half of red wines have an *Acidity* < 8 (below the decision boundary) and are therefore falsely classified as *white*.

Note that in Figure 4.2 and the following Figures 4.3 and 4.4 we use the training data in the absence of testing data to evaluate predictive quality. This is not appropriate! However, since the purpose of this section is to visualize basic ideas, we ignore this fact for now.

To analyze the results in more detail, we can use what is called a confusion matrix:

```
##              Truth
## Prediction  red white
##       red   510    80
##     white   609  1039
```

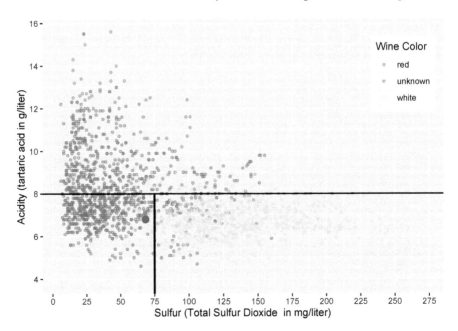

FIGURE 4.3 Sub-Space Boundaries for Acidity and Sulfur in Wine

Usually, in a *confusion matrix* for two classes (e.g., *red* and *white*) the column labels refer to the truth. In our case, the first column shows counts of wines that are actually *red*, while the second column shows counts for wines that are actually *white*.

In contrast, the row labels refer to the Predictions. In the *confusion matrix* above, the first row shows counts for wines predicted as *red*, while the second row shows counts for wines predicted as *white*.

Now that you understand the structure of the *confusion matrix*, we can interpret the matrix's four entries (cells).

- The first row shows all wines that are predicted as *red*:

  - The first cell contains wines that are predicted correctly as *red* because they are actually *red* (510 wines).

  - The second cell contains wines that are predicted falsely as *red* because they are actually *white* (80 wines).

- The second row shows all wines that are predicted as *white*:

  - The first cell contains wines that are predicted falsely as *white* because they are actually *red* (609 wines).

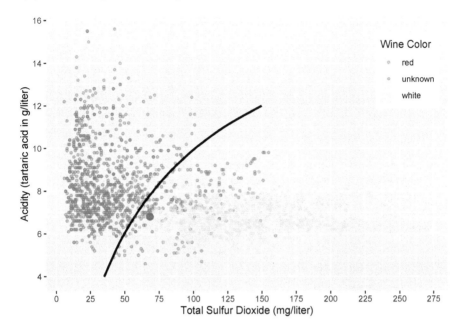

FIGURE 4.4 Curved Decision Boundary for Acidity and Sulfur in Wine

– The second cell contains wines that are predicted correctly as *white* because they are actually *white* (1039 wines).

Since all observations fall in one of the four cells in the *confusion matrix*, the sum of the four cells equals the number of observations. In addition, the sum of the cells on the main diagonal of the *confusion matrix* reflects the correctly predicted observations. This allows us to calculate our first performance metrics (*accuracy*) from the *confusion matrix*:

$$Accuracy = \frac{510 + 1039}{510 + 80 + 609 + 1039} = 0.69$$

More about the *confusion matrix* and the related performance metrics in Section 4.8.

Can we improve the prediction quality further?

Yes, we can improve quality by dividing the area below the horizontal line in Figure 4.2 by adding a vertical decision boundary. A vertical decision boundary below the horizontal decision boundary is akin to dividing the wines with an *Acidity* < 8 by total sulfur dioxide (*Sulfur*) contained in the wine. A value of *Sulfur* = 75 seems to be reasonable for this decision boundary, and the resulting sub-spaces are displayed in Figure 4.3:

The decision boundaries in Figure 4.3 create three sub-spaces:

1. An area for wines with $Acidity > 8$ mainly containing red wines. Therefore, any wine falling into this area would be predicted as *red*.

2. An area with wines with $Acidity < 8$ and $Sulfur < 75$ mainly containing red wines. Therefore, any wine falling into this area would be predicted as *red*. The *unknown* wine symbolized by the *blue* point would also be classified as *red*.

3. An area with wines with $Acidity < 8$ and $Sulfur > 75$ mainly containing white wines. Therefore, any wine falling into this area would be predicted as *white*.

The resulting *confusion matrix* is displayed below:

```
##              Truth
## Prediction   red white
##       red    1016   145
##     white    103   974
```

You can see that the *accuracy* (based on the training data) has improved:

$$Accuracy = \frac{1016 + 974}{1016 + 145 + 103 + 974} = 0.89$$

Another approach to classifying the wines in *red* and *white* could be to draw a non-linear decision boundary like in Figure 4.4. Wines in the upper-left of the curved decision boundary would be classified as *red*, and all others would be classified as *white*. The resulting *confusion matrix* would be similar to the one shown in the example with sub-spaces. The *blue* point in Figure 4.4 would be classified as white wine (again, we do not know if this is correct).

The visualizations in Figures 4.3 and 4.4 were chosen for a reason. Creating sub-spaces like in Figure 4.3, is the underlying idea behind *Decision Tree* and *Random Forest* machine learning models (see Chapter 10 for details). Generating a non-linear decision boundary like in Figure 4.4 is the underlying idea behind *Neural Network* models (see Chapter 9 for details).

The idea behind *k-Nearest Neighbors* will be visualized and explained in what follows.

4.5 The Idea Behind k-Nearest Neighbors

The following two sections will explain the idea behind *k-Nearest Neighbors*. In Section 4.5.1, we start with the most basic *k-Nearest Neighbors* model ($k = 1$). It predicts the class (wine color) for a new observation (wine with unknown *WineColor*) by finding the observation closest to it — the nearest neighbor. Then the class (*WineColor*) of the nearest neighbor observation is used to predict the unknown observation's class ($\widehat{WineColor}$).

If *k-Nearest Neighbors* considers more than one neighboring point ($k > 1$), e.g., the four nearest neighbors ($k = 4$), the class of the majority of these neighbor points is the predicted class. In case of a tie, the prediction is chosen randomly (see Section 4.5.2 for a visualization of a *k=4 Nearest Neighbors* model).

In a *k-Nearest Neighbors* model, the *hyper-parameter* k determines the number of neighbors to be considered. k is called a *hyper-parameter* because, in contrast to parameters that are determined based on data, it has to be chosen at the design stage of the model.

4.5.1 k-Nearest Neighbors for k=1

We start with $k = 1$, which means that *k-Nearest Neighbors* focuses only on the closest neighbor.

To introduce the idea, it is best to zoom in from Figure 4.1 closer to the wine we would like to predict (the *blue* point). This makes it easier to identify the neighbor closest to the *blue* point.

Figure 4.5 shows the result after zooming in. Eyeballing makes it easy to identify the nearest neighbor to the *blue* point. The nearest neighbor is the wine (the point) connected with the bold magenta line to the wine we want to predict (the *blue* point). Since the closest neighbor's wine color is *red*, *k-Nearest Neighbors* with $k = 1$ predicts *red* for the wine with the unknown wine color.

Eyeballing is a good tool when working with diagrams. Still, for a machine learning model like *k-Nearest Neighbors*, we have to find a way to measure the distances between the point (the wine) we like to predict and all points in the training dataset. This is the only way to find the nearest neighbor programmatically.

In Figure 4.5, the two black lines and the magenta line form a right-angled triangle, which means *Pythagoras* is here to help. If we name the *blue* point with an index p (for predict) and the *red* point we want to calculate the distance to with an index i, then the length of the triangle's leg a equals $Sulfur_i - Sulfur_p$, and the length of leg b equals $Acid_i - Acid_p$. The length

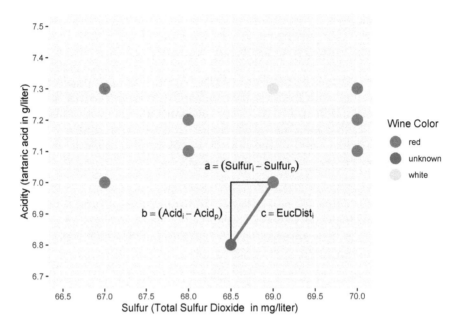

FIGURE 4.5 Predicting Wine Color with k-Nearest Neighbors (k=1)

of the magenta line labeled c is the distance between the red and the blue point (called **Euclidean Distance**). To calculate this distance, we can use the *Pythagorean* theorem:

$$c^2 = a^2 + b^2$$

When we substitute a and b with the *Sulfur* and *Acid* differences between the wine we want to predict (*blue* point) and the wine symbolized by the red dot in the triangle in Figure 4.5, we can calculate the *Euclidean Distance* (*EucDist*) as follows:

$$\underbrace{EucDist_i^2}_{c^2} = \underbrace{(Sulfur_i - Sulfur_p)^2}_{a^2} + \underbrace{(Acid_i - Acid_p)^2}_{b^2}$$

$$\Longleftrightarrow$$

$$EucDist_i = \sqrt{(Sulfur_i - Sulfur_p)^2 + (Acid_i - Acid_p)^2} \quad (4.1)$$

The formula above can be used to calculate the *Euclidean Distance* between the wine we want to predict (p) and any other wine (i) in the training dataset. This is because we know the values of the predictor variables for the point we like to predict as well as the predictor values for all observations in the training dataset. Calculating *Euclidean Distances* from wine p to all wines in the training data allows us to find the wine with the smallest distance to wine p. This wine's color will then become the predicted color for wine p.

Calculate Euclidean Distance for Three or More Variables

Assume our observations have two different predictor variables x and y, like in the example above. We can then apply the logic from Equation (4.1) and calculate the (*Euclidean*) distance between a point we like to predict and any point i as follows:

$$EucDist2_i = \sqrt{(x_i - x_p)^2 + (y_i - y_p)^2}$$

$EucDist2_i$ is the distance between the two observations in two-dimensional space.

How does the formula change when considering a third predictor variable z? We just add the new variable under the square root in a similar way as we did it for the other variables:

$$EucDist3_i = \sqrt{(x_i - x_p)^2 + (y_i - y_p)^2 + (z_i - z_p)^2}$$

Interestingly, when considering three variables, $EucDist3_i$ represents the length of the shortest straight-line between two points in three-dimensional space.

If we consider more variables, a straightforward geometric interpretation is not possible anymore. However, we just add the squared difference of a new variable between the prediction point and a point i under the square root. For example, in Section 4.10, we will consider 784 variables resulting in a pretty long formula under the square root, but this is no problem for a computer.[a]

The formula below shows how the *Euclidean Distance* is calculated between the prediction point p and a point i when N predictor variables $(v_1, v_2, ..., v_j, ..., v_N)$ are considered:

$$EucDistN_i = \sqrt{\sum_{j=1}^{N}(v_{i,j} - v_{p,j})^2}$$

---

[a]To avoid writing very long formulas, a programmer who creates a *k-Nearest Neighbors* algorithm would most likely use matrix algebra.

Now that you know how to calculate the *Euclidean Distance* between any two observations for any number of predictor variables, we can demonstrate how the *k-Nearest Neighbors* model predicts and how its performance can be measured using the testing dataset:

Step 1: Take the first observation from the testing dataset and calculate the distance from this record to all observations in the training dataset.

Step 2: Find the observation that has the smallest distance to the testing observation.

Step 3: The predicted class (e.g., *red* or *white*) for the observation from the testing dataset is the same as the class from its nearest neighbor.

Step 4: For the observation from the testing dataset, we actually know the true class — although we never showed it to the model. Therefore, we can compare the true class of the testing observation with the prediction to find out if the prediction was true or false.

Step 5: Depending on the prediction (*red* or *white*) and whether it was correct, we update one of the four cells in the *confusion matrix*.

We repeat Steps 1 – 5 for all observations from the testing dataset.

Note, in *production* — when values for the outcome class (e.g., *WineColor*) are unknown, Steps 4 and 5 are omitted.

4.5.2   k-Nearest Neighbors for k>1

So far, we have considered only $k = 1$, but this can be problematic in some cases. Please take a look at Figure 4.6: We used a different wine to predict (*blue* point) that has a slightly higher acid content (*Acid* = 7.3 instead of *Acid* = 6.8). Therefore, compared to Figure 4.5 the *blue* point is now located higher and is nearest to a point (observation) representing a white wine (see N_1 in Figure 4.6). Consequently, the prediction of *k-Nearest Neighbors* (k=1) would be *white*. However, in Figure 4.6, red wine observations surround the wine that we try to predict, and the closest white wine seems to be an exception. Intuitively, we would predict the unknown wine as being *red*.

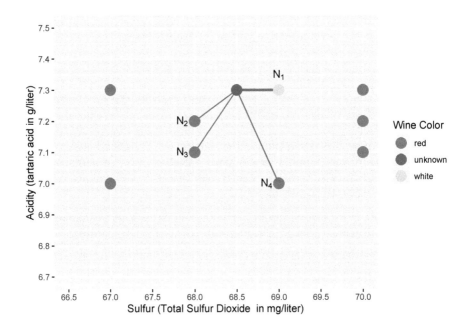

FIGURE 4.6 Predicting Wine Color with k-Nearest Neighbors ($k = 4$)

A *k-Nearest Neighbors* analysis that considers only one neighbor (the nearest; see N_1 and the bold magenta line in Figure 4.6) might suffer from this type of exception. Therefore, we might consider more than one neighbor ($k > 1$).

Figure 4.6 shows an example for a $k = 4$ Nearest Neighbors model. The four nearest neighbors to the *blue* prediction point (N_1, N_2, N_3, N_4) and their distance to the prediction point are marked with four magenta lines. The majority of these 4-nearest neighbors are red wines (3 compared to 1). Consequently, the prediction is *red*, which is compatible with our intuition. We can also say that the probability of the unknown wine being *red* is 75% ($\frac{3}{4} = 0.75$), and the probability of being *white* is 25% ($1 - 0.75 = 0.25$).

If one of the three red wines were *white*, we would end up with a tie. In this case, the predicted wine color would be determined randomly.

In a real-world application, you have to choose the value for the *hyper-parameter k* in the *model design* stage. The chosen k is then valid for all model predictions. This raises the question: How do we find an appropriate value for k? The answer is: We use a systematic *trial-and-error* process called "tuning".

Tuning the *hyper-parameter k* for a *Nearest Neighbors* model is covered in detail in Chapter 6, Section 6.7.

Right now, you might be tempted to run the model for different values of k and then use the testing dataset to see which k delivers the best prediction performance. However, this is not an appropriate way to optimize hyper-parameters. Using the testing dataset to optimize hyper-parameters can lead to overfitting.

Overfitting occurs when a prediction model performs well on the training data, but when it is used for preditions based on new data that the model has "never seen before", it performs poorly. Therefore, we have to find ways to limit ourselves to the training data when optimizing *hyper-parameters* such as the k in *k-Nearest Neighbors* (see Section 6.7 for methods, for how we can do this).

In general, a k that is too low is prone to be influenced by isolated outliers, although the surrounding neighborhood would suggest otherwise. On the other hand, a k that is too high would consider a neighborhood so large that it does not represent the neighborhood surrounding the prediction point anymore.

4.6   Scaling Predictor Variables

Before we build a *k-Nearest Neighbors* model in R, we have to solve one more problem that can be best illustrated when visualizing the wine data for $k = 1$ again in Figure 4.7.

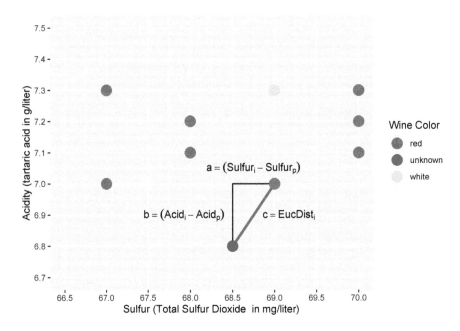

FIGURE 4.7 Predicting Wine Color with k-Nearest Neighbors ($k = 1$)

Figure 4.7 shows the *blue* prediction point and its nearest neighbor. The idea behind *k-Nearest Neighbors* ($k = 1$) is to find the most similar point (observation) to the prediction point.

First, look at the similarities and dissimilarities between the *blue* prediction point and its nearest neighbor. At a first glance, it seems in Figure 4.7, the two wines (points) are more dissimilar in terms of *Acidity* than in terms of *Sulfur* — the length of the vertical leg of the triangle is double the length of the horizontal leg. However, this impression is misleading as it only relates to the scale chosen for the diagram.

In contrast, if we plug in the values for *Acidity* and *Sulfur* into the *Euclidean Distance* equation,

$$
\underbrace{\frac{EucDist_i^2}{c^2}}_{} \;=\; \underbrace{\frac{(Sulfur_i - Sulfur_p)^2}{68.5-69}}_{} + \underbrace{\frac{(Acid_i - Acid_p)^2}{6.8-7}}_{}
$$

$$
\Longleftrightarrow
$$

$$
EucDist_i \;=\; \sqrt{0.25 + 0.04}
$$

we can see that the influence of the variable $Sulfur$ on the $Euclidean\ Distance$ is six times greater than the one of $Acidity$. Why is this? The variable $Sulfur$ is measured as sulfur dioxide concentration in the wine in $mg/liter$, while the variable $Acidity$ is measured as tartaric acid concentration in the wine in $g/liter$ (with 1 g equal to 1,000 mg). These different scales artificially increase the values of sulfur by a factor of 1,000, contributing to the greater importance of the variable $Sulfur$ when calculating $Euclidean\ Distance$.

To get a less biased representation of both variables when calculating $Euclidean\ Distance$, we need to scale the two predictor variables to the same or at least a similar range. This would give both variables the appropriate importance in the $Euclidean\ Distance$ formula.

There are several scaling techniques available to accomplish this task. Asaithambi (2017) is a good source for comparing common scaling techniques. He explains in detail why scaling might be needed, for which type of machine learning model scaling should be used, and how the most common scaling techniques work.

Here, we will only introduce two commonly used scaling techniques (see keyword $Feature\ Scaling$ in Wikipedia contributors (2023c) for more details):

Rescaling:

This technique generates a variable y_i that is scaled to a range between 0 and 1. The calculation is based on the original variable's value x_i, its minimum x_{min}, and its maximum x_{max}:

$$
y_i = \frac{x_i - x_{min}}{x_{max} - x_{min}}
$$

You can see how this works when you take a closer look at the extreme values for x: If x_i is equal to the smallest value in the dataset ($x_i = x_{min}$), the numerator and thus the scaled value y_i becomes 0. If x_i is equal to the largest value in the dataset ($x_i = x_{max}$), the numerator becomes $x_{max} - x_{min}$, and the scaled value becomes 1. Therefore, all scaled values are between 0 and 1. If we scale several predictor variables this way, they will end up in the same range (0 – 1) for all predictor variables.

Z-Score Normalization:

Z-score uses a variable's mean and the standard deviation for scaling. First, we calculate the mean $\bar{x}$ for the original variable x, and then the standard deviation s. To scale the variable x to the variable z, we use the following formula:

$$z_i = \frac{x_i - \overline{x}}{s}$$

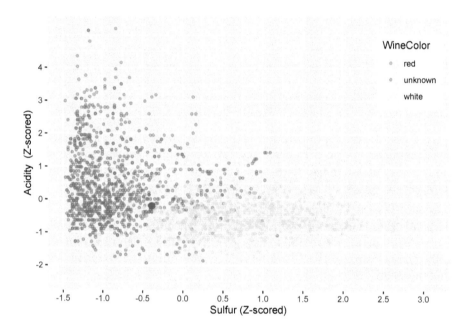

FIGURE 4.8 Z-Normalized Variables Acidity and Sulfur

The resulting Z-score expresses by how many standard deviations a data point deviates negatively or positively from the mean. In theory, Z-scores can be between $-\infty$ and $+\infty$. In reality, in almost all cases, Z-scores range from the mid-negative single digits to the mid-positive single digits. For example, the probability for a normal-distributed variable to have a Z-score greater than 5 or smaller than -5 is 0.000057%.

Therefore, *Z-score normalization* scales different variables to a similar range, preserves the spread, and does not rely heavily on the largest and smallest values. These properties make *Z-score normalization* a good candidate for scaling variables before they are used with *k-Nearest Neighbors*. In Figure 4.8 you can see the Z-score-scaled wine training dataset. The scale for *Acidity* and *Sulfur* is similar, and the shape of the data is preserved (compare with Figure 4.4).

4.7 Using Tidymodels for k-Nearest Neighbors

This section will use R and a *k-Nearest Neighbors* model to classify wines into red and white wines based on only two chemical properties (*Acidity* and *Sulfur*). In Section 4.9, you will work with an interactive project and extend the analysis using more chemical properties.

4.7.1 The tidymodels Package

In the following chapters of this book, we will utilize the R `tidymodels` package for our analysis. Therefore, before we develop our first machine learning model, we will provide a brief overview about the `tidymodels` package.

The `tidymodels` package allows working with a unified syntax and workflow for a wide variety of machine learning models and data engineering tasks. This avoids learning new commands and workflows each time you use a new machine learning model or R package.

The `tidymodels` package provides a standardized workflow with standardized commands for the following tasks:

- Randomly dividing observations into training and testing datasets.

- Pre-processing data with *recipes* where each *recipe* contains one or more `step_`-commands to successively pre-process the training and testing data in exactly the same way. These `step_`-commands are available for various tasks. For example, `step_naomit()` can be used to remove incomplete observations or to perform *Z-score-normalization*, `step_normalize()` can be used. You can find a list of data pre-processing steps at: https://www.tidymodels.org/find/recipes/

- Creating machine learning model-designs with only three standardized commands. At the time of the writing of this book, `tidymodels` supported more than 40 different machine learning models. Rather than building and coding these models separately, the `tidymodels` package provides *wrappers* around existing machine learning packages and their models. The *wrapper* translates the standardized `tidymodels` commands internally to a code required by the related package (machine learning model) and then executes the machine learning model. You can find a list of available machine learning models at: https://www.tidymodels.org/find/parsnip/#models)

- Tuning Hyper-parameters to choose *hyper-parameters* that need to be determined before the model is calibrated with the training data.

- Assessing prediction quality of trained machine learning models with a set of predefined metrics.

The following sections will cover all of these tasks except for *hyper-parameter tuning*, which will be covered in detail in Chapter 6.

Kuhn and Silge, two of the developers of `tidymodels`, provide a comprehensive guide to `tidymodels`, its functionality, and its philosophy (see Kuhn and Silge (2022)).

4.7.2 Loading and Splitting the Data

In the code block further below, we start with loading the needed R packages `rio`, `janitor`, and `tidymodels`.

Note that `tidymodels` is a meta-package comprising various other packages, including most packages from the `tidyverse`. Therefore, it is usually not necessary to load the `tidyverse` package separately.

After loading the packages, we use the same wine dataset as in Section 4.5 and again select only the predictors *TotalSulfurDioxide* (renamed to *Sulfur*) and *Acidity* to predict the outcome variable *WineColor* (see `import()` and `select()`).

Many machine learning models that perform *classification* (including *k-Nearest Neighbors*) require the outcome variable to be an R `factor` variable (see Section 3.5.1 for details about R `factor` variables). In the wine dataset, *WineColor* is a `character` variable. Therefore, we have to use `mutate()` to transform *WineColor* to a factor variable using the `as.factor()` command:

```
library(rio); library(janitor); library(tidymodels)
DataWine=import("https://ai.lange-analytics.com/data/WineData.rds") |>
        clean_names("upper_camel") |>
        select(WineColor, Sulfur=TotalSulfurDioxide, Acidity) |>
        mutate(WineColor=as.factor(WineColor))
head(DataWine)
```

```
##    WineColor Sulfur Acidity
## 1        red     37    10.8
## 2      white    213     6.4
## 3      white    139     9.4
## 4      white     90     8.2
## 5      white    183     6.4
## 6        red     38     6.7
```

After importing the wine data and selecting the variables for analysis, we need to split the dataset into training and testing data. In the code below, we start with initializing the random number generator with `set.seed(876)` to make the randomization process reproducible. Then we use the `initial_split()` command to define how the split should be performed. By setting `prop=0.7`,

R will randomly assign 70% of the observations to the training data and the
rest to the testing data. The argument `strata=WineColor` uses *WineColor* as
the stratifying variable to ensure that red and white wines are approximately
equally represented in the training and testing data.

Finally, we extract the training and testing data from the R object `Split7030`
and assign them to `DataTrain` and `DataTest`, respectively:

```
set.seed(876)
Split7030=initial_split(DataWine, prop=0.7, strata=WineColor)
DataTrain=training(Split7030)
DataTest=testing(Split7030)

head(DataTrain)
```

```
##    WineColor Sulfur Acidity
## 1        red     37    10.8
## 2        red     38     6.7
## 3        red     12     7.5
## 4        red     25     7.1
## 5        red    114     8.0
## 6        red     66     7.6
```

The first six records of `DataTrain` are printed above for reference. If you like
to review the details about splitting a dataset into training and testing data,
go to Section 4.3.

Remember that we need to initialize R's random number generator to ensure
that the randomly generated training and testing datasets are the same each
time we run the code (see Section 4.3 for more details).

4.7.3 Recipe for Data Pre-Processing

In this section and throughout the book, we will use *recipes* from the `tidy-`
`models` package to pre-process our data. This will simplify data pre-processing
and, in addition, clearly show the pre-processing structure.

You can compare a *tidymodels recipe* to a recipe in a cookbook. First, the
ingredients are listed, and then you find the steps to use these ingredients to
cook the meal.

```
RecipeWine=recipe(WineColor~Acidity+Sulfur, data=DataTrain) |>
          step_normalize(all_predictors()) |>
          step_naomit()
```

Analogous, a *tidymodels recipe* starts with the command `recipe()` that selects all variables (ingredients) used in the analysis. The outcome variable is separated from the predictor variables with a tilde symbol (~). In order to separate the predictor variables from each other, a plus sign (+) is used. It is essential to understand that the + sign is unrelated to any type of addition. It is just used as a symbol to separate the predictor variables.

The second required argument in the *recipe* command is a `data=` argument that determines which data frame is used for the pre-processing. This data frame is usually the training data frame.

The `recipe()` command is followed by instructions on how to process the data step by step. Each step starts with `step_`, indicating that the instruction (command) is part of a *recipe*.

The `recipe()` command and all steps used in a *recipe* are connected with the *piping* operator (`|>`) to form the *recipe*. A *recipe* is usually saved into an *R* object. See, for example, the code block above where the *recipe* is saved into the *R* object`RecipeWine`. We started the object name with the word `Recipe` to indicate that the object contains a *recipe*.

The `recipe()` command in the code block above lists the predictor variables *Sulfur* and *Acidity* explicitly separated by a + sign. There is also a short form for defining variables as outcome and predictor variables that can be used when the processed data frame exclusively contains the outcome and predictor variables. That is, there are no extra unused variables in the data frame.

We use the short form in the code below to replicate the *recipe* above. As you can see, there is only a minimal change in the first argument of the `recipe()` command — called the *formula*. We still list the outcome variable `WineColor` followed by the ~ symbol. But on the right-side of the ~ symbol, we simply add a dot (`.`) instead of listing the predictor variables. The `.` represents all other variables in the data frame (`DataTrain`) that are not outcome variables — all predictor variables.

```
RecipeWine=recipe(WineColor~., data=DataTrain) |>
        step_naomit() |>
        step_normalize(all_predictors())
```

Previously, you learned that predictor variables must be scaled before using them in a *k-Nearest Neighbors* model. Scaling avoids variables with greater values having a stronger influence on the prediction results than variables with lower values. Recall that previously *Z-score normalization* was introduced as an effective scaling method (see Section 4.6 for details).

The package `tidymodels` provides a command `step_normalize()` that performs *Z-score normalization* and can be added to a *recipe*. We can add the variables that need to be *Z-score normalized* as arguments into the `step_normalize()`

command, such as `step_normalize(Sulfur, Acidity)`. This is fine when you only have two predictor variables, but it can become tedious if you have many predictor variables. Therefore, `tidymodels` allows us to use a broader definition for the variables that need to be pre-processed. In the code block below, we use `step_normalize(all_predictors())` to normalize all of our predictor variables.

We also add `step_naomit()` to the *recipe* above. This ensures that incomplete observations are deleted. It is good practice to add this step and to monitor which and how many observations are deleted.

When we print the *recipe* `RecipeWine`, we can see that two variables were assigned the predictor *role*, and one was assigned the outcome *role*. We can also see the *steps* that we had defined:

```
print(RecipeWine)

##
## -- Recipe ----------------------------------
##
## -- Inputs
## Number of variables by role
## outcome:   1
## predictor: 2
##
## -- Operations
## * Removing rows with NA values in: <none>
## * Centering and scaling for:
##    all_predictors()
```

It is important to realize that the *recipe* above does not process any data at this point; it only holds the instructions on which variables are outcome/predictor variables and how to process them later when executing the *recipe*. Again, a *recipe* in *R* can be compared to a recipe in a cookbook. A cookbook recipe does not make the meal. It only gives instructions on how to make the meal We will use a `workflow()` later in Section 4.7.5 to automatically prepare the *recipe* for execution, generate the pre-processed data, and finally use the pre-processed data as input for a machine learning model.[2]

---
[2]In case you need to prepare and execute a *recipe* manually, you can follow these steps: i) prepare the *recipe* for execution: `RecipeWinePrep=RecipeWine |> prep()`, ii) using the `bake()` command to (pre-)process the data as determined by the *recipe*, e.g., the testing data: `DataTestProc=bake(RecipeWinePrep, new_data=DataTest)`.

You might have noticed that the `select()` and the `mutate()` commands were used right after the data was loaded with `import()` — before the *recipe* `RecipeWine` was even defined. This raises the question:

When should we use `select()` and `mutate()`, and when should we use a recipe to pre-process data?

Here are some suggestions:

1. Generally, using a *recipe* is advisable because we can reuse a *recipe* on other data frames.

2. It is good practice to use `select()` before a *recipe* to reduce the columns of an original data frame to only those columns (variables) that are required for the analysis. This allows us to use the `.`-notation in the formula argument of the `recipe()` command.

3. When transforming *outcome variables*, it is advised to always do this outside of a *recipe*. For example, in the *R* code above, we used `mutate()` to convert the outcome variable *WineColor* from a `char`-acter data type to a `factor` data type outside the *recipe*. If a *recipe* is later used on another dataset for prediction, this dataset might not contain a column for the outcome variable.[3] More about why *recipes* should not be used on outcome variables in Kuhn and Silge (2022), Section 8.4.

4.7.4   Creating a Model-Design

A *model design* determines which machine learning model from which *R* package should be used for the analysis.

To define a *model design* within the `tidymodels` environment, only three commands (connected with `|>`) are required. The following code block shows how to generate a machine learning *model design* for a *k-Nearest Neighbors* model:

```
ModelDesignKNN=nearest_neighbor(neighbors=4,
                           weight_func="rectangular") |>
               set_engine("kknn") |>
               set_mode("classification")
```

As you can see, the *k-Nearest Neighbors* model is designed with only three commands:

---

[3]Even if the dataset does contain the outcome variable, such as the testing data, some `step_` commands, including `step_normalize()`, ignore the outcome variable to avoid *data leakage*. *Data Leakage* occurs when information from the training process is used (often inadvertently) in the testing phase of the model. This can lead to poor prediction quality when the model is used in the production phase.

1. A command determining the name of the machine learning algorithm (in this case `nearest_neighbor()`) and optionally *hyper-parameter* for the model. Here we used `neighbors=4` to determine the value for *k* (number of neighbors), and `weight_function=rectangular` to ensure that the original *k-Nearest Neighbors* algorithm is used.

2. A `set_engine()` command to provide the name of the package that performs the machine learning algorithm (in this case, `set_engine("kknn")`). Note there is no need to load the package via `library()` because this is done internally by the `set_engine()` command, but the package must be installed before you use it.

3. A `set_mode()` command that indicates if we perform a *classification* or a *regression*.

The *model design* is then stored in an *R* object (`ModelDesignKNN`). As the name suggests, `ModelDesignKNN` is only a *design* for a model, like a blueprint. A *model design* like `ModelDesignKNN` only contains a model description, and no data are fitted to the model at this point of the development. Consequently, `ModelDesignKNN` in its current state cannot be used for predictions.

When we print the *model design*, we get some basic information about the *model design*.

```
print(ModelDesignKNN)
```

```
## K-Nearest Neighbor Model Specification (classification)
##
## Main Arguments:
##   neighbors = 4
##   weight_func = rectangular
##
## Computational engine: kknn
```

To find detailed information about how *k-Nearest Neighbors* is implemented through the `kknn` package, we refer to Hechenbichler and Schliep (2004). To find more details about *model design* in `tidymodels` see Kuhn and Silge (2022), Chapter 6.

4.7.5 Creating and Training a Workflow

In the two previous sections, we defined a *recipe* and a *model design*. In this section, we will put it all together in a *workflow*. A *workflow* combines a recipe for data pre-processing with a *model design* into a *workflow*. Afterward, the *workflow* needs to be fitted (calibrated) to the training data before it can be used to predict (more about fitted vs. *unfitted* machine learning models will be covered in Section 5.4.2).

In the code block below, we start with the `workflow()` command, and we add the *recipe* (`add_recipe(RecipeWine)`) and the *model design* (`add_model(ModelDesignKNN)`) to the *workflow*. Then we fit the *workflow* to the training data with `fit(DataTrain)` and save the fitted *workflow model* into the R object `WFModelWine`. We decided to begin the object name with WFModel to indicate that this R object is a *workflow* model ready to be used for predictions.

```
WFModelWine=workflow() |>
          add_recipe(RecipeWine) |>
          add_model(ModelDesignKNN) |>
          fit(DataTrain)
```

4.7.6   Predicting with a Fitted Workflow Model

In this section, we will use the fitted *workflow model* from the previous section to predict the *WineColor* for the observations of the testing dataset `DataTest`.

We use the testing rather than the training dataset because we want to assess the model's prediction quality rather than how well the model can approximate the training data.

To predict the wine color of different wines based on their *acidity* and *sulfur dioxide* content, we can use the `predict()` command. As you can see in the code block below, the `predict()` command only requires two arguments: the name of the trained *workflow* object (`WFModelWine`) and the name of the data frame that contains the predictor variables for the prediction (`DataTest`):

```
DataPred=predict(WFModelWine, DataTest)
```

The `predict()` command pre-processes the testing data as defined in the *recipe* and then uses the fitted *workflow model* (`WFModelWine`) to predict the *WineColor*. The predictions can be assigned to a data frame (in this case, `DataPred`).

You can see the predictions for the first six wines in the testing dataset in the printout below:

```
head(DataPred)
```

```
## # A tibble: 6 x 1
##    .pred_class
```

```
##    <fct>
## 1 white
## 2 red
## 3 white
## 4 white
## 5 white
## 6 red
```

The variable with the prediction is automatically named *.pred_class*. However, we cannot see if the predictions are correct because we cannot easily compare the estimate (*.pred_class*; stored in DataPred) to the truth (*WineColor*; stored in DataTest).

It would be great if the data frame DataTest could be *augmented* with the predictions from the *workflow*. Then we could observe estimate and truth together. This is precisely what the augment() command does.

The augment() command predicts first and then adds the prediction column(s) to the data frame used to predict. It requires the same arguments as the predict() command: First, the name of the fitted *workflow* object, and second the name of the data frame containing the predictor variables. When executing the augment() command, it performs the predictions and combines the resulting prediction results with the data frame that was used for the prediction (e.g., DataTest). The result is usually saved in a new data frame (e.g., *DataTestWithPred*):

```
DataTestWithPred=augment(WFModelWine, DataTest)

head(DataTestWithPred)
```

```
## # A tibble: 6 x 6
##   WineColor Sulfur Acidity .pred_class .pred_red
##   <fct>      <dbl>   <dbl> <fct>           <dbl>
## 1 white         90     8.2 white            0.25
## 2 red           19    11.8 red              1
## 3 white        220     6.7 white            0
## 4 red          131     7.8 white            0.25
## 5 white        161     7   white            0
## 6 red           41     9.9 red              1
## # i 1 more variable: .pred_white <dbl>
```

The printout of the first six observations from the data frame DataTestWith-Pred shows the truth in the outcome variable *WineColor* and the estimate in the variable *.pred_class*. Five of the six observations are predicted correctly, while one (the fourth observation) is mispredicted.

The augment() command also calculates the probabilities for each observation to be a *red* or a *white* wine and stores them in the variables *.pred_red* and *.pred_white*, respectively. These probabilities result from the voting process of the *k-Nearest Neighbors*. Remember, we considered the four nearest neighbors. Therefore, the vote for the color *red* could be either 25%, 50%, 75%, or 100%, which is reflected in the probabilities of the variable *.pred_red*. The probabilities for white wine follow from $.pred\_white = 1 - .pred\_red$

4.7.7   Assessing the Predictive Quality with Metrics

The tidymodels package provides several commands to calculate *metrics* that reflect predictive performance. Most of these commands compare the estimate with the truth and then calculate the related metrics.

For example, we can use the con_mat() command from tidymodels to create a *confusion matrix*. The command requires three arguments:

1. The name of the data frame that contains the estimate and the truth (e.g., DataTestWithPred).

2. The variable that contains the truth (e.g., *DataWine*)

3. The variable that contains the estimate (e.g., *.pred_class*)

The code block below uses conf_mat() in combination with the data frame DataTestWithPred to generate a *confusion matrix*:

```
ConfMatrixWine=conf_mat(DataTestWithPred, truth=WineColor,
                        estimate=.pred_class)

print(ConfMatrixWine)


##          Truth
## Prediction red white
##      red   436    46
##    white    44   434
```

The sum of the counts of the main-diagonal elements of the *confusion matrix* (the counts of correctly predicted wines) is very high, compared to the sum of the counts of the off-diagonal elements (the counts of the falsely predicted wines). This is the first indicator for a good prediction quality. However, as the following section will show, we have to analyze the *confusion matrix* in more depth to gain an accurate, objective assessment about the prediction quality.

4.8   Interpreting a Confusion Matrix

In the previous section, a *confusion matrix* was created to assess the predictive quality of the *k-Nearest Neighbors* model. The first classification class (*red* in our example) listed in a *confusion matrix* is usually called the Positive Class, while the second class listed is the Negative Class (*white* in our example). However, which class is considered *positive* and which one is considered *negative* is arbitrary and mostly not important as long as we agree on which one is *positive* and which is *negative*.[4]

The *confusion matrix* from the previous section is printed below. For easier readability, the four entry fields are labeled as *True Positives (TP)*, *False Positives (FP)*, *False Negatives (FN)*, and *True Negatives (TN)*:

```
##              Truth
## Prediction red      white
##       red    TP: 436 FP: 46
##       white FN: 44   TN: 434
```

Both entries (cells) in the first row of the *confusion matrix* represent the counts for predicting a wine as *red* (the *positive* class). The first entry shows 436 wines predicted as red which are actually red (*True Positives; TP*). On the other hand, the second entry of the first row represents 46 red wines that are predicted as *red*, and are therefore falsely predicted because they are actually *white* (*False Positives; FP*).

We can make similar statements for the second row in the *confusion matrix*. The second row represents the two counts for wines that are predicted as *white* (the *negative* class). 44 wines are predicted as *white*, but because they are actually *red*, they are falsely predicted (*False Negatives; FN*), while 434 are correctly predicted as *white* (*True Negatives; TN*).[5]

We can calculate testing data *accuracy* and see that the result has improved compared to our visual attempts in Section 4.4:

$$Accuracy = \frac{TP+TN}{TP+FP+TN+FN} = \frac{436+434}{960} = 0.91$$

Warning: Be careful when interpreting accuracy as a single metric!

---

[4]In tidymodels, the positive class is the one that is listed first in the factor levels.

[5]Hint: When trying to find out which cells in a *confusion matrix* represent *TP, FP, TN,* and *FN*, start with interpreting the rows (the *predictions*) and then interpret the columns (the *truth*).

Confusion Matrix: Be Careful with Accuracy

The following made-up story demonstrates a problem when only *accuracy* is used to evaluate a machine learning model:

Dr. Nebulous offers what he calls a *97% Machine Learning Gambling Prediction*. Here is how it works: Gamblers can buy a prediction from Dr. Nebulous for a fee of $5. Dr. Nebulous will then run his famous machine learning model and send a closed envelope with the prediction. The gambler is supposed to open the envelope in the casino right before placing a bet of $100 on a number in roulette. The envelope contains a message that states either "You will win" or "You will lose", which allows the gambler to act accordingly by either placing or not placing the bet.

Dr. Nebulous claims that a "clinical trial" performed by 1,000 volunteers, who opened the envelope after they had bet on a number in roulette, shows an *accuracy* of 97.3%.

How could Dr. Nebulous have such a precise model? The trick is that his machine learning model uses what is called a *naive prognosis*: It always predicts "You will lose".

Let us take a look at the *confusion matrix* from the 1,000 volunteers' trial:

```
##           Truth
## Prediction Win Lose
##      Win    0    0
##      Lose  27  973
```

Roulette has (including the zero) 37 numbers to bet on. Consequently, the chance to win is $\frac{1}{37} = 0.027$. This means that out of the 1000 volunteers, 27 are expected to win, and 973 are expected to lose. You can see that in the *confusion matrix* above, the *accuracy* promised by Dr. Nebulous is correct: When you divide the sum of the diagonal elements of the matrix by the observations, you get 0.973 ($\frac{0+973}{1000}$).

However, when we look at the correct positive and negative rates separately, we see that Dr. Nebulous's *accuracy* rate (although correct) makes little sense.

The correct negative rate (specificity) is 100% (out of 973 volunteers who lost, all were correctly predicted as "You will lose"). But, the correct positive rate (sensitivity) is 0% (out of the 27 winners, all were falsely predicted as "You will lose"). This example shows:

When interpreting the confusion matrix, you must look at accuracy, sensitivity, and specificity simultaneously.

In the example above, Dr. Nebulous intentionally misused the *confusion matrix*'s interpretation to his financial advantage.

However, you can unintentionally run into the same problem because sometimes machine learning models "choose the easiest way" to generate a successful prediction, which can be the *naive prognosis*.

This is especially true when the outcome variable in the classification model is unbalanced, meaning that values for one of the classes (*negative* or *positive*) occur dramatically more often than others. You will learn how to identify unbalanced datasets and how to mitigate the problem in Chapter 8.

To make sure the high *accuracy* rate from our *k-Nearest Neighbors* model is not misleading, we will separately calculate sensitivity — the rate of correctly predicted positives (red wines) and specificity — the rate of correctly predicted negatives (white wines).

We start with calculating *sensitivity* from the *confusion matrix*: 480 wines (the sum of the left column) in the testing dataset are red wines (positive class). From these red wines, 436 were predicted correctly. Therefore we can calculate *sensitivity* as follows:

$$Sensitivity = \frac{TP}{TP + FN} = \frac{436}{436 + 44} = 0.9083$$

Specificity is calculated similarly, but we focus on the right column of the *confusion matrix*: 480 wines (the sum of the entries in the right column) in the testing dataset are white wines (negative class). From these white wines, 434 were predicted correctly. Therefore we can calculate *specificity* as follows:

$$Specificity = \frac{TN}{FP + TN} = \frac{434}{46 + 434} = 0.9042$$

To summarize, based on the testing dataset, the overall *accuracy* (proportion of overall correctly predicted wines) was 90.62%, *sensitivity* (proportion of correctly predicted red wines) was 90.83%, and *specificity* the (proportion of correctly predicted white wines) was 90.42%. These are pretty good results.[6]

For the analysis in this section, we used only two predictor variables (sulfur dioxide content and acidity of the wines). In the following section, you will repeat the analysis with your own model, but you will use all available predictor variables to improve the predictive quality further.

4.9 ◐ Project: Predicting Wine Color with Several Chemical Properties

Interactive Section

In this section, you will find content together with R code to execute, change, and rerun in RStudio.

The best way to read and to work with this section is to open it with *RStudio*. Then you can interactively work on R code exercises and R projects within a web browser. This way you can apply what you have learned so far and extend your knowledge. You can also choose to continue reading either in the book or online, but you will not benefit from the interactive learning experience.

---

[6]Besides *accuracy*, *sensitivity*, and *specificity*, many other metrics can be calculated from a *confusion matrix*. Lyer (2021) provides a good overview together with an introduction to confusion matrices.

To work with this section in *RStudio* in an interactive environment, follow these steps:

1. Ensure that both the `learnR` and the `shiny` package are installed. If not, install them from RStudio's main menu (Tools -> Install Packages ...).

2. Download the `Rmd` file for the interactive session and save it in your `project` folder. You will find the link for the download below.

3. Open the downloaded file in RStudio and click the `Run Document` button, located in the editing window's top-middle area.

For detailed help for running the exercises including videos for Windows and Mac users we refer to: https://blog.lange-analytics.com/2024/01/interactsessions.html

Do not skip this interactive section because besides providing applications of already covered concepts, it will also extend what you have learned so far.

Below is the link to download the interactive section:

https://ai.lange-analytics.com/exc/?file=04-KNearNeighExerc200.Rmd

In what follows, you will develop your own *k-Nearest Neighbors* model to predict the color of wines based on chemical properties. In contrast to the previous section, you will extend the analysis to use all chemical properties available in the wine dataset.

Below you can see all variables available in the wine dataset. The first variable *WineColor* is the outcome variable, followed by the predictor variables that indicate the chemical properties of a wine. The last variable *Quality* reflects how consumers rated the quality of the wines. This variable is not a chemical property and is likely irrelevant for predicting a wine's color. Therefore, *Quality* should not be used as a predictor.

```
##  [1] "WineColor"         "Acidity"
##  [3] "VolatileAcidity"   "CitricAcid"
##  [5] "ResidualSugar"     "Chlorides"
##  [7] "FreeSulfurDioxide" "TotalSulfurDioxide"
##  [9] "Density"           "PH"
## [11] "Sulphates"         "Alcohol"
## [13] "Quality"
```

The code block below loads the wine dataset, changes variable names to *UpperCamel* notation, unselects the variable *Quality* from the data, renames *TotalSulfurDioxide* to *Sulfur*, and defines *WineColor* as `factor` data type.

After the random number generator has been initialized, the data are split into training and testing data (see Section 4.3 for details).

Now it is your turn: Please complete the two commands that extract training

and testing data from the split to assign them to the data frames `DataTrain`
and `DataTest`.

```
library(tidymodels); library(rio); library(janitor)
DataWine=import("https://ai.lange-analytics.com/data/WineData.rds") |>
          clean_names("upper_camel") |>
          select(-Quality) |>
          rename(Sulfur=TotalSulfurDioxide) |>
          mutate(WineColor=as.factor(WineColor))

set.seed(876)
Split7030=initial_split(DataWine, prop=0.7, strata=WineColor)

DataTrain=...(...)
DataTest=...(...)

head(DataTrain)
```

Next, by executing the code block below, you will create the *recipe*. The command is the same as before, and the results will be saved into the *R* object
`RecipeWine`:

```
RecipeWine=recipe(WineColor~., data=DataTrain) |>
          step_naomit() |>
          step_normalize(all_predictors())

print(RecipeWine)


##

## -- Recipe ---------------------------------

##

## -- Inputs

## Number of variables by role

## outcome:   1
## predictor: 11

##

## -- Operations

## * Removing rows with NA values in: <none>

## * Centering and scaling for:
##    all_predictors()
```

The commands to create the *model design* are also the same as before. When you execute the code block below, the *model design* will be created and saved into the R object ModelDesignKNN:

```
ModelDesignKNN=nearest_neighbor(neighbors=4,
                                weight_func="rectangular") |>
            set_engine("kknn") |>
            set_mode("classification")

print(ModelDesignKNN)


## K-Nearest Neighbor Model Specification (classification)
##
## Main Arguments:
##    neighbors = 4
##    weight_func = rectangular
##
## Computational engine: kknn
```

You are now tasked with adding the *recipe* and the *model design* to a *work-flow* and then fitting the *workflow* to the training data. Note that the *recipe* RecipeWine, the *model design* ModelDesignKNN, and the data frame DataTrain have already been loaded in the background. Please complete the code block below and execute it.

```
WFModelWine=workflow() |>
          add_recipe(...) |>
          add_model(...) |>
          fit(...)

print(WFModelWine)
```

Because the *workflow* model is fitted to the training data, we can use it for predictions. Instead of using the predict() command, we again use the more comprehensive augment() command, which predicts *WineColor* based on the predictor variables from the testing dataset and then adds the predictions as a new variable named *.pred_class* to DataTest. The complete result is saved in the R object DataTestWithPred.

Since the R object DataTestWithPred contains the predictions (estimate) for the wine color and also the truth, stored in variable *WineColor*, we can use it as the data argument for metrics commands. An example is the conf_mat() command that generates a *confusion matrix*. The related code is already prepared. You just have to execute it.

```
DataTestWithPred=augment(WFModelWine, DataTest)
conf_mat(DataTestWithPred, truth=WineColor, estimate=.pred_class)
```

```
##             Truth
## Prediction red white
##       red   474    2
##     white     6  478
```

A first glance at the diagonal elements of the *confusion matrix* already indicates an improvement over the model with two predictor variables.

The tidymodels package can help you to calculate metrics such as *accuracy*, *sensitivity*, and *specificity*. Instead of calculating these metrics separately you can streamline the process by creating a *metric set* first.

In the code block below, the command metric_set() creates a new command to calculate accurracy, sensitivity, and specificity. We name the new command MetricsWine.

The newly created command MetricWine() can be used similarly to the conf_mat() command, but instead of creating a *confusion matrix*, it creates all the metrics previously specified with metric_set() simultaneously. This saves you some typing effort.

Give it a try with the code block below (note, the data frame DataTest and the fitted *workflow model* WFModelWine have already been loaded in the background):

```
DataTestWithPred=augment(WFModelWine, DataTest)

MetricsWine=metric_set(accuracy, sensitivity, specificity)
MetricsWine(DataTestWithPred, truth=WineColor, estimate=.pred_class)
```

```
## # A tibble: 3 x 3
##   .metric     .estimator .estimate
##   <chr>       <chr>          <dbl>
## 1 accuracy    binary         0.992
## 2 sensitivity binary         0.988
## 3 specificity binary         0.996
```

As the *confusion matrix* and the three metrics above confirm, we reached an almost perfect prediction quality.

Try changing the arguments in the metric_set() command to different metrics and see what happens.

Predicting the wine color from the wine dataset is a notoriously easy task. Therefore, the next section will approach a more realistic problem. We will try to identify the ten digits (0 – 9) from handwriting. This is also known as *OCR* (*Optical Character Recognition*).

4.10 ◎ Project: Recognize Handwriten Numbers

In this section, you will develop a machine learning model based on *k-Nearest Neighbors* for a real-world application. The goal is to recognize handwritten digits from images. You will use the *MNIST* dataset, a standard dataset for image recognition. The *MNIST* dataset is publicly available and contains 60,000 images for training and 10,000 images for testing purposes. LeCun et al. (2005) developed the *MNIST* dataset based on two datasets from handwritten digits obtained from census workers and high school students.

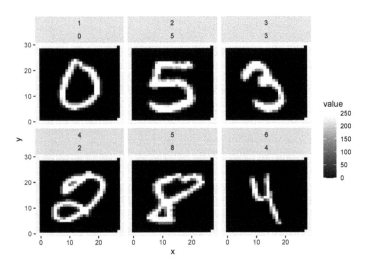

FIGURE 4.9 First Six Handwritten Numbers of the MNIST Dataset

Figure 4.9 shows a printout of the first six images from the *MNIST* dataset, giving you an idea of how the census workers and high school students wrote the numbers.

Rather than using the complete *MNIST* dataset, in this project, we will use only a subset (the first 500 images/rows of the original *MNIST* dataset) to speed up the training time. In the digital resources section (see Section 4.12) of this chapter, you will find links for sample images of 500, 1,000, and 10,000, as well as the link to the original dataset. This allows you to modify the code below to use more observations.

The machine learning model in this section recognizes only handwritten digits. Other more advanced but similar applications recognize numbers and characters from scanned documents. *OCR* in the Adobe PDF app is one of these examples.

4.10.1   How Images Are Stored

Before working with a *k-Nearest Neighbors* model, we first need to understand the problem we are trying to solve. This is when domain knowledge plays an important role. *Domain knowledge* is the knowledge about a specific field or discipline outside of machine learning. In the case of image recognition, *domain knowledge* involves understanding how images can be stored in a dataset.

In general, a gray-scale image can be stored in a raster format. A raster is a grid with two dimensions. The *MNIST* images are stored in a grid of 28 rows and 28 columns. Each entry in this grid (called a pixel) indicates the brightness of the cell on a scale from 0 to 255. A value of 0 indicates black, a value of 255 indicates white, and values between 0 and 255 indicate some degree of gray.

Figure 4.10 shows an example of how a handwritten "9" can be stored in an image file. The background colors in the cells of Figure 4.10 are only for demonstration purposes. An image file would only contain numbers between 0 and 255 organized in rows and columns separated by commas.

There is a problem when working with images in a machine learning model. Machine learning models usually require that each observation is within a row of a data frame and that the columns represent predictor variables. As explained above, images are stored in a 2D grid.

The solution is to combine all the rows of an image into one long row of pixels. In our case, we start with the first row, append the second row of the image raster, append the third row, and so on, until we finally append the 28th row. Because the images initially have 28 rows and 28 columns, each image would then be converted to one long row consisting of 784 ($28 \cdot 28$) columns. This was done with the *MNIST* dataset. Each image is stored in one row. Each of the 784 pixels of an image is stored in one of 784 columns. These columns will become the 784 predictor variables. The outcome variable (called *Label*) is stored in the first column of the data frame. It contains each image's digit.

Take a look at Table 4.1, which shows an excerpt from the *MNIST* data frame for the first six images. Note that the table does not show all 784 predictor variables (pixels). Instead, it only shows the pixel values for the first three pixels and the last two pixels for the six images. These pixels represent the left-upper and the right-lower corner for each of the six images. They are all 0 (black) because the digits were written with a white pen, and the corresponding pixels are more in the center of the image.

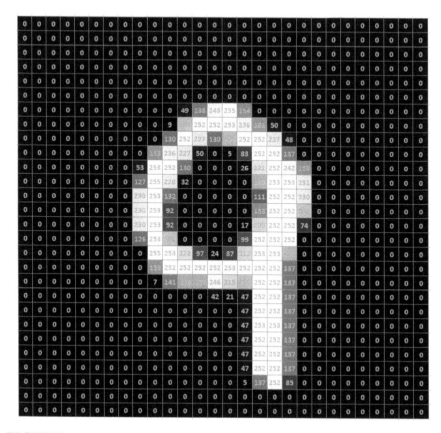

FIGURE 4.10 Raster Image of a Nine

TABLE 4.1 How Images are Stored in the MNIST Dataset

Label	PIX1	PIX2	PIX3	...	PIX783	PIX784
0	0	0	0	...	0	0
5	0	0	0	...	0	0
3	0	0	0	...	0	0
2	0	0	0	...	0	0
8	0	0	0	...	0	0
4	0	0	0	...	0	0

4.10.2 Build Recipe, Model-Design, and Workflow

Interactive Section

In this section, you will find content together with *R* code to execute, change, and rerun in RStudio.

The best way to read and to work with this section is to open it with *RStudio*. Then you can interactively work on *R* code exercises and *R* projects within a web browser. This way you can apply what you have learned so far and extend your knowledge. You can also choose to continue reading either in the book or online, but you will not benefit from the interactive learning experience.

To work with this section in *RStudio* in an interactive environment, follow these steps:

1. Ensure that both the learnR and the shiny package are installed. If not, install them from RStudio's main menu (Tools -> Install Packages ...).

2. Download the Rmd file for the interactive session and save it in your project folder. You will find the link for the download below.

3. Open the downloaded file in RStudio and click the Run Document button, located in the editing window's top-middle area.

For detailed help for running the exercises including videos for Windows and Mac users we refer to: https://blog.lange-analytics.com/2024/01/interactsessions.html

Do not skip this interactive section because besides providing applications of already covered concepts, it will also extend what you have learned so far.

Below is the link to download the interactive section:

https://ai.lange-analytics.com/exc/?file=04-KNearNeighExerc300.Rmd

Now that you know how the images of the *MNIST* dataset are stored, you can start the machine learning project by importing the data. The first line in the code block further below imports a data frame with the first 500 images from the original *MNIST* dataset. Each image is stored in a row with the label indicating which of the ten digits it represents.

Please complete the code block below in the interactive version of this section in *RStudio*. Here are a few hints:

- The *Label* for each image is stored as an integer data type, but *k-Nearest Neighbors* only accepts a factor data type for the outcome variable. Therefore, you must transform the outcome variable *Label* to factor data type.

- When splitting the dataset into training and testing data, you can use strata= to indicate that the numbers stored in *Label* are approximately equally represented in the training and the testing dataset. After you have completed the commands in the code block, the head(DataTrain) command will show you the first six observations of the training dataset.

```
DataMnist=import("https://ai.lange-analytics.com/data/MN500.rds") |>
mutate(Label=as.factor(...))
set.seed(123)
Split7030=initial_split(DataMnist, 0.70, strata=...)
DataTrain=training(...)
DataTest=...(...)
```

```
head(DataTrain)
```

When developing a machine learning model with `tidymodels`, you can always follow the same process:

1. Define a *recipe* to pre-process the data and define which variables are *outcome* and which are *predictor* variables (for details about *recipes* see Section 4.7.1).

2. Define the *model design* that determines which machine learning model to use and which *R* package contains the model (for details about *model design* see Section 4.7.1).

3. Add the *recipe* and the *model design* to a *workflow* and use the training data to fit the machine learning model. The resulting *workflow* model can then be used for predictions (for details about *workflows* see Section 4.7.5).

The code block below completes Steps 1 and 2. The first line creates the *recipe*, and it is stored in an *R* object that is named `RecipeMnist`. We can use `Label~.` to determine that *Label* is the outcome variable, and all other variables are predictor variables because the data frame `DataTrain` contains exclusively outcome and predictor variables. Normalization with `step_normalize()` is unnecessary because the predictor variables are already in the same range (from 0 for *black* to 255 for *white*). Also, all observations are complete. Therefore, `step_naomit()` is not needed either.

The second step is your task. Please complete the command that defines the *model design* and store the result in the *R* object `ModelDesignKNN`. Use the model `nearest_neighbor()` from the *R* package `kknn` and remember that the model is a *classification* rather than a *regression* model.

After completing and executing the code block, *R* will print a summary of the *recipe* and the *model design*.

```
RecipeMnist=recipe(Label~., data=DataTrain)
```

```
ModelDesignKNN=...(neighbors=5, weight_func="rectangular") |>
```

```
                    set_engine("...") |>
                    set_mode("...")
```

```
print(RecipeMnist)
print(ModelDesignKNN)
```

Now, you can move to the third step to create a fitted *workflow model*. In the code block below, you add the *recipe* (`RecipeMnist`) and the *model design* (`ModelDesignKNN`) to a *workflow*, and then you fit the *workflow* with the training data stored in `DataTrain`. The fitted *workflow model* is then saved in the object `WFModelMnist`. When you print the fitted *workflow model*, R will provide information about the *recipe* and the fitted model. This might take a moment. So, be a little patient.

```
WFModelMnist=workflow() |>
            add_recipe(...) |>
            add_model(...) |>
            fit(...)
```

```
print(WFModelMnist)
```

Since `WFModelMnist` is a fitted *workflow model*, you can use it to predict the images in the testing dataset (`DataTest`). Again, you will use the command `augment()` instead of `predict()`. Consequently, the testing dataset will be augmented with a new column `.pred_class` that contains predicted digits for each image. The result will then be saved into the data frame `DataTestWithPred`.

```
DataTestWithPred=augment(..., ...)
```

```
head(DataTestWithPred |> select(Label, .pred_class, everything()))
```

The head command prints the first six observations. You will see that `DataTestWithPred` now contains for each observation both the predictions (*.pred_class*) and the true value (in this case, *Label*).

Remember, this is crucial for assessing a model's prediction quality because many `tidymodels` commands that assess predictive quality require a variable for a `truth` argument (in this case, `truth=Label`) and a variable for the `estimate` argument (in this case `estimate=.pred_class`). The `conf_mat()` command, which generates the *confusion matrix*, is an example (note that the data frame `DataTestWithPred` has already been loaded in the background):

```
conf_mat(DataTestWithPred, truth=Label, estimate=.pred_class)
```

```
##             Truth
## Prediction  0  1  2  3  4  5  6  7  8  9
##          0  9  0  1  0  0  0  1  0  0  0
##          1  0 18  3  1  2  2  1  1  0  0
##          2  0  0 10  0  0  0  0  0  0  0
##          3  1  0  1 11  0  0  0  0  0  0
##          4  1  0  0  1 16  0  0  0  0  1
##          5  0  0  0  1  0 12  2  0  0  0
##          6  0  0  0  0  0  0 11  0  0  0
##          7  0  0  1  0  0  0  0  7  0  2
##          8  0  0  0  0  0  0  0  0 11  0
##          9  0  0  0  0  1  1  0  7  2 13
```

Again, counts for correct predictions are aligned in the cells on the main diagonal. For example, Row 3 contains counts for cases where three was predicted. Column 3 contains counts for observations where the label was actually three. Consequently, the count in Row 3 and Column 3 shows the count of correct predictions (11).

To calculate other metrics for the testing data, we again use the `metric_set()` command and require to calculate `accuracy`, `sensitivity`, and `specificity`. The resulting R command is saved in the R object `MetricsSetMnist`.

Then, in the second line of code, we execute the `MetricsSetMnist()` command with the same arguments that we used to create the confusion metrics.

```
MetricsSetMnist=metric_set(accuracy, sensitivity, specificity)
MetricsSetMnist(DataTestWithPred, truth=Label, estimate=.pred_class)
```

```
## # A tibble: 3 x 3
##    .metric      .estimator .estimate
##    <chr>        <chr>          <dbl>
## 1 accuracy     multiclass     0.776
## 2 sensitivity  macro          0.773
## 3 specificity  macro          0.975
```

The calculated metrics confirm the overall good prediction quality. The *accuracy* of the model is 77.6%. This is a good result compared to a simple guess that would generate an *accuracy* of about 10%. *Sensitivity* (*True Positive* rate) and *specificity* (*True Negative* rate) also indicate good predictive quality. Note that these metrics were calculated as averages over all ten digits (indicated by the term *macro* in the printout).[7]

You can improve the result by using more observations from the *MNIST* dataset. In the digital resource section (see Section 4.12) you can download

---

[7]See (Mohajon (2020)) for an intuitive explanation and (Vaughan (2022)) for details about how multi-class metrics are calculated in `tidymodels`.

an *R* script that contains the code used in this section. That *R* script allows you to use *MNIST* samples with more observations (1,000 and 10,000) to improve the predictive results.

4.11 When and When Not to Use kNN Models

- *k-Nearest Neighbors* can be used to solve *classification* problems similar to the ones in this section. *k-Nearest Neighbors* usually produces good prediction results.

- In principle, *k-Nearest Neighbors* can also be used for regression problems. First, it finds the k nearest neighbor observations. Afterward, the mean of the outcome variable of the k nearest neighbors is used to generate the prediction. However, *k-Nearest Neighbors* is rarely used for regression models because other machine learning models, such as *Ordinary Least Square* (*OLS*) regression , *Neural Networks*, or *Random Forest* models, usually perform better.

- Besides using *k-Nearest Neighbors* for prediction purposes, it is also useful to identify similar observations. For example, when somebody is using a dating website, the website often searches its database for similar partners in terms of age, income, education, and interests. If 20 partner recommendations are required, *k-Nearest Neighbors* ($k = 20$) finds the 20 most compatible potential partners (similar in terms of *Euclidean Distance*).

  Some video recommendation systems work similarly. The machine learning algorithm would first find customers with a similar viewing history and then recommend videos that these customers had watched and rated high.

- A disadvantage of *k-Nearest Neighbors* models is their slow performance. When the number of predictor variables and/or the number of observations becomes large, *k-Nearest Neighbors* can be prohibitively slow.

  Consider that the original *MNIST* dataset consists of 60,000 training observations and 10,000 testing observations. This means that *k-Nearest Neighbors* needs to compare each of the 10,000 testing images with all of the 60,000 training images for each of the 784 pixels. This would lead to 470,400,000,000 ($10,000 \cdot 60,000 \cdot 784$) pixel comparisons. While this is still possible with a fast computer, a faster comparison algorithm, and a lot of patience, it becomes very problematic when we consider images with better resolution — e.g., 1280×1024. This would lead to ($10,000 \cdot 60,000 \cdot 1280 \cdot 1024$) pixel comparisons. You do the math.

4.12   Digital Resourses

Below you will find a few digital resources related to this chapter such as:

- Videos
- Short articles
- Tutorials
- *R* scripts

These resources are recommended if you would like to review the chapter from a different angle or to go beyond what was covered in the chapter.

Here we show only a few of the digital resourses. At the end of the list you will find a link to additonal digital resources for this chapter that are maintained on the Internet.

You can find a complete list of digital resources for all book chapters on the **companion website:** https://ai.lange-analytics.com/digitalresources.html

---

R Script and Data Sources for MNIST Data Analysis

The material provided below allows you to experiment with recognizing handwritten notes from the MNIST dataset using k-Nearest Neighbors.

You can use the import() command from the rio package together with the links below to import random subsets of the MNIST dataset as well as the complete MNIST dataset:

- 500 sample observations (R data frame):
  https://ai.lange-analytics.com/data/MN500.rds
- 1,000 sample observations (R data frame):
  https://ai.lange-analytics.com/data/MN1000.rds
- 10,000 sample observations (R data frame):
  https://ai.lange-analytics.com/data/MN10000.rds
- Complete MNISTdataset as (R list object):
  https://ai.lange-analytics.com/data/MN.rds

Example:
library(rio)
DataMnist=import("https://ai.lange-analytics.com/data/MN500.rds")

Alternatively, you can download an R script that you can use as a template to work with the various MNIST data subsets. See the link below.

Link: https://ai.lange-analytics.com/dr?a=360

Free DataCamp Course About k-Nearest Neighbors

This is a free course from *DataCamp* that introduces *k-Nearest Neighbors*. It is interactive, and it provides exercises. The course covers other classification models as well, but they are not free.

Link: https://ai.lange-analytics.com/dr?a=338

A Video Tutorial for k-Nearest Neighbors to Recognize Handwriting

This R tutorial video by Carsten Lange shows how handwritten digits from images of the MNIST dataset can be classified using *k-Nearest Neighbors*.

Link: https://ai.lange-analytics.com/dr?a=320

More Digital Resources

Only a subset of digital resources is listed in this section. The link below points to additional, concurrently updated resources for this chapter.

Link: https://ai.lange-analytics.com/dr/knearneigh.html

5

Linear Regression — Key Machine Learning Concepts

This chapter focuses on linear regression. Linear regression is a machine learning algorithm just like *k-Nearest Neighbors* (see Chapter 4), *Random Forests* (see Section 10.4), or *Neural Networks* (see Chapter 9). Assuming that most readers are familiar with the basics of linear regression, we will use linear regression as an example to introduce important machine learning concepts.

Therefore, even if you already have a good understanding of linear regression, you should read this chapter carefully as it introduces new machine learning concepts used in later chapters.

Section 5.4 introduces linear regression for a univariate (one predictor variable) approach. Based on a mockup dataset, two different approaches are used to optimize the regression parameters:

1) **Ordinary Least Squares (OLS)**, which allows for calculating the regression parameters based on a formula.

2) **Trial-and-Error** algorithms which systematically try different regression parameters to improve the predictions.

   We will introduce **Grid Search** and an **Optimizer** based *trial-and-error* algorithm. These algorithms are widely used for more advanced machine learning models. This chapter will explain both algorithms, which allows us to treat them as *black box* concepts when working with other machine learning models in the following chapters.

In the interactive Section 5.5, you will work on an interactive project to extend the univariate model to a multivariate model using several predictor variables to estimate housing prices.

5.1   Learning Outcomes

This section outlines what you can expect to learn in this chapter. In addition, the corresponding section number is included for each learning outcome to help you to navigate the content, especially when you return to the chapter for review.

In this chapter, you will learn:

- The basic concepts of linear regression (see Section 5.3).

- How to calibrate parameters in a machine learning model to improve predictive quality (see Section 5.3).

- How to calculate optimal regression parameters using OLS (see Section 5.4.2).

- How to distinguish between unfitted and fitted models (see Section 5.4.2).

- How to use a *trial-and-error* algorithm called Grid Search in *R* to find optimal regression parameters (see Section 5.4.3.1).

- How to use an Optimizer *trial-and-error* algorithm in *R* to find optimal regression parameters (see Section 5.4.3.2).

- How to leverage the R tidymodels package to process data (`recipes`), to define a linear model (*model design*), to create a *workflow*, and to calibrate the *workflow* to the training data (see Section 5.4.2).

- How to transform categorical data such as the survival of a *Titanic* passenger (*died/survived*) or the waterfront location of a house (*yes/no*) into numerical dummy variables (see Section 5.5).

- How to distinguish between dummy encoding and one-hot encoding (see Section 5.5).

5.2   R Packages Required for the Chapter

This section lists the *R* packages that you need when you load and execute code in the interactive sections in *RStudio*. Please install the following packages using `Tools -> Install Packages ...` from the *RStudio* menu bar (you can find more information about installing and loading packages in Section 3.4):

- The `rio` package (Chan et al. (2021)) to enable the loading of various data formats with one `import()` command. Files can be loaded from the user's hard drive or the Internet.

- The `janitor` package (Firke (2023)) to rename variable names to *Upper-Camel* and to substitute spaces and special characters in variable names.

- The `tidymodels` package (Kuhn and Wickham (2020)) to streamline data engineering and machine learning tasks.

- The `kableExtra` (Zhu (2021)) package to support the rendering of tables.

- The `learnr` package (Aden-Buie et al. (2022)), which is needed together with the `shiny` package (Chang et al. (2022)) for the interactive exercises in this book.

- The `shiny` package (Chang et al. (2022)), which is needed together with the `learnr` package (Aden-Buie et al. (2022)) for the interactive exercises in this book.

5.3 The Basic Idea Behind Linear Regression

The basic idea behind linear regression is to use a linear function with one (univariate) or more (multivariate) predictor variables x_j to predict a continuous outcome variable y.

Equations (5.1) and (5.2) are examples of predicting the outcome y_i with one and two predictor variables, respectively. Because regression Equations (5.1) and (5.2) generate predictions for the true outcome variable y_i, the variables on the left of the equations are marked with a *hat* (see $\hat{y}_i$) to indicate that the left-hand-sides of Equations (5.1) and (5.2) are the results of predictions:[1]

$$\hat{y}_i = \beta_1 x_i + \beta_2 \tag{5.1}$$
$$\hat{y}_i = \beta_1 x_{1,i} + \beta_2 x_{2,i} + \beta_3 \tag{5.2}$$

We know the numerical values for the predictor variables $x_{j,i}$ for any given observation in the training and testing dataset. Consequently, we can plug in the numerical values for the predictors $x_{j,i}$ into Equations (5.1) or (5.2) and calculate a prediction for the outcome $(\hat{y}_i)$.

However, this only works if and only if we know the values for the parameters (the βs). Finding optimal values for the parameters that result in the best prediction quality is the central objective for linear regression. It is similarly important for most machine learning algorithms.

---

[1]Strictly speaking, the βs are also estimates and should be written as $\hat{\beta}_j$. For simplicity, in what follows, we omit the hats on model-parameters.

In linear regression the term *coefficients* instead of *parameters* is often used for the β values. We choose the term *parameters* to be compatible with other machine learning algorithms in upcoming chapters.

We will introduce two methodologies for finding the optimal βs:

Method 1: Using **Ordinary Least Squares (OLS)** to calculate optimal values for the parameters β. *OLS* is the default method for almost all statistical programs for linear regression, including R.

Method 2: Using a **systematic trial-and-error process** to find optimal β parameters.

Both methods lead to approximately the same results. Therefore, it seems redundant to introduce a *trial-and-error* method when we can calculate the results precisely with *OLS*.

The reason for introducing *trial-and-error* approaches is that more complex machine learning algorithms do not allow us to calculate the optimal parameters, and we have to fall back onto *trial-and-error* approaches.

This chapter introduces two *trial-and-error* algorithms. This will allow us to treat these algorithms as a *black box* when we use them in the following chapters.

In the previous chapter, we used the *confusion matrix* to assess prediction quality. With linear regression, this is not possible because our outcome variable is continuous. Various metrics (see Section 6.4) are available to measure prediction quality for a continuous variable. For simplicity, throughout this chapter, we will only use the *Mean Squared Error* (*MSE*) to quantify prediction quality:

$$MSE = \frac{\sum_{i=1}^{N}(\hat{y}_i - y_i)^2}{N}$$

Looking at the formula above, you can see why this metric is called *Mean Squared Error*. The term $(\hat{y}_i - y_i)^2$ quantifies the (squared) error for each observation. So, summing over all squared errors and dividing by the number of observations gives us the **Mean Squared Error**.

5.4   Univariate Mockup: Study Time and Grades

To illustrate the *OLS* approach (see Section 5.4.2) and two different *trial-and-error* approaches (*Grid Search* in Section 5.4.3.1 and an *Optimizer* approach in Section 5.4.3.2), we use an extremly simplified mockup dataset consisting of only five observations. In the real-world five observations are surely not

TABLE 5.1 Mockup Training Dataset

i	y_i Grade	x_i StudyTime	$\hat{y}_i$ PredGrade	$\hat{y}_i - y_i$ Error	$(\hat{y}_i - y_i)^2$ ErrorSq
1	65	2	69	4	16
2	82	3	73	-9	81
3	93	7	89	-4	16
4	93	8	93	0	0
5	83	4	77	-6	36

enough to perform a reliable data analysis! However, to keep it simple, we will ignore this fact for now.

The goal is to estimate the outcome of an exam based on students' study time. The predicted outcome variable is $\widehat{Grade}_i$ (similar to $\hat{y}_i$ in Equation (5.1)) and the only predictor variable is $StudyTime_i$ (similar to x_i in Equation (5.1)).

Table 5.1 displays the five observations for both variables, *Grade* and *StudyTime*, in Columns 2 and 3.

5.4.1   Predictions and Errors

Before we analyze the relationship between *StudyTime* and *Grade* with linear regression, let us briefly introduce a few selected concepts related to predictions and the resulting errors:

Univariate Linear Regression assumes we can predict an outcome based on a linear relationship between the outcome variable and one predictor variable. This can be expressed in a prediction equation such as:

$$\hat{y}_i = \beta_1 x_i + \beta_2 \tag{5.3}$$

When numerical values for β_1 and β_2 are selected, we can use Equation (5.3) to predict the outcome $\hat{y}_i$ for each observation in the training or testing dataset (note, for simplicity, we do not consider a testing dataset here, but we will in Section 5.5).

The goal is to find optimal values $\beta_{1,opt.}$ and $\beta_{2,opt.}$ that maximize prediction quality.

Prediction quality can be measured through the Mean Square Error, which is defined as:

$$MSE = \frac{\sum_{i=1}^{N}(\hat{y}_i - y_i)^2}{N}$$

The linear prediction equation for predicting the outcome *Grade* with the predictor *StudyTime* is:

$$\widehat{Grade}_i = \beta_1 StudyTime_i + \beta_2 \tag{5.4}$$

Given a numerical pair of parameters (β_1 and β_2), it is possible to predict a *Grade* for any value of the predictor variable *StudyTime*. Let us arbitrarily choose $\beta_1 = 4$, $\beta_2 = 61$, and store the $\beta's$ in the R vector object VecBeta.

```
VecBeta=c(4, 61)
DataTable=DataMockup |>
        mutate(PredGrade=VecBeta[1]*StudyTime+VecBeta[2])
```

The code block above shows how the predicted grade (*PredGrade*) in Column 4 of Table 5.1) was calculated: In the mutate() command the values for β_1 and β_2 where extracted from VecBeta as VecBeta[1] (first element) and VecBeta[2] (second element) to calculate the variable *PredGrade*.

Let us verify the predicted grade for the first observation in Table 5.1:

$$PredGrade_1 = 4 \cdot 2 + 61 = 69$$

The predicted grade for a student who studies for 2 hours is predicted to be 69 points. Similarly, you can predict the grades for all other observations in the training dataset (see Column 4 of Table 5.1). Try to verify at least one other observation's *PredGrade*!

Figure 5.1 shows the *StudyTime/Grade* data from Table 5.1 plotted as blue points. The red line reflects the prediction equation for the arbitrarily chosen $\beta_1 = 4$ and $\beta_2 = 61$. Consequently, all predicted *StudyTime/PredGrade* combinations (black dots) are on the red line.

To measure the prediction error for each of the five observations (see Column 5 in Table 5.1), we have to calculate the difference between the prediction and the true value of the outcome variable:

$$Error = PredGrade - Grade$$

These errors are visualized in Figure 5.1 as the vertical difference between the blue points (true grades) and the black points (predicted grades).

In the code block below, the last two mutate() commands show how the values for the *Error* and the *ErrorSq* columns of Table 5.1 are calculated. You can also see that the (*MSE*) is calculated from the mean of the observations squared error (*ErrorSq*):

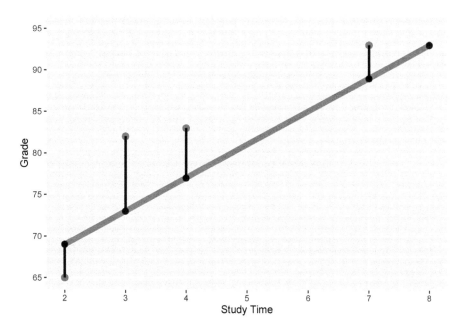

FIGURE 5.1 *StudyTime/Grade* Regression for $\beta_1 = 4$ and $\beta_2 = 61$

```
DataMockup=
  import("https://ai.lange-analytics.com/data/DataStudyTimeMockup.rds")

VecBeta=c(4, 61)
DataTable=DataMockup |>
          mutate(PredGrade=VecBeta[1]*StudyTime+VecBeta[2]) |>
          mutate(Error=PredGrade-Grade) |>
          mutate(ErrorSq=Error^2)
MSE=mean(DataTable$ErrorSq)
cat("The MSE for VecBeta[1]=4 and VecBeta[2]=61 is:", MSE )

## The MSE for VecBeta[1]=4 and VecBeta[2]=61 is: 29.8
```

We can also calculate the *MSE* algebraically:

$$MSE \;=\; \frac{1}{N}\sum_{i=1}^{N}(\hat{y}_i - y_i)^2$$

$$\Longleftrightarrow$$

$$MSE \;=\; \frac{1}{N}\sum_{i=1}^{N}(\underbrace{\overbrace{\beta_1 x_i + \beta_2}^{\text{Prediction } i} - y_i}_{\text{Error } i})^2 \tag{5.5}$$

At this point, you can already see that smaller prediction errors (i.e., absolute smaller values for $\hat{y}_i - y_i$) lead to a smaller MSE. Therefore, our error function is well suited as a metric to measure a model's predictive quality and can be used to find optimal β parameters for the model later on.

Equation (5.5) allows us to calculate the MSE for any set of parameters (β_1, β_2) because based on the training dataset, all values for the predictor variable (x_i) and the outcome variable (y_i) are known — leaving only β_1 and β_2 to be determined.

This can be shown for the mockup dataset, if we resolve the summation sign ($\sum$) in Equation (5.5) and also substitute y_i and x_i with the training data observations from Table 5.1 (remember, i is the index for the observation), we get Equation (5.6):

$$MSE = \frac{(\beta_1 x_1 + \beta_2 - y_1)^2 + (\beta_1 x_2 + \beta_2 - y_2)^2 + \cdots + (\beta_1 x_5 + \beta_2 - y_5)^2}{5}$$

$$\Longleftrightarrow$$

$$MSE = \frac{1}{5}\left[(\underbrace{\overbrace{\beta_1 \cdot 2 + \beta_2}^{\text{Prediction 1}} -65)^2}_{\text{Error 1}} + (\underbrace{\overbrace{\beta_1 \cdot 3 + \beta_2}^{\text{Prediction 2}} -82)^2}_{\text{Error 2}} \right.$$

$$+ (\underbrace{\overbrace{\beta_1 \cdot 7 + \beta_2}^{\text{Prediction 3}} -93)^2}_{\text{Error 3}} + (\underbrace{\overbrace{\beta_1 \cdot 8 + \beta_2}^{\text{Prediction 4}} -93)^2}_{\text{Error 4}}$$

$$\left. + (\underbrace{\overbrace{\beta_1 \cdot 4 + \beta_2}^{\text{Prediction 5}} -83)^2}_{\text{Error 6}} \right] \tag{5.6}$$

Equation (5.6) shows that when the training data are given, the MSE is only based on the choice of the parameters — the βs.

Consequently, if you now substitute the previously arbitrary chosen values, $\beta_1 = 4$ and $\beta_2 = 61$, into Equation (5.6), you can take a calculator and find that $MSE = 29.8$. This is very cumbersome, but it might be a good exercise to fully understand the importance of Equation (5.6).

Although calculating the MSE is cumbersome for a human, writing a function in R to calculate the MSE based on a pair of β-values and a training dataset is relatively easy. Since such a function will be needed in the following sections, we created an R function (`FctMSE()`) to calculate the MSE. This function can be imported in your R code with the `import()` command (see the code block further below).

For those who are interested in the underlying code and how to program a function in R, a link to a blog post is provided in the Digital Resource Section 5.7.

How to use the function `FctMSE()` is shown in the code block below:

```
library(rio)
FctMSE=import("https://ai.lange-analytics.com/source/FctMSE.rds")
VecBeta=c(4, 61)
MSE=FctMSE(VecBeta, data=DataMockup)
cat("The MSE for VecBeta[1]=4 and VecBeta[2]=61 is:", MSE)
```

```
## The MSE for VecBeta[1]=4 and VecBeta[2]=61 is: 29.8
```

First, the code for the function is downloaded with `import()` and stored in the *R* object `FctMSE`. Next, the values for β_1 and β_2 are stored in the *R* vector object `VecBeta`. Finally, the function calculates the *MSE* based on `VecBeta` and the mockup dataset `DataMockup`. The result is printed with the `cat()` command.

In the printout above, you can see that the *MSE* calculated by `FctMSE()` is the same as the one we calculated manually previously.

Takeaways from the MSE

The *MSE* for a univariate *OLS* regression with N observations can be calculated as:

$$MSE = \frac{1}{N} \sum_{i=1}^{N} (\beta_1 x_i + \beta_2 - y_i)^2 \text{ with: } x_i \text{ and } y_i \text{ known from the training dataset.}$$

1. When the training data are given, only the choice of the β parameters determines the *MSE*. Since both — the values for x_i and y_i — are part of the training dataset, the *MSE* depends only on the chosen values for the β parameters.

2. Since different values for β_1 and β_2 generate different *MSE*s, the goal is to find a pair of β parameters that leads to the smallest possible *MSE*.

In the following Section 5.4.2, you will learn how to calculate the optimal values $\beta_{1,opt.}$ and $\beta_{2,opt.}$ for the mockup example using *OLS*. Afterward, in Section 5.4.3, we will introduce two algorithms that a computer can use for a systematic *trial-and-error* approach to find the optimal values $\beta_{1,opt.}$ and $\beta_{2,opt.}$.

5.4.2   Calculate Optimal Parameter Values Based on *OLS*

The most common method to find optimal values for the parameters (such as β_1 and β_2) in linear regression is based on the Ordinary Least Squares (*OLS*) method. With *OLS*, a linear regression's optimal βs can be determined using formulas (closed-form solution). Unfortunately, *OLS* works only for

TABLE 5.2 Mockup Training Dataset with Columns for $y_i x_i$ and x_i^2

i	y_i Grade	x_i StudyTime	$y_i x_i$ GradeXStudyTime	x_i^2 StudyTimeSquared
1	65	2	130	4
2	82	3	246	9
3	93	7	651	49
4	93	8	744	64
5	83	4	332	16

linear regression, and we have to rely on *trial-and-error* for most other machine learning models.

Below are the formulas for the optimal βs for a univariate regression based on a training dataset with N observations. As before, we abbreviate the outcome variable *Grade* with y and the only predictor variable *StudyTime* with x:[2]

$$\beta_{1,opt} = \frac{N \sum_{i=1}^{N} y_i x_i - \sum_{i=1}^{N} y_i \sum_{i=1}^{N} x_i}{N \sum_{i=1}^{N} x_i^2 - \left(\sum_{i=1}^{N} x_i\right)^2} \quad (5.7)$$

$$\beta_{2,opt.} = \frac{\sum_{i=1}^{N} y_i - \beta_1 \sum_{i=1}^{N} x_i}{N} \quad (5.8)$$

You can see that the values for $\beta_{opt,1}$ and $\beta_{opt,2}$ are only based on data from the training dataset. The two equations might look pretty scary to some readers unfamiliar with summation notation. However, it is actually not that difficult to calculate the values for $\beta_{opt,1}$ and $\beta_{opt,2}$ if we use R.

Again, we use the mockup dataset (see Columns 2 and 3 of Table 5.2) to demonstrate how $\beta_{opt,1}$ and $\beta_{opt,2}$ can be calculated with R based on Equations (5.7) and (5.8).

We start with the summation $\sum_{i=1}^{N} x_i$. The term $\sum_{i=1}^{N} x_i$ means that we sum up all x_i considering that i takes values starting from 1 and ending with N (N being 5 in our case). Because i is the row number in Table 5.1, $\sum_{i=1}^{N} x_i$ stands for the sum of the x column in Table 5.1. The same applies to $\sum_{i=1}^{N} y_i$.

With this knowledge, we can already use R to calculate $\sum_{i=1}^{N} x_i$ and $\sum_{i=1}^{N} y_i$:

```
SumOfX=sum(DataMockup$StudyTime)
SumOfY=sum(DataMockup$Grade)
```

---

[2]In the Digital Resource Section 5.7 you can find a link to a short blog article that shows how Equations (5.7) and (5.8) can be derived.

At this point, we are not ready yet to calculate $\beta_{1,opt}$ according to Equation (5.7) because the formula also requires calculating the sum from the product of the observations for y_i and x_i ($\sum_{i=1}^{N} y_i x_i$) as well as the sum of the squares of the x_i values ($\sum_{i=1}^{N} x_i^2$). However, we can use the mutate() command to add these variables to the data frame DataMockup and call the new resulting data frame DataTable:

```
DataTable=DataMockup |>
  mutate(GradeXStudyTime=Grade*StudyTime) |>
  mutate(StudyTimeSquared=StudyTime^2)
```

Table 5.2 shows the resulting data frame DataTable.

Next, we calculate the sums of $\sum_{i=1}^{N} y_i x_i$ and $\sum_{i=1}^{N} x_i^2$ (see the code block below). When we plug in these sums together with the previously calculated sums $\sum_{i=1}^{N} x_i$ and $\sum_{i=1}^{N} y_i$ and the value for N ($N = 5$) into Equation (5.7) we get $\beta_{1,opt}$:

```
N=5
SumOfY=sum(DataTable$Grade)
SumOfX=sum(DataTable$StudyTime)
SumOfXY=sum(DataTable$GradeXStudyTime)
SumOfXSq=sum(DataTable$StudyTimeSquared)

Beta1opt=(N*SumOfXY-SumOfX*SumOfY)/(N*SumOfXSq-SumOfX^2)

cat("Based on the training dataset the optimal value for Beta1 =",
    Beta1opt)

## Based on the training dataset the optimal value for Beta1 = 3.963
```

Afterward, we can plug in the value of $\beta_{1,opt}$ into Equation (5.8) together $\sum_{i=1}^{N} y_i$ and $\sum_{i=1}^{N} x_i$ to calculate $\beta_{2,opt}$:

```
Beta2opt= (SumOfY-Beta1opt*SumOfX)/N
cat("Based on the training dataset the optimal value for Beta2 =",
    Beta2opt)

## Based on the training dataset the optimal value for Beta2 = 64.18
```

Hurrah, you just used *OLS* to find the optimal β-values for the mockup regression! The good news is that you do not need to memorize these formulas. They are already integrated into the statistical software R. To find the optimal parameters with R, you can use the command linear_reg() from the tidymodels package. The R code to create a *linear regression workflow* is mostly

the same as the one explained in detail in the previous chapter (see Section
4.7.3):

```
library(tidymodels)
RecipeMockup=recipe(Grade~StudyTime, data=DataMockup)

ModelDesignLinRegr=linear_reg() |>
                set_engine("lm") |>
                set_mode("regression")

WFModelMockup=workflow() |>
            add_recipe(RecipeMockup) |>
            add_model(ModelDesignLinRegr) |>
            fit(DataMockup)
```

1. Define and save the *recipe* that indicates which variable is the out-
    come and which is the predictor variable, together with the data
    argument. Note that we do not add any `step_` commands for data
    pre-processing since we can use the mockup data as is.

2. Define the *model design* in three steps that determine:

    i) The name of the machine learning model (`linear_reg()`).

    ii) The *R* package used for that model (`lm`).

    iii) The mode used — which is either "classification" or "regres-
    sion".

3. Add the *recipe* and the *model design* to the *workflow* and fit the
    workflow to the data.

Note that we did not split the data into training and testing data. Consequently, we fit the *workflow* with the complete dataset `DataMockup` as the
training dataset. This is only acceptable because our example is a mockup. In
a real-world application splitting into training and testing data is an absolute
must to avoid *overfitting* (more on *overfitting* in Chapter 6).

Fitting the *workflow* with `fit(DataMockup)` is when the parameters for the
model design are calculated and saved within the *workflow* model `WFModel-`
`Mockup`. A (*workflow*) model where the values for the parameters have been
determined is called a *fitted model*. A *fitted model* can be used for prediction.

Fitted Model vs. Unfitted Model

An unfitted model is a prediction equation like Equation (5.4) in Section 5.4.1 or a model *workflow* that has not been fitted to the training data (i.e., if we omit fit(DataTrain) in the *workflow* code). An unfitted model already contains the rule of how predictions are built. Still, because the numerical values for the parameters (βs) are not determined — an unfitted model cannot be used to predict.

When we determine the optimal values for the parameters (βs) by minimizing the MSE, we calibrate (*fit*) the model to the training data. The model becomes a fitted model.

A fitted model can be directly used for predictions because the numerical values for its parameters (βs) have been determined.

We can use the tidy() command to extract the parameters and other useful information. In general, the tidy() command extracts *important* information from various types of R objects and returns a data frame that can be saved for further processing. Here we output the data frame to the *Console*:

```
tidy(WFModelMockup)
```

```
## # A tibble: 2 x 5
##   term         estimate std.error statistic p.value
##   <chr>           <dbl>     <dbl>     <dbl>   <dbl>
## 1 (Intercept)      64.2      6.06      10.6 0.00180
## 2 StudyTime        3.96      1.14      3.48 0.0399
```

As you can see in the column titled estimate, the value for the parameter related to StudyTime ($\beta_{1,opt.}$) and the one related to the intercept of the prediction function (Intercept; $\beta_{2,opt.}$) are the same as the ones we calculate manually above. Using a real-world dataset, we will interpret the other columns from the tidy() output later in Section 5.5.

5.4.3 Trial-and-Error to find Optimal Parameters

The following sections will use two *trial-and-error* approaches to find the optimal $\beta's$. Since we calculated $\beta_{1,opt.}$ and $\beta_{2,opt.}$ already in the previous section, we can use the results as a benchmark to see how well the *trial-and-error* approaches are performing.

$$MSE \quad = \quad \frac{1}{N} \sum_{i=1}^{N} (\hat{y}_i - y_i)^2$$

$$\Longleftrightarrow$$

$$MSE \quad = \quad \frac{1}{N} \sum_{i=1}^{N} (\underbrace{\overbrace{\beta_1 x_i + \beta_2}^{\text{Prediction } i} - y_i}_{\text{Error } i})^2 \qquad (5.9)$$

Equation (5.9) provides again the formula to calculate the MSE. For a given training dataset (all y_i and x_i are known), we can choose any pair β_1 and β_2, and use Equation (5.9) to calculate the related *mean squared error* (see Section 5.4 for details). However, rather than arbitrarily choosing values for β_1 and β_2, we will use more systematic approaches.

In Section 5.4.3.1, we will use **Grid Search**: First, we generate two vectors β_1 and β_2 containing various values, respectively. Then we will use R to generate all possible combinations for the β_1 and β_2 values. For each of the resulting pairs of β_1 and β_2, we will calculate the MSE and finally choose the pair with the lowest MSE.

In Section 5.4.3.2, we will use an **Optimizer** to find optimal values for β_1 and β_2. An *Optimizer* is an iterative computer algorithm that can find optimal parameters to minimize or maximize a target function. In our case the MSE function (5.9) is the target function.

5.4.3.1   Finding Optimal Parameters Using Grid Search

This section uses the *Grid Search* algorithm to find the pair of $\beta_{1,opt}$ and $\beta_{2,opt}$ that minimizes the MSE.

Let us start by deciding on a range for β_1 and β_2 and on how many values we would like to test for each β. At the beginning of this section, we used $\beta_1 = 4$ and $\beta_2 = 61$, and the prediction results were not too bad. So, why not use a range around these values. We choose a range from $3 - 5$ for β_1 and a range from $50 - 70$ for β_2. For each, β_1 and β_2, we will generate about 20 values in the chosen range.

In the code block below, we generate a sequence of values for β_1 ranging from 3 to 5 with an increment of 0.1. For β_2, we choose values ranging from 50 to 70 with an increment of 1 resulting in 21 values for each, β_1 and β_2. These values are then assigned to the R vector objects `VecBeta1Values` and `VecBeta2Values`, respectively.

```
VecBeta1Values=seq(3, 5, 0.1)
VecBeta2Values=seq(50, 70, 1)
```

```
cat("First 5 values for beta1:",VecBeta1Values[1:5],"\n",
    "Last 5 values for beta1:",VecBeta1Values[17:21],"\n",
    "First 5 values for beta2:",VecBeta2Values[1:5],"\n",
    "Last 5 values for beta2:",VecBeta2Values[17:21])
```

```
## First 5 values for beta1: 3 3.1 3.2 3.3 3.4
##  Last 5 values for beta1: 4.6 4.7 4.8 4.9 5
##  First 5 values for beta2: 50 51 52 53 54
##  Last 5 values for beta2: 66 67 68 69 70
```

As you can see above, we printed the first and the last five values for each vector object `VecBeta1Values` and `VecBeta2Values`.

Now we need all possible pairwise combinations of the values generated for β_1 and β_2. Because we generated 21 values for each β_1 and β_2, we will end up with a total of 441 ($21 \cdot 21$) combinations. Fortunately, we do not have to generate these combinations manually. The R command `expand.grid()` can generate the 441 combinations for us. We store the result in the data frame `GridBetaPairs` and print the first and last five pairs of β_1 and β_2:

```
GridBetaPairs=expand.grid(Beta1=VecBeta1Values, Beta2=VecBeta2Values)
print(GridBetaPairs[c(1,2,3,4,5,437,438,439,440,441),])
```

```
##      Beta1 Beta2
## 1      3.0    50
## 2      3.1    50
## 3      3.2    50
## 4      3.3    50
## 5      3.4    50
## 437    4.6    70
## 438    4.7    70
## 439    4.8    70
## 440    4.9    70
## 441    5.0    70
```

For each pair of β_1 and β_2 (each row in `GridBetaPairs`), we must calculate the MSE to find the pair with the smallest MSE. Because this method is comprehensive but not computationally efficient, *Grid Search* is sometimes called a **Brute Force** approach.

Calculating the MSE for the β_1 and β_2 pairs is accomplished in the following code block with the `apply()` command. It *applies* a function (in this case, `FctMSE()`; see Section 5.4.1 for details about `FctMSE()`) to each of the rows of the data frame `GridBetaPairs` using the β_1 and β_2 pairs in each row together

with the data frame `DataMockup` to calculate the related $MSEs$.[3] These MSE
values are then stored in the R vector object `VecMSE` and appended to the
data frame `GridBetaPairs` as a new column using `mutate()`.

```
FctMSE=import("https://ai.lange-analytics.com/source/FctMSE.rds")
VecMSE=apply(GridBetaPairs, FUN=FctMSE, data=DataMockup, MARGIN=1)
```

```
GridBetaPairs=mutate(GridBetaPairs, MSE=VecMSE)
```

```
head(GridBetaPairs)
```

```
##    Beta1 Beta2   MSE
## 1    3.0    50 379.2
## 2    3.1    50 360.4
## 3    3.2    50 342.2
## 4    3.3    50 324.5
## 5    3.4    50 307.4
## 6    3.5    50 290.9
```

The printout above shows the structure of the data frame `GridBetaPairs` after
the $MSEs$ for each β-pair have been appended.

We will not use the `apply()` command in the following chapters. Therefore, it
is sufficient to understand that `apply()` calculates the MSE for each of the
rows of `GridBetaPairs`.

The last step is to find the β-pair with the smallest MSE. This is a little
tricky: We first find the smallest MSE (using `min(MSE)`) and then use this
smallest MSE to filter the data frame (`MSE==min(MSE)`). The result is the row
with the smallest MSE, which we save as `BestModel` and print afterward.

```
BestModel=filter(GridBetaPairs, MSE==min(MSE))
```

```
print(BestModel[1,])
```

```
##    Beta1 Beta2  MSE
## 1      4    64 20.8
```

As you can see in the printout, we get $\beta_1 = 4$ and $\beta_2 = 64$ with an $MSE = 20.8$. This deviates slightly from the calculated values from Section 5.4.2 where
we obtained $\beta_{opt,1} = 3.96$ and $\beta_{opt,2} = 64.18$. This deviation should not come
as a surprise. For the β_1 range, we used an increment of 0.1, and for the β_2
range, an increment of 1, leaving us with a coarse grid. Still, this coarse grid
already had 441 rows for which the $MSEs$ needed to be calculated.

---

[3]The argument `Margin=1` ensures that the function `FctMSE()` is applied to the rows rather
than the columns.

We suggest that you try a finer grid. Copy the code block further below into an R script. The code includes all commands we used before but uses a finer grid by changing the increment for β_1 from 0.1 to 0.01, creating 201 different β_1 values ranging from 3 to 5 in steps of 0.01. The increment for β_2 is changed from 1 to 0.1, creating 201 different β_2 values ranging from 50 to 70 in steps of 0.1. Now the grid GridBetaPairs is more granular, but it also contains 40,401 rows $(201 \cdot 201)$ with pairs of βs. This means R has to calculate the MSE for 40,401 pairs of βs. When you execute the new code, it will take a while. It took about 15 minutes on a computer with four cores and an *Intel i5* processor — enjoy a coffee while waiting.

Spoiler alert: In the end, you will get parameters very close to the ones we calculated in Section 5.4.2 with OLS.[4]

```
library(rio); library(tidyverse)
FctMSE=import("https://ai.lange-analytics.com/source/FctMSE.rds")
DataMockup=
  import("https://ai.lange-analytics.com/data/DataStudyTimeMockup.rds")

VecBeta1Values=seq(3, 5, 0.01) #creates 201 beta1 values
VecBeta2Values=seq(50, 70, 0.1)#creates 201 beta2 values

GridBetaPairs=expand.grid(Beta1=VecBeta1Values, Beta2=VecBeta2Values)
cat("GridBetaPairs has", nrow(GridBetaPairs), "rows.")

VecMSE=apply(GridBetaPairs, FUN=FctMSE,data=DataMockup,MARGIN=1)

GridBetaPairs=mutate(GridBetaPairs, MSE=VecMSE)

BestModel=filter(GridBetaPairs, MSE==min(MSE))
print(BestModel)
```

In summary, we can say that *Grid Search* finds optimal parameters if the solution is within the range used for the search and if the grid is fine enough. On the other hand, a more refined grid, unfortunately, increases computing time exponentially because the MSE for all combinations needs to be calculated.

We will use *Grid Search* in Chapter 6 when tuning *hyper-parameters*.

---

[4]For those who like to push it a little further: Install the future.apply package and load it at the beginning of the code block with library(future.apply). Also, execute the command plan(multisession). Now when you rerun the code and change the apply() command to the future_apply() command (all arguments stay as they are), your code will be executed on different cores of your computer and should be much faster - assuming your computer has two or more cores.

5.4.3.2   Finding Optimal Parameters Using an Optimizer

The *Grid Search* algorithm tries all possible pairwise βs combinations. However, as you saw, it can be very slow. This raises the question if it is really necessary to calculate the MSE for all pairs or if there is a more systematic approach.

Different types of *Optimizers* fill this void. In general, the process for an *Optimizer* to find an MSE-minimum can be described in four steps:

1. The *Optimizer* uses a first guess for the parameters to start the *Optimizer* process.

    For example, we use $\beta_1 = 4$ and $\beta_2 = 61$ as a first guess.

2. The *Optimizer* uses the error function to calculate the target MSE-value for the chosen parameters.

    We will use the function FctMSE() to calculate the MSE based on the training data and the β_1 and β_2 parameters.

3. The *Optimizer* changes the parameters slightly so that the new parameters result in a lower target value (a slightly lower MSE).

4. Repeat Steps 2 and 3 until the target value (MSE) approximately reaches a minimum.

The process described above leads to a *local minimum*. A *local minimum* guarantees that no β-combination with a lower MSE exists in the close vicinity of the minimum (similar βs). However, it is possible that the minimum found is not unique and other *local minima* exist. Some or all of these other *local minima* have a smaller MSE.

In practice, the problem of a *local minimum* often is negligible. In some cases (including linear regression), we already know that only one minimum exists. In other cases, the predictive quality is already good, and it is not very relevant if we can further improve.

Most importantly, a very high approximation of the training data might lead to *overfitting* — approximating the training data well but predicting the testing data poorly (more in Chapter 6). Therefore, finding the lowest local minimum (global minimum) for the MSE for the training data might not be in our best interest. The old saying "Perfect is the enemy of the good", applies.

The good message is that *Optimizers* are already integrated into almost all machine learning algorithms. They are executed automatically and can be treated as a *black box*.

In addition, R (like most statistical software packages) provides an *Optimizer* as a command that we can use to minimize error functions. The command is called `optim()`, and we will only use it in this section to find the optimal parameters for the $\beta's$ for the mockup example.

In its default mode, the `optim()` command requires three arguments:

1. A vector with the initial guess of the values for the βs. Here we use $\beta_1 = 4$ and $\beta_2 = 61$ (if you like, you can try to run the *Optimizer* with a different initial guess).

2. The name (without the parentheses) of the R function to be minimized. In this case, `FctMSE`.

3. The name of the data frame that contains the training data. In this case, `data=DataMockup`

```
library(tidymodels)
VecBetaFirstTrial=c(4, 61)
BestModel=optim(VecBetaFirstTrial, FctMSE, data=DataMockup)
cat("Optimal parameters values fo beta1 and beta2:", BestModel$par)
```

```
## Optimal parameters values fo beta1 and beta2: 3.963 64.18
```

```
cat("Minuimum MSE:", BestModel$value)
```

```
## Minuimum MSE: 20.79
```

The `optim()` command's output is stored in the R object `BestModel`. We can extract the optimal parameters with `BestModel$par` and the minimal MSE with `BestModel$value`.

You can see that the optimal parameters $\beta_{opt,1}$ and $\beta_{opt,2}$ are similar to what we calculated in Section 5.4.2 with *OLS*. Remember, these parameters were found by *trial-and-error* and were not calculated using the *OLS* formula.

Optimizers as a Black Box

Most machine learning models have built-in *Optimizers*. We can treat them as *black boxes*:

An Optimizer is a black box. It finds the best parameters for an error function that only depends on the training data and a set of parameters.

This is all you need to know to understand the fitting process of machine learning models.

The `fit(DatTrain)` command from the `tidymodels` package pushes the training data to an internal *Optimizer*. Then the *Optimizer* finds the optimal parameter values for the βs and creates a fitted *workflow* that can be used for prediction.

5.5 ⊘ Project: Predict House Prices with Multivariate Regression

Interactive Section

In this section, you will find content together with R code to execute, change, and rerun in RStudio.

The best way to read and to work with this section is to open it with *RStudio*. Then you can interactively work on R code exercises and R projects within a web browser. This way you can apply what you have learned so far and extend your knowledge. You can also choose to continue reading either in the book or online, but you will not benefit from the interactive learning experience.

To work with this section in *RStudio* in an interactive environment, follow these steps:

1. Ensure that both the learnR and the shiny package are installed. If not, install them from RStudio's main menu (Tools -> Install Packages ...).

2. Download the Rmd file for the interactive session and save it in your project folder. You will find the link for the download below.

3. Open the downloaded file in RStudio and click the Run Document button, located in the editing window's top-middle area.

For detailed help for running the exercises including videos for Windows and Mac users we refer to: https://blog.lange-analytics.com/2024/01/interactsessions.html

Do not skip this interactive section because besides providing applications of already covered concepts, it will also extend what you have learned so far.

Below is the link to download the interactive section:

https://ai.lange-analytics.com/exc/?file=05-LinRegrExerc100.Rmd

Now that you learned some details about **OLS**, **Grid Search**, and **Optimizers** based on a mockup dataset, it is time to work with a real-world scenario. In this section, you will work on a project to estimate housing prices with linear regression using the so-called **King County House Sale** dataset (Kaggle (2015)). This dataset contains house sale prices from May 2014 to May 2015 for King County in Washington State, including Seattle, WA.

As predictor variables, you will use:

Sqft: The living square footage of a house. This variable is called *SqftLiving* in the original dataset and therefore needs to be renamed to *Sqft*.

Grade: Indicates the condition of a house ranging from 1 (worst) to 13 (best).

Waterfront: Indicates if a house is located at the waterfront. Being at a waterfront location is coded in the original dataset as $(Waterfront = yes)$ otherwise as $(Waterfront = no)$.

In the code block below, we import the complete King County dataset with all 21,613 observations using import(). Then we convert the variable names to *UpperCamel* style with clean_names("upper_camel") and select the variables *Price*, *Sqft* (renamed from *SqftLiving*), *Grade*, and *Waterfront*.

It is unnecessary for a linear regression model to normalize the predictors as we did for the *k-Nearest Neighbors* model. The reason is that *OLS* adjusts the coefficients (β parameters) to changing dimensions. You find more information on why it is not necessary to normalize predictors for linear regression in the *Digital Resource* section for this chapter.

As in Chapter 4, we will split the data into training and testing data by randomly assigning observations to either the training or the testing data. As a reminder, only the training data are used to train the model (finding optimal parameters). The testing dataset is a holdout dataset exclusively used to assess the predictive quality after training has been completed.

```
library(tidyverse); library(rio); library(janitor); library(tidymodels)
DataHousing=
  import("https://ai.lange-analytics.com/data/HousingData.csv") |>
  clean_names("upper_camel") |>
  select(Price, Sqft=SqftLiving, Grade, Waterfront)
set.seed(777)
Split7030=initial_split(DataHousing, prop=0.7, strata=Price, breaks=5)
DataTrain=training(Split7030)
DataTest=testing(Split7030)
head(DataTrain)
```

```
##      Price Sqft Grade Waterfront
## 1 221900 1180     7         no
## 2 180000  770     6         no
## 3 189000 1200     7         no
## 4 230000 1250     7         no
## 5 252700 1070     7         no
## 6 240000 1220     7         no
```

In the initial_split() command, the first argument (0.7) determines the proportion of observations randomly assigned to the training dataset (consequently, 30% are assigned to the testing dataset). The second argument (data=DataHousing) determines the data frame to be used as a source for the split. Like in Chapter 4, we choose one variable (strata=Price) that should be proportionally presented in the training and testing dataset. Since *Price* is a continuous variable rather than a categorical variable, we split the range of the housing prices into quintiles using breaks=5. This ensures observations from each quintile are proportionally represented in training and testing data. In the printout above, you can see the first six records of the training dataset.

The linear regression model is represented by the following equation:

$$\widehat{Price} = \beta_1 Sqft + \beta_2 Grade + \beta_3 Waterfront\_yes + \beta_4 \qquad (5.10)$$

OLS assumes that all predictor variables have an additive and independent impact on the outcome variable. The related βs scale the strength of these impacts.

Before using *OLS* to find the optimal numerical values for the βs, we have to solve one more problem: The $Waterfront$ variable in the data frame `DataTrain` is not numerical. Instead, it contains the values "yes" and "no". To tackle this problem, we can turn $Waterfront$ into a *dummy variable* using `step_dummy()` in the *recipe*. The command `step_dummy()` assigns a value of 1 when the value of the $Waterfront$ variable is "yes" and a value of 0 when it is "no". There is no definite rule about which value 1 or 0 is assigned to "yes" or "no", but it is common practice to assign 1 to "yes" and 0 to "no".

The *recipe* in the code block below determines the variables used for the analysis and converts $Waterfront$ into a dummy variable. First, *Price* is defined as the outcome variable, and all other variables (*Sqft*, *Grade*, and *Waterfront*) are defined as predictor variables using the .-notation. Then `step_dummy(Waterfront)` converts the categorical variable $Waterfront$ into the dummy variable $Waterfront\_yes$.

```
library(tidymodels)
RecipeHouses=recipe(Price~., data=DataTrain) |>
          step_dummy(Waterfront)
```

Note that `step_dummy` changes the variable name (the column name in the data frame) to indicate which category is set to "1". Since waterfront "yes" is assigned to 1, the command `step_dummy()` renames $Waterfront$ to $Waterfront\_yes$. Consequently, if $Waterfront\_yes = 1$, a house is located at the waterfront.

Dummy Variables and One-Hot Encoding

A dummy variable is called a *dummy* because it fills in for the presence of a category. For example, the 1 of the dummy variable $Waterfront\_yes$ indicates with a numerical value that a *waterfront* is present and with 0 that a waterfront is not present.

In the *waterfront* case, creating the dummy variable seems straightforward. However, in the case of red and white wines, one might create two dummy variables $WineColor\_white$ and $WineColor\_red$ with a value of $WineColor\_white = 1$ for white wines (0 otherwise) and $WineColor\_red$ for red wines (0 otherwise). Creating a variable for each state of a categorical variable is called one-hot encoding.

One-hot encoding can be advantageous for some machine learning models (e.g., *Random Forest*) because it allows for a more straightforward interpretation of the variables. In OLS regressions *one-hot encoding* leads to a situation that makes it mathematically impossible to calculate the βs (*dummy trap*).

The *dummy trap* occurs when using *one-hot encoding* for *OLS* because one dummy variable is redundant. For example, in the case of white and red wines, when we know that $WineColor\_white = 1$, it follows that $WineColor\_red = 0$ (an observation (a wine) can be either *white* or *red*). This redundancy is also reflected in an algebraic property: If we know the values for $WineColor\_white$, we can calculate the values for $WineColor\_red$ ($WineColor\_red = 1 - WineColor\_white$). If we can calculate one predictor from one or more other predictor variables, these variables are *perfectly correlated*. The absence of *perfect correlation* is one of the conditions to be fulfilled for *OLS* regression.

Consequently, for *OLS*, if we have n categories, we will only consider $n - 1$ dummy variables. So, for example, in the case of the $Waterfront$ categorical variable with two categories ("yes" and "no"), we will consider only one dummy variable $Waterfront\_yes$ but not the other $Waterfront\_no$ to avoid *perfect correlation*.

The multivariate *model design* for the housing analysis does not differ from the univariate *model design* in Section 5.4.2. From the package lm, we use the model linear_reg() with mode "Regression".

Please substitute the ... in the code block below and execute the code. If everything is correct, R prints information about the *model design*:

```
ModelDesignHouses=linear_reg() |>
  set_engine("...") |>
  set_mode("...")
print(ModelDesignHouses)
```

Next, you will use a pipe to add the recipe and the *model design* to a *workflow* and fit the *workflow* model to the training data.

Please substitute the ... in the code block below and execute the code. If everything is correct, R will print information about the fitted *workflow* model. The printout includes the optimal values for the βs:

```
WFModelHouses=workflow() |>
            add_recipe(...) |>
            add_model(...) |>
            fit(...)
print(WFModelHouses)
```

Another way to extract the optimal β values from the *workflow* object WFModelHouses is to use the tidy() command:

```
ResultsTidy=tidy(WFModelHouses)
print(ResultsTidy)
```

```
## # A tibble: 4 x 5
##    term             estimate std.error statistic   p.value
##    <chr>               <dbl>     <dbl>     <dbl>     <dbl>
## 1 (Intercept)      -570056.  15133.             -37.7 6.63e-297
## 2 Sqft                180.      3.25             55.2 0
## 3 Grade             95214.   2548.              37.4 1.65e-292
## 4 Waterfront_yes   868338.  22200.              39.1 7.12e-319
```

The tidy() command returns the optimal β values and other information in a data frame. The resulting data frame is printed above. The *estimate* column contains values for the parameters for *Sqft* (β_1), *Grade* (β_2), *Waterfront_yes* (β_3), and the intercept (β_4).

If we plug in the optimal βs in Equation (5.10), we get the prediction equation:

$$
\begin{aligned}
\widehat{Price} \;=\; & 180 \cdot Sqft + 95214 \cdot Grade + \\
& 868338 \cdot Waterfront\_yes + (-570056) \quad (5.11)
\end{aligned}
$$

If we know the values for the predictor variables, we can estimate the housing price. For example, if we want to predict the price of a house with 1,500 square feet ($Sqft = 1500$), a building condition grade of 9 ($Grade = 9$), and the house is not located at the waterfront ($Waterfront\_yes = 0$), we can plug in these values into the prediction Equation (5.11). As a result we get 556,870 as the predicted house price ($\widehat{Price} = 556{,}870$).

Try it out in the code block below. Substitute *Sqft*, *Grade*, and *Waterfront_yes* with the corresponding values and execute the code to get the predicted price ($\widehat{Price}$).

```
180*Sqft+95214*Grade+868338*Waterfront_yes-570056
```

Equation (5.11) also helps to interpret the βs. The β parameters indicate the predicted price change when the related predictor variable increases by one unit.

Suppose the living square footage increases by one unit (one extra square foot), then the estimated price of a house changes by about 180 units ($180) because the change of one unit is multiplied by 180 ($\beta_1 = 180$). You can verify this when you return to the code block above and substitute $Sqft$ with 1501 instead of 1500 (leave $Grade = 9$ and $Waterfront\_yes = 0$ unchanged). You will see that the estimated price will be $557,050 instead of $556,870, a change of $180.

The same interpretation is true for β_2, the parameter for a building's condition. If $Grade$ increases by one unit (one grade), then the estimated price of that house increases by about $95,214 (confirm this in the code block above).

The interpretation of the parameter for the dummy variable $Waterfront\_yes$ is a bit tricky. Technically, if the dummy variable $Waterfront\_yes$ increases by one unit, the estimated housing price would increase by $868,338.

To better interpret this increase, we have to consider the limited range of a dummy variable: A dummy variable can only increase by one unit when it switches from 0 to 1. In the case of the $Waterfront\_yes$ dummy, this means $Waterfront\_yes = 0$ increases by one unit to $Waterfront\_yes = 1$. In short, if we would hypothetically place a house that is not at the waterfront ($Waterfront\_yes = 0$) to a location at the waterfront ($Waterfront\_yes = 1$), the dummy variable $Waterfront\_yes$ would increase by one unit — the estimated housing price would increase by $868,338. In other words, houses at the waterfront are expected to be $868,338 more expensive, on average.

Lastly, we need to check if the parameters are significant. The P values in the rightmost column from the `tidy()` command output above show the probabilities of the true parameters being zero (i.e., being irrelevant). Since the P values are all very close to zero, this probability is extremely low, meaning the parameters are significant.

The parameters' interpretability and significance are strong points of linear regression. Unfortunately, most other machine learning models do not allow us to interpret their parameters directly. This is the reason why in the past these models were called *black box models*.

However, dramatic progress has been made in recent years that allows us to explain the predictions of machine learning models. We will introduce some important algorithms to better interpret the predictions of machine learning models in Chapter 11.

To assess the predictive quality of the fitted model based on the testing dataset ($DataTest$), we again use the `augment()` command. It predicts the housing price and appends the predictions as column `.pred` to the testing data. The resulting data frame is saved as `DataTestWithPred`:

```
DataTestWithPred=augment(WFModelHouses, DataTest)
head(DataTestWithPred)
```

```
## # A tibble: 6 x 5
##      Price  Sqft Grade Waterfront    .pred
##      <dbl> <int> <int> <chr>         <dbl>
## 1 1230000  5420    11 no         1450647.
## 2  257500  1715     7 no          404430.
## 3  291850  1060     7 no          286802.
## 4  229500  1780     7 no          416103.
## 5  530000  1810     7 no          421491.
## 6  650000  2950     9 no          816645.
```

You can see that the first observation has a predicted house price of $1,450,647. Since the testing dataset also includes the true value for the outcome variable *Price*, you can calculate the prediction error (e.g., $Error = 1450647 - 1230000 = 220647$). The house was over-estimated by $ 220,647.

You might wonder why the data frame contains the character variable *Waterfront* and not the dummy variable *Waterfront_yes*. The answer is that predictions generated by augment() were appended to the original data frame DataTest, which contains the original categorical variable *Waterfront* with the values "yes" and "no".

Since the data frame DataTestWithPred includes both the *truth* (*Price*) and the *estimate* (*.pred*), it allows using the metrics() command to evaluate the fitted model's predictive quality for the testing data. Again, we only have to provide the truth=Price and estimate=.pred together with the date frame DataTestWithPred, and the metrics() command will calculate default metrics for the regression analysis:

```
metrics(DataTestWithPred,truth=Price, estimate=.pred)
```

```
## # A tibble: 3 x 3
##    .metric .estimator  .estimate
##    <chr>   <chr>           <dbl>
## 1 rmse     standard     244656.
## 2 rsq      standard       0.549
## 3 mae      standard     163358.
```

As you can see above, the metrics() command calculates the *root mean squared error* ($\sqrt{MSE}$; rmse), the r^2 (rsq), and the mean absolute error (mae).

The rmse is closely related to the *MSE*. A minimal *MSE* also implies a minimal *root mean squared error*. The importance of the *MSE* stems from the fact that it is used as a criterion to find the best parameters. However, the MSE and the `rmse` numerical values are not well suited for interpretation.

The r^2 (`rsq`) expresses the proportion of the variance of the outcome variable (*Price*) explained by the prediction equation. In our case, the regression can explain 54% of the *Price* variance.

The most intuitive of the metrics calculated above is the mean absolute error (`mae`). The analysis performed here shows that based on the observations from the testing data, the model over/underpredicted the true housing price on average by \$163,358.

5.6 When and When not to use Linear Regression

- An OLS regression can predict an underlying linear relationship between a continuous variable and one or more predictor variables. The resulting parameters are interpretable, and significance tests are possible if certain conditions (the Gauss-Markov conditions) are fulfilled (see Gujarati and Porter (2009) for more details).

- Linear regression is not a good choice if we face a *classification* problem like predicting if a wine is *red* or *white*. In Chapter 8 when *Logistic Regression* is covered, we will explain in detail why linear regression is ill-suited for *classification*.

- If the *true* relationship between the outcome and predictor variable(s) is non-linear, OLS regression is, in most cases, not a good tool to use. Although we can introduce some degree of non-linearity into a linear regression by transforming underlying data logarithmically before utilizing them as predictor and outcome variables, more complex non-linear relationships are unsuitable for OLS regression.

  You can see the problem in Figure 5.2, where the underlying relationship between the outcome variable Y and the predictor variable X follows a parabolic trend (see the blue data points). Using OLS on the data in Figure 5.2 would give us the red regression function. You can see that this regression function systematically underestimates for smaller predictor values ($x \leq 120$), overestimates for values in the middle ($120 < x \geq 165$), and underestimates again for larger values ($x \geq 180$).

- It is possible to model basic interactions between predictor variables with OLS by transforming the data and thus indirectly introducing non-linearities (Chapter 7 provides an example).

  However, when using interaction terms, researchers must decide upfront

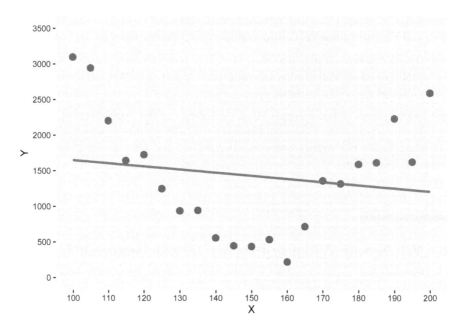

FIGURE 5.2 Estimating a Parabolic Trend with OLS Regression

which interactions to consider. In addition, interpreting the significance of the interaction terms can be problematic.

If the goal is to consider more complex interactions and upfront assumptions about the type of interactions are difficult, other machine learning algorithms such as *Neural Networks* (see Chapter 9) or *tree-based* algorithms (see Chapter 10) are superior to *OLS*.

• In many cases it is a good idea to use linear regression as a benchmark and then evaluate if other more advanced machine learning models can deliver better predictive quality.

5.7   Digital Resources

Below you will find a few digital resources related to this chapter such as:

• Videos
• Short articles
• Tutorials
• *R* scripts

These resources are recommended if you would like to review the chapter from a different angle or to go beyond what was covered in the chapter.

Here we show only a few of the digital resoures. At the end of the list you will find a link to additonal digital resources for this chapter that are maintained on the Internet.

You can find a complete list of digital resources for all book chapters on the companion website: https://ai.lange-analytics.com/digitalresources.html

Linear Regression, Clearly Explained!!!

A video from *StatQuest* by Josh Starmer. The video explains the fundamentals of linear regression.

Link: https://ai.lange-analytics.com/dr?a=363

FctMSE() - An R Function to Calculate the Mean Squared Error

A blog post by Carsten Lange describes how to program an R function. It uses the *R* function FctMSE() which was used in the book *Practical Machine Learning with R* as an example. FctMSE() calculates the *MSE* for a dataset based on the provided parameter values for slope and intercept of a univariate prediction function.

Link: https://ai.lange-analytics.com/dr?a=362

Deriving the Formulas for Parameters in Univariate Linear Regression Using OLS

A blog post by Carsten Lange describes how optimal parameters for a univariate linear regression can be derived using the Ordinary Least Square method (*OLS*).

Link: https://ai.lange-analytics.com/dr?a=430

Why Predictors for Linear Regression Do Not Need Normalisation

This blog post by Carsten Lange describes why OLS linear regression data do not need to be normalized. The article includes an example with R code showing how OLS parameters (coefficients) adjust when dimensions change.

Link: https://ai.lange-analytics.com/dr?a=431

tidymodels Part 1: Running a Machine Learning Model in Three Easy Steps

This blog post by Carsten Lange shows that processing data, creating an OLS model design, and running the model requires only three steps in *tidymodels*. The blog post also shows that adjusting the code to use a different machine learning model requires only minimal modifications.

Link: https://ai.lange-analytics.com/dr?a=429

More Digital Resources

Only a subset of digital resources is listed in this section. The link below points to additional, concurrently updated resources for this chapter.

Link: https://ai.lange-analytics.com/dr/linregr.html

6

Polynomial Regression — Overfitting/Tuning Explained

The importance of creating training and testing data, and how this can be done in R, was emphasized in the previous chapters. Splitting the data into training and testing data is necessary because you cannot use the same data to train (calibrate) a model's parameters and assess a model's predictive quality. If you did that, your model would be *overfitted*!

Overfitting is a situation where a fitted model approximates the training data well, but fails on new observations, which it has never seen before.

In this chapter, we first explain the problem of *overfitting* in more detail (see Section 6.3). Then in Section 6.4, we use a univariate *Polynomial Model* to demonstrate *overfitting* with an example. This model will predict house prices based on various powers of the predictor variable square footage (e.g., $Sqft$, $Sqft^2$, $Sqft^3$, ...).

Polynomial Model

A model that expresses the relationship between the predicted outcome and the predictor variable(s) as a polynomial function is called a Polynomial Model. A *Polynomial Model* involving one predictor variable is called a univariate *Polynomial Model*. In contrast a *Polynomial Model* involving two or more predictor variables is called a multivariate *Polynomial Model*.

Example - Univariate *Polynomial Model* with predictor variable x:

$$\hat{y} = \beta_1 x + \beta_2 x^2 + \beta_3 x^3 + \beta_4$$

Example - Multivariate *Polynomial Model* with two predictor variables (x_1 and x_2):

$$\hat{y} = \beta_1 x_1 + \beta_2 x_1^2 + \beta_3 x_1 x_2 + \beta_4 x_2 + \beta_5 x_2^2 + \beta_6$$

The term $x_1 x_2$ is called an *interaction term*. This is because the term $x_1 x_2$ only has a high value (high influence on the outcome) if x_1 and x_2 have high values. For example, to predict *wage* the two numerical predictors *skill level* and *years of experience* could be modeled as an interaction term because it requires both skill and experience to earn a high wage.

In what follows, we will work with a univariate *Polynomial Model*. We will use a very small training dataset to calibrate the model parameters. The small training dataset in connection with the *Polynomial Model* will lead to an *overfitting* scenario.

In Section 6.4, the *overfitting* scenario will allow us to visualize why *overfitting* can occur and why it is problematic for predicting new observations.

In Section 6.5, we will introduce hyper-parameter tuning, an iterative procedure that helps to avoid *overfitting*. *Hyper-parameter tuning* will help us to find the best model complexity (degree of the *power* for $Sqft$) for the *Polynomial Model*.

In Section 6.6 we will introduce a tuning template based on the R tidymodels package. This template will allow you to use the concept of *hyper-parameter tuning* with any machine learning model as long as it is supported by tidymodels.

In Section 6.7 you can apply the template from Section 6.6 to work on an interactive project. You will try to find the best value for the *hyper-parameter* k for the *k-Nearest Neighbors* model that was used in Chapter 4 to classify wines into red and white wines.

6.1   Learning Outcomes

This section outlines what you can expect to learn in this chapter. In addition, the corresponding section number is included for each learning outcome to help you to navigate the content, especially when you return to the chapter for review.

In this chapter, you will learn:

1. To identify under which circumstances overfitting likely occurs (see Section 6.3).

2. To apply a Polynomial Model to predict house prices (see Section 6.4).

3. How to explain overfitting in detail (see Section 6.4).

4. How overfitting can compromise the prediction quality for new data (see Section 6.4).

5. How to use hyper-parameter tuning to avoid *overfitting* (see Section 6.5).

6. How to work with the 10-Step Tuning Template to tune *hyper-parameters* for various types of machine learning models (see Section 6.5).

7. How to work with a real-world dataset and apply the tuning template from Section 6.5 to find the best value for the *hyper-parameter k* in a *k-Nearest Neighbors* model (see Section 6.7).

6.2 R Packages Required for the Chapter

This section lists the *R* packages that you need when you load and execute code in the interactive sections in *RStudio*. Please install the following packages using `Tools -> Install Packages ...` from the *RStudio* menu bar (you can find more information about installing and loading packages in Section 3.4):

- The `rio` package (Chan et al. (2021)) to enable the loading of various data formats with one `import()` command. Files can be loaded from the user's hard drive or the Internet.

- The `janitor` package (Firke (2023)) to rename variable names to *Upper-Camel* and to substitute spaces and special characters in variable names.

- The `tidymodels` package (Kuhn and Wickham (2020)) to streamline data engineering and machine learning tasks.

- The `kableExtra` (Zhu (2021)) package to support the rendering of tables.

- The `learnr` package (Aden-Buie et al. (2022)), which is needed together with the `shiny` package (Chang et al. (2022)) for the interactive exercises in this book.

- The `shiny` package (Chang et al. (2022)), which is needed together with the `learnr` package (Aden-Buie et al. (2022)) for the interactive exercises in this book.

- The `kknn` package (Schliep and Hechenbichler (2016)) to run *k-Nearest Neighbors* models.

6.3 The Problem of Overfitting

Machine learning aims to develop models that can be used to predict outcomes in the future. However, data scientists can only develop machine learning models based on data from the past (training data).[1] They use the training data to calibrate a machine learning model's parameters.

This approach is not without problems. When *too successfully* calibrating a machine learning model to the training data (i.e., the error based on the training data is very small), the model is extremely specialized in approximating the training data, but it fails with new observations that are not part of the training dataset. This is the core problem of overfitting.

To avoid *overfitting* while in the stage of model development by adjusting the *model design* (i.e., choosing *hyper-parameter* values) is not easy. When we cannot use the testing data to asses different designs, since the testing data can only be used to evaluate the finalized model.

Without being able to use the testing data, a *second-best* approach to minimize *overfitting* is *Cross-Validation*. This procedure utilizes the training data and randomly chooses part of the training data as a holdout validation dataset, to validate different *model designs*. This process is repeated on a rolling base until each observation was assigned once to the validation dataset (more about *Cross-Validation* in Section 6.5.2).

Circumstances that Can Lead to Overfitting

Identifying conditions that make *overfitting* more likely helps with developing strategies to avoid it. In general, *overfitting* is more likely to occur:

1. When the training dataset does not have a sufficient number of observations.
2. When the model considers many variables and consequently contains many parameters to calibrate.
3. When the underlying machine learning model is highly non-linear.

6.4   Demonstrating Overfitting with a Polynomial Model

To demonstrate how *overfitting* occurs and which problems result from *overfitting*, we will use a *Polynomial Model* to predict housing prices.

As in the interactive Section 5.5, we utilize the King County House Sale dataset (Kaggle (2015)) and split the data into training and testing data:

---

[1]This is at least true for *supervised models*. *Unsupervised models* like *reinforcement models* that can improve during the *production stage* exceed the scope of this book. In an *IBM* blog article Delua (2021) provides a brief comparison between *supervised* and *unsupervised* machine learning models.

```
library(tidymodels); library(rio); library(janitor)
DataHousing=
   import("https://ai.lange-analytics.com/data/HousingData.csv") |>
   clean_names("upper_camel") |>
   select(Price, Sqft=SqftLiving)

set.seed(777)
Split001=DataHousing |>
         initial_split(prop=0.001, strata=Price, breaks=5)
DataTrain=training(Split001)
DataTest=testing(Split001)
```

Note that the argument `prop=0.001` in the `initial_split()` command assigns only 20 observations to the training data. The remaining 21,593 observations will be used as testing data. The reason to consider only 20 observations for training, although enough observations are available to create a bigger training dataset, is that we will purposely create circumstances that can lead to an *overfitting* scenario. In real-world analysis, where we work with bigger training datasets, *overfitting* is often more subtle and difficult to identify.

We use the prediction equation below to estimate the price of a house based on living square footage (*Sqft*). The model is polynomial because *Sqft* is considered with various powers:

$$\widehat{Price} = \beta_1 Sqft + \beta_2 Sqft^2 + \beta_3 Sqft^3 + \beta_4 Sqft^4 + \beta_5 Sqft^5 + \beta_6 \quad (6.1)$$

Since the price of a house ($\widehat{Price}$) is estimated based only on its square footage, the model is classified as univariate. A univariate model was chosen because it will allow us to present the results in a 2D diagram with the price on the vertical and square footage on the horizontal axis.[2]

As you see in Equation (6.1) the predictor variable *Sqft* is used with powers ranging from $1 - 5$, which makes the model non-linear.[3]

If you look at the circumstances that likely lead to *overfitting* in the info box at the end of the previous section, you can see that all conditions are fulfilled here:

1. The training dataset does not have a sufficient number of observations (20 observations in our case).

2. The model contains many variables and, thus many parameters to calibrate (five variables and six parameters to calibrate is usually

---

[2]A multivariate real estate model will be covered in Chapter 7.
[3]Later in this chapter, *Polynomial Models* with various degrees will be used.

not considered many, but compared to only 20 observations the number of parameters can be considered as large).

3. The model is highly non-linear (a polynomial of degree 5 is highly non-linear).

To create the *Polynomial Model* with `tidymodels` we use the same *model design* as in the interactive Section 5.5. To introduce non-linearity we use the *recipe* (the data):

```
ModelDesignLinRegr=linear_reg() |>
                set_engine("lm") |>
                set_mode("regression")

RecipeHouses=recipe(Price~., data=DataTrain) |>
            step_mutate(Sqft2=Sqft^2, Sqft3=Sqft^3,
                        Sqft4=Sqft^4,Sqft5=Sqft^5)
```

The *recipe* utilizes `step_mutate()` to create four additional variables that are calculated as the square, cubic, quartic, and quintic of the variable $Sqft$:

- `Sqft2`$=Sqft^2$,
- `Sqft3`$=Sqft^3$,
- `Sqft4`$=Sqft^4$,
- `Sqft5`$=Sqft^5$.

Because $Sqft$ is not only used in its original form, but also with various powers (squared, cubic, quartic, and quintic), the model is non-linear (in the data).

When looking at Equation (6.1) you can see why the model is *linear in its parameters*: If we treat the variables $Sqft, Sqft^2, ..., Sqft^5$ the same as any other variable in a multivariate linear *OLS* model, then each variable is multiplied by a parameter $\beta_1 - \beta_5$ and added to the equation. Thus Equation (6.1) is a linear function as long as we interpret the different powers of $Sqft$ as separate variables.

A Polynomial Model is linear in parameters but non-linear in data.

Consequently, the *Polynomial Model* from Equation (6.1) can still be optimized the same way as a regular *OLS* model because it is still linear in its parameters, when we treat each power of $Sqft$ as separate variables.

We optimize by adding the *recipe* and the linear *model design* to the *workflow* `WFModelHouses`, which is then fitted to the 20 observations in the training dataset with `fit(DataTrain)`:

```
WFModelHouses=workflow()  |>
               add_recipe(RecipeHouses)  |>
               add_model(ModelDesignLinRegr)  |>
               fit(DataTrain)
```

Since the *workflow* WFModelHouses is fitted to the training data, we can use it to predict and measure the model's predictive performance. We start with measuring the performance regarding the training data.

As before, we use the augment() command to append the predictions to the training dataset and then we use the metrics() command to calculate predictive performance metrics (see Sections 4.7.6 and 4.7.7 for details):

```
DataTrainWithPred=augment(WFModelHouses, DataTrain)
metrics(DataTrainWithPred, truth=Price, estimate=.pred)
```

```
## # A tibble: 3 x 3
##    .metric .estimator  .estimate
##    <chr>   <chr>           <dbl>
## 1 rmse     standard    136432.
## 2 rsq      standard         0.715
## 3 mae      standard    104047.
```

The metrics() command by default calculates the *root mean square error* (rmse), r^2 (rsq), and the *mean average error* (mae), when provided with the column names for the estimate (.pred) and the truth (Price) in the data frame DataTrainWithPred.

You can see that based on the training data, the *Polynomial Model* performs well. For example, based on the mae, the model under/overestimates on average by $104,000 (for comparison, a linear model with *Sqft* as the only predictor variable would create a *mean average error* of $139,000).

The good results for the *Polynomial Model* based on the training data are also confirmed in Figure 6.1 where we plotted the 20 training data observations (red) together with a linear prediction function (blue) and the prediction function for the *Polynomial Model* (magenta).

You can see that the magenta line (the *Polynomial Model*) approximates the training data better than the blue line (the linear model). This is because the non-linearity of the *Polynomial Model* gives the magenta line more flexibility. The magenta line bends downwards to better predict lower-priced houses between 1,300 sqft and 2,200 sqft. Then it bends upwards to approximate higher priced houses with square footage between 2,500 sqft and 4,000 sqft. Finally, it bends down again to almost perfectly approximate the low-priced outlier house point with about 4,500 sqft.

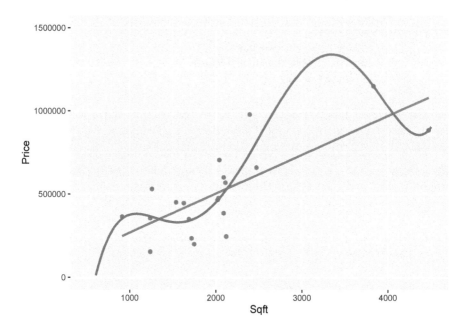

FIGURE 6.1 Approximating Training Data with Polynomial (Degree 5)

In contrast, the blue line representing the linear benchmark cannot bend and therefore is located in the center of the training data.

The question remains, if the *Polynomial Model* (the magenta line in Figure 6.1) can also predict the testing data well.

To generate predictive metrics for the testing data, we again use the `augment()` and the `metrics()` commands, but this time we provide the data frame `DataT-est` to the `augment()` command::

```
DataTestWithPred=augment(WFModelHouses, DataTest)
metrics(DataTestWithPred, truth=Price, estimate=.pred)
```

```
## # A tibble: 3 x 3
##    .metric .estimator      .estimate
##    <chr>   <chr>               <dbl>
## 1 rmse     standard      99940240.
## 2 rsq      standard         0.0215
## 3 mae      standard       1719470.
```

You can see that the *Polynomial Model* that performed so well on the training data performs poorly on the testing data. The *mean average error* (`mae`) shows that the model under/overestimates on average by $1,719,000 (!!!) based on the testing data (for comparison, a linear model with $Sqft$ as the only predictor variable would create a *mean average error* of $168,000 based on the testing data).

Why *overfitting* occurred and why the testing data were predicted so poorly by the *Polynomial Model* can be seen in Figure 6.2. The figure shows the training data (red dots), the testing data (small black dots) together with the prediction functions for the *Polynomial Model* (magenta line), and the linear benchmark (blue line).

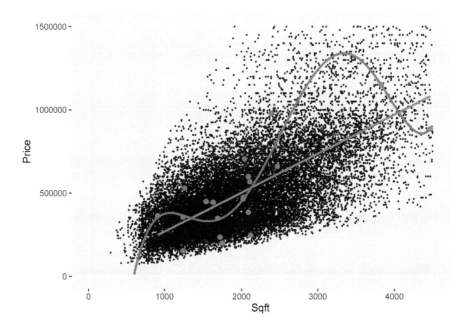

FIGURE 6.2 Model Performance on Testing and Training Data

The flexibility of the magenta line (the non-linearity of the *Polynomial Model*) allows to approximate the training data very well, but the strong focus on the training data fails to represent the general trend of the remaining data (testing data). This is exactly the problem of *overfitting*.

In contrast, the blue linear line cannot bend (the linear one-predictor benchmark model can only produce a straight line). This prevents the model from *overfitting* (over-approximating the training data).

The problems with *overfitting* can further be demonstrated when extending the *Degree-5 Polynomial Model* to a *Degree-10 Polynomial* Model. This means that in the prediction equation, exponents all the way up to 10 are considered for $Sqft$:

$$\widehat{Price} = \beta_1 Sqft + \beta_2 Sqft^2 + \beta_3 Sqft^3 + \beta_4 Sqft^4 + \cdots + \beta_9 Sqft^9 + \beta_{10} Sqft^{10} + \beta_{11}$$

Thanks to the `tidymodels` package, it is fairly easy to repeat the analysis for a *Degree-10 Polynomial Model* by only modifying the *recipe*. Instead of using `step_mutate()` to generate new predictor variables with various powers of *Sqft*, we now use `step_poly()` to generate 10 new variables for the 10 different powers of *Sqft*:

```
RecipeHousesPoly10=recipe(Price~., data=DataTrain) |>
                step_poly(Sqft, degree=10,
                        options=list(raw=TRUE))
```

By default (`options=list(raw=FALSE)`) the command `step_poly()`, transforms the calculated polynomials to *orthogonal polynomials*, which allows for better interpretation of the regression parameters (βs). Since the *Polynomial Regression* model we use here is too complex to allow any interpretation of its parameters and since orthogonal polynomials exceed the scope of this book, we will work with the original polynomials in what follows (`options=list(raw=TRUE)`). The predictions are the same regardless of whether you use original or *orthogonal polynomials.*[4]

If we graph the resulting prediction function of the *Degree-10 Polynomial Model* (magenta line in Figure 6.3), you can see the complete disaster of extreme *overfitting*.

The *Degree-10 Polynomial Model* represented by the magenta line approximates the 20 training observations (red dots) almost perfectly but totally fails to predict the testing data (small black dots).

For example, the *Degree-10 Polynomial Model* predicts extremely high housing prices for houses with small square footage, predicts negative housing prices for houses with square footage in the ranges of 1,000 – 1,200 sqft and 2,700 – 3,700 sqft, and predicts extremely high prices for houses with 3,900 – 4,400 sqft.

From Figure 6.3, it is obvious to see why *overfitting* occurred. However, in almost all real-world cases we will not be able to generate a graph like in Figure 6.3. Therefore, comparing performance between training and testing data is the only way to identify *overfitting*.

---

[4]For more details about *Orthogonal Polynomial Regression* see Narula (1979).

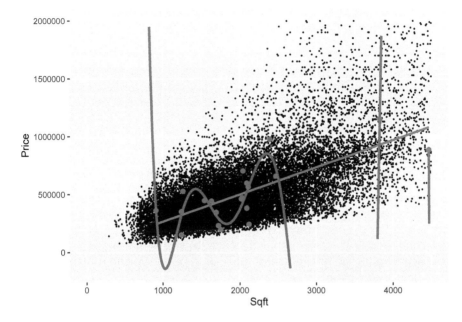

FIGURE 6.3 Model Performance on Testing and Training Data

Overfitting Summary

Overfitting occurs when a highly non-linear (flexible) model adjusts almost perfectly to a relatively small number of training observations, but the adjustment is so specific that the model fails when predicting the testing data.

Overfitting is sometimes compared to human learning behavior, when somebody learns facts by heart rather than understanding the underlying theory.

If — after the completion of model development — a comparison of training and testing data reveals overfitting, the model development needs to start from scratch.

The new model development includes generating new sets of training and testing data (change of the value in `set.seed()`). Otherwise, we risk extending the *overfitting* from the training to the testing data.

6.5 Tuning the Complexity of a Polynomial Model

In the previous section, *overfitting* occurred in the *Degree-5 Polynomial Model* and to an extreme degree in the *Degree-10 Polynomial Model*. The linear model (blue line in Figures 6.2 and 6.3) seemed to be superior to the *Degree-5* and *Degree-10 Polynomial Model*.

However, this does not mean a linear model is always the best choice. For example, when the underlying pattern that generated the data is non-linear, a linear regression model is sub-par to fit the non-linear pattern.

This raises the question:

How can we choose the right degree for a Polynomial Model?

6.5.1   Hyper-Parameters vs. Model Parameters

The appropriate degree for a *Polynomial Model* cannot be found with the *Optimizer* that calibrates the β-parameters (*model parameters*) because in order to run the *Optimizer*, we have to choose the model first — including the polynomial degree. Therefore parameters like the polynomial degree, that need to be determined before the model calibration, are called *hyper-parameters* rather than *model parameters*.

Hyper-Parameters

1. *Hyper-parameters* are parameters that change the design of a machine learning model or the data pre-processing in a *recipe*. For example, the *hyper-parameter k* in a *k-Nearest Neighbors model design* or the degree of a *Polynomial Model* in a *recipe*.

2. *Hyper-parameters* often control the degree of non-linearity, and thus the flexibility of the prediction function. Therefore, we often face a trade-off between model flexibility and the risk of *overfitting*.

3. *Hyper-parameters* cannot be determined with an *Optimizer* based on training data like a model's β parameters. Therefore, we must utilize a *trial-and-error* process to find suitable *hyper-parameters*. This process is called hyper-parameter tuning.

4. We cannot utilize the testing data for *hyper-parameter tuning* because this can extend *overfitting* into the testing data!

Finding the best *hyper-parameter* values is not specific to *Polynomial Models* only; we ran into this challenge already in Chapter 4 when deciding on the parameter k (the number of neighbors to consider) for *k-Nearest Neighbors*. Later, in Chapter 9, when covering *Neural Network* models, we have to decide how many neurons to consider when building a *Neural Network*. The number of neurons in a *Neural Network* is also considered a *hyper-parameter*. In fact, most machine learning models require finding best *hyper-parameters* at the *model design* stage. This process is called hyper-parameter tuning.

6.5.2 Creating the Tuning Workflow

In this and the following sections, we will tune the *hyper-parameter* for the polynomial degree of the model covered in Section 6.4 using the same dataset. The only exception is the number of observations assigned to the training data. Instead of using an extremely small training dataset, we will use a more realistic training dataset size. In the code block below, we again import the **King County House Sale** dataset (Kaggle (2015)), but now split the 21,613 observations into 80% training and 20% testing data:

```
library(tidymodels); library(rio); library(janitor)

DataHousing=
  import("https://ai.lange-analytics.com/data/HousingData.csv") |>
  clean_names("upper_camel") |>
  select(Price, Sqft=SqftLiving)

set.seed(987)

Split80=DataHousing |>
        initial_split(prop=0.8, strata=Price, breaks=5)
DataTrain=training(Split80)
DataTest=testing(Split80)
```

Building the *workflow* for the analysis follows almost the same steps as in the previous section. We create a recipe and a *model design*. Afterward, we add both to a *workflow*:

```
RecipeHousesPolynomOLS=recipe(Price~., data=DataTrain) |>
                  step_poly(Sqft, degree=tune(),
                            options=list(raw=TRUE))

ModelDesignLinRegr=linear_reg() |>
                  set_engine("lm") |>
                  set_mode("regression")

TuneWFModelHouses=workflow() |>
                  add_model(ModelDesignLinRegr) |>
                  add_recipe(RecipeHousesPolynomOLS)
```

However, there are two differences compared to the *workflow* in Section 6.4:

1. In `step_poly()` where the argument `degree=` determines the highest power of $Sqft$ in the prediction equation, we do not assign a number

for the degree. This makes sense because the aim of *hyper-parameter tuning* is to find this number (the degree of the *Polynomial Model*).

Since the argument `degree=` needs somehow to be determined, we use `tune()` as a placeholder. It is important not to over-interpret the meaning of `tune()`. It is only a placeholder that, later, will get replaced by the values for `degree` when we try and evaluate different values for `degree`.

2. The *workflow* does not contain a `fit()` command to fit the model parameters to the training data. This also makes sense: Because the `degree` for the polynomial function is not determined, fitting the model is not possible. Consequently, the *workflow* cannot be used for predictions. It is only a blueprint for the tuning process that we will later perform. To clarify that the *workflow* is used for tuning only, the related *R* object name is prefixed with the word `Tune` (`TuneWFModelHouses`).

In order to evaluate the performance of several different degrees for the *Polynomial Model*, we have to decide which degrees we would like to try out. This is an arbitrary decision.

Nevertheless, the `tidymodels` package can still provide some guidance. For most *hyper-parameters* a related command exists that returns a recommended *hyper-parameter* value range. The name of the command is often the same as the name of the *hyper-parameter*. For example, you can use the command `degree()` to find a recommended range for the *hyper-parameter* `degree`:

```
degree()
```

```
## Polynomial Degree (quantitative)
## Range: [1, 3]
```

The command returns a recommended range for the *hyper-parameter* `degree` from 1 – 3. We will extend this range and evaluate *polynomial degrees* from 1 – 10.

For tuning purposes, the `tidymodels` package expects a data frame with the values for each *hyper-parameter* in the columns. The column names must be the same as the name of the respective *hyper-parameter*. Since we tune only one *hyper-parameter* in this case, the data frame `ParGridHouses` contains only one column named `Degree` with the values from 1 – 10:

```
ParGridHouses=data.frame(degree=c(1:10))
print(ParGridHouses)
```

```
##    degree
```

```
## 1        1
## 2        2
## 3        3
## 4        4
## 5        5
## 6        6
## 7        7
## 8        8
## 9        9
## 10      10
```

Later, during the tuning process, the *hyper-parameter* values above will be pushed one by one to the tuning *workflow* `TuneWFModelHouses`. Each value will fill in for the placeholder `tune()` and the *workflow* will be fitted. Next, its predictive quality will be evaluated. The *workflow* (the *polynomial degree*) with the best performance constitutes the *best model*.

6.5.3 Validating the Tuning Results

To find the *best model*, we need to validate each *hyper-parameter* value from the tuning results (each *hyper-parameter* combination in case we tune more than one *hyper-parameter*). This raises the question:

Which dataset should be used to validate the tuning results?

You might be tempted to use the testing dataset to validate different values for *hyper-parameters*. However, keep in mind that the testing dataset should never be used for any type of optimization — including *hyper-parameter* tuning.

If you ignore this rule, you might get a good performance on the testing data. But because now the optimization is specialized for the testing data, you likely will get poor predictive results in the production stage when you confront your model with new data, which it had never seen before. This would be an example of pushing the *overfitting* problem from the training to the testing data.

Using the complete training dataset to find the best *hyper-parameter* value is also not an option because the best performing *hyper-parameter* value would be the one that triggers the highest degree of *overfitting*.

In what follows, we will introduce two strategies to assess various values of *hyper-parameters* without using the testing dataset or the complete training dataset:[5]

---

[5]In what follows, we show how to create a *validation dataset* and how to perform *Cross-Validation*. For other procedures such as *Bootstrapping* or *Leave-One-Out* we refer to Kuhn and Silge (2022).

Validation Dataset

One option is to randomly choose a number of observations from the training dataset, exclude them from training, and assign them to an additional holdout dataset called the validation dataset.

The *validation dataset* will never be used for training. Instead, the observations in the *validation dataset* are set aside to assess the predictive performance for different *hyper-parameter* values.

A *validation* dataset is very similar to a *testing* dataset since both are used to assess the performance of a specific model. The difference is that the assessment is performed at different stages of development. While the *validation* dataset is used during the *model design* stage to find the best *hyper-parameter* values, the *testing* dataset is used after the development of the machine learning model is finalized to assess overall predictive quality.

The validation_split() command in the code block below can be used to split the training data into observations that are used for training (analysis observations) and those that are used to assess the predictive performance for various *hyper-parameter* settings (assessment observations). The command validation_split() is similar to the command initial_split(). The argument prop=0.85 determines the percentage of observations leftover for training and the argument strat=Price ensures that different housing price levels are proportionally distributed between training and assessment. The splitted observations are then stored in the data frame DataValidate:

```
set.seed(879)
DataValidate=validation_split(DataTrain, prop = 0.85, strat=Price)
```

The resulting data frame DataValidate includes the complete training dataset, but observations are internally earmarked with analysis to indicate that an observation will be used for training, and with assessment to indicate that the observation will be used as validation data to assess *hyper-parameter* performance.

Using a validation dataset to compare *hyper-parameter* performance is appropriate for large datasets. For smaller datasets, there are a couple of disadvantages:

1. Excluding observations from the training process and earmarking them for *hyper-parameter* assessment reduces the number of observations that are available for training.

2. The observations used for the assessment of *hyper-parameters* are randomly chosen. This bears the risk that, by accident, an unusual validation dataset might be created (the risk is higher for smaller training datasets). Evaluating *hyper-parameters* based on unusual

assessment observations might lead to a sub-par choice of *hyper-parameter* values.

Cross-Validation

Instead of using one dataset where observations are earmarked for training or *hyper-parameter* assessment, the *Cross-Validation* procedure creates multiple training/assessment datasets called *folds* or *resamples*. These folds differ only by which observations are chosen for training and which ones are used for *hyper-parameter* assessment. Figure 6.4 shows the basic idea behind *Cross-Validation* for four folds.

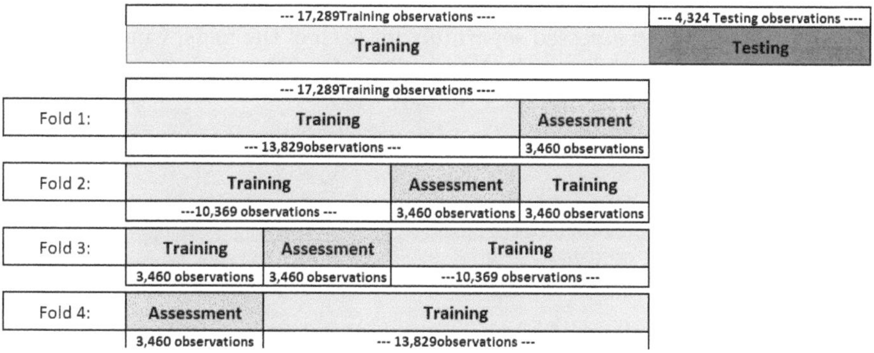

FIGURE 6.4 The Basic Idea Behind Cross-Validation

Cross-Validation shuffles the training dataset and then copies it N times, assigning each copy to one of N folds. Each of these folds has a different set of observations excluded from the training and used for the assessment of the various *hyper-parameter* combinations.

Figure 6.4 shows an example for four folds. The shuffled training dataset is copied four times into Folds 1 – 4. In Fold 1, the last quarter of observations, is assigned to the assessment dataset. The remaining observations are used for training. In Fold 2, the third quarter of observation is designed to the *assessment* dataset, and the remaining observations are used for training. In Fold 3, the second quarter of observations is assigned to the assessment dataset, and in Fold 4, the first quarter. This assures that every observation is exactly used once in an assessment dataset.

When a model is *tuned*, each of the *hyper-parameter* values is assessed for all four folds (requires training of the model for each fold). The overall performance for a *hyper-parameter* value is calculated as the mean performance of the assessment observations in folds 1, 2, 3, and 4. The same process is then repeated for the other *hyper-parameter* values.

It is common to choose ten folds if the training dataset is sufficiently big. For smaller datasets, a lower number of folds can be selected. To compensate for a low number of folds, the process of shuffling the training data, creating folds, and training/assessing the models can be repeated several times. This requires setting the `repeat=` argument for the related `vfolds_cv()` command to a value > 1 (the default is `repeat=1`).

The advantage of Cross-Validation is that different sets of observations are used for assessment (the mean prediction error is used to assess overall performance) and all observations of the training data at some stage of model assessment are used for *validation*. Therefore, the risk of an unusual assessment dataset is mitigated.

The disadvantage of Cross-Validation is that each *hyper-parameter* setup needs to be trained and assessed separately for each of the folds. Computation time increases exponentially with the number of *hyper-parameters* tried out and proportionally with the number of folds used.

Using the R code block below, you can create the *Cross-Validation* folds for our *Polynomial Model*:

```
set.seed(987)
FoldsHouses=vfold_cv(DataTrain, v=4, strata=Price)
```

For simplicity reasons we generate only four folds, although our dataset would be big enough to choose the common 10-fold setup. The command `vfold_cv()` creates the four folds (see the argument `v=4`). The `strata` argument ensures that the different house prices are proportionally represented in the various assessment folds.

6.5.4 Executing the Tuning Process

Now that we have stored the four folds for *training* and *hyper-parameter assessment* in the R object `FoldsHouses` and the *hyper-parameters* to be tried out in `ParGridHouses`, we can use the command `tune_grid()` to evaluate each of the ten parameter values (degree $1 - 10$). Given four folds and ten parameter values to evaluate, the `tune_grid()` command has to train and assess a total of 40 model/data variations.

The command `tune_grid()` executes the tuning process (see the R code block below). It requires the name of the tuning *workflow* (`TuneWFModelHouses`) as the first argument. Then the data frame with the *hyper-parameter* values to be tried out must be provided with the `grid=` argument (in our case: `grid=ParGridHouses`). Finally, an argument for the R object that holds the folds for training and assessment (`resamples=FoldsHouses`) is required. The `metrics` argument is optional. In the R code below, the argument `metrics=metric_set(rmse,rsq,mae)` determines that performance metrics for the *root mean squared error* (rmse), r^2 (rsq), and the *mean average error* (mae) are calculated for each parameter value and for each fold:[6]

```
TuneResultsHouses=tune_grid(TuneWFModelHouses, resamples=FoldsHouses,
                            grid=ParGridHouses,
                            metrics=metric_set(rmse,rsq,mae))
```

Tuning a *workflow* can take a while, from a few seconds to a day or more depending on the number of *hyper-parameters* to tune and the number of folds used for validation. In the code block above, the results from `tune_grid()` for each parameter value, each fold, and each performance metric are saved in the *R* object `TuneResultsHouses`.

There are several ways to extract information from the *R* object `TuneResultsHouses`. For example, you can use the command `autoplot()` to create a graphical overview of the performance for the different *hyper-parameter* values (see Figure 6.5).

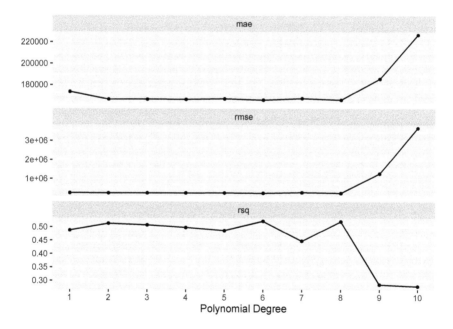

FIGURE 6.5 Performance Metrics During Tuning

The plots in Figure 6.5 indicate that a linear equation (`degree=1`) performs not as well as some of the polynomials with a `degree>1`.

---

[6]If you prefer to use the validation dataset that we developed at the beginning of this section you can change the `resamples=` argument to `resamples=DataValidate`.

The performance for `degree` 2 – 8 is similar for the three metrics (with the exception of degree=7 for the `rsq` metric).

Polynomials with degrees 9 and 10 have a poor predictive performance based on the assessment from the *Cross-Validation* folds.

To see more details, we extract the *hyper-parameter* value rankings from the *workflow* `TuneResultsHouses` based on the three performance measures. We start with the best five *hyper-parameters* using the metric *root mean squared error* (`rmse`):

```
show_best(TuneResultsHouses, metric="rmse")
```

```
## # A tibble: 5 x 7
##    degree .metric .estimator     mean     n std_err
##     <int> <chr>   <chr>         <dbl> <int>   <dbl>
## 1       6 rmse    standard     251993.     4   6179.
## 2       8 rmse    standard     252979.     4   5971.
## 3       2 rmse    standard     255965.     4   7243.
## 4       3 rmse    standard     257680.     4   7875.
## 5       4 rmse    standard     260994.     4   9911.
## # i 1 more variable: .config <chr>
```

The best (lowest) `rmse` was 251,993 for a polynomial `degree` of 6. The linear model (`degree=1`) did not make it to the top five.

The ranking of the five best-performing models based on r^2 is the same as the one for `rmse`:

```
show_best(TuneResultsHouses, metric="rsq")
```

```
## # A tibble: 5 x 7
##    degree .metric .estimator mean     n std_err .config
##     <int> <chr>   <chr>     <dbl> <int>   <dbl> <chr>
## 1       6 rsq     standard  0.522     4  0.0304 Prepro~
## 2       8 rsq     standard  0.521     4  0.0110 Prepro~
## 3       2 rsq     standard  0.513     4  0.0277 Prepro~
## 4       3 rsq     standard  0.508     4  0.0226 Prepro~
## 5       4 rsq     standard  0.498     4  0.0295 Prepro~
```

The ranking for *mean average error* `mae` is slightly different. However, the best-performing model is still the *Degree-6 Polynomial Model*:

```
show_best(TuneResultsHouses, metric="mae")
```

```
## # A tibble: 5 x 7
```

```
##    degree .metric .estimator    mean    n std_err
##     <int> <chr>   <chr>        <dbl> <int>   <dbl>
## 1       6 mae     standard    165798.    4   1924.
## 2       8 mae     standard    165868.    4   1764.
## 3       4 mae     standard    166325.    4   2137.
## 4       3 mae     standard    166434.    4   1863.
## 5       2 mae     standard    166546.    4   1840.
## # i 1 more variable: .config <chr>
```

Since all three performance measures ranked a *Polynomial Model* of degree 6 as the best model, it does not matter which performance measure we choose to extract the `degree` for the best model. For example, to extract the best-performing *hyper-parameter* to minimize `rmse`, we can use:

```
BestHyperPar=select_best(TuneResultsHouses, "rmse")
print(BestHyperPar)
```

```
## # A tibble: 1 x 2
##   degree .config
##    <int> <chr>
## 1      6 Preprocessor06_Model1
```

The printout of `BestHyperPar` shows that the best-performing *hyper-parameter* value is saved in the data frame column `degree` as the first and only entry.

We will use this data frame to create a model (the best one) with the best *hyper-parameter* (`degree=6`).

To do this, we add the best *hyper-parameter* to the tune *workflow* with `final-ize_workflow()`. This command substitutes the `tune()` placeholder with the optimal *hyper-parameter* value that is stored in `BestHyperPar`. Afterward, we add the `fit()` command to the pipe to train the *workflow* model:

```
BestWFModelHouses=TuneWFModelHouses |>
                finalize_workflow(BestHyperPar) |>
                fit(DataTrain)
print(BestWFModelHouses)
```

```
## == Workflow [trained] =====================
## Preprocessor: Recipe
## Model: linear_reg()
##
## -- Preprocessor ---------------------------
## 1 Recipe Step
##
## * step_poly()
```

```
##
## -- Model ----------------------------------
##
## Call:
## stats::lm(formula = ..y ~ ., data = data)
##
## Coefficients:
## (Intercept)  Sqft_poly_1  Sqft_poly_2  Sqft_poly_3
##   -1.30e+04     6.57e+02    -4.90e-01     2.05e-04
## Sqft_poly_4  Sqft_poly_5  Sqft_poly_6
##   -3.76e-08     3.18e-12    -9.93e-17
```

The printout above from the fitted *workflow* confirms that WFModelHouses is a fitted *workflow* because it contains the values for the estimated *model-parameters* (see *Coefficients*). Consequently, WFModelHouses can be used for predictions. We use the augment() command to predict based on the testing dataset and the metrics() command to calculate the related *metrics*:

```
DataTestWithPredBestModel=augment(BestWFModelHouses, DataTest)
metrics(DataTestWithPredBestModel, truth=Price, estimate=.pred)
```

```
## # A tibble: 3 x 3
##    .metric .estimator  .estimate
##    <chr>   <chr>            <dbl>
## 1 rmse     standard       240706.
## 2 rsq      standard          0.586
## 3 mae      standard       164987.
```

Given that we used a univariate model with $Sqft$ being the only variate, the results look quite good. Based on the testing data $r^2 = 0.5857$. The *mean average error* shows that the housing price is, on average, under/overestimated by \$164,987 (for comparison, a linear model with $Sqft$ as the only predictor variable would create a *mean average error* of \$173,000 based on the testing data).

Figure 6.6 ilustrates why the *Degree-6 Polynomial Model* (magenta line) performs better than a linear regression (blue line) and why it does not lead to *overfitting*: Although a polynomial function of *Degree-6* is potentially very flexible, you can see in Figure 6.6 that it differs only slightly from the linear prediction function for houses smaller than 3,000 sqft. For houses larger than 3,000 sqft, the *Degree-6* prediction function estimates higher valued houses much better than the linear function.

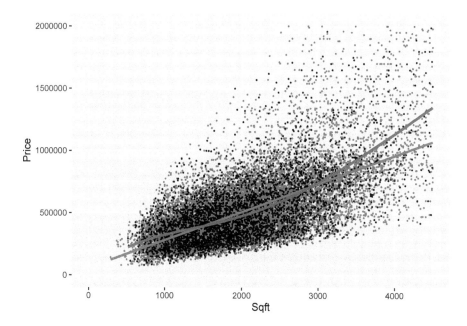

FIGURE 6.6 Poynomial Degree-6 vs. Linear Prediction Functions

6.6   10-Step Template to Tune with tidymodels

In the previous section, we used the `tidymodels` package to tune a polynomial machine learning model. Since `tidymodels` provides a unified analysis framework independent of the machine learning model, you can use the same set of commands for many other machine learning models.

In this section, we provide a *10-Step Template* to make it easy for you to develop a complete machine learning analysis that includes tuning *hyperparameters* and also assessing the final results based on the testing data. You can use the template for all machine learning models covered in this book and for other machine learning models not covered here as well.[7]

Below you will find the *10-Step Template* together with sample code. In the Digital Resources section for this chapter (see Section 6.10), you will find an *R* script that contains the *R* code for the *10-Step Template* together with an example.

---

[7]At the writing of this book, `tidymodels` supported more than 30 machine learning models (see https://parsnip.tidymodels.org/reference).

Step 1 - Generate Training and Testing Data: Note, it is assumed that the data frame `MyData` contains the data you are analyzing.

```
set.seed(987)
Split80=MyData |>
    initial_split(prop=0.8, strata=<OUTCOME VARIABLE>, breaks=5)
DataTrain=training(Split80)
DataTest=testing(Split80)
```

Substitute `<OUTCOME VARIABLE>` with the name of your outcome variable for the `strata=` argument. This ensures that the distribution of your outcome variable is similar in the training and testing data.

Step 2 - Create a Recipe: In the code block below, substitute `<OUTCOME VARIABLE>` with your outcome variable and `<PREDICTOR VARIABLE(S)>` with a list of your predictor variables separated by "+"-signs.

Alternatively, you can use a "." on the right of the "~"-sign to use all predictor variables from the related data frame.

```
Recipe=recipe(<OUTCOME VARIABLE>~<PREDICTOR VARIABLE(S)>,
              data=DataTrain) |>
        step_<NAME OF STEP>(<ARGUMENT(S) OF STEP>)
```

Note that `step_<NAME OF STEP>()` stands for an optional pre-processing step of the predictor variables. `<ARGUMENT(S) OF STEP>` represents optional arguments for the related `step_` command.

If you plan to tune a *hyper-parameter* in a recipe you have to assign the `tune()` placeholder rather than a value to the related argument. For example, `degree=tune()` in `step_poly()`.

You can find a list of available step commands together with their names at: https://recipes.tidymodels.org/reference.

Step 3 - Create a Model Design: Substitute `<NAME OF ML-COMMAND>` with the command name for the related machine learning model and optional with arguments for `<ARGUMENT(S) OF COMMAND>`.

Then substitute `<PACKAGE NAME>` in the `engine()` command with the package name for the machine learning model and `<MODE>` in the `set_mode()` command with either *regression* or *classification*.

```
ModelDesign=<NAME OF ML-COMMAND>(<ARGUMENT(S) OF COMMAND>) |>
            set_engine("<PACKAGE NAME>") |>
            set_mode("<MODE>")
```

If you plan to tune a *hyper-parameter* in a *model design*, you have to assign the `tune()` placeholder rather than a value to the related argument. For example, `neighbors=tune()` in the `nearest_neighbor()` command.

You can find the command names for various machine learning models together with the related package names for the `set_engine()` command at: https://parsnip.tidymodels.org/reference.

Step 4 - Add the Recipe and the Model Design to a Workflow: In the code block below the *recipe* (named: `Recipe`) and the *model design* (named: `ModelDesign`) are added to the *workflow* `TuneWFModel`:

```
TuneWFModel=workflow() |>
          add_recipe(Recipe) |>
          add_model(ModelDesign)
```

Step 5 - Create a Hyper-Parameter Grid: The *hyper-parameter* values that need to be tried out must be listed in a data frame column named with the same name as the *hyper-parameter*:

```
ParGrid=data.frame(<HYPER-PAR1>=c(<LIST OF VALUES>),
          <HYPER-PAR2>=c(<LIST OF VALUES>), <ETC>)
```

The `data.frame()` command is one way to create the required data frame. `<HYPER-PAR1>` is the name of a *hyper-parameter*, and the `c()` command can be utilized to provide a list of values. If you tune more than one *hyper-parameter*, add these in the same way.

If you tune only one *hyper-parameter*, for example, only the number of `neighbors` in a *k-Nearest Neighbors* model, the code could look like this:

```
ParGrid=data.frame(neighbors=c(1,3,6))
```

Step 6 - Create Resamples for Cross-Validation: To create the `resamples` for *Cross-Validation*, you can use the following code:

```
FoldsForTuning=vfold_cv(DataTrain, v=10, strata=<OUTCOME VARIABLE>)
```

A typical *Cross-Validation* setup includes ten folds. If you like to work with a smaller number of folds, especially for smaller datasets, change `v=10` accordingly to reflect the number of folds.

To ensure the outcome variable is similarly distributed in each section of the folds, substitute `<OUTCOME VARIABLE>` with the name of your outcome variable.

Step 7 - Tune the Workflow and Train All Models: The   command `tune_grid()` trains models for all *hyper-parameter* combinations stored in the data frame `ParGrid` using all `resamples` stored in the previous step in `FoldsForTuning`.

```
TuneResults=tune_grid(TuneWFModel, resamples=FoldsForTuning,
grid=ParGrid, metrics=metric_set(<LIST OF METRICS>)),
control_grid(verbose=TRUE))
```

The optional `metrics` argument specifies the metrics that are calculated. For example, substitute `metric_set(<LIST OF METRICS>)` with `metric_set(rmse, rsq, mae)` for a regression or with `metric_set(accuracy, sensitivity, specificity)` for a classification problem.

The argument `control_grid(verbose=TRUE)` is optional. When used like here with `verbose=TRUE`, the tuning reports its progress to the *R Console*.

Step 8 - Extract the Best Hyper-Parameter(s): Because   all   assessment results for the specified metrics are stored in the *tuning* object `TuneResults`, we can use `select_best()` to extract the best *hyper-parameter(s)* for the metric we are interested in:

```
BestHyperPar=select_best(TuneResults, "<METRIC>")
```

You need to specify which metric should be used to identify the best-performing model by substituting `<METRIC>` with the metric of your choice. Note that only metrics specified previously in Step 7 can be chosen.

Step 9 - Finalize and Train the Best Workflow Model: You can use the command `finalize_workflow()` to substitute the `tune()` in `TuneWFModel` with the values from `BestHyperPar`. Afterward, the command `fit(DataTrain)` trains the finalized *workflow* model with the training data:

```
BestWFModel=TuneWFModel |>
         finalize_workflow(BestHyperPar) |>
         fit(DataTrain)
```

Step 10 - Assess Prediction Quality Based on the Testing Data: This step should only be performed after the model is completed and no further changes are planned because otherwise, you cannot use the testing data.

```
DataTestWithPredBestModel=augment(BestWFModel, DataTest)
metrics(DataTestWithPredBestModel, truth=<OUTCOME VARIABLE>,
    estimate=.pred)
```

The `augment()` command writes the predictions into a column named `.pred` and augments the testing data frame with that column. The resulting data frame is saved as `DataTestWithPredBestModel`.

Since the `metrics()` command needs to compare these predictions with the true values to calculate the metrics, the name of the outcome variable also needs to be provided by substituting `<OUTCOME VARIABLE>` accordingly.

6.7 ◎ Project: Tuning a k-Nearest Neighbors Model

Interactive Section

In this section, you will find content together with R code to execute, change, and rerun in RStudio.

The best way to read and to work with this section is to open it with *RStudio*. Then you can interactively work on R code exercises and R projects within a web browser. This way you can apply what you have learned so far and extend your knowledge. You can also choose to continue reading either in the book or online, but you will not benefit from the interactive learning experience.

To work with this section in *RStudio* in an interactive environment, follow these steps:

1. Ensure that both the `learnR` and the `shiny` package are installed. If not, install them from RStudio's main menu (Tools -> Install Packages ...).

2. Download the `Rmd` file for the interactive session and save it in your `project` folder. You will find the link for the download below.

3. Open the downloaded file in RStudio and click the `Run Document` button, located in the editing window's top-middle area.

For detailed help for running the exercises including videos for Windows and Mac users we refer to: https://blog.lange-analytics.com/2024/01/interactsessions.html

Do not skip this interactive section because besides providing applications of already covered concepts, it will also extend what you have learned so far.

Below is the link to download the interactive section:

https://ai.lange-analytics.com/exc/?file=06-TrainTestExerc100.Rmd

In Section 4.9, you used a *k-Nearest-Neighbor* model to predict the color of a wine. We arbitrarily set $k = 4$ to consider the four nearest neighbors.

In this section, you will work on the same problem with an interactive project, but you will tune the *hyper-parameter k* with *Cross-Validation* to find an optimal k (good approximation of the training data without *overfitting*). You will use the *10-Step Template* from Section 6.6 to make it easy to setup the code.

In the Digital Resources section for this chapter (see Section 6.10) you find a link to a blog post that describes how to use the *10-Step Template* in detail. The blog post also provides the *R* code for the template.

Step 1 - Generating Training and Testing Data: As before, you use the wine dataset and split the data into training (`DataTrain`) and testing data (`DataTest`). Since you use the same value in the `set.seed()` command, the (random) split will be identical to the one we used before with the $k = 4$ *Nearest Neighbor* model. The code below has been executed already.

```
library(tidymodels); library(rio); library(janitor)
DataWine=import("https://ai.lange-analytics.com/data/WineData.rds") |>
        clean_names("upper_camel") |>
        rename(Sulfur=TotalSulfurDioxide) |>
        mutate(WineColor=as.factor(WineColor))

set.seed(876)
Split7030=initial_split(DataWine, prop=0.7, strata=WineColor)
DataTrain=training(Split7030)
DataTest=testing(Split7030)

head(DataTrain)
```

```
##    WineColor Acidity VolatileAcidity CitricAcid
## 1        red    10.8           0.320       0.44
## 2        red     6.7           0.855       0.02
## 3        red     7.5           0.380       0.57
## 4        red     7.1           0.270       0.60
## 5        red     8.0           0.580       0.28
## 6        red     7.6           0.400       0.29
##    ResidualSugar Chlorides FreeSulfurDioxide Sulfur
## 1            1.6     0.063                16     37
## 2            1.9     0.064                29     38
## 3            2.3     0.106                 5     12
## 4            2.1     0.074                17     25
## 5            3.2     0.066                21    114
## 6            1.9     0.078                29     66
##    Density   PH Sulphates Alcohol Quality
## 1   0.9985 3.22      0.78   10.00       6
## 2   0.9947 3.30      0.56   10.75       6
## 3   0.9960 3.36      0.55   11.40       6
## 4   0.9981 3.38      0.72   10.60       6
## 5   0.9973 3.22      0.54    9.40       6
```

```
## 6   0.9971 3.45      0.59    9.50       6
```

Step 2 - Create a Recipe: Here, you will create a *recipe* and store it in the *R* object Recipe. Use step_rm() to remove the predictor variable *Quality* because it is not related to *WineColor*, and the command step_normalize() to normalize all remaining predictors. Please, substitute <THESE> placeholders accordingly and execute the code. Note that the data frame DataTrain has already been loaded in the background:

```
Recipe=recipe(WineColor~., data=DataTrain) |>
      step_<NAME OF STEP>(<ARGUMENT OF STEP>) |>
      step_<NAME OF STEP>(all_predictors())
print(Recipe)
```

Step 3 - Create a Model Design: Next, you will create the *model design* and store it into the *R* object ModelDesign. Since you plan to tune the argument neighbors= (stands for the *k* in *Nearest Neighbors*), you have to add it as an argument into the nearest_neighbor() command by substituting <ARGUMENT(S) OF COMMAND> with the argument and its value. Remember that you cannot set neighbors to a specific numerical value because you want to tune the *hyper-parameter* neighbors later on. Therefore you have to assign the placeholder tune() to the argument neighbors.

```
ModelDesign=nearest_neighbor(<ARGUMENT(S) OF COMMAND>) |>
            set_engine("kknn") |>
            set_mode("classification")
print(ModelDesign)
```

Step 4 - Add the Recipe and the Model Design to a Workflow: The code block below adds the *R* object Recipe and the model design object ModelDesign to a *workflow* model named TuneWFModel. The *R* code has been executed already.

```
TuneWFModel=workflow() |>
            add_recipe(Recipe) |>
            add_model(ModelDesign)
print(TuneWFModel)


## == Workflow ================================
## Preprocessor: Recipe
## Model: nearest_neighbor()
##
## -- Preprocessor ----------------------------
## 2 Recipe Steps
```

```
##
## * step_rm()
## * step_normalize()
##
## -- Model ----------------------------------
## K-Nearest Neighbor Model Specification (classification)
##
## Main Arguments:
##   neighbors = tune()
##
## Computational engine: kknn
```

You can see in the printout above that the *workflow* is not *finalized* because the number of `neighbors` has not been set in the *model design*. The *hyper-parameter* `neighbors` is set to `tune()` instead and will later, in Step 7, be replaced in a trial and error process with different values for `neighbors`.

Step 5 - Create a Hyper-Parameter Grid: Later, when tuning is executed in Step 7, values reaching from 1 – 15 for the *hyper-parameter* `neighbors` shall be tried out.

You need to provide these values in a data frame column that is named the same as the *hyper-parameter*. Below, replace the `<LIST OF VALUES>` to define a column `neighbors` in the data frame `ParGrid`. The column should contain values from 1 – 15:

```
ParGrid=data.frame(neighbors=c(<LIST OF VALUES>))
print(ParGrid)
```

Step 6 - Creating Resamples for Cross-Validation: The values you have created above for k (*hyper-parameter* `neighbors`) will be evaluated later using five folds (*resamples*). Each fold contains the complete training data, but different sections are used for training and assessment in each fold.

Please create five folds below by substituting `<NUMBER OF FOLDS>` accordingly.

The folds will be saved in the R object `FoldsForTuning`:

```
set.seed(123)
FoldsForTuning=vfold_cv(DataTrain, v=<NUMBER OF FOLDS>,
                        strata=WineColor)
print(FoldsForTuning)
```

Step 7 - Tune the Workflow and Train All Models: Now it is time to run the tuning procedure using the `tune_grid()` command. Be patient because it will take some time to fully execute. Since we have to try out 15 parameters and use five folds for each model, the `tune_grid()` command has to fit 75 models ($15 \cdot 5 = 75$).

Please substitute `<LIST OF METRICS>` with a list of metrics to be calculated. Use the metrics *accuracy*, *specificity*, and *sensitivity*.

After the tuning is finished, all results are stored in the R object `TuneResults`, and they can be evaluated by different *metrics* commnands.

For example the command `autoplot()` provides a diagrammatic overview of the results for all three *metrics*.

```
TuneResults=tune_grid(TuneWFModel, resamples=FoldsForTuning,
grid=ParGrid, metrics=metric_set(<LIST OF METRICS>))
autoplot(TuneResults)
```

The three graphs that you will create in the exercise above are also displayed in Figure 6.7. They show for each *metric* the related *accuracy*, *specificity*, and *sensitivity* for all tried out *hyper-parameters* (`neighbors`). The results for the five folds are averaged.

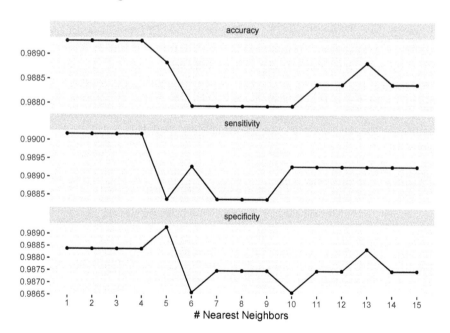

FIGURE 6.7 Tuning Results for Various k Values

You can see that `neighbors` values between 1 and 4 produce the best results for *accuracy* (predicting red and white wines (positive and negative class) correctly) and *sensitivity* (predicting red wines (positive class) correctly). If you look at *specificity* (predicting white wines (negative class) correctly), you can see that $k = 5$ produces the best result. However, $k = 5$ also leads to a sharp decrease in *sensitivity* and a decrease in *accuracy* as well.

It seems reasonable to use the best result for *accuracy*, which means choosing a k between 1 and 4.

Step 8 - Extract the Best Hyper-Parameter(s): All assessment results for the specified metrics are stored in the *tuning* object `TuneResults`. Choose the metric *accuracy* by substituting `<METRIC>` accordingly. Afterward, when you execute the code the `select_best()` command extracts the best *hyper-parameter* (value for `neighbors`) for the metric you specified:

```
BestHyperPar=select_best(TuneResults, "<METRIC>")
print(BestHyperPar)
```

As you will see in the printout after executing the R code, the best value for the *hyper-parameter* `neighbors` based on *accuracy* is 1. It is saved in the data frame `BestHyperPar`.

You can try other metrics in the code block above and see if the result changes. Why would the metric `rmse` cause an error?

Step 9 - Finalize and Train the Best Workflow Model: The   code block below is executed already. The `finalize_workflow()` command used the value from `BestHyperPar` to substitute the `tune()` placeholder in the R object `TuneWFModel` (created in Steps 2 – 4). The *hyper-parameter* is now set to 'neighbors=`1 completing the *workflow*. The command `fit(DataTrain)` calibrates the *workflow* to the training data and the result is saved into `WFModelBest`.

```
WFModelBest=TuneWFModel |>
          finalize_workflow(BestHyperPar) |>
          fit(DataTrain)

print(WFModelBest)


## == Workflow [trained] ======================
## Preprocessor: Recipe
## Model: nearest_neighbor()
##
## -- Preprocessor ---------------------------
## 2 Recipe Steps
##
## * step_rm()
## * step_normalize()
```

```
##
## -- Model ----------------------------------
##
## Call:
## kknn::train.kknn(formula = ..y ~ ., data = data, ks = min_rows(1L,
##
## Type of response variable: nominal
## Minimal misclassification: 0.009383
## Best kernel: optimal
## Best k: 1
```

At the end of the printout above, you can see that (k) was set to 1 rather than tune(). You can also see that WFModelBest is fitted to the training data because the "Minimum missclassification" is reported (based on the training data).

Step 10: Assess Prediction Quality Based on the Testing Data:
Since WFModelBest is a fitted model, you can use it for predictions. In this last step, you use the augment() command to predict WineColor. The augment() command will then add the prediction results as column .pred to the testing data.

The conf_mat() command compares the predictions in column .pred to the true values to create a *confusion matrix*. But before, you have to substitute <OUTCOME VARIABLE> with the variable name (column name) for the outcome variable.

```
DataTestWithPredBestModel=augment(WFModelBest, DataTest)
conf_mat(DataTestWithPredBestModel, truth=<OUTCOME VARIABLE>,
         estimate=.pred_class)
```

You will see in the *confusion matrix* that based on the testing data from 480 red wines, only six were misclassified. Likewise, from the 480 white wines, only seven were misclassified. Given that the classification was only based on the chemical properties of the wines, the results are excellent.

Most likely, a true wine expert might have reached a similar impressive result, but it would have taken them a long time to classify 960 wines.

6.8 When and When not to Use Polynomial Regression

- *Polynomial Regression* is a straightforward but not a sophisticated machine learning procedure. Therefore, it should only be used for basic non-linear relationships where possible interactions between predictor variables are known.

- Regular *OLS* models and basic *Polynomial Models* have the advantage that the coefficients are directly interpretable. This is not true anymore even for slightly more complex *Polynomial Models*.

Since the advantage of direct coefficient interpretability is lost for more complex *Polynomial models*, it is recommended to use more powerful machine learning models such as *Neural Networks* (see Chapter 9) or tree based models like *Random Forest* (see Chapter 10) when analyzing complex regression problems.

6.9   When and When not to Use Tuning

- Anytime a machine learning model has *hyper-parameters* from which you believe they have an impact on the predictive quality, you should use tuning.

- Even if you have a small dataset, you can use tuning. Although the tuning procedures described here are not well suited for small datasets you can use procedures like *Bootstrapping* or *Leave-One-Out* (see Kuhn and Silge (2022) for more details) for smaller datasets.

- Deciding which *hyper-parameters* to tune and how many values to try can be challenging. This is especially true when you tune more than one *hyper-parameter*. In that case, you have to try different combinations of the values for each *hyper-parameter*, and consequently, the number of models to tune can get very big very fast. The number of models the tuning has to fit equals the number of folds times the number of *hyper-parameter* value combinations. For example, if you have ten folds and three *hyper-parameters* with five values each, and you want to try out all combinations of these *hyper-parameter* values, you have to fit 1,250 model/data combinations ($10 \cdot 5 \cdot 5 \cdot 5 = 1,250$).

6.10   Digital Resources

Below you will find a few digital resources related to this chapter such as:

- Videos
- Short articles
- Tutorials
- *R* scripts

These resources are recommended if you would like to review the chapter from a different angle or to go beyond what was covered in the chapter.

Here we show only a few of the digital resourses. At the end of the list you will find a link to additonal digital resources for this chapter that are maintained on the Internet.

You can find a complete list of digital resources for all book chapters on the companion website: https://ai.lange-analytics.com/digitalresources.html

Polynomial Regression Video

Mike X. Cohen provides a YouTube video that explains the basic idea of Polynomial Regression.

Link: https://ai.lange-analytics.com/dr?a=369

The Danger of Overfitting

This video by Cassie Kozyrkov, former Chief Decision Scientist at Google, explains why splitting data into training and testing data is important. She also explains why overfitting is a problem.

Link: https://ai.lange-analytics.com/dr?a=348

Supported Recipe Steps for Preprocessing

Here is a list of all recipe step_() commands that can be piped with |> to a recipe. The linked website will tell you which steps are available for which preprocessing purpose.

Link: https://ai.lange-analytics.com/dr?a=325

Supported Machine Learning Models from tidymodels

Here is a list of all supported tidymodels machine learning models. The linked website will tell you for each model:

- the model name
- the package name(s) for the *set_engine()* command
- the hyper-parameters that you can tune

Link: https://ai.lange-analytics.com/dr?a=324

A 10-Step Template to Create, Tune, and Assess a Machine Learning Model with tidymodels

The link below will open a blog article by Carsten Lange. The article provides a *tidymodels* 10-step template for creating, tuning, and assessing machine learning models. The template is explained in detail and a link for downloading the related *R* script is provided.

Link: https://ai.lange-analytics.com/dr?a=323

More Digital Resources

Only a subset of digital resources is listed in this section. The link below points to additional, concurrently updated resources for this chapter.

Link: https://ai.lange-analytics.com/dr/traintest.html

7

Ridge, Lasso, and Elastic-Net —
Regularization Explained

In the previous chapter, you learned how to adjust *hyper-parameters* during the *model design* stage to avoid *overfitting* while still getting a good approximation of the training data.

In this chapter, we will introduce *regularization*. Regularization is another technique to avoid *overfitting*, and it is applied at the training stage of a machine learning algorithm — when the optimal β parameters are determined. *Regularization* adds penalties for large parameters to a machine learning model's target function. Here we will cover the most common penalty types Lasso, Ridge, and Elastic-Net. The latter is a combination between *Lasso* and *Ridge*. These penalties limit the flexibility of the underlying regression model during the optimization phase by eliminating or significantly weakening *model-parameters* (βs) that are not crucial for the prediction quality. We will explain the idea behind *regularization* in Section 7.4.

In Section 7.4.1, a *Lasso* regularized univariate *Polynomial Regression* model will be introduced, and in Section 7.4.2, a *Ridge* regularized *Polynomial Regression* model will be presented. Section 7.4.3 shows how *Ridge* and *Lasso* models can be combined into the *Elastic-Net* approach.

In the interactive Section 7.5, you will use a multivariate *Elastic-Net* regression model to estimate house prices. You can experiment with the *hyper-parameters* that control the mix of *Ridge* and *Lasso* in an *Elastic-Net* regression model. Afterward, you will tune the *Elastic-Net* model to optimize predictive quality.

7.1 Learning Outcomes

This section outlines what you can expect to learn in this chapter. In addition, the corresponding section number is included for each learning outcome to help you to navigate the content, especially when you return to the chapter for review.

In this chapter, you will learn:

- The basic idea behind regularization (see Section 7.4)

- The difference between the penalty terms for Lasso and Ridge regression models (see Section 7.4)

- How the target function for Lasso regularized regression models differs from the MSE function of an unregularized model (see Section 7.4.1)

- How to create a workflow for a Lasso regularized regression using the R tidymodels framework (see Section 7.4.1)

- How *Lasso* regularized parameter estimates are affected by the value of the Lasso penalty *hyper-parameter* (see Section 7.4.1)

- How the target function for Ridge regularized regression model differs from the MSE function of an unregularized model (see Section 7.4.2)

- How to create a workflow for a Ridge regularized model using the R tidymodels framework (see Section 7.4.2)

- How *Ridge* regularized parameter estimates are affected by the value of the Ridge penalty *hyper-parameter* (see Section 7.4.2)

- How Elastic-Net *regularization* combines elements of both *Lasso* and *Ridge* to create a more flexible *regularization* function (see Section 7.5.3).

- How to create a workflow for a Elastic-Net regularized model using the R tidymodels framework (see Section 7.5.3)

- How to tune Elastic-Net hyper-parameters and how to measure the final predictive performance (see Section 7.5.4)

7.2   R Packages Required for the Chapter

This section lists the R packages that you need when you load and execute code in the interactive sections in *RStudio*. Please install the following packages using Tools -> Install Packages ... from the *RStudio* menu bar (you can find more information about installing and loading packages in Section 3.4):

- The rio package (Chan et al. (2021)) to enable the loading of various data formats with one import() command. Files can be loaded from the user's hard drive or the Internet.

- The janitor package (Firke (2023)) to rename variable names to *Upper-Camel* and to substitute spaces and special characters in variable names.

- The tidymodels package (Kuhn and Wickham (2020)) to streamline data engineering and machine learning tasks.

- The `kableExtra` (Zhu (2021)) package to support the rendering of tables.

- The `learnr` package (Aden-Buie et al. (2022)), which is needed together with the `shiny` package (Chang et al. (2022)) for the interactive exercises in this book.

- The `shiny` package (Chang et al. (2022)), which is needed together with the `learnr` package (Aden-Buie et al. (2022)) for the interactive exercises in this book.

- The `glmnet` package (Friedman et al. (2010), Tay et al. (2023)), which is needed to execute *Lasso*, *Ridge*, and *Elastic-Net* regression models.

7.3 Unregularized Benchmark Model

To demonstrate the idea behind *regularization*, we start by comparing an unregularized model that we introduce in this section to three different regularized models in Section 7.4.

As in Chapter 6, our goal is to predict house prices based on the **King County House Sale** dataset (Kaggle (2015)). The code block below imports the dataset and selects the predictor variables. Afterward, the observations are split into training and testing datasets. Both datasets will be used for the unregularized model in this section as well as for the three regularized models in Section 7.4.

```
library(tidymodels); library(rio); library(janitor)
DataHousing=
  import("https://ai.lange-analytics.com/data/HousingData.csv") |>
  clean_names("upper_camel") |>
  select(Price, Sqft=SqftLiving)

set.seed(777)
Split001=initial_split(DataHousing, prop=0.001, strata=Price, breaks=5)
DataTrain=training(Split001)
DataTest=testing(Split001)
```

Note that we set `prop=0.001`, resulting in a training dataset with only 20 observations. We use such a small training dataset purposely to create a scenario where *overfitting* becomes problematic, allowing us to show how *regularization* can mitigate an *overfitting* problem later.

As in Chapter 6, we use a *Degree-5 Polynomial Regression* model:

$$\widehat{Price}_i = \beta_1 Sqft_i + \beta_2 Sqft_i^2 + \beta_3 Sqft_i^3 + \beta_4 Sqft_i^4 + \beta_5 Sqft_i^5 + \beta_6 \quad (7.1)$$

For an unregularized model, like the one here, the *model-parameters* are determined by the *Optimizer* with the goal to minimize the error function — the Mean Squared Error (*MSE*):

$$MSE \;\; = \;\; \frac{1}{20} \sum_{i=1}^{20} \left(\widehat{Price}_i - Price_i \right)^2 \qquad\qquad (7.2)$$

with: $\widehat{Price}_i = \beta_1 Sqft_i + \beta_2 Sqft_i^2 + \beta_3 Sqft_i^3 + \beta_4 Sqft_i^4 + \beta_5 Sqft_i^5 + \beta_6$

When you substitute the estimated price ($\widehat{Price}_i$) for a house observation i in the error function (7.2) with the prediction function (also shown in equation (7.2)), you can see that the *MSE* only depends on the *model-parameters* (the βs). This is because the training data already determines all other values ($Price_i$ and $Sqft_i$).

Consequently, the *Optimizer* can reach the goal of minimizing the *MSE* by finding the optimal model parameters ($\beta_{j,opt.}$) with a systematic *trial-and-error* approach.

The code block further below shows that there is little difference between WFModelBenchmark and the *workflow* we created in Section 6.4 for a *Polynomial Regression* model.

Only the *recipe* is different because we use step_normalize(all_predictors()) to *Z-score normalize* all predictors (see Section 4.6 for details about normalizing predictor variables).

Normalization is usually not required for a *Polynomial Regression* model. Still, here we normalize the predictors because we will use this *workflow model* as a benchmark to compare with three regularized regression models — *Lasso* (see Section 7.4.1), *Ridge* (see Section 7.4.2), and *Elastic-Net* (see 7.4.3). Since all three models require *normalization*, the benchmark model must also use normalized predictors to be comparable.

To find out why regularized models need normalization, go to the Digital Resources section for this chapter (see Section 7.7).

```
library(tidymodels)
ModelDesignBenchmark=linear_reg() |>
                set_engine("lm") |>
                set_mode("regression")


RecipeHouses=recipe(Price~., data=DataTrain) |>
            step_mutate(Sqft2=Sqft^2,Sqft3=Sqft^3,
```

```
                        Sqft4=Sqft^4,Sqft5=Sqft^5) |>
           step_normalize(all_predictors())

WFModelBenchmark=workflow() |>
                 add_model(ModelDesignBenchmark) |>
                 add_recipe(RecipeHouses) |>
                 fit(DataTrain)
```

Since the code above creates a fitted *workflow model* for the *Degree-5 Polynomial* model, we can extract the β-parameters from the fitted *workflow model* for the house price analysis by utilizing the `tidy()` command:

```
tidy(WFModelBenchmark)
```

```
## # A tibble: 6 x 5
##     term            estimate  std.error  statistic  p.value
##     <chr>              <dbl>      <dbl>      <dbl>    <dbl>
## 1 (Intercept)       509945.     36463.      14.0    1.28e-9
## 2 Sqft             8853783.  10515448.       0.842  4.14e-1
## 3 Sqft2          -50947114.  54352075.      -0.937  3.64e-1
## 4 Sqft3          112589222. 111217647.       1.01   3.29e-1
## 5 Sqft4         -106894260. 101985738.      -1.05   3.12e-1
## 6 Sqft5           36592435.  34688741.       1.05   3.09e-1
```

We will come back to these values later on. For now, keep in mind that the individual β parameters (see the `estimate` column) are not interpretable. This is because a univariate *Degree-5 Polynomial* model is already too complex to allow for the interpretation of its β parameters. However, try to remember that with the exception of the intercept (β_0) most β values are in the one to three-digit million range. You will later see how *regularization* can lower some of these values or even set them to zero.

Now, let us look at the predictive quality of the unregularized benchmark model (`WFModelBenchmark`). We start with evaluating the training data with the R code shown in the code block below. The `augment()` command creates the predictions and augments them to the training data. Afterward, the `metrics()` command calculates the *root mean squared error* (`rmse`), r^2 (`rsq`), and the *mean absolute error* (`mae`) from the data frame `DataTrainWithPredBenchmark` which includes both the predicted and the true price for the training observations:

```
DataTrainWithPredBenchmark=augment(WFModelBenchmark, DataTrain)
metrics(DataTrainWithPredBenchmark, truth=Price, estimate=.pred)
```

```
## # A tibble: 3 x 3
##    .metric .estimator   .estimate
##    <chr>   <chr>             <dbl>
## 1 rmse     standard      136432.
## 2 rsq      standard         0.715
## 3 mae      standard      104047.
```

To evaluate the predictive quality based on the testing data, we use the same code applied to the testing data:

```
DataTestWithPredBenchmark=augment(WFModelBenchmark, DataTest)
metrics(DataTestWithPredBenchmark, truth=Price, estimate=.pred)
```

```
## # A tibble: 3 x 3
##    .metric .estimator      .estimate
##    <chr>   <chr>                <dbl>
## 1 rmse     standard      99940240.
## 2 rsq      standard          0.0215
## 3 mae      standard       1719470.
```

The average over/underestimation (mae) based on the training data is about $104,000 while the same metric based on the testing data is about $1,719,500. This is a strong indication of an *overfitting* problem.

7.4   The Idea Behind Regularization

In Chapter 6, we tuned *hyper-parameters* to avoid *overfitting*. In this chapter, we will tackle the problem with *regularization*.

Regularization

Regularization is a technique applied during a model's calibration. The goal is to generate optimal *model-parameters* (βs) that are smaller than the ones from the related unregularized model — possibly zero.

Small *model-parameters* weaken the influence of the associated predictor variables or eliminate their influence if the parameter is zero.

A model with fewer variables or seriously weakened influence of some variables is less flexible, and therefore *overfitting* becomes less likely.

In essence, *regularization* minimizes or eliminates the influence of predictor variables with little explanatory power on the output variable, thereby improving predictive performance.

The goal of *regularization* — to generate smaller or zero β parameters — leads to the following question:

How can we influence the Optimizer to produce smaller *model-parameters* than the ones that minimize the *Mean Squared Error*?

The answer is that we must give the *Optimizer* a different goal. Such a goal is formalized in the target function below:

$$T^{arget} \;=\; \frac{1}{20}\sum_{i=1}^{20}\left(\widehat{Price}_i - Price_i\right)^2 + \lambda P^{enalty} \tag{7.3}$$

with: $\quad \widehat{Price}_i = \beta_1 Sqft_i + \beta_2 Sqft_i^2 + \beta_3 Sqft_i^3 + \beta_4 Sqft_i^4 + \beta_5 Sqft_i^5 + \beta_6$

You can see that now the target function consists of the MSE and a *penalty* term (P^{enalty}). Hence, we call it an *target function* rather than an *error function*. The goal for the *Optimizer* is now twofold:

1) Minimizing the MSE.

2) Minimizing a *penalty* value which is high when the *model-parameters* (the βs) are large and low otherwise.

The MSE and the P^{enalty} still only depend on the values for the βs. Therefore, the *Optimizer* can minimize the target function (7.3) as before with systematic *trial-and-error*.

The *hyper-parameter* λ ($0 \le \lambda < +\infty$) determines the strength of the P^{enalty} relative to the MSE.

Two major approaches exist to quantify the *penalty*:

Lasso: The *penalty* is calculated as the sum of all (absolute) β values, except the one for the intercept (β_6):

$$P^{enalty}_{Lasso} = \sum_{j=1}^{5} |\beta_j| \tag{7.4}$$

Note that reducing a large or a small β parameter by the same amount has the same impact on the *penalty*.

Ridge: The *penalty* is calculated as the sum of all squared β values, except the one for the intercept (β_6):

$$P^{enalty}_{Ridge} = \sum_{j=1}^{5} \beta_j^2 \tag{7.5}$$

Note that because of the squaring of the βs, large parameters have an over-proportional impact on the *penalty*. Thus, reducing a large β parameter by one unit has a bigger impact on the *penalty* than reducing a smaller β parameter by one unit. We will see later that this is an important difference between *Lasso* and *Ridge*.

7.4.1 Lasso Regularization

When you substitute the definition for the *Lasso penalty* from equation (7.4) into the target function (7.3) you get the target function for the *Lasso* approach:

$$T_{Lasso}^{arget} = \underbrace{\frac{1}{20}\sum_{i=1}^{20}\left(\widehat{Price}_i - Price_i\right)^2}_{MSE_{OLS}} + \lambda\underbrace{\sum_{i=j}^{5}|\beta_j|}_{P_{Lasso}^{enalty}} \tag{7.6}$$

with: $\widehat{Price}_i = \beta_1 Sqft_i + \beta_2 Sqft_i^2 + \beta_3 Sqft_i^3 + \beta_4 Sqft_i^4 + \beta_5 Sqft_i^5 + \beta_6$

You can see again that the target (T_{Lasso}^{arget}) only depends on the β values because the values for the prices of the houses $(Price_i)$ and their square footage $(Sqft_i)$ are known from the training data. Consequently, the *Optimizer* can again use a systematic *trial-and-error* process to find the β values that minimize the target function (7.6).

During the process, the *Optimizer* considers both the MSE and the P_{Lasso}^{enalty} simultaneously. Therefore for all $\lambda > 0$ the optimal β parameters will be smaller than in the case of an unregularized optimization $(\lambda = 0)$.

Below you will find the R code to create a *Lasso model design* and a fitted *workflow model*. For the *recipe* that created the various powers of the $Sqft$ and normalized the resulting predictors, we used the *recipe* from Section 7.3:

```
library(glmnet)
set.seed(777)
ModelDesignLasso=linear_reg(penalty=500, mixture=1) |>
                set_engine("glmnet") |>
                set_mode("regression")


WFModelLasso=workflow() |>
                add_model(ModelDesignLasso) |>
                add_recipe(RecipeHouses) |>
                fit(DataTrain)
```

Note, for the *model design* we again used the `linear_reg()` command, but in contrast to Section 7.3, where we used the `lm` package to create the unregularized model, we now use the `glmnet` package (see `set_engine("glmnet")`) to create a regularized model.

The `glmnet` package is a highly efficient package developed by Friedman et al. (2010). It supports multiple machine learning algorithms including *Lasso* (with `linear_reg(mixture=1)`) and *Ridge* with (with `linear_reg(mixture=0)`). We will discuss the *hyper-parameter* `mixture` in more detail in Section 7.4.3. In the code block above, we set `mixture=1` to work with a *Lasso* model.

The other *hyper-parameter* `penalty=` in the code block above stands for the λ in Equation (7.6). This `tidyverse` *hyper-parameter* name is a little confusing because it determines the strength of the *penalty* but not the *penalty* itself. Just remember, `penalty` and λ are essentially the same.

The *hyper-parameter* named `penalty` can either be set to a specific numerical value or be determined in a tuning process. In the latter case, tuning and *regularization* are combined. In the interactive project in Section 7.4.3 you will tune the `penalty` (the $\$\lambda$). In the code block above, we arbitrarily chose `penalty=500` to keep things simple.

Since the *workflow* `WFModelLasso` is a fitted *workflow model* (it was calibrated with the training data), we can extract the model parameters with the `tidy()` command:

```
tidy(WFModelLasso)
```

```
## # A tibble: 6 x 3
##    term         estimate penalty
##    <chr>           <dbl>   <dbl>
## 1 (Intercept)   509945.     500
## 2 Sqft         -460508.     500
## 3 Sqft2        1171967.     500
## 4 Sqft3              0      500
## 5 Sqft4              0      500
## 6 Sqft5        -560318.     500
```

Notice that after including the *Lasso penalty*, the β parameters (see column `estimate`) are smaller than those from the unregularized benchmark model in Section 7.3.[1] Two *model-parameters* (β_3 and β_4) are equal to zero, essentialy eliminating the related predictor variables $Sqft^3$ and $Sqft^4$ from the prediction equation. This is more obvious when you plug in the *Lasso* β values into Equation (7.1):

---

[1]Other than comparing the size of the parameters between the two models, the individual β parameters are not interpretable. This is because a univariate *Degree-5 Polynomial* model is already too complex to be interpreted.

$$\widehat{Price}_i = -460508 \cdot Sqft_i + 1171967 \cdot Sqft_i^2 + 0 \cdot Sqft_i^3 +$$
$$0 \cdot Sqft_i^4 + (-560318) \cdot Sqft_i^5 + 509945$$
$$\widehat{Price}_i = -460508 \cdot Sqft_i + 1171967 \cdot Sqft_i^2 + (-560318) \cdot Sqft_i^5 + 509945$$

The equation above is simpler and has smaller β parameters than the related prediction equation for an unregularized model which explains why *overfitting* is less likely.

To compare the predictive quality of the *Lasso* model to the benchmark model from Section 7.3, we first calculate the *metrics* based on the training for the *Lasso* model:

```
DataTrainWithPredLasso=augment(WFModelLasso,DataTrain)
metrics(DataTrainWithPredLasso, truth=Price, estimate=.pred)
```

```
## # A tibble: 3 x 3
##    .metric .estimator   .estimate
##    <chr>   <chr>            <dbl>
## 1 rmse     standard     144976.
## 2 rsq      standard       0.679
## 3 mae      standard     110007.
```

Then, we calculate the *metrics* for the *Lasso* model based on the testing data:

```
DataTestWithPredLasso=augment(WFModelLasso, DataTest)
metrics(DataTestWithPredLasso, truth=Price, estimate=.pred)
```

```
## # A tibble: 3 x 3
##    .metric .estimator    .estimate
##    <chr>   <chr>             <dbl>
## 1 rmse     standard     4723086.
## 2 rsq      standard        0.0296
## 3 mae      standard      303118.
```

Let us look at the average over/underestimation of the house prices (mae) and compare the *Lasso* model to the unregularized benchmark model from Section 7.3. You can see that based on the training data the mae increased from about $104,000 to $110,000 but more importantly based on the testing data the mae decreased from about $1,719,500 to $303,100. These results suggest better predictive performance of the *Lasso* model and, more importantly, indicate that the *overfitting* problem is most likely mitigated.

So far, we have only developed β estimates for a penalty of $\lambda = 500$. Figure 7.1

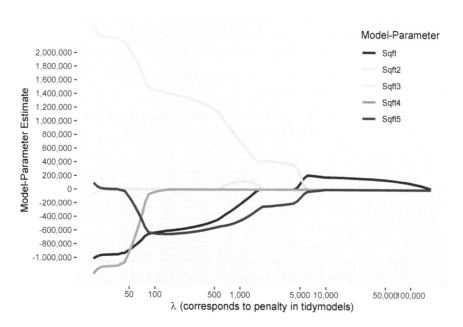

FIGURE 7.1 Parameter Estimates for Different Lasso Penalty Estimates

shows the β estimates for the related predictor variables based on penalty values ranging from $\lambda = 19$ to $\lambda = 190900$.[2]

As expected, when the penalty (λ; corresponds to *hyper-parameter* penalty in tidymodels) increases, the sum of the calibrated absolute β values decreases. You can also see that all βs decrease eventually to zero when the λ increases enough. However, before this happens to all β values, some βs decrease to zero already at a lower λ level, successively eliminating the related predictor variable from the analysis.

Let us explain this phenomenon with an example. When $\lambda = 500$, the parameters for the predictor variables $Sqft^3$ and $Sqft^4$ are already zero ($\beta_3 = 0$ and $\beta_4 = 0$), the β values for β_1, β_2, and β_5 are -460508, 1171967 and -560318, respectively. You can confirm this in Figure 7.1 when you imagine a vertical line at $\lambda = 500$.

When you move rightwards in the diagram in Figure 7.1, λ increases, and with it, the influence of P_{Lasso}^{enalty} on T_{Lasso}^{arget} in the target function (7.6). To compensate the *Optimizer* needs to lower one or more β values. Since it does

---

[2]The linear_reg() command from the glmnet package does not only calibrates the β parameters based on the λ chosen (penalty=500), it also, by default, calibrates for 100 other λ values. The results for Figure 7.1 were extracted with the command extract_fit_engine(WFModelLasso). We do not use these results for tuning because we will use the more advanced tidymodels tuning approach later in Section 7.5.

not matter for P_{Lasso}^{enalty} which parameter will be lowered, the *Optimizer* will successively lower those β parameters that create the smallest damage to the MSE when lowered.

7.4.2   Ridge Regularization

In this section, we will work with *Ridge regularization*. As you will see, this approach differs only slightly from the *Lasso* approach we introduced in Section 7.4.1.

The most significant difference is that *Ridge* uses a different method to penalize large β values. Instead of adding up the absolute values to calculate the *penalty*, *Ridge* squares the β values before adding them up to calculate the *Ridge penalty* (P_{Ridge}^{enalty}).

This becomes more obvious when you substitute the definition for the *Ridge penalty* from equation (7.5) into the target function (7.3) resulting in the target function for the *Ridge* approach:

$$T_{Ridge}^{arget} = \underbrace{\frac{1}{20} \sum_{i=1}^{20} \left(\widehat{Price}_i - Price_i \right)^2}_{MSE} + \underbrace{\lambda \sum_{i=j}^{5} \beta_j^2}_{P_{Ridge}^{enalty}} \qquad (7.7)$$

with: $\widehat{Price}_i = \beta_1 Sqft_i + \beta_2 Sqft_i^2 + \beta_3 Sqft_i^3 + \beta_4 Sqft_i^4 + \beta_5 Sqft_i^5 + \beta_6$

Since the β parameters are now squared when contributing to the *Ridge* penalty, larger β values have an over-proportional impact on the *penalty*, a major difference compared to the *Lasso* approach.

When using the *Ridge* model with `tidymodels`, we can use the same code as in the *Lasso* Section 7.4.1. The only two changes are that we set the argument `mixture=` in the `linear_reg()` command to `mixture=0`, indicating that we use a *Ridge* model[3] and that we arbitrarily set the argument `penalty=1000000` ($\lambda = 1000000$).

```
set.seed(777)
ModelDesignRidge=linear_reg(penalty=1000000, mixture=0) |>
                 set_engine("glmnet") |>
                 set_mode("regression")


WFModelRidge=workflow() |>
             add_model(ModelDesignRidge) |>
             add_recipe(RecipeHouses) |>
             fit(DataTrain)
```

---

[3]More about the `mixture=` argument in Section 7.4.3.

For the *recipe* that creates the various powers of the $Sqft$ and normalizes the resulting predictors, we again use the *recipe* from Section 7.3.

Since the *workflow* WFModelRidge is a fitted *workflow model* (it was calibrated with the training data), we can extract the model parameters with the tidy() command:

```
tidy(WFModelRidge)
```

```
## # A tibble: 6 x 3
##    term        estimate penalty
##    <chr>          <dbl>   <dbl>
## 1 (Intercept)  509945. 1000000
## 2 Sqft          25790. 1000000
## 3 Sqft2         23133. 1000000
## 4 Sqft3         19885. 1000000
## 5 Sqft4         16968. 1000000
## 6 Sqft5         14570. 1000000
```

The β parameters (see column estimate) are smaller than the ones from the unregularized benchmark model in Section 7.3. However, none of the β parameters is equal to zero. So, none of the predictor variables is eliminated. This is a major difference between *Ridge* and *Lasso*.

To evaluate the *Ridge* model's predictive quality and to compare the performance with the benchmark model from Section 7.3 and the *Lasso* model from Section 7.4.1 we calculate the *Ridge* model's *metrics* based on the testing data:

```
DataTestWithPredRidge=augment(WFModelRidge, DataTest)
metrics(DataTestWithPredRidge, truth=Price, estimate=.pred)
```

```
## # A tibble: 3 x 3
##   .metric .estimator  .estimate
##   <chr>   <chr>           <dbl>
## 1 rmse    standard      330485.
## 2 rsq     standard        0.237
## 3 mae     standard      186431.
```

Let us look at the average over/underestimation of the house prices (mae) and compare the *Ridge* model to the *Lasso* model. You can see that based on the testing data, the mae for the *Ridge* model is about \$186,400 which is lower than the one for the *Lasso* model (\$303,100). Both models outperform by far the unregularized model from Section 7.3, which produced a testing data mae of about \$1,719,500, likely due to *overfitting*.

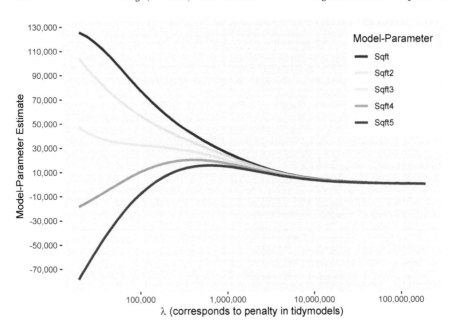

FIGURE 7.2 Parameter Estimates for Different Ridge Penalty Estimates

Figure 7.2 shows the β estimates of the related predictor variables for penalty multipliers ranging from $\lambda = 19,089$ to $\lambda = 190,885,312$.[4]

As in the *Lasso* model, when λ increases, the calibrated β values have a tendancy to move towards zero. In contrast to the *Lasso* model (see Figure 7.1), individual predictor variables are not eliminated (individual β values are not set to zero). Instead, you can see in Figure 7.2 that the paths for the β values converge to a common value. Afterward, when further increasing λ, this common value decreases further, until all β values reach zero — none of the βs reaches zero individually like in the *Lasso* case. Consequently, none of the predictor variables are eliminated individually.

This phenomenon can be explained by the *Ridge penalty* term. When λ is large, the *penalty* term has a high weight compared to the MSE. Consequently, the *Optimizer* focuses mainly on the *penalty* term. Since larger (in absolute terms) β values impact the *penalty* over-proportionally, the *Optimizer* has an incentive to lower these values first. This leads to a situation where β values converge to simlar values in Figure 7.2, for large λ values.

---

[4]The `linear_reg()` command from the `glmnet` package does not only calibrate the β parameters based on the λ chosen (`penalty=1000000`), it also calibrates 100 other λ values. The results for Figure 7.2 were extracted with the command `extract_fit_engine(WFModelLasso)`. We do not use these results for tuning because we will use the more advanced `tidymodels` *tuning* approach later in Section 7.5.

7.4.3 Elastic-Net — Combining Lasso and Ridge

In the previous two sections, we introduced *Lasso* and *Ridge*. *Lasso* tends to reduce β parameter values to zero. Consequently, it eliminates predictors from the model and makes *overfitting* less likely. It is the model of choice if you want to reduce the number of predictors to those with the strongest explanatory power. In contrast, *Ridge* lowers the β parameter values of all predictor variables to avoid *overfitting* without eliminating predictor variables. If you like to keep all predictor variables in the model, *Ridge* is the model of choice to avoid *overfitting*.

Often, we are ambivalent about keeping all predictor variables or not. The goal is to maximize predictive performance and to minimize *overfitting*. Therefore, it is often difficult to determine which algorithm is superior. So, why not combine *Lasso* and *Ridge*?

This is exactly what the *Elastic-Net* approach does. It uses both — the penalty for *Lasso* and the one for *Ridge* — and adds their weighted average to the *MSE* in the target function:

$$T^{arget}_{Elastic} = \underbrace{\frac{1}{20}\sum_{i=1}^{20}\left(\widehat{Price}_i - Price_i\right)^2}_{MSE} + \lambda\left(\overbrace{\alpha P^{enalty}_{Lasso} + (1-\alpha)P^{enalty}_{Ridge}}^{P^{enalty}_{Elastic}}\right) \quad (7.8)$$

$$T^{arget}_{Elastic} = \underbrace{\frac{1}{20}\sum_{i=1}^{20}\left(\widehat{Price}_i - Price_i\right)^2}_{MSE} + \lambda\left(\overbrace{\alpha\underbrace{\sum_{i=j}^{5}|\beta_j|}_{P^{enalty}_{Ridge}} + (1-\alpha)\underbrace{\sum_{i=j}^{5}\beta_j^2}_{P^{enalty}_{Lasso}}}^{P^{enalty}_{Elastic}}\right) \quad (7.9)$$

with: $\widehat{Price}_i = \beta_1 Sqft_i + \beta_2 Sqft_i^2 + \beta_3 Sqft_i^3 + \beta_4 Sqft_i^4 + \beta_5 Sqft_i^5 + \beta_6$

In Equation (7.8) you can see that the penalty for $P^{enalty}_{Elastic}$ is calculated as a weighted average from the penalties P^{enalty}_{Lasso} and P^{enalty}_{Ridge}. The *hyper-parameter* α $(0 \le \alpha \le 1)$ determines the share of the *Lasso penalty*. For example, if $\alpha = 0.5$ then the share of the *Lasso penalty* is 50% and the share of the *Ridge penalty* $((1-\alpha) = 0.5)$ is also 50%. If $\alpha = 0.3$ then the share of the *Lasso* penalty is 30%, and the share of the *Ridge penalty* $((1-\alpha) = 0.7)$ is 70%.

The *hyper-parameter* α corresponds to the argument `mixture=` in the `linear_reg()` command. You worked with it already in Section 7.4.1 when you set `mixture=1` assigning a share of 100% to the *Lasso penalty* and a share of 0% $((1-\alpha) = 0)$ to the *Ridge penalty* — basically running a pure *Lasso* model.

In Section 7.4.2 you ran a pure *Ridge* model by setting `mixture=0` $(\alpha = 0)$ and thus implying that the share of the *Ridge penalty* is 100% $((1-\alpha) = 1)$.

The advantage of the *Elastic-Net* approach is that you can run any mixture of *Lasso* and *Ridge regularization*. The disadvantage is that you get with α (`mixture`) another *hyper-parameter* that either needs to be set in the `linear_reg()` command or that needs to be *tuned* together with the *hyper-parameter* λ (`penalty`).

You will tune these *hyper-parameters* later in an interactive project in Section 7.5. Here, in this section, we implement *Elastic-Net* into `tidymodels` by arbitrarily setting the *hyper-parameters* to keep things simple.

The commands to set up a `tidymodels` *workflow* for the *Elastic-Net* model are almost the same as in the previous section, except that we arbitrarily set `penalty=10000` and `mixture=0.5`.

```
set.seed(777)
ModelDesignElastNet=linear_reg(penalty=10000, mixture=0.5) |>
                    set_engine("glmnet") |>
                    set_mode("regression")


WFModelElastNet=workflow() |>
                add_model(ModelDesignElastNet) |>
                add_recipe(RecipeHouses) |>
                fit(DataTrain)
```

For the *recipe* that creates the various powers of the $Sqft$ and normalizes the resulting predictors, we again use the *recipe* from Section 7.3.

Since the *workflow* `WFModelRidge` is a fitted *workflow model* (it was calibrated with the training data), we can extract the model parameters with the `tidy()` command:

```
tidy(WFModelElastNet)
```

```
## # A tibble: 6 x 3
##    term          estimate penalty
##    <chr>            <dbl>   <dbl>
## 1 (Intercept)    509945.    10000
## 2 Sqft           151417.    10000
## 3 Sqft2           89828.    10000
## 4 Sqft3               0     10000
## 5 Sqft4               0     10000
## 6 Sqft5          -58923.    10000
```

As expected, the β parameters (see `estimate` column) are much smaller than those from the unregularized benchmark model in Section 7.3. The β_3 and β_4 parameters were set to zero, eliminating the related predictor variables

$Sqft^3$ and $Sqft^4$ from the prediction equation. This reflects the influence of the *Lasso* approach. The *model-parameters* β_1, β_2, and β_5 are reduced to a similar range when ignoring the sign. This reflects the influence of the *Ridge* approach.

To evaluate if the *Elastic-Net* with *Lasso* and *Ridge* equally presented (mixture=0.5) can outperform the individual models, we will assess the *Elastic-Net* model's predictive performance based on the testing data and compare with the performance of the *Lasso* and *Ridge* models:

Like before, we calculate the model's *metrics* for the testing data using the augment() and metrics() commands:

```
DataTestWithPredElastNet=augment(WFModelElastNet, DataTest)
metrics(DataTestWithPredElastNet, truth = Price, estimate = .pred)
```

```
## # A tibble: 3 x 3
##    .metric .estimator    .estimate
##    <chr>   <chr>             <dbl>
## 1 rmse     standard      600767.
## 2 rsq      standard        0.00664
## 3 mae      standard      180716.
```

As you can see, based on the testing data, the *Elastic-Net* model over/underestimates the house prices on average by about $180,700 (mae). For comparison the mae for *Lasso* was $303,100 and the mae for *Ridge* was $186,400.

7.5 ⊘ Project: Predicting House Prices with Elastic-Net

Interactive Section

In this section, you will find content together with *R* code to execute, change, and rerun in RStudio.

The best way to read and to work with this section is to open it with *RStudio*. Then you can interactively work on *R* code exercises and *R* projects within a web browser. This way you can apply what you have learned so far and extend your knowledge. You can also choose to continue reading either in the book or online, but you will not benefit from the interactive learning experience.

To work with this section in *RStudio* in an interactive environment, follow these steps:

1. Ensure that both the `learnR` and the `shiny` package are installed. If not, install them from RStudio's main menu (Tools -> Install Packages ...).
2. Download the `Rmd` file for the interactive session and save it in your `project` folder. You will find the link for the download below.
3. Open the downloaded file in RStudio and click the `Run Document` button, located in the editing window's top-middle area.

For detailed help for running the exercises including videos for Windows and Mac users we refer to: https://blog.lange-analytics.com/2024/01/interactsessions.html

Do not skip this interactive section because besides providing applications of already covered concepts, it will also extend what you have learned so far.

Below is the link to download the interactive section:

https://ai.lange-analytics.com/exc/?file=07-RidgeLassoExerc100.Rmd

In the previous section, we worked with a univariate *Polynomial Model* to demonstrate *regularization* and to evaluate *overfitting* scenarios. In the real world, data scientists usually use multivariate models to include more than one variable in their analysis. Therefore, this interactive exercise will teach you how to use a multivariate approach.

7.5.1   The Data

You will again predict house prices using the **King County House Sale** dataset (Kaggle (2015)). In the code block below, the dataset is loaded. Instead of selecting only one variable to predict the price of a house ($Price_i$), we use the `select()` command to choose the number of bedrooms ($Bedr_i$) and the year a house was built ($Year$), together with the house's square footage ($Sqft$). We filter out houses with a price of more than \$1,300,000 and square footage 4,500 sqft or more, which are outliers:

```
library(tidymodels); library(rio); library(janitor); library(glmnet)

DataHousing=
  import("https://ai.lange-analytics.com/data/HousingData.csv")|>
  clean_names("upper_camel") |>
  select(Price, Sqft=SqftLiving, Bedr=Bedrooms, Year=YrBuilt) |>
  filter(Price<=1300000, Sqft<4500)

set.seed(777)
```

```
Split005=initial_split(DataHousing, prop=0.005, strata=Price, breaks=5)
DataTrain=training(Split005)
DataTest=testing(Split005)
```

Note when creating the training dataset, we use the argument `prop=0.005`, leading to a training dataset with about 100 observations. This size is small, but in general realistic for a training dataset. However, given a total of 20,699 available observations, we could have used the more common `prop=0.7`. In that case, we would end up with 14,489 observations for the training dataset. With such a large training dataset, the unregularized model we use later in this section would likely not lead to *overfitting*, and thus *regularization* would no longer be needed — which would defeat the purpose of this interactive exercise.

7.5.2 Unregularized Benchmark Model

As a benchmark, we begin with an unregularized model. In this case, a multi-variate *Degree-2 Polynomial Model*. It includes the variables *Sqft*, *Bedr*, and *Year*. They are used in their original form, squared, and as various *interaction terms*:

$$
\begin{aligned}
Price \;=\; & \beta_1 Sqft + \beta_2 Bedr + \beta_3 Year \\
+\; & \beta_4 Sqft^2 + \beta_5 Bedr^2 + \beta_6 Year^2 \\
+\; & \beta_7 SqftBedr + \beta_8 SqftYear + \beta_9 BedrYear \\
+\; & \beta_{10} Sqft^2 Bedr + \beta_{11} SqftBedr^2 + \beta_{12} Sqft^2 Bedr^2 \\
+\; & \beta_{13} Sqft^2 Year + \beta_{14} SqftYear^2 + \beta_{15} Sqft^2 Year^2 \\
+\; & \beta_{16} Bedr^2 Year + \beta_{17} BedrYear^2 + \beta_{18} Bedr^2 Year^2 \quad (7.10)
\end{aligned}
$$

As before, we use a *recipe* to generate and normalize the additional predictors:

```
RecipeHousesMultivar=recipe(Price~., data=DataTrain) |>
              step_mutate(Sqft2=Sqft^2,Bedr2=Bedr^2,Year2=Year^2,
                 SqftxBedr=Sqft*Bedr,SqftxYear=Sqft*Year,
                 BedrxYear=Bedr*Year,Sqft2xBedr=Sqft2*Bedr,
                 SqftxBedr2=Sqft*Bedr2,Sqft2xBedr2=Sqft2*Bedr2,
                 Sqft2xYear=Sqft2*Year,SqftxYear2=Sqft*Year2,
                 Sqft2xYear2=Sqft2*Year2,Bedr2xYear=Bedr2*Year,
                 BedrxYear2=Bedr*Year2,Bedr2xYear2=Bedr2*Year2) |>
              step_normalize(all_predictors())
```

Afterward, we create the *model design* (`ModelDesignBenchmark`), the *workflow model* (WFModelBenchmark), and we calibrate WFModelBenchmark to the training data:

```
ModelDesignBenchmark=linear_reg() |>
                set_engine("lm") |>
                set_mode("regression")

WFModelBenchmark=workflow() |>
                add_model(ModelDesignBenchmark) |>
                add_recipe(RecipeHousesMultivar) |>
                fit(DataTrain)
```

When you execute the tidy() command in the code block below, you will see that all predictor variable parameters (βs), except the one for the intercept, are in the multi-million range, and some even in the multi-billion range (see column estimate).

```
tidy(WFModelBenchmark)
```

When you execute the code block below, the model's training and testing data predictions are compared to the true values ($Price_i$), and the related metrics are calculated:

```
DataTrainWithPredBenchmark=augment(WFModelBenchmark,DataTrain)
print("Metrics for Training Data:")
metrics(DataTrainWithPredBenchmark, truth=Price, estimate=.pred)

DataTestWithPredBenchmark=augment(WFModelBenchmark,DataTest)
print("Metrics for Testing Data:")
metrics(DataTestWithPredBenchmark, truth=Price, estimate=.pred)
```

After executing the code above, you will see that the mae for the training data is about \$111,700 and the mae for the testing data is about \$142,800. Such a low training mae, when compared to the testing mae, strongly indicates *overfitting*.

In the following section, you will use an *Elastic-Net* model to improve the predictive quality.

7.5.3   Regularized Elastic-Net Polynomial Model

When you substitute the ... after mixture= and penalty= in the code further below with values of your choice and execute, the model's β values will be calibrated and printed. Also, the metrics for the testing data are calculated and printed.

Recall, if `mixture=0`, you will run a *Ridge* model; if `mixture=1`, you will run a *Lasso* model. For anything in between, you will run a *mixed* model.

Finding an appropriate value for the argument `penalty=` is more tricky. For the *Ridge penalty*, values between 15,000 and 154,000,000 will work. For the *Lasso penalty*, values between 15 and 154,000 will work.[5]

Try a few settings and see how the results are changing. For example, use `mixture=1` (*Lasso*) and `penalty=100000`. Afterward, increase and decrease `penalty=` and leave `mixture=1` constant. How are the results changing? Then try `mixture=0` and leave `penalty=100000` to see the different results for a *Ridge* model. You can also set `mixture=0.5` or `mixture=0.7` to try out different *Elastic-Net* models. Playing with different *hyper-parameter* values and observing the resulting βs and *metrics* will help you to better understand the *Ridge*, *Lasso*, and *Elastic-Net* approaches.

```
ModelDesignRegularized=linear_reg(penalty=... , mixture=...) |>
                        set_engine("glmnet") |>
                        set_mode("regression")


WFModelRegularized=workflow() |>
                    add_model(ModelDesignRegularized) |>
                    add_recipe(RecipeHousesMultivar) |>
                    fit(DataTrain)

print("Beta Values (see Column Estimate:)")
tidy(WFModelRegularized)

DataTestWithPredRgularized=augment(WFModelRegularized, DataTest)
print("Metrics for Testing Data:")
metrics(DataTestWithPredRgularized, truth=Price, estimate=.pred)
```

Warning: In the code block above, you changed *hyper-parameters* and evaluated the effects based on the testing data to better understand *regularization*. Never use the testing data to find the best hyper-parameters. Otherwise, you end up with a model that is highly specialized to the testing data, but when used on new data in the production phase, it would likely perform very poorly.

---

[5]These recommendations are based on the 100 λ values that `glmnet` analyzes by default, depending on the model and the training data. Values outside these ranges might produce surprising results.

Instead, use validation data derived from the training dataset to evaluate the performance of *hyper-parameters*. This is the underlying principle of *tuning*, and in the next section, you will tune the *workflow model* to improve performance.

7.5.4   Tuning the Elastic-Net Polynomial Model

In this section, you will use the *10-Step Template* to tune the *hyper-parameters* `penalty` and `mixture`.

Step 1 - Generate Training and Testing Data: The training and testing data have already been generated (see Section 7.5.3 above).

Step 2 - Create a Recipe: The *recipe* to create the predictors for the multivariate *Degree-2 Polynomial* model (`RecipeHousesMultivar`) was created in connection with the unregularized model and can be reused here. It establishes the predictors with various powers and the interaction terms.

Step 3 - Create a Model Design: The *model design* from the previous section needs slight modifications. We have to add the `tune()` placeholder for the *hyper-parameters*:

```
ModelDesignElastNetTune =linear_reg(penalty=tune(), mixture=tune()) |>
                         set_engine("glmnet") |>
                         set_mode("regression")
```

Step 4 - Add the Recipe and the Model Design to a Workflow: As before, we add the *recipe* and the (modified) *model design* to the *workflow*:

```
TuneWFModel=workflow() |>
            add_recipe(RecipeHousesMultivar) |>
            add_model(ModelDesignElastNetTune)
```

Step 5 - Create a Hyper-Parameter Grid: Previously, when only one *hyper-parameter* was tuned, you added the values to be tried out in a data frame column named with the same name as the *hyper-parameter*. When you have more than one *hyper-parameter*, it gets a little more complicated because you want to try out different combinations of *hyper-parameters*.

If you decide to try out all combinations of the values from two or more *hyper-parameters*, you can use the `crossing()` command. The arguments of the `crossing()` command are the *hyper-parameters* you would like to try out. The assigned values to these arguments are the values you want to try out for each of the *hyper-parameters*. They are assigned to each argument as R `vector` objects. The `crossing()` command then generates all possible combinations for the values of the *hyper-parameters*.

For example, in this project you will later try 66 *penalty* values from 15,000 to 80,000 with an increment of 1,000 and three *mixture* values (0, 0.5, and 1). You can use the crossing() command to generate all possible combinations:

```
ParGridHouses=crossing(mixture=c(0, 0.5, 1),
                       penalty=seq(15000, 80000, 1000))
print(ParGridHouses)


## # A tibble: 198 x 2
##     mixture penalty
##       <dbl>   <dbl>
## 1         0   15000
## 2         0   16000
## 3         0   17000
## 4         0   18000
## 5         0   19000
## 6         0   20000
## 7         0   21000
## 8         0   22000
## 9         0   23000
## 10        0   24000
## # i 188 more rows
```

The R vector object assigned to mixture is created with the c() command by listing the related values. The R vector object assigned to penalty is created with the seq() command. The first value in seq() determines where the sequence starts (15,000) and the second where it ends (80,000). The third argument determines the increment (the step size; 1,000).

You can see in the printout above that crossing() generates all possible combinations of the *penalty* values and the *mixture* values. Each of these 198 combinations will be tried out when you tune the *workflow* later on.

The crossing() command is very helpful when you combine multiple *hyper-parameters* with several values each. Imagine you want to create a grid with all combinations of five *hyper-parameters* with ten values each, crossing() would create 100,000 parameter combinations ($10 \cdot 10 \cdot 10 \cdot 10 \cdot 10 = 10^5$) for you. Be advised, tuning 100,000 *hyper-parameter* combinations would use a lot of computing time.

In general, computing time increases exponentially with the number of *hyper-parameters*, while computing time increases proportionally when the values for each *hyper-parameter* increase. These facts must be considered when deciding how many *hyper-parameters* you want to tune and how many values you like to consider for each *hyper-parameter*.

Step 6: - **Create Resamples for Cross-Validation:** To create *resamples* for *Cross-Validation*, we use the vfold() command. However, although usually recommended, creating ten *Cross-Validation* folds creates a problem. Given that we have only 101 observations, the validation set of each fold would consist only of about ten observations. Therefore, we will create sets of three folds (v=3), which leaves about 30 observation for each validation dataset. To offset the small number of folds, we repeat the process of creating folds ten times (see the argument repeats=10) creating a total of 30 folds:

```
FoldsForTuning=vfold_cv(DataTrain, v=3, strata=Price, repeats=10)
```

Step 7 – Step 10:

Now, you are ready to finalize the tuning process in the interactive project. The training and testing data (from Step 1), the *workflow* including the *recipe* and the *model design* (from Steps 2 – 4), as well as the *resamples* for validation (from Step 6) have already been loaded in the background.

In the code block below, you only have to define the data frame with the *parameter grid* as explained in Step 5 to try out various combinations for the *hyper-parameters* penalty= and mixture=.

For the first time you run the code, it is recommended to use the values as determined in Step 5 (you can later change them). Note, executing the code can take a while because penalty=seq(15000,80000,1000) will create 66 *penalty* values, and mixture=seq(0,1,0.5) will create 3 *mixture* values. The crossing() command will then create 198 combinations ($66 \cdot 3$) which will be all tried out and evaluated in the tuning process in Step 7.

When R outputs the results, look carefully at the β parameters, the plot generated by autoplot() after Step 7, and the metrics for the testing data. Then change the c() and seq() commands that generate the *hyper-parameter* values for penalty= and mixture=. Afterward, execute the code again and see how the results change.

Please recall, that for this setup *Ridge penalty* values between 15,000 and 154,000,000 will work and *Lasso penalty* values between 15 and 154,000 will work.[6]

```
# Step 5 - Create a Hyper-Parameter Grid:
#
# ParGridHouses contains the hyper-parameter combinations to be
# tried out.
```

---

[6]These recommendations are based on the 100 λ values that glmnet tries by default, depending on the model and the training data. Values outside these ranges might produce surprising results.

```
# Change the values for the seq() commands to try out different values.
ParGridHouses=crossing(penalty=seq(15000, 80000, 1000),
                       mixture=seq(0, 1, 0.5))
print("Hyper-Parameter Combinations to be Tried Out:")
ParGridHouses

# Step 7: Tune the Workflow and Train All Models
set.seed(777)
TuneResultsElastNet=tune_grid(WFModelElastNetTune,
                              resamples=FoldsForTuning,
                              grid=ParGridHouses,
                              metrics = metric_set(rmse))

# The diagram shows how the  *root mean squared error* (`rmse`)
# changes with increasing regularization:
autoplot(TuneResultsElastNet)

# Step 8 - Extract the Best Hyper-Parameter(s):
BestHyperPara=select_best(TuneResultsElastNet, "rmse")
print("Best values for the Hyper-Parameters")
BestHyperPara

# Step 9: Finalize and Train the Best Workflow
BestWFModel=finalize_workflow(WFModelElastNetTune, BestHyperPara) |>
            fit(DataTrain)

print("Optimal Beta Parameters (see estimate column)")
tidy(BestWFModel)

# Step 10: Assess Prediction Quality Based on the Testing Data:
DataTestBestWFModelWithPred=augment(BestWFModel, DataTest)
print("Metrics for the Testing Data")
metrics(DataTestBestWFModelWithPred, truth = Price, estimate = .pred)
```

7.6 When and When Not to Use Ridge and Lasso Models

- *Regularization* can be used for a wide range of machine learning models to avoid *overfitting*. Every machine learning model with an *error function* that depends on *model-parameters* (βs) can use *regularization*.

Regularization will decrease the values of *model-parameters* possibly all the way to zero. Smaller *model-parameters* will weaken (or eliminate) the influence of the related predictor variables and thus help to avoid *overfitting*.

- Considering computing resources you should also consider that *regularization* adds one or more *hyper-parameters* that need to be tuned (one extra *hyper-parameter* for *Lasso* or *Ridge* and two for *Elastic-Net*).

- If you have a large training dataset compared to the number of *model-parameters* to be optimized, *regularization* might not be necessary. However, you can still use *regularization* in an attempt to improve predictive quality further.

- Using *regularization* for one or more *hyper-parameters* is often a judgment call that should be guided by the required computing time, and the expectation that smaller *model-parameters* improve predictive quality.

- If you use *regularization*, the question arises which *regularization* approach to use.

  - Use *Lasso* if your goal is to eliminate predictor variables from the model.

  - Use *Ridge* to lower the values of all β parameter values without eliminating predictor variables.

  - Use *Elastic-Net* to combine *Lasso* and *Ridge* when you have no preference about eliminating predictor variables or not, and your main goal is to improve predictive performance and to lower *overfitting*. Consider that *Elastic-Net* adds an additional *hyper-parameter* (mixture) that might need tuning.

- Some models, like *k-Nearest Neighbors*, do not optimize an error function and are thus unsuitable for *regularization*.

7.7 Digital Resources

Below you will find a few digital resources related to this chapter such as:

- Videos
- Short articles
- Tutorials
- R scripts

These resources are recommended if you would like to review the chapter from a different angle or to go beyond what was covered in the chapter.

Here we show only a few of the digital resourses. At the end of the list you will find a link to additonal digital resources for this chapter that are maintained on the Internet.

You can find a complete list of digital resources for all book chapters on the companion website: https://ai.lange-analytics.com/digitalresources.html

Regularization in R Tutorial: Ridge, Lasso and Elastic Net

A free DataCamp tutorial about *Ridge*, *Lasso*, and *ElasticNet* regularization that also discusses the trade-off between bias and variance in machine learning.

Link: https://ai.lange-analytics.com/dr?a=371

Lasso Regression Using tidymodels with data for "The Office"

A video and article by Julia Silge published in her blog TidyTuesday. The post describes how to use *tidymodels* to analyze data from the TV series "The Office". A Lasso approach is tuned to regularize the *model-parameters* for a linear regression.

Link: https://ai.lange-analytics.com/dr?a=372

Regularization: What? Why? and How? (Part 1)

The first part of two articles by Siddant Rai in MLearning.ai. The author describes requirements for *regularization* in Part 1 and *regularisation* techniques in Part 2.

Link: https://ai.lange-analytics.com/dr?a=370

Linear Regression Does Not Need Normalization but Ridge/Lasso Regression Does

This blog post by Carsten Lange discusses normalization. It shows that although *normalization* is not needed for linear *OLS* regression, it is needed when a penalty term is used, including *Lasso*, *Ridge*, and *Elastic-Net* regressions. The blog post article is interactive and provides an *R* script with an intuitive example.

Link: https://ai.lange-analytics.com/dr?a=374

More Digital Resources

Only a subset of digital resources is listed in this section. The link below points to additional, concurrently updated resources for this chapter.

Link: https://ai.lange-analytics.com/dr/ridgelasso.html

8

Logistic Regression — Handling Imbalanced Data

Logistic Regression is a machine learning algorithm that can be used to classify binary categories such as *Yes/No*, *Present/Not-Present*, or *Red Wine/White Wine*. *Logistic Regression* is one of the classic machine learning algorithms for classification problems. The basic idea dates back almost 200 years (Verhulst (1845)). Nevertheless, *Logistic Regression* is among the most used algorithms for classifying binary events and is often successful in machine learning competitions.

8.1 Learning Outcomes

This section outlines what you can expect to learn in this chapter. In addition, the corresponding section number is included for each learning outcome to help you to navigate the content, especially when you return to the chapter for review.

In this chapter, you will learn:

- What are the basic ideas behind *Logistic Regression* (see Section 8.3).

- Why Logistic Regression is better suited than OLS for predicting categorical variables (see Section 8.3).

- How to distinguish between probabilities and odds (see Section 8.3).

- How to convert probabilities to odds (see Section 8.3).

- How you can transform the Logistic Regression equation into a form that is similar to the linear *OLS* regression equation (see Section 8.3).

- How you can use the transformed equation to interpret a Logistic Regression's model-parameters (see Section 8.3).

- How to to create a tidymodels workflow for Logistic Regression to analyze churn at the *TELCO* telecommunications company (see the interactive Section 8.4).

- How to identify problems related to imbalanced data — unequal distribution of the binary classification variable (see the interactive Section 8.4).

- How to troubleshoot an imbalanced Logistic Regression, when predictive quality varies dramatically between *sensitivity* and *specificity*[1] (see the interactive Section 8.5).

- How to use downsampling and upsampling to adjust an imbalanced dataset (see the interactive Section 8.5).

8.2   R Packages Required for the Chapter

This section lists the *R* packages that you need when you load and execute code in the interactive sections in *RStudio*. Please install the following packages using `Tools -> Install Packages ...` from the *RStudio* menu bar (you can find more information about installing and loading packages in Section 3.4):

- The `rio` package (Chan et al. (2021)) to enable the loading of various data formats with one `import()` command. Files can be loaded from the user's hard drive or the Internet.

- The `janitor` package (Firke (2023)) to rename variable names to *Upper-Camel* and to substitute spaces and special characters in variable names.

- The `tidymodels` package (Kuhn and Wickham (2020)) to streamline data engineering and machine learning tasks.

- The `kableExtra` (Zhu (2021)) package to support the rendering of tables.

- The `learnr` package (Aden-Buie et al. (2022)), which is needed together with the `shiny` package (Chang et al. (2022)) for the interactive exercises in this book.

- The `shiny` package (Chang et al. (2022)), which is needed together with the `learnr` package (Aden-Buie et al. (2022)) for the interactive exercises in this book.

- The `glm2` package (Friedman et al. (2010) and Tay et al. (2023)), which is needed to execute *Logistic Regression*.

- The `themis` package (Hvitfeldt (2023)) to *up-* and *downsample* imbalanced datasets with advanced algorithms.

---

[1]See Section 4.8 for the concepts of *sensitivity* and *specificity*.

8.3   The Idea Behind Logistic Regression

The basic idea behind *Logistic Regression* can be best demonstrated with an example. Let us start with creating a synthetic dataset based on a made-up story:

After quite a few years past graduation, 11 college friends reunite. Financially, some of them are doing very well, while others are just doing OK. In Table 8.1, you find the yearly salaries (in $1,000) for 10 of our 11 friends together with their names and an indicator if they own a yacht ($Yacht = 1$) or not ($Yacht = 0$). Note that there are only 10 rows in Table 8.1 as one of the 11 friends, Nina, has yet to arrive. We will talk more about Nina later on.

Our objective is to find a machine learning algorithm that can predict for the 10 friends whether or not they own a yacht. In Table 8.1, you can see that except for Jack, all friends who own a yacht had a six-figure income, and the ones who do not own a yacht have a lower income. Therefore, finding a machine learning algorithm that uncovers this rule should be relatively easy.

To keep the example simple and because we do not aim to predict yacht ownership outside the group of our friends, we use all of the data from Table 8.1 as training data and do not use a testing dataset.

TABLE 8.1 Income and Yacht Ownership

Name	Income	Yacht
Jack	45	1
Sarah	50	0
Carl	55	0
Eric	60	0
Zoe	67	0
James	250	1
Enrico	280	1
Erica	320	1
Stephanie	370	1
Susan	500	1

An obvious — but as it turns out later, sub-optimal — approach is a linear regression. We could use *OLS* to find a regression line with slope β_1 and intercept β_2 that best approximates the data (minimizing the *MSE*). Figure 8.1 shows the resulting regression line for the data in Table 8.1 and Equation (8.1) shows the related prediction equation:

$$P_i^{rob} = \beta_1 Inc_i + \beta_2$$
$$P_i^{rob} = 0.0023 Inc_i + 0.1418 \qquad (8.1)$$

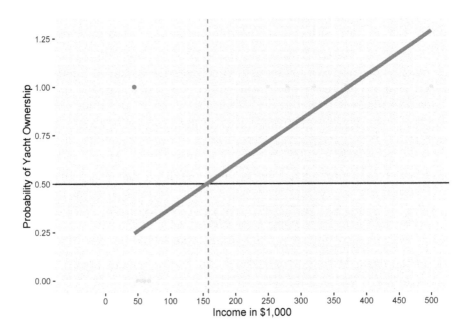

FIGURE 8.1 Linear Function for Binary Classification

As you can see from the regression line in Figure 8.1, the underlying regression assigns continuous numbers to different income levels rather than assigning categorical values such as 1 ("yacht owner: yes") or 0 ("yacht owner: no"). Therefore, we interpret the continuous predictions from the regression as **probabilities** for being a yacht owner (P_i^{rob}). Consequently, the underlying methodology is called the *Linear Probability Model (LPM)*.[2]

The linear regression line in Figure 8.1 as well as the underlying prediction Equation (8.1) from the *LPM* can be used to predict the probability of a person beeing a yacht owner based on their income.

For example, a person with an income of 300 ($300,000) has a probability of nearly 80% ($0.0023 \cdot 300 + 0.1418$) to own a yacht. In comparison, a person with an income of 100 ($100,000) has a probability of about 35% ($0.0023 \cdot 100 + 0.1418$) to be a yacht owner (see Figure 8.1 as well as Equation (8.1)).

Whenever the outcome variable (the probability) of the prediction equation is greater than 0.5,[3] we predict "yacht owner: yes" otherwise, "yacht owner:

---

[2]See Wooldridge (2020), Section 7.5.
[3]We neglect the problem of a probability being precisely 0.5.

no". For example, a person with an income of 75 ($75,000) is predicted to not own a yacht. We get this result by using the regression line (or the prediction equation) to find the related probability for an income of 75, which is a probability of 0.31 ($0.0023 \cdot 75 + 0.1418 = 0.3143$). Since 0.31 is smaller than 0.5 (see the black horizontal line in Figure 8.1), we predict "yacht owner: no".

Here is a shortcut to see quickly which incomes are predicted as "yacht owner: no" and which are predicted as "yacht owner: yes". You can later use the same shortcut to identify other binary predictions from a diagram:

1. Find the intersection point between the prediction function and the horizontal 0.5 probability line.

2. Draw a vertical line through the intersection point (see the dashed blue line in Figure 8.1). This line is called a decision boundary, because it reflects the boundary between predicted classes.

3. All incomes left of the *decision boundary* (income smaller than 158) are predicted as "no". All incomes right of the *decision boundary* (income greater than 158) are predicted as "yes".

Based on the *decision boundary* in Figure 8.1, you can see that persons with an income greater than 158 ($158,000) are predicted to own a yacht. Five of our friends have an income greater than 158, and all own a yacht (see the five correctly predicted points in the upper-right section of the diagram). On the other hand, persons with an income smaller than 158 ($158,000) are predicted not to own a yacht. Five of our friends have an income smaller than 158, and four of those do not own a yacht (see the four correctly predicted points in the left lower section of the diagram). One person's yacht ownership was mispredicted. Jack has an income of 45 ($45,000), which is left of the dashed line. His yacht ownership was consequently predicted as "No", but he does own a yacht (see the incorrectly predicted red point in the upper left section of the diagram). Jack's case seems to be a special case. He earns the lowest income but still owns a yacht. Maybe Jack loves boats so much that he spends almost all his money on his boat. Perhaps he lives on the boat to save rent or he inherited the yacht. We don't know.

In any case, with predicting only one out of ten observations incorrectly so far, linear regression seems to work well to predict categorical variables. In what follows, we will show the drawbacks of using linear regression to predict categorical variables, and we will provide a better alternative.

The first drawback of using linear regression to predict categorical variables is already evident in Figure 8.1. All incomes greater than 375 ($375,000) lead to probabilities greater than 1 (100%). For example, the probability of owning a yacht with an income of 500 ($500,000) is predicted to be 1.29 (129%). That makes no sense since probabilities take on values between 0 and 1. With different data, we could also end up with a regression line that predicts negative probabilities, which also does not make sense.[4]

If we are willing to give up the linearity requirement, the problems mentioned above can be avoided. We could use a non-linear prediction line as shown in Figure 8.2 (see the magenta curve). A non-linear prediction line can bend for greater income values downwards and thus avoid exceeding 1. For small income values, the prediction line can bend upwards and thus avoid falling below 0. When incomes exceed 250, the curve approaches 1, but never exceeds 1. The curve approaches 0 for very small incomes but never falls below 0.

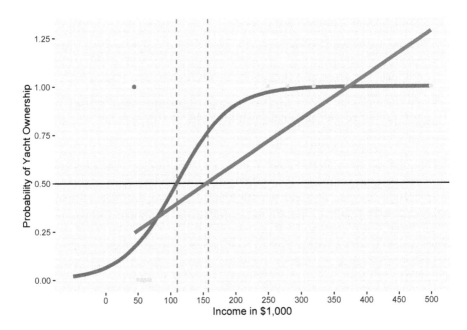

FIGURE 8.2 Comparing Linear and Logistic Function

Since the magenta curve looks like a step of a staircase, first horizontal, then (almost) vertical, and finally horizontal again, these types of curves are often called step-functions. The scientific term is **Sigmoid functions**. Examples include:[5]

- The *Logistic* function[6]
- The *Hyperbolic Tangent* function
- The *Arc Tangent* function

---

[4]A mitigation could be to define all probabilities greater than 100% as 100% and all negative probabilities as 0%. However, this would lead to a kinked prediction line and is also not a good solution for other reasons.

[5]See Wikipedia contributors (2023d).

[6]Confusingly the *Logistic* function is sometimes also called the *Sigmoid function.*

As you can probably guess from the name, the Logistic function is used for Logistic Regression.

The equation below shows the prediction equation for a Logistic Regression with one predictor variable x_i (income in our example) and P_i^{rob} the probability for an event occurring (e.g., yacht ownership: "yes"):

$$P_i^{rob} = \frac{1}{1 + e^{-(\beta_1 x_i + \beta_2)}} \tag{8.2}$$

In Equation (8.2) the parameter β_2 shifts the related curve horizontally, and the parameter β_1 determines the steepness of the step in the step-function graph. An *Optimizer* can be used to calibrate β_1 and β_2 to ensure the best prediction quality for the training data.

Note that *Logistic Regression* does not use the *mean squared error* (MSE) for the error function. Instead, an error based on a function called Logistic Loss is used. For now, just remember that *Logistic Regression* does not minimize the MSE and uses a different function instead.

In Figure 8.2, the magenta curve shows the *Logistic* prediction function with optimized βs. When you apply the technique outlined above to create a *decision boundary*, you can see that every income greater than 110 (right of the magenta dashed *decision boundary*) is predicted as yacht ownership "yes", and any income smaller than 110 (left of the magenta dashed *decision boundary*) is predicted as yacht ownership "no".

The position of the decision boundary for the *Logistic Regression* is slightly different from that for the linear regression — 110 vs. 158. However, the predictions are the same, and the yacht ownership of all friends is predicted correctly again, except for Jack.

A big drawback of linear regression is that it is not well suited for classification because it is sensitive to outliers. This can be best demonstrated with an example:

The 11th friend, Nina, arrives late (her Porsche had a flat tire). That is the reason that her data was initially not considered. Nina's yearly income is $2.5 million, and *yes*, she owns a yacht. This is what we would expect from our previous estimate. Therefore, adding the observation for Nina should keep the predictions approximately the same.

As you will see, Nina's high income combined with her yacht ownership will (as expected) keep the predictions from the *Logistic Regression* very much the same. However, Nina's exceptionally high income (outlier) combined with her yacht ownership will change the predictions from the linear regression so much that they become useless.

To demonstrate this, let us add Nina's observation to the training data and

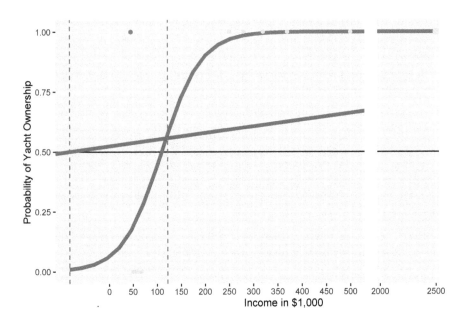

FIGURE 8.3 The Impact of an Oulier on Linear and Logistic Prediction Functions

see what happens. Given Nina's income ($2.5 million) and the fact that she owns a yacht ($Yacht = 1$), we get a new observation with an x-axis value of 2,500 far to the right and a y-value of 1 because Nina owns a yacht. Adding the observation for Nina to the training data changes both the logistic and the linear prediction function (see Figure 8.2):

- The new curve for the *Logistic Regression* (magenta) shifts a little to the right when adding the observation for Nina, but the shift is minimal. The decision boundary is now at 122 instead of 110. Therefore, the predictions from the *Logistic Regression*'s decision boundary have mostly stayed the same: Six of our friends with income greater than 122 are predicted correctly as yacht owners, including Nina's prediction. Five of our friends with an income of less than 122 are predicted as not owning a yacht, which is correct for four of our friends but again not for Jack (red point).

- The new linear regression line — to better approximate the new data point — is much flatter than the original one (see the blue solid line). Consequently, the new decision boundary for the linear regression is now at an income of negative 83 (blue dashed line). This changes the predictions of the new linear prediction function dramatically compared to when the observation for Nina (the outlier) was not considered. All 11 observations are predicted as yacht owners because all 11 observations have an income greater than negative

83. This overly simplistic prediction leaves four observations with wrong predictions (compared to one with the *Logistic Regression*).

Linear regression is unsuitable for predicting categorical variables, because it is sensitive to outliers.

The question remaining is:

What is the advantage of the Logistic function compared to other Sigmoid (step) functions?

To approach this question, we must distinguish between *odds* and *probabilities*. You probably heard about *odds* already in connection with sports betting.

Probabilities vs. Odds

Both *probabilities* and *odds* measure the chance of a *success* (e.g., getting heads in a coin flip or rolling a six with a die).

A probability measures the ratio between the expected number of *successes* occurring in relation to the total number of possible events. For example, the probability of getting a head (*success*) in a coin flip is $\frac{1}{2} = \frac{\#Successes}{\#Events}$, since we expect one head when we flip the coin twice. The probability of rolling a six with a die is $\frac{1}{6} = \frac{\#Successes}{\#Events}$.

$$P^{rob}_{yes} = \frac{\#Successes}{\#Successes + \#NoSuccesses} \qquad (8.3)$$

In contrast, odds measure the ratio between the number of *successes* occurring in relation to the number of *no-successes* occurring. One could also say *odds* are the number of events with "something happening" in relation to the number of events with "something not happening".

For example, the *odds* in a coin flip for heads are $\frac{1}{1} = \frac{\#Successes}{\#NoSuccesses}$. The *odds* for rolling a six with a die are $\frac{1}{5} = \frac{\#Successes}{\#NoSuccesses}$. We would say that the *odds* for heads are 1 to 1, often expressed as 1:1, and that the *odds* of rolling a six with a die are 1 to 5, often expressed as 1:5. You can calculate *odds* as:

$$O^{dds}_{yes} = \frac{\#Successes}{\#NoSuccesses} \qquad (8.4)$$

To derive how to convert *probabilities* to *odds*, we start with dividing numerator and denominator in Equation (8.4) by ($\#Successes + \#NoSuccesses$):

$$O^{dds}_{yes} = \frac{\frac{\#Successes}{\#Successes+\#NoSuccesses}}{\frac{\#NoSuccesses}{\#Successes+\#NoSuccesses}} = \frac{P^{rob}_{yes}}{P^{rob}_{no}} \qquad (8.5)$$

You can see now that the main numerator in Equation (8.5) equals P^{rob}_{yes} and the main denominator equals P^{rob}_{no}. Therefore, we can convert *probabilities* to *odds* as follows:

$$O^{dds} = \frac{P^{rob}_{yes}}{P^{rob}_{no}} = \frac{P^{rob}_{yes}}{1 - P^{rob}_{yes}} \quad \text{with: } P^{rob}_{no} = 1 - P^{rob}_{yes} \qquad (8.6)$$

Now that you know what *odds* are, we can show you what makes the *Logistic* function so special. We start with the *Logistic* function from Equation (8.2):

$$P_{yes,i}^{rob} = \frac{1}{1 + e^{-(\beta_1 \cdot x_i + \beta_2)}}$$

and take the reciprocal on both sides of the equation:

$$\frac{1}{P_{yes,i}^{rob}} = 1 + e^{-(\beta_1 \cdot x_i + \beta_2)}$$

Then we subtract 1 on both sides:

$$\frac{1}{P_{yes,i}^{rob}} - 1 = e^{-(\beta_1 \cdot x_i + \beta_2)}$$

When we consider that $-1 = -\frac{P_{yes,i}^{rob}}{P_{yes,i}^{rob}}$ and substitute -1 accordingly, we get (after simplification):

$$\frac{1 - P_{yes,i}^{rob}}{P_{yes,i}^{rob}} = e^{-(\beta_1 \cdot x_i + \beta_2)}$$

Now we take again the reciprocal on both sides and get:

$$\frac{P_{yes,i}^{rob}}{1 - P_{yes,i}^{rob}} = e^{\beta_1 \cdot x_i + \beta_2}$$

According to Equation (8.6) in the yellow box above, $\frac{P_{yes,i}^{rob}}{1-P_{yes,i}^{rob}} = O_{yes,i}^{dds}$. If we substitute accordingly, we get:

$$O_{yes,i}^{dds} = e^{\beta_1 \cdot x_i + \beta_2} \tag{8.7}$$

Equation (8.7) is the prediction equation for *odds* rather than *probabilities* as in Equation (8.2).

But there is another benefit from all the transformations. We can show this when we take the logarithm on both sides of Equation (8.8), resulting in Equation (8.8):

$$\ln(O_{yes/ln,i}^{dds}) = \beta_1 x_i + \beta_2 \tag{8.8}$$

The right-hand side of Equation (8.8) now shows a typical linear regression equation with one predictor variable. This allows us to interpret the coefficients, in our case β_1, in a familiar way: We can say if x increases by one unit, the log odds on the left-hand side of Equation (8.8) increase by β_1 units.

In addition, since the logarithmic change of a variable represents its percentage change, we can say that if x increases by one unit, then the odds increase by β_1 percent. This means:

The coefficients in a Logistic Regression are directly interpretable.

One last comment before applying *Logistic Regression* to a real dataset: Unfortunately, we cannot use a formula, like in linear OLS, to calculate the optimal coefficients. Instead, we have to rely on an *Optimizer* to find the optimal βs by *trial-and-error*. However, this does not matter for practical purposes because the *Optimizer* is already built into the algorithm used by statistical software such as *R*.

8.4 ◎ Analyzing Churn with Logistic Regression

Interactive Section

In this section, you will find content together with *R* code to execute, change, and rerun in RStudio.

The best way to read and to work with this section is to open it with *RStudio*. Then you can interactively work on *R* code exercises and *R* projects within a web browser. This way you can apply what you have learned so far and extend your knowledge. You can also choose to continue reading either in the book or online, but you will not benefit from the interactive learning experience.

To work with this section in *RStudio* in an interactive environment, follow these steps:

1. Ensure that both the `learnR` and the `shiny` package are installed. If not, install them from RStudio's main menu (Tools -> Install Packages ...).

2. Download the `Rmd` file for the interactive session and save it in your `project` folder. You will find the link for the download below.

3. Open the downloaded file in RStudio and click the `Run Document` button, located in the editing window's top-middle area.

For detailed help for running the exercises including videos for Windows and Mac users we refer to: https://blog.lange-analytics.com/2024/01/interactsessions.html

Do not skip this interactive section because besides providing applications of already covered concepts, it will also extend what you have learned so far.

Below is the link to download the interactive section:

https://ai.lange-analytics.com/exc/?file=09-LogRegrExerc100.Rmd

Now that you have learned how *Logistic Regression* works, it is time to apply what you learned to a "real-world" problem.

In this interactive section, you are tasked to analyze churn behavior for customers of the *Telco* company. *Telco* is a fictional telecommunications company that offers various phone and Internet services. For your analysis, you will use the IBM *Telco* customer churn dataset (see IBM (2021)). In this dataset, the *Churn* column indicates if a customer departed within the last month (*Churn* = *Yes*) or not (*Churn* = *No*). Other columns contain various predictor variables for each of the 7,043 customers, such as *Gender* (*Female* or *Male*), *SeniorCitizen* (0 for *No* or 1 for *Yes*), *Tenure* (months of membership), as well as *MonthlyCharges* (in U.S.-$).[7]

The code block below has already been executed in the background for you. It loads the required libraries and the data, which then are stored in the *R* object `DataChurn`. Afterward, `clean_names()` changes the variable names to *UpperCamel*, and `select()` chooses the variables for the analysis. Finally, `mutate()` converts the outcome variable *Churn* to type `factor`, which is necessary because almost all `tidymodels` classification models require the outcome variable to be of type `factor`. The argument `levels=c("Yes","No")` ensures that "Yes" is treated as the positive class and "No" as the negative class. This is important when you later interpret metrics such as *sensitivity* and *specificity*:

```
library(rio); library(janitor); library(tidymodels)
DataChurn=import("https://ai.lange-analytics.com/data/TelcoData.csv") |>
         clean_names("upper_camel") |>
         select(Churn,Gender, SeniorCitizen, Tenure, MonthlyCharges) |>
         mutate(Churn=factor(Churn, levels=c("Yes", "No")))
head(DataChurn)
```

```
##    Churn Gender SeniorCitizen Tenure MonthlyCharges
## 1    No Female             0      1          29.85
## 2    No   Male             0     34          56.95
## 3   Yes   Male             0      2          53.85
## 4    No   Male             0     45          42.30
## 5   Yes Female             0      2          70.70
## 6   Yes Female             0      8          99.65
```

In the code block above, we used the mutate command to convert the outcome variable *Churn* into a `factor` variable. Why did we not use a *recipe* to accomplish the same goal? The reason is that conversion of outcome variables should always be done before splitting the data because manipulations of outcome variables are sometimes not executed on the test dataset when defined in a *recipe*. We already discussed this in Section 4.7.3. In addition, you can find more information about why *recipes* should not be used on outcome variables in Kuhn and Silge (2022), Section 8.4.

---

[7]Note this dataset is from 2018 (Kaggle (2018)). If the data were collected today, most likely more *Gender* categories were considered.

Now, it is your turn to split the data into training and testing data. You know how — right? Just substitute the ... (note that the data frame `DataChurn` has already been loaded in the background):

```
set.seed(789)
Split3070=...(..., prop=0.7, strata=...)

DataTrain=...(...)
DataTest=...(...)
head(DataTrain)
```

Before you create the *recipe*, the *model design*, and the *workflow*, you should take a look at the structure of the training dataset first. To show the structure of the *R* object `DataTrain`, we use the `str()` command on the data frame `DataTrain` in the code block below:

```
str(DataTrain)
```

```
## 'data.frame':    4929 obs. of  5 variables:
## $ Churn         : Factor w/ 2 levels "Yes","No": 2 2 2 2 2 2 2 2 2 2 ...
## $ Gender        : chr  "Female" "Male" "Male" "Female" ...
## $ SeniorCitizen : int  0 0 0 0 0 0 0 0 0 0 ...
## $ Tenure        : int  1 45 22 10 62 13 58 25 21 12 ...
## $ MonthlyCharges: num  29.9 42.3 89.1 29.8 56.1 ...
```

You can see that *Churn* is a `factor` variable, which is what we want. *SeniorCitizen* is an `integer` dummy variable with 1 for senior citizens and 0 otherwise — no transformation needed. However, *Gender* should be a numerical dummy variable but is a `character` variable. Therefore, you need a `step_dummy()` in the *recipe* that transforms *Gender* into a dummy variable.

The other variables *Tenure* and *MonthlyCharges* are of type `integer` and `double`, respectively. Since this makes both variables `numerical`, no transformation is needed. Also, the *Logistic Regression* algorithm you will use later does not require *normalization*.

Consequently, the *recipe* has only one step — `step_dummy()` to convert *Gender* into a dummy variable. Please substitute the ... and then click `Run Code` to define `RecipeChurn` (note that the data frame `DataTrain` has already been loaded in the background):

```
RecipeChurn=recipe(...~., data=DataTrain) |>
          step_...(Gender)
print(RecipeChurn)
```

To define the *model design*, you must set the algorithm's name, the engine, and the mode. All of this is prepared for you in the code block below, and the code is already executed:

```
ModelDesignLogisticRegr=logistic_reg() |>
                        set_engine("glm") |>
                        set_mode("classification")

print(ModelDesignLogisticRegr)


## Logistic Regression Model Specification (classification)
##
## Computational engine: glm
```

The printout above shows details about the *model design*. Now, you are ready to put it all together and fit the training data using the *Optimizer* to find the best βs. Note that the *recipe* (RecipeChurn), the *model design* (ModelDesignLogisticRegr), and the training dataset (DataTrain) have already been loaded in the background:

```
WFModelChurn=workflow() |>
            add_recipe(...) |>
            add_model(...) |>
            fit(...)
print(WFModelChurn)
```

After you execute the code above, the *workflow model* WFModelChurn can be used for predictions. We created WFModelChurn already in the background and again use the augment() command to predict the outcome variable based on the predictor variables from the testing dataset DataTest.

```
DataTestWithPred=augment(WFModelChurn, new_data=DataTest)
str(DataTestWithPred)


## tibble [2,114 x 8] (S3: tbl_df/tbl/data.frame)
## $ Churn         : Factor w/ 2 levels "Yes","No": 2 2 2 2 2 1 1 2 2 1 ...
## $ Gender        : chr [1:2114] "Male" "Male" "Female" "Female" ...
## $ SeniorCitizen : int [1:2114] 0 0 0 0 0 1 0 1 0 0 ...
## $ Tenure        : int [1:2114] 34 16 69 52 71 1 1 71 27 5 ...
## $ MonthlyCharges: num [1:2114] 57 18.9 113.2 20.6 106.7 ...
## $ .pred_class   : Factor w/ 2 levels "Yes","No": 2 2 2 2 2 1 2 2 2 1 ...
## $ .pred_Yes     : num [1:2114] 0.1242 0.1027 0.1066 0.015 0.0801 ...
## $ .pred_No      : num [1:2114] 0.876 0.897 0.893 0.985 0.92 ...
```

You can see in the printout that the data frame `DataTestWithPred` now includes columns for both the `truth` (*Churn*) and the `estimate` (*.pred_class*). Consequently, we can use `DataTestWithPred` to generate a *confusion matrix*:

```
conf_mat(DataTestWithPred, truth=Churn, estimate=.pred_class)
```

```
##              Truth
## Prediction  Yes   No
##        Yes  239  150
##         No  322 1403
```

Next, we create a new metrics command that we call `FctMetricsSet`. The `FctMetricsSet()` command takes the same arguments as the `conf_mat()` command and then outputs *accuracy*, *sensitivity*, and *specificity*:

```
FctMetricsSet=metric_set(accuracy, sensitivity, specificity)
FctMetricsSet(DataTestWithPred, truth=Churn, estimate=.pred_class)
```

```
## # A tibble: 3 x 3
##    .metric      .estimator .estimate
##    <chr>        <chr>          <dbl>
## 1 accuracy     binary         0.777
## 2 sensitivity  binary         0.426
## 3 specificity  binary         0.903
```

At a first glance, everything looks good. *Accuracy* is about 78%, *specificity* is even 90%. However, the result for *sensitivity* is not good. Only 43% of the customers who churned were correctly identified. Simply flipping a coin to determine if a customer churns or not would have given us a *sensitivity* of about 50%!

What went wrong?

Using the `count()` command in the code block below provides the answer:

```
count(DataTrain, Churn)
```

```
##   Churn    n
## 1   Yes 1308
## 2    No 3621
```

You can see the training dataset is not balanced. The number of observations in the training dataset for customers, who did not churn, is triple the number of observations for customers that did churn. This imbalanced dataset leads to a biased *Optimizer* with a tendency to predict *Churn = No*.[8]

---

[8]The info box in Section 4.8 provides further details about how imbalanced datasets can cause prediction problems.

The following section will introduce three algorithms that can help to fully or partially balance an imbalanced dataset. Afterward, in the interactive Section 8.6, you will apply your knowledge and repeat the *Logistic Regression* analysis performed in this section but with a more balanced dataset.

8.5   Balancing Data with Downsampling, Upsampling, and SMOTE

In the previous section, due to an imbalanced dataset, predictions were biased toward the over-represented $Churn = No$ class, called the *majority class*. The majority class represents the most prevalent classification in a dataset. In contrast, the minority class represents the classification that occurs less often or rarely in a dataset ($Churn = Yes$ in the *Telco* dataset).

A slightly imbalanced dataset usually does not cause any problems, but a dataset like the *Telco* dataset with 3,621 observations for the majority class and only 1,308 observations in the minority class (see Table 8.2 further below) can cause predictions biased toward the majority class.

The two most common approaches to work with imbalanced datasets are removing observations from the majority class (*downsampling*) and/or adding observations to the minority class (*upsampling*):

Downsampling: This procedure randomly deletes observations from the majority class until the ratio of the observations from the majority and the minority class reaches the desired ratio (e.g., 1:1).

Upsampling: In its simplest version, *upsampling* creates new observations for the minority class by copying randomly chosen observations from the minority class until the ratio of the observations from the majority and the minority class reaches the desired ratio (e.g., 1:1).

Often, a combination of *downsampling* and *upsampling* is performed.

Before working with *up-* and *downsampling*, we must decide whether to balance both the training and testing data or only the training data. The right decision is to balance the training data but not the testing data. This is because when the model is fully trained, the testing data are used to assess how the model will perform in the real world when facing new data in the production stage. Therefore, since the real world contains imbalanced data, the testing data should also contain imbalanced data neither treated with *downsampling* nor with *upsampling*.

In what follows, we will introduce one *downsampling* and two *upsampling* methods. These methods can be used in combination or individually. The themis package provides the related commands `step_downsample()`, `step_upsample()`, and `step_smote()`. These commands process, by default, only the training data but not the testing data.[9]

Let us start with **downsampling**: In the code block below, we first load the `themis` package (Hvitfeldt (2023)) and then add `step_downsample()` to the *recipe* that we already used in Section 8.4 for the *churn* model.

```
library(themis)
set.seed(678)
RecipeChurn=recipe(Churn~., data=DataTrain) |>
            step_dummy(Gender)|>
            step_downsample(Churn)
```

Later, we will add a similar *recipe* to a *workflow*, and the *workflow* will execute the *recipe* and thus balance the minority and majority classes.

At this point, we want to find out if the *recipe* successfully changes the composition of the training data. To test this, we must explicitly apply the updated *recipe* to the training data and store the results in a new data frame (`DataTrainBal`) for further analysis.

For this step, we can use the `juice()` command.[10] It extracts the training data from the *recipe* like a juicer squeezes lemon juice out of a lemon. Note, you have to add `prep()` (prepare) after the *recipe* to ensure its execution before the data are extracted with `juice()`.

```
DataTrainBal=RecipeChurn |>
             prep() |>
             juice()
count(DataTrainBal, Churn)
```

```
## # A tibble: 2 x 2
##    Churn       n
##    <fct> <int>
## 1 Yes      1308
## 2 No       1308
```

After using the `count()` command, you can see above that the dataset is now perfectly balanced. But when you compare the data from `DataTrainBal` with

---

[9]The `skip=` argument determines if a `step_()` command is applied to the testing data or if the testing data will be *skipped*. For most `step_()` commands, the default is `skip=FALSE` because usually, we want a `step_()` to be applied to the training and testing data. However, the default for `step_downsample()`, `step_upsample()`, and `step_smote()` is `skip=TRUE` to *skip* the testing data. You can change the default values for `skip=`, but it is not recommended.

[10]In the book's following chapters, we will not use `juice()`. Therefore, you do not need to memorize the `juice()` command.

TABLE 8.2 Churn Count for Original Telco Training Dataset

Churn	n	Proportion
Yes	1308	0.2654
No	3621	0.7346

the original *Telco* training data (see Table 8.2), you also can see that we lost observations from the majority class because the majority class was reduced to 1,308 observations from 3,621 observations. Of course, losing so many records means losing a lot of information.

This brings us to upsampling. The idea behind *upsampling* is to randomly copy observations in the minority class until the number of observations in the minority class reaches the desired number of observations (the default is the same number as the majority class). The code block below is almost identical to the code blocks above, except that we use `step_upsample()` instead of `step_downsample()`:

```
library(themis)
set.seed(678)
RecipeChurn=recipe(Churn~., data=DataTrain) |>
            step_dummy(Gender)|>
            step_upsample(Churn)

DataTrainBal=RecipeChurn |>
             prep() |>
             juice()
count(DataTrainBal, Churn)


## # A tibble: 2 x 2
##   Churn     n
##   <fct> <int>
## 1 Yes    3621
## 2 No     3621
```

As you can see when comparing the printout above with the contents of Table 8.2, the data set is balanced. However, we did not lose any observations because we increased the observations in the minority class.

In this context, it is important to point out that we do not gain any new information, although we now have more observations. This is because we copied existing observations to increase the minority class. The information contained in the training data did not increase!

Many data scientists believe that having multiple identical observations from *upsampling* in the minority class is not the best solution. Consequently, improved methods are needed to increase the number of observations in the minority class. One of these methods is **SMOTE** (Synthetic Minority Oversampling Technique; see Chawla et al. (2002)). The idea behind *SMOTE* is to artificially generate new observations for the minority class, which are similar but not identical to existing observations. The *SMOTE* algorithm is implemented by the `Themis` package through `step_smote()` and works as follows:

1. Randomly choose an observation from the minority class.

2. Find the nearest neighbor to this observation using *k-Nearest Neighbors* (see Section 4 for details about the *k-Nearest Neighbors* algorithm).

3. Calculate a randomly weighted average for each predictor variable from the chosen observation from Step 1 and its nearest neighbor.

4. Use the calculated values for the predictor variables to create a new observation for the minority class.

Repeat Steps 1 – 4 until the number of observations in the minority class reaches the desired number of observations (the default is the same number as the majority class).

The code block below is identical to the code blocks above, except that we use `step_smote()`:

```
library(themis)
set.seed(678)
RecipeChurn=recipe(Churn~., data=DataTrain) |>
            step_dummy(Gender)|>
            step_smote(Churn)

DataTrainBal=RecipeChurn |>
             prep() |>
             juice()
count(DataTrainBal, Churn)


## # A tibble: 2 x 2
##    Churn     n
##    <fct> <int>
## 1 Yes     3621
## 2 No      3621
```

The result in terms of observations in the minority and majority classes is the same as the one we got with `step_upsample()`. The improvement with *SMOTE* is that the observations in the minority class are now augmented with similar observations rather than identical copies of existing observations.

Later, in Section 8.6, you can experiment with the balancing methods introduced here, such as step_downsample(), step_upsample(), step_smote(), and you can combine them as you wish.

For the *down-* and *upsampling* commands step_downsample(), step_upsample(), and step_smote(), you can also set the desired ratio between the majority and minority class.

The Downsampling command uses the argument under_ratio= for the desired ratio. under_ratio is defined as:

$$under\_ratio = \frac{N_{major}}{N_{minor}}$$

with: N_{major} := final number of observations for the majority class

and N_{minor} := number of observations for the minority class

For example, under_ratio=1 (the default) means that after *downsampling* is completed, the minority and the majority class have the same number of observations. under_ratio=1.2 means that *downsampling* will be stopped when the number of majority observations is 20% bigger than the number of minority observations.

For the two upsampling commands, step_upsample() and step_smote() the desired ratio is determined by the argument over_ratio=, which is defined as:

$$over\_ratio = \frac{N_{minor}}{N_{major}}$$

with: N_{minor} := final number of observations for the minority class

and N_{major} := number of observations for the majority class

For example, over_ratio=1 (the default) means that after *upsampling* is completed, the minority and the majority class have the same number of observations. over_ratio=0.9 means that *upsampling* will be stopped when the number of minority observations reaches 90% of the number of observations of the majority class.

8.6 ○ Repeating the Churn Analysis with Balanced Data

When analyzing churn for the *Telco* company in Section 8.4 your results were biased toward predicting that customers do not churn ($Churn = No$). This happened because the number of observations in the *Telco* dataset was biased toward customers who did not churn (the negative class).

As a reminder, due to the imbalanced dataset, *specificity* (prediction quality of the negative class) was 90%, while *sensitivity* (prediction quality of the positive class) was only 43%.

In this section, you will repeat the analysis from Section 8.4, but you will balance the training data before you perform the *Logistic Regression* analysis to improve the results. You will use the same training/testing data and the same commands (except for the *recipe's* definition).

To give you an idea about how to modify the *recipe*, we present a first trial in the code block below. We use `step_downsample(Churn, under_ratio=2)` and `step_smote(Churn, over_ratio=0.75)`:

```
set.seed(789)
RecipeChurn=recipe(Churn~., data=DataTrain) |>
            step_dummy(Gender)|>
            step_downsample(Churn, under_ratio=2) |>
            step_smote(Churn, over_ratio=0.75)

DataTrainBal=RecipeChurn |>
            prep() |>
            juice()
count(DataTrainBal, Churn)


## # A tibble: 2 x 2
##    Churn      n
##    <fct> <int>
## 1 Yes     1962
## 2 No      2616
```

How did we get the data frame `DataTrainBal`? First, `step_downsample(Churn, under_ratio=2)` randomly deletes observations from the majority class of the training data frame (`DataTrain`), until the number of observations in the majority class is reduced to double the size of the minority class (1,308 observations for $Churn = Yes$ and 2,616 observations for $Churn = No$); initially the majority class was almost triple the size of the minority class. Afterward, `step_smote(Churn, over_ratio=0.75)` creates new observations for the minority class until the number of observations in the minority class reaches 75% of the number of observations of the majority class (1,962 observations for $Churn = Yes$ and 2,616 observations for $Churn = No$).

Using this somehow more ballanced dataset, we get (based on the testing data), the following *confusion matrix*:

```
##            Truth
## Prediction  Yes   No
##        Yes  350  338
##         No  211 1215
```

The *confusion matrix* above implies a *specificity* of 78% but still only a *sensitivity* of 62%. This is an improvement compared to the analysis with the imbalanced dataset, but maybe you can improve the results even further.

You will use the code block further below to improve the results. It contains the *recipe* definition from above and is otherwise identical to the code we used for the imbalanced dataset before. The training dataset `DataTrain` and the testing dataset `DataTest` have already been loaded in the background.

When you execute the code block below unchanged, you will get the same results as in the example above. Try this first and then try to improve the results further by changing the under_ratio and the over_ratio values. You can also try to use only *undersampling* or only *oversampling*:

```
# Recipe
set.seed(789)
RecipeChurn=recipe(Churn~., data=DataTrain) |>
            step_dummy(Gender)|>
            step_downsample(Churn, under_ratio=2) |>
            step_smote(Churn, over_ratio=0.75)

# Model Design
ModelDesignLogisticRegr=logistic_reg() |>
                        set_engine("glm")|>
                        set_mode("classification")

# Building Fitting Workflow
WFModelChurn=workflow() |>
  add_recipe(RecipeChurn) |>
  add_model(ModelDesignLogisticRegr) |>
  fit(DataTrain)

# Prediction with augment()
DataTestWithPred=augment(WFModelChurn, new_data=DataTest)

# Printing counts for traingdata after down- and upsampling
DataTrainBal=RecipeChurn |>
            prep() |>
            juice( )

print("Count for balanced training data:")
print(count(DataTrainBal,Churn))

# Creating Metrics Based on DataTest
ConfMatrix=conf_mat(DataTestWithPred,truth=Churn, estimate=.pred_class)

print("*confusion matrix*")
print(ConfMatrix)

FctMetricsSet=metric_set(accuracy, sensitivity, specificity)
FctMetricsSet(DataTestWithPred, truth=Churn, estimate=.pred_class)
```

8.7 When and When Not to Use Logistic Regression

- *Logistic Regression* is a straightforward algorithm and a good choice for predicting binary categorical variables. Because of its simplicity, *Logistic Regression* is also a fast algorithm in terms of required computing resources. Therefore, it can be used for large datasets.

- If it is crucial to interpret the impact of predictor variables in addition to predicting an outcome, *Logistic Regression* is a good choice. This is because, in contrast to many other classification algorithms, *Logistic Regression* allows the interpretation of its parameters.

- When logarithmic *odds* are estimated, *Logistic Regression* is algebraically similar to linear regression. This limits the non-linearity of the general prediction function. However, it also allows for a more straightforward interpretation of the predictor estimates.

- *Logistic Regression* might not be a well-suited method for complex or highly non-linear estimation problems. The reason is that the *Logistic* function, in its middle section, is almost linear. Consequently, for highly non-linear estimation problems, models such as *Random Forest* (see Chapter 10) or *Neural Networks* (see Chapter 9) are likely to be better alternatives.

- In general, a good strategy for classification problems is to start with *Logistic Regression* as a benchmark and then try to improve the results with other machine learning algorithms.

- *Probit* and *Tobit* algorithms (see Hanck et al. (2023) and McDonald and Moffitt (1980)) are closely related to *Logistic Regression*. Because of their similarity with *Logistic Regression* they have similar strengths and weaknesses.

8.8 Digital Resources

Below you will find a few digital resources related to this chapter such as:

- Videos
- Short articles
- Tutorials
- *R* scripts

These resources are recommended if you would like to review the chapter from a different angle or to go beyond what was covered in the chapter.

Here we show only a few of the digital resources. At the end of the list you will find a link to additonal digital resources for this chapter that are maintained on the Internet.

You can find a complete list of digital resources for all book chapters on the companion website: https://ai.lange-analytics.com/digitalresources.html

Logistic Regression

A video from *StatQuest* by Josh Starmer. The video explains *Logistic Regression* in a fundamental and intuitive way.

Link: https://ai.lange-analytics.com/dr?a=393

Odds and Log(Odds), Clearly Explained!!!

A video from *StatQuest* by Josh Starmer. The video explains the difference between *probabilities* and *odds*. It also provides intuition for *log-odds*.

Link: https://ai.lange-analytics.com/dr?a=394

Undersampling, Oversampling, and SMOTE

An article by Joos Korstanje in *Towards Data Science*. The article introduces the problem of unbalanced data and explains *undersampling, oversampling*, as well as *SMOTE*. Although the examples are programmed in *Python*, they are easy to understand.

Link: https://ai.lange-analytics.com/dr?a=351

More Digital Resources

Only a subset of digital resources is listed in this section. The link below points to additional, concurrently updated resources for this chapter.

Link: https://ai.lange-analytics.com/dr/logregr.html

9

Deep Learning — MLP Neural Networks
Explained

Deep Learning is an *Artificial Intelligence (AI)* methodology. It performs tasks that we all believed just a few years ago, could only be performed by humans.

Deep Learning models are used in many different applications. For example, researchers use *Deep Learning* to analyze medical images to improve cancer diagnosis (image recognition); Amazon's *Alexa* uses *Deep Learning* to understand human languages (*Natural Language Processing (NLP)*); and you can use Conversational Generative Pre-training Transformers (short: chatbots) like *ChatGPT* from *OpenAI* or *Bard* from *Google* to compose written text or just have a chat. These technologies are all based on *Deep Learning*.

Deep Learning uses *Neural Networks* as integral part. There would be no *Deep Learning* without *Neural Networks*. The term *Neural Networks* originated from early attempts of researchers (see for example McCulloch and Pitts (1943)) to create machine learning models that resemble the human brain.

The human brain processes information as electric currents through neurons, and then passes it on to other neurons connected by dendrites in a complex network with endless layers of neurons. Similarly, a *Neural Network* contains layers of interconnected nodes — like neurons in the human brain. Each of these nodes, or *artificial neurons*, performs a mathematical operation on the data it receives, and then passes the results on to other neurons in the network.

Neural Networks research today focuses on improving predictive quality rather than attempting to resemble the human brain. Consequently, in what follows, we will not discuss how little or how much a *Neural Network* is similar to a human brain. For a brief discussion of this topic, see Haykin (1999), Section 1.2 and Lange (2003), Chapter 2.

The word "deep" in *Deep Learning* refers to the number of layers in the *Neural Network* structure. In general, *Deep Learning* algorithms are extremely complex with many layers and a very high number of parameters to estimate (sometimes billions or trillions of parameters!).[1] Here are some examples of deep *Neural Networks*:

---

[1] For example, it is believed that *GPT-4* is trained on 1.7 trillion parameters.

- *Convolutional Neural Networks (CNN)*: for image recognition and classification.

- *Recurrent Neural Networks (RNN)*: for sequence processing.

- *Long short-term memory (LSTM)*: a more advanced type of *RNN* for tasks that require sequence processing, such as speech recognition and sentiment analysis.

- *Generative Adversarial Networks (GANs)*: for semantic image editing, style transfer, image synthesis.

- Generative *AI*: a field that is still developing. Applications so far reach from generating reports, papers and art; all the way to simulation of scientific experiments. The end of future applications is not in sight.

Due to the complexity and the demanding computational resources, *Deep Neural Networks* are beyond the scope of this chapter. Instead, we will explain the basic underlying concepts of *Deep Learning* using a simpler *Neural Network* type called *Multi-Layer Perceptron (MLP)*.

MLP Neural Networks were among the first *Neural Networks* to be developed. The principles of *MLP Neural Networks* can also be applied to more complex and sophisticated *Neural Networks*. After reading this chapter you will have a good idea about the basic functionality of *Deep Neural Networks*.

MLP Neural Networks consist of one or more layers, each layer contains at least one neuron. The layers in *MLP Neural Networks* are fully connected, meaning that each neuron in one layer can pass information to each neuron in the following layer. Figure 9.1 in Section 9.4.1 shows a basic example of a fully connected *MLP Neural Network* with an input layer (2 neurons), a hidden layer[2] (2 neurons), and an output layer (1 neuron).

Neural Networks can be used for classification and regression tasks. Here, we will focus on regression tasks. Throughout this chapter, we will use the `diamonds` dataset[3] to predict diamond prices based on a diamond's physical properties. We will introduce the `diamonds` dataset in more detail in Section 9.3.

In what follows, *MLP Neural Networks* are covered in four parts:

In Section **9.4**, we introduce the idea behind *Neural Networks* in an intuitive way. We show the structure of a simplified *Neural Network*, demonstrating how a *Neural Network* predicts, and we describe the basic principle (*Back Propagation/Steepest Gradient Descent*) used by the *Optimizer* to find the best β parameters for a *Neural Network*.

In Section **9.5** we use the `nnet` *R* package (Venables and Ripley (2002))

---

[2]All layers between the input and the output layers are called hidden layers.
[3]This dataset is built into the `ggplot2` *R* package (Wickham (2016)).

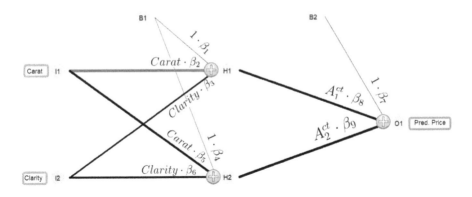

FIGURE 9.1 Graphical Representation of a Neural Network

together with tidymodels and the diamonds dataset to predict diamond prices using a *MLP Neural Networks* model. The nnet package has been around for a long time, and more advanced packages have been developed. However, we use nnet in Section 9.4 because it supports *Sigmoid* activation functions, which allows us to introduce basic ideas of *Neural Network* algorithms in a straightforward way.

In Section 9.6 we compare the *R* nnet package and *PyTorch*, another open source machine learning library using *Neural Networks*. The latter is implemented through the brulee package (Kuhn and Falbel (2022)) into *R*. *PyTorch* is a machine learning framework initially developed by Facebook (now *Meta AI*). It provides *MLP Neural Network* functionality that supports more advanced activation functions (e.g., the *Rectified Linear Unit (ReLU)* activation function) and more tuning parameters to optimize predictive performance.

In the interactive Section 9.7 you will use *PyTorch* to estimate diamond prices in a real-world setting. We will provide a template that allows you to try various *hyper-parameter* settings for tuning the *Neural Network* model.

9.1 Learning Outcomes

This section outlines what you can expect to learn in this chapter. In addition, the corresponding section number is included for each learning outcome to help you to navigate the content, especially when you return to the chapter for review.

In this chapter, you will learn:

- How to work with a **graphical representation of a Neural Network** (see Section 9.4.1).

- How to transform the graphical representation into a **Neural Network prediction function** (see Section 9.4.2).

- How to use an **Optimizer in a Neural Network** to change the network's parameters to step-wise improve the approximation quality (the underlying method is called *Steepest Gradient Decent* or *Back Propagation Algorithm*; see Section 9.4.4)

- Why *Neural Networks* have **outstanding approximation qualities** that allow them to approximate any continuous function with any degree of accuracy (see Section 9.5).

- How and why the outstanding approximation quality of *Neural Networks* makes them prone to **overfitting** (see Section 9.5).

- How to work with the **R nnet package** and with **PyTorch** to design and run a *Neural Network* (see Section 9.5 and Section 9.7).

- Why a *Neural Network* with **ReLU** (**Rectified Linear Unit**) activation functions has the same outstanding approximation properties as a *Neural Network* with classic *Sigmoid* activation functions (see Section 9.6).

- Why *ReLU* functions mitigate the possible inability of the *Optimizer* to change the values for the β parameters (**Vanishing Gradient** problem; see Section 9.6).

- How to use *PyTorch* in an **interactive project** to estimate the prices of more than 50,000 diamonds based on four common predictors used in the appraisal industry (*Carat*, *Clarity*, *Cut*, and *Color*; see Section 9.7).

9.2   R Packages Required for the Chapter

This section lists the *R* packages that you need when you load and execute code in the interactive sections in *RStudio*. Please install the following packages using `Tools -> Install Packages ...` from the *RStudio* menu bar (you can find more information about installing and loading packages in Section 3.4):

- The `rio` package (Chan et al. (2021)) to enable the loading of various data formats with one `import()` command. Files can be loaded from the user's hard drive or the Internet.

- The `janitor` package (Firke (2023)) to rename variable names to *Upper-Camel* and to substitute spaces and special characters in variable names.

- The `tidymodels` package (Kuhn and Wickham (2020)) to streamline data engineering and machine learning tasks.

- The `kableExtra` (Zhu (2021)) package to support the rendering of tables.

- The `learnr` package (Aden-Buie et al. (2022)), which is needed together with the `shiny` package (Chang et al. (2022)) for the interactive exercises in this book.

- The `shiny` package (Chang et al. (2022)), which is needed together with the `learnr` package (Aden-Buie et al. (2022)) for the interactive exercises in this book.

- The `nnet` package (Venables and Ripley (2002)) to create and optimize basic *MLP Neural Networks*.

- The `brulee` package (Kuhn and Falbel (2022)) to create and optimize *MLP Neural Networks* based on the *Python* library *PyTorch*. Regarding the `brulee` package, it is important to mention that the *PyTorch* software needs to be installed after the package is installed. Installing the *PyTorch* software is straightforward: When the package is used for the first time (i.e., with `library(brulee)`) a popup window asks to download and install the required software. After confirming with "Yes", the software will be installed.

9.3 Data

For training and testing, we use the well-known `diamonds` dataset. The `diamonds` dataset contains information on $53,940$ diamonds and is included in the *R* package `ggplot2` (Wickham (2016)). You can learn more about the `diamonds` dataset by typing `"? diamonds"` into the *R Console*. Since `ggplot2` is automatically loaded with the `tidymodels` package, the command `library(ggplot2)` is not required.

In the code block below, we first load the `tidymodels` and `janitor` libraries. Then we convert the column names in the `diamonds` data frame to *UpperCamel*, select the variables *Price*, *Carat*, *Clarity*, *Cut*, and *Color* for the analysis, and save the result into the data frame `DataDiamonds`. Afterwards, we use the `str()` command to take a look at the structure of the data frame:

```
library(tidymodels); library(janitor)
DataDiamonds= diamonds |>
            clean_names("upper_camel") |>
            select(Price, Carat, Clarity, Cut, Color)
str(DataDiamonds)
```

```
## tibble [53,940 x 5] (S3: tbl_df/tbl/data.frame)
## $ Price  : int [1:53940] 326 326 327 334 335 336 336 337 337 338 ...
## $ Carat  : num [1:53940] 0.23 0.21 0.23 0.29 0.31 0.24 0.24 0.26 0.22
## $ Clarity: Ord.factor w/ 8 levels "I1"<"SI2"<"SI1"<..: 2 3 5 4 2 6 7
## $ Cut    : Ord.factor w/ 5 levels "Fair"<"Good"<..: 5 4 2 4 2 3 3 3 1
## $ Color  : Ord.factor w/ 7 levels "D"<"E"<"F"<"G"<..: 2 2 2 6 7 7 6 5
```

The output of the `str()` command shows that the data frame `DataDiamonds` contains 53,940 observations and five different variables (columns) that describe various properties of the diamonds together with their prices (in U.S.-$).

The variables *Carat, Clarity, Cut*, and *Color* chosen as predictors are also known as the four *Cs* of diamond appraisal:[4]

1. Carat: A measurement unit used to describe a diamond's weight. It is measured in metric grams (1 *carat* equal to 0.2 *g*) and is the most visually apparent factor when comparing diamonds.

2. Clarity: A measurement for the visibility of natural microscopic inclusions and imperfections within a diamond. Diamonds with little to no inclusions are considered particularly rare and highly valued. The clarity of the diamond is rated in eight categories measuring how clear the diamond is (*I1* (worst), *SI2, SI1, VS2, VS1, VVS2, VVS1, IF* (best)).[5]

3. Cut: Refers to a diamond's facets, symmetry, and reflective qualities. The cut of a diamond is directly related to its overall sparkle and beauty. The cut of a diamond is rated in five categories as *Fair, Good, Very Good, Ideal*, and *Super Ideal*.

4. Color: Refers to the natural color or lack of color visible within a diamond. The closer a diamond is to "colorless", the more expensive the diamond is. Color is rated in seven categories from *D* (best) to *J* (worst).

From the `str()` command output above, you can see that *Clarity, Cut*, and *Color* are stored as *R factor-data-type* with 8, 5, and 7 *factor-levels*,

---

[4] The following description was retrieved from the *Brilliant Earth* website (`https://www.brilliantearth.com/diamond/buying-guide/`).

[5] The *clarity* rating in the `diamonds` dataset is in line with the rating categories from the *Gemological Institute of America* (`https://4cs.gia.edu/en-us/diamond-clarity/`), except that the Flawless (*IF*) and the Inclusion (*I*) categories are not divided in specific grades.

respectively. Since we need numerical values for the analysis, we use the `as.integer()` command in the code block below to extract the *factor-levels* as integer values:

```
DataDiamonds=DataDiamonds |>
            mutate(Clarity=as.integer(Clarity)) |>
            mutate(Cut=as.integer(Cut)) |>
            mutate(Color=as.integer(Color))
head(DataDiamonds)
```

```
## # A tibble: 6 x 5
##    Price Carat Clarity   Cut Color
##    <int> <dbl>   <int> <int> <int>
## 1    326  0.23       2     5     2
## 2    326  0.21       3     4     2
## 3    327  0.23       5     2     2
## 4    334  0.29       4     4     6
## 5    335  0.31       2     2     7
## 6    336  0.24       6     3     7
```

9.4 The Idea Behind Neural Network Models

This section introduces some of the principle ideas behind *Neural Networks*. We start in Section 9.4.1 with a graphical representation of a simplified *Neural Network* that predicts the *Price* of a diamond based on two predictor variables (*Carat* and *Clarity*). In Section 9.4.2, we will show how the graphical representation of a *Neural Network* can be transformed into the prediction equation of the *Neural Network*. In Section 9.4.3 we use a numerical example to show how the *Neural Network* can predict the price of a given diamond based on its *carat* and *clarity* when the values for the β values are determined. Finally, in Section 9.4.4, we try to shed some light on how the *Optimizer* in a *Neural Network* can find the β parameters that lead to the best prediction quality (minimizing the MSE for the training data).

9.4.1 Graphical Representation of a Neural Network Explained

Let us start with a graphical approach by demonstrating how a *Neural Network* can predict continuous outcome variables such as the *Price* of a diamond based on two predictor variables (*Carat* and *Clarity*).

Figure 9.1 demonstrates the process. The figure shows a *Neural Network* with an input layer at the left of the network consisting of two input neurons ($I1$ and $I2$), a hidden layer in the middle of the network composed of two hidden neurons ($H1$ and $H2$), and an output layer at the right of the network with one output neuron that will later contain the diamond's predicted price ($O1$).

The three layers (input, hidden, and output) are fully connected with the red and black lines, meaning that each neuron of a previous layer is connected with each neuron of the following layer. Considering that *perceptron* is a different term for *neuron*, you can see where the name *Multi Layer* (input, hidden, output) *Perceptron* comes from. The *MLP* in Figure 9.1 has only one hidden layer, but more complex *MLP* networks can have multiple hidden layers with many neurons inside each layer.

A *Neural Network* processes observations one by one and creates a prediction at the output neuron ($O1$) for each observation. We will use Figure 9.1 to show how a *Neural Network* can generate a prediction from the values of the predictor variables of a given observation i. For now, we assume that values for the parameters (the βs) are provided and known:

Step 1: At the beginning of the prediction process, the values for the predictor variables of observation i are loaded into the input neurons ($I1$ and $I2$). For example, for a diamond with 0.3 carats ($Carat_i = 0.3$) and clarity rating of *SI1* ($Clarity_i = 3$), the input neuron $I1$ contains a value of 0.3, and the input neuron $I2$ contains a value of 3.

Step 2: The values of the input neurons are transmitted to each of the hidden neurons ($H1$ and $H2$), but before they arrive, their values are weighted (multiplied) with the parameters β_2, β_3, β_5, and β_6, respectively. This way, the original value from the input neurons are amplified or weakened, depending on whether the absolute values for the βs are greater or smaller than one. Negative β parameter values reverse the signs of the predictor variable values.

In addition to the weighted input values ($Carat_i \cdot \beta_2$, $Clarity_i \cdot \beta_3$, $Carat_i \cdot \beta_5$, and $Clarity_i \cdot \beta_6$) that arrive at the hidden neurons $H1$ and $H2$, the bias neuron $B1$ sends a value that is equal to β_1 to hidden neuron $H1$ and a value of β_4 to hidden neuron $H2$. Because these values are independent of the values for the predictor variables ($B1$ and $B2$ always contain a value of one), the neurons $B1$ and $B2$ are called *bias neurons*.

Step 3: As you can see in Figure 9.1 at the green $\oplus$ signs in front of the hidden neurons $H1$ and $H2$, three different weighted values arrive at each hidden neuron before they are further processed. For each hidden neuron, the three related values are aggregated to single values called the *effective inputs* of the hidden neurons by simply adding them up. This is symbolized by the green $\oplus$ signs in front of $H1$ and $H2$ in Figure 9.1. The *effective inputs* ($I_{1,i}^{eff}$ and $I_{2,i}^{eff}$) for the hidden neuron $H1$ and $H2$ are:

$$I_{1,i}^{eff} = \beta_1 + \beta_2 Carat_i + \beta_3 Carity_i$$

and

$$I_{2,i}^{eff} = \beta_4 + \beta_5 Carat_i + \beta_6 Carity_i$$

Step 4: These two *effective inputs* — one for each of the hidden neurons — are now plugged into non-linear functions (called *activation functions*) inside hidden neuron $H1$ and $H2$. The two results are called the *activities* ($A_{1,i}^{ct}$ and $A_{2,i}^{ct}$) of the neurons $H1$ and $H2$. We will talk more about *activation functions* in a minute.

Steps 5: The *activities* of the hidden neurons $A_{1,i}^{ct}$ and $A_{2,i}^{ct}$ are transmitted to the output neuron ($O1$), but before they arrive, their values are weighted with β_8 and β_9, respectively.

Steps 6: Three values arrive at the green $\oplus$ sign in front of the output neuron ($O1$): the two weighted *activities* from the hidden neurons ($\beta_8 A_{1,i}^{ct}$ and $\beta_9 A_{2,i}^{ct}$) and the value from the bias neuron $B2$, which equals β_7. These three values are aggregated (added up) to a single value, which is the value of the output neuron $O1$ and, at the same time, the predicted price for the related diamond.

In more complex networks, the output neuron $O1$ may also contain an activation function, but here what goes into the output neuron comes out without any transformation ($O1 = I_{O1}^{eff}$).

The steps above, in connection with Figure 9.1 provide a basic idea about how a Neural Network processes values from predictor variables to generate a prediction for an outcome variable. If the *Neural Network* contains more input and hidden neurons, or more layers, the process is more complex, but the underlying idea is the same.

However, two questions have not been answered so far:

Question 1: We assumed that the values for the β parameters are known. But how are they determined?

Answer: The answer to this question is simple for the initial values of the βs: The parameters are determined randomly (usually with $-1 < \beta_j < 1$). This makes it possible to generate initial predictions for all observations in the training dataset. The resulting initial predictions are usually not very good. They need improvement by updating the β parameters in an iterative process. This updating process — called training the *Neural Network* — is a little more complex. We will discuss the underlying basics in Section 9.4.4 after we cover a numerical example for a prediction in Section 9.4.3.

Question 2: How are the *activation functions* inside the hidden neurons $H1$ and $H2$ transforming the *effective input values* ($I_{1,i}^{eff}$ and $I_{2,i}^{eff}$) into the *activities* of the hidden neurons ($A_{1,i}^{ct}$ and $A_{2,i}^{ct}$)?

Answer: This is a bit more tricky: Various *activation functions* can be used inside a hidden neuron to transform the *effective inputs* $I_{j,i}^{eff}$ into a neurons' activity $A_{j,i}^{ct}$ (j stands for the hidden neuron number and i for the observation number). Here, we use the *Logistic* function — the same function we used for *Logistic Regression* in Chapter 8. We plug the *effective inputs* $I_{1,i}^{eff}$ and $I_{2,i}^{eff}$ into the *Logistic* function and calculate the *activities* $A_{1,i}^{ct}$ and $A_{2,i}^{ct}$ for the hidden neurons $H1$ and $H2$:

$$A_{1,i}^{ct} = \frac{1}{1 + e^{-I_{1,i}^{eff}}} \tag{9.1}$$

$$A_{2,i}^{ct} = \frac{1}{1 + e^{-I_{2,i}^{eff}}} \tag{9.2}$$

9.4.2 Transforming the Graphic Approach Into a Prediction Equation

Figure 9.1 shows the graphical structure of a *Neural Network*, but for using a computer to make predictions, the graph needs to be transformed into a prediction equation, which is the goal of this section.

Figure 9.1 and Step 3 above show how the *effective inputs* for the two hidden neurons are calculated from the weighted predictor variables and the bias neurons. For an observation i, this can be expressed in the following two equations determining $I_{1,i}^{eff}$ and $I_{2,i}^{eff}$:

$$I_{1,i}^{eff} = \beta_1 + \beta_2 Carat_i + \beta_3 Clarity_i \tag{9.3}$$

$$I_{2,i}^{eff} = \beta_4 + \beta_5 Carat_i + \beta_6 Clarity_i \tag{9.4}$$

We can substitute $I_{1,i}^{eff}$ and $I_{2,i}^{eff}$ according to Equations (9.3) and (9.4) into the activation functions (9.1), and (9.2) and we get the *activities* for the hidden neurons:

$$A_{1,i}^{ct} = \frac{1}{1 + e^{-(\beta_1 + \beta_2 Carat_i + \beta_3 Clarity_i)}} \tag{9.5}$$

$$A_{2,i}^{ct} = \frac{1}{1 + e^{-(\beta_4 + \beta_5 Carat_i + \beta_6 Clarity_i)}} \tag{9.6}$$

Note, the *effective inputs* ($I_{1,i}^{eff}$ and $I_{2,i}^{eff}$) for the two hidden neurons are highlighted to make the equations easier to read.

Equations (9.5) and (9.6) show that we can calculate the *activities* for the hidden neurons $H1$ and $H2$ entirely based on the predictor values of an observation if we know the numerical values for the βs (and we do!).

After transforming the *activities* ($A_{1,i}^{ct}$ and $A_{2,i}^{ct}$) of the two hidden neurons into formulas, we are only two steps away from predicting the price of a diamond. As shown before in Steps 5 and 6, the predicted price can be calculated from the *activities* of the hidden neurons and the bias neuron as follows:

$$\widehat{Price}_i = \beta_7 + \beta_8 A^{ct}_{1,i} + \beta_9 A^{ct}_{2,i} \qquad (9.7)$$

If we now substitute $A^{ct}_{1,i}$ and $A^{ct}_{2,i}$ according to Equations (9.5) and (9.6), we get the **Neural Network's prediction function**:

$$\widehat{Price}_i = \beta_7 + \overbrace{\frac{1}{1 + e^{-(\beta_1 + \beta_2 Carat_i + \beta_3 Clarity_i)}}}^{\text{Activity of Hidden Neuron 1}} \cdot \beta_8$$

$$+ \overbrace{\frac{1}{1 + e^{-(\beta_4 + \beta_5 Carat_i + \beta_6 Clarity_i)}}}^{\text{Activity of Hidden Neuron 2}} \cdot \beta_9 \qquad (9.8)$$

Again, for readability, the *effective inputs* ($I^{eff}_{1,i}$ and $I^{eff}_{2,i}$) for the two hidden neurons are highlighted.

Deriving the prediction function in Equation (9.8) was a little tedious. You might want to go back to Steps 1 – 6 and read again carefully. It is worth the effort because the prediction equation in (9.8) indicates how a *Neural Network* can predict based on the predictor values when the β parameters are known. If you understand this concept, you will realize that the predictive quality of the *Neural Network* only depends on the right choice of the parameters (the βs).

The takeaways so far are:

1. The *Neural Network* from Figure 9.1 can be transformed into a prediction equation (see Equation (9.8)).

2. The predicted price for a diamond following Equation (9.8) depends only on the predictor values (*Carat* and *Clarity*) and the values for the β parameters.

3. Since we know the values for the βs, either from randomly choosing them or as part of the optimization process, we can predict the price for any diamond based on *Carat* and *Clarity*.

4. The initial prediction with a random parameter choice is likely not good, but we can gradually improve the prediction by adjusting the β parameters iteratively. How this can be done will be explained in Section 9.4.4.

If not all details are clear to you at this point, do not worry. We will follow up with a numerical example in the next section.

9.4.3   Numerical Example: Predicting Prices for Diamonds with a Neural Network

In this section, we will choose an individual diamond (see Table 9.1) and predict its price based on the *Neural Network* displayed in Figure 9.2 and also based on the prediction Equation (9.8).

TABLE 9.1 Sample Diamond from DataDiamonds

Price	Carat	Clarity
506	0.3	3

Table 9.1 shows that the diamond has 0.3 carats $(Carat_i = 0.3)$ and a clarity of 3 $(Clarity_i = 3)$. All other predictors are omitted for now. We assume for the initial prediction that the values of the β parameters are already randomly determined as:

$$\beta_1 = 0.1, \beta_2 = -0.9, \beta_3 = 0.5, \beta_4 = -0.1, \beta_5 = 0.8, \beta_6 = 0.6,$$
$$\beta_7 = 0.1, \beta_8 = 0.8, \beta_9 = 0.9$$

The prediction process is displayed in Figure 9.2. The color of the connectors between the neurons shows if the related parameter is positive (black) or negative (red). The connector's thickness reflects whether the parameter — in absolute terms — is big or small. As an exercise, compare the connectors in Figure 9.2 with the randomly chosen β values.

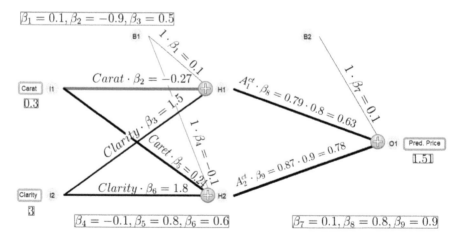

FIGURE 9.2 Graphical Representation of a Fitted Neural Network Structure

Starting in the very left in Figure 9.2, you can see that the input neurons $I1$

and $I2$ hold the predictor values for the diamond, 0.3 and 3, respectively. Both input values are transmitted to the hidden neuron $H1$ and weighted with β_2 and β_3, resulting in values of $0.3 \cdot (-0.9) = -0.27$ and $3 \cdot 0.5 = 1.5$, respectively. In addition, the weighted value from the bias neuron $B1$ $(1 \cdot \beta_1 = 0.1)$ also arrives at the hidden neuron $H1$. These three values are aggregated (added up) to the *effective input* of hidden neuron $H1$:

$$I_{1,i}^{eff} = \underbrace{1 \cdot 0.1}_{1 \cdot \beta_1 = 0.1} + \underbrace{0.3 \cdot (-0.9)}_{Carat_i \cdot \beta_2 = -0.27} + \underbrace{3 \cdot 0.5}_{Clarity_i \cdot \beta_3 = 1.5} = 1.33$$

The *effective input* for the hidden neuron $H2$ is calculated similarly, except that $Carat_i$ is weighted with β_5, $Clarity_i$ is weighted with β_6, and the value from the bias neuron $B1$ is weighted with β_4. Adding up these value leads to the *effective input* for the hidden neuron $H2$:

$$I_{2,i}^{eff} = \underbrace{1 \cdot (-0.1)}_{1 \cdot \beta_4 = -0.1} + \underbrace{0.3 \cdot 0.8}_{Carat_i \cdot \beta_5 = 0.24} + \underbrace{3 \cdot 0.6}_{Clarity_i \cdot \beta_6 = 1.8} = 1.94$$

The *effective inputs* ($I_{1,i}^{eff}$ and $I_{2,i}^{eff}$) together with the logistic activation functions (see Equations (9.1) and (9.2)) are used to calculate the *activities* ($A_{1,i}^{ct}$ and $A_{2,i}^{ct}$) for the hidden neurons:

$$A_{1,i}^{ct} = \frac{1}{1 + e^{-I_{1,i}^{eff}}}$$

$$A_{1,i}^{ct} = \frac{1}{1 + e^{-1.33}} = 0.79$$

$$A_{2,i}^{ct} = \frac{1}{1 + e^{-I_{2,i}^{eff}}}$$

$$A_{2,i}^{ct} = \frac{1}{1 + e^{-1.94}} = 0.87$$

Now that we know the *activities* for the hidden neurons $H1$ and $H2$, we can weigh them with β_8 and β_9, respectively (see Figure 9.2). Then we add up the weighted *activities* together with the bias $B2$ according to Equation (9.7) and we get the predicted price ($\widehat{Price}_i$) for the diamond from Table 9.1:

$$\widehat{Price}_i = \beta_7 + \beta_8 A_{1,i}^{ct} + \beta_9 A_{2,i}^{ct}$$
$$\widehat{Price}_i = 0.1 + 0.8 \cdot 0.79 + 0.9 \cdot 0.87 = 1.51$$

The prediction (obviously) does not change if we use the prediction Equation (9.8). We can show this in two steps. First, we plug the numerical β values into the prediction Equation (9.8):

$$\widehat{P}_i \;=\; 0.1 + \overbrace{\frac{1}{1 + e^{-(\,0.1 - 0.9Carat_i + 0.5Clarity_i\,)}}}^{\text{Activity of Hidden Neuron 1}} \cdot 0.8$$

$$+ \; \underbrace{\frac{1}{1 + e^{-(\,-0.1 + 0.8Carat_i + 0.6Clarity_i\,)}}}_{} \cdot 0.9$$

Next, we substitute $Carat_i$ and $Clarity_i$ with the values from Table 9.1 (0.3 and 3, respectively):

$$1.51 \;=\; 0.1 + \overbrace{\frac{1}{1 + e^{-(\,0.1 - 0.9 \cdot 0.3 + 0.5 \cdot 3\,)}}}^{\text{Activity of Hidden Neuron 1}} \cdot 0.8$$

$$+ \; \overbrace{\frac{1}{1 + e^{-(\,-0.1 + 0.8 \cdot 0.3 + 0.6 \cdot 3\,)}}}^{\text{Activity of Hidden Neuron 2}} \cdot 0.9$$

Note the *effective inputs* are highlighted for better readability.

The predicted price for the diamond is again \$1.51. Don't get your hopes up, you won't find a diamond for that little money.

As Table 9.1 shows, the actual price of the diamond is \$506 ($Price = 506$). The high prediction error (an underestimation of \$504.49) should not surprise us because we randomly chose the β parameters.

At this point, we can summarize: With the β values given, we are able to create a prediction for any observation — including all observations from the training dataset. Since we also know the actual price for the observations, we can calculate the (squared) error for any observation in the training dataset.

For example, the squared prediction error for the observation from Table 9.1 is:

$$\begin{aligned} Error_i^2 &= (\widehat{Price}_i - Price_i)^2 \\ &= (1.51 - 506)^2 = 254510.20 \end{aligned}$$

If we can use the *Neural Network* to generate a prediction for each of the observations from the training dataset and consequently can calculate the squared error for each of these observations, we can calculate the *Mean Squared Error (MSE)* for the training data — for any given set of β values. This raises the question:

How can we iteratively change the βs to gradually improve the Neural Network's predictive quality — minimizing the MSE?

This is what we will cover in the following section.

9.4.4 How the Optimizer Improves the Parameters in a Neural Network

For most regression[6] tasks, the *Optimizer* in a *Neural Network* (integrated in the `tidymodels` *workflow*) aims to minimize the MSE[7] by adjusting the β values.

To give you a basic idea of how the *Optimizer* adjusts the β values, we will use the first iteration (the first adjustment of the β values) as an example. We start with the randomly chosen β values (see Section 9.4.3) and show how the *Optimizer* changes these values to get a slightly lower MSE. This process can then be iteratively repeated until the MSE is reasonably low.

So, let us assume the following β values are already randomly chosen at the beginning of the adjustment process:

$$\beta_1 = 0.1, \beta_2 = -0.9, \beta_3 = 0.5, \beta_4 = -0.1, \beta_5 = 0.8, \beta_6 = 0.6,$$
$$\beta_7 = 0.1, \beta_8 = 0.8, \beta_9 = 0.9$$

Then we can use the definition of the MSE in connection with prediction Equation (9.8) to calculate the MSE for the initial set of βs for the training dataset. This MSE will be the benchmark when the *Optimizer* adjusts the βs to produce a new set of βs that (slightly) improves the MSE. For the set of randomly chosen β parameters, the equation to calculate the MSE is:

$$MSE = \frac{\sum_{i=1}^{N}(\widehat{Price}_i - Price_i)^2}{N} \tag{9.9}$$

with:

$$\widehat{Price}_i = 0.1 + \overbrace{\frac{1}{1 + e^{-(\,0.1 - 0.9Carat_i + 0.5Clarity_i\,)}}}^{\text{Activity of Hidden Neuron 1}} \cdot 0.8$$

$$+ \overbrace{\frac{1}{1 + e^{-(\,-0.1 + 0.8Carat_i + 0.6Clarity_i\,)}}}^{\text{Activity of Hidden Neuron 2}} \cdot 0.9$$

---

[6]Classification applications use different metrics to measure the predictive quality in a *Neural Network* but this exceeds the scope of this chapter.

[7]See Section 5.4 for details about the MSE.

Note the *effective inputs* are highlighted for better readability.

We start with using the prediction equation to calculate the predicted price for the first observation in the training dataset $(\widehat{P_1})$. Since we know the true price (P_1) for this diamond from the training data, we can calculate the related squared error as $(\widehat{P_1} - P_1)^2$.

Continuing with the other observations, we calculate the predicted price and the related squared error for the complete training dataset and then calculate the mean from all squared errors. This gives us the MSE for the training dataset related to the initial set of βs. This calculation shows again:

For a given training dataset, we can calculate the MSE for any set of chosen β values.

Next, we increase only β_1 by a very small amount, leaving all other β values unchanged, and calculate the new MSE using Equation (9.9). Consequently, the MSE will either decrease or increase compared to the benchmark MSE. This provides us with information in which direction β_1 should be changed. If increasing β_1 was successful and the MSE decreased, mark β_1 to be increased. Otherwise, mark β_1 for a decrease.

Next, we reset the value for β_1 and use the same procedure for β_2 to find out if β_2 should be increased or decreased.

We do the same for all other β parameters, and consequently, we will know for each β parameter if it should be increased or decreased.

The amount of the actual increase or decrease for each of the β parameters is proportional to the change of the MSE they triggered when individually changed. In addition, to ensure that the changes are not too large, we multiply these changes with a learning rate — a constant number smaller than one, for example, 0.01.[8]

This procedure results in a new set of βs with a slightly smaller MSE. This new set of βs becomes the new benchmark and the procedure above is repeated.

After each iteration (also called *epoch*), the MSE slightly improves. We continue until the MSE is lowered to the desired level or until a preset number of *epochs* is reached.

The process described above would work in most cases but is inefficient. In reality, the *Optimizer* uses a more sophisticated algorithm based on the *Steepest Gradient Descent* algorithm (sometimes called the *Back Propagation* algorithm). The *Steepest Gradient Descent* algorithm follows the ideas outlined

---

[8]Changing the β parameters by too much, will still move them in the right direction, but they might overshoot the optimum — leading to an oscillating and possibly exploding MSE. How to find an appropriate learning rate to adjust the change of the β parameters exceeds the scope of this book. For more details see Manassa (2021).

above but utilizes calculus (i.e., partial derivatives) to estimate the change of the MSE when a specific β value is changed.[9]

9.5 Build a Simplified Neural Network Model

Now it is time to see a *Neural Network* in action. This section uses the R nnet package (Venables and Ripley (2002)) to show a real-world application for *Neural Networks*. In what follows, we will emphasize the outstanding approximation properties of *Neural Networks* but also show how susceptible *Neural Networks* are to *overfitting*.

We use the nnet package in this section, although more advanced packages such as *PyTorch* have been recently implemented into R. You will use *PyTorch* in the interactive Section 9.7.

The reason to use nnet here is to stay compatible with Section 9.4. That is, the nnet package supports *Sigmoid* activation functions. In contrast, *PyTorch* only supports more advanced activation functions such as *Rectified Linear Activation Unit (ReLU)* functions (more about *ReLU* in Section 9.7).

As before, we start with loading the data and generating training and testing data:

```
library(tidymodels); library(janitor)
set.seed(777)
DataDiamonds=diamonds |>
          clean_names("upper_camel") |>
          select(Price, Carat, Clarity) |>
          mutate(Clarity=as.numeric(Clarity)) |>
          sample_n(500)

Split005= initial_split(DataDiamonds, prop=0.05)
DataTrain=training(Split005)
DataTest=testing(Split005)
```

As you can see, we use only 500 observations from the diamond dataset and assign only 25 observations (prop=0.05; 0.05·500=25) to the training dataset. A training dataset with 25 observations is extremely small for a *Neural Network* application, but it is well suited to demonstrate the *overfitting* problem later on.

---

[9]You can find more information about *Gradient Descent*, including the mathematics behind the algorithm, in Manassa (2021).

Next, we define the `recipe()`. It will later be added to a `workflow()` for the analysis:

```
RecipeDiamonds=recipe(Price~., data=DataTrain) |>
              step_normalize(all_predictors())
```

As you can see, we normalize the predictor variables. Most *Neural Network* applications require scaling of the predictor variables. Why this is the case is explained with the help of Figure 9.3 and in the info box that follows.

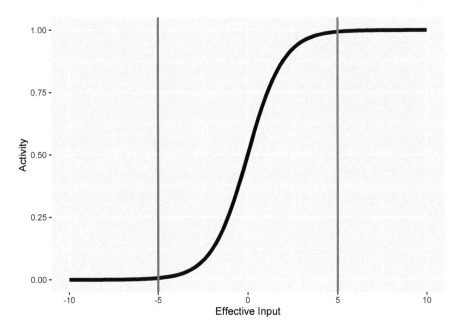

FIGURE 9.3 The Sigmoid Function

Consequently, for predictor variables with large input values such as the *GDP*, a *Neural Network* will likely create *activities* of either 0 or 1 for all observations. Afterward, between the hidden and the output layer (see Figure 9.1), these 0 or 1 *activities* will be multiplied with the related β values but because the *activities* do not change for the different observations (they stay 0 or 1), the output of the *Neural Network* will be constant regardless of which observation is processed.

If this is not bad enough, the optimization process used in *Neural Networks* (most of the times a variation of the *Steepest Gradient Descent* algorithm) has difficulties changing the βs when the slope of the activation functions is 0. Consequently, the βs that multiply the inputs would not change (get smaller) during the iterations.[a] The training process gets stuck.

To see a numerical example, you can process two very different diamonds through the *Neural Network* in Figure 9.2 ($Carat_1 = 0.1$, $Clarity_1 = 5$ and $Carat_2 = 0.4$, $Clarity_2 = 6$). Both diamonds will generate $A_1^{ct} = A_2^{ct} = 1$ and thus, despite being different, will have exactly the same predicted price.

As a rule of thumb: When you get the same or very similar predictions for all or most of your training data, it is often due to a lack of scaling or inappropriate scaling.

---

[a]The *Steepest Gradien Descent* algorithm changes βs based on partial derivatives. When the slope of the activation functions is zero, the partial derivatives are also zero, and so is the change of the βs.

In the *recipe* above, we used `step_normalize()` and thus applied *Z-score Normalization* (see Section 4.6 for more details). The *Z-score Normalization* scaling method is often used for *Neural Networks*. *Z-score Normalization* is unlikely to produce values smaller than -5 or greater than 5.[10] Additionally, the scaled inputs are multiplied by absolute β values smaller than one. Consequently, *effective input* values are not large and have a good chance to impact the activation function at different points in the middle section. In this section the slope is not zero and the generated *activities* discriminate between different input values (see Figure 9.3). Consequently, the *Neural Network* generates different outputs for different observations.

Next, we create a *model design* for the *Neural Network* analysis:

```
ModelDesignNN= mlp(hidden_units=50, epochs=10000, penalty=0) |>
               set_engine("nnet") |>
               set_mode("regression")
```

The model command for an *MLP* network is `mlp()`, and we use the `nnet` package (see `set_engine("nnet")`). The argument `hidden_units=50` determines that we use a hidden layer with 50 hidden neurons, `epochs=10000` determines that the *Optimizer* runs 10,000 *epochs* (iterations), and `penalty=0` determines

---

[10]For example, a normal-distributed variable's probability of having a Z-score greater than 5 or smaller than -5 is 0.000057%.

that we do not use *regularization*. The package nnet supports *regularization* similar to *Ridge regularization*, and the value assigned to penalty determines how the penalty term and the *MSE* are weighted in the target function. All three arguments can optionally be tuned by assigning tune(). Here, we keep it simple and do not tune the *Neural Network*, but in the interactive Section 9.7, you will tune a *Neural Network* using *PyTorch*.

To fit a workflow() model with the training data, we must add the *recipe* and the *model design* to a *workflow* and use the built-in *Optimizer* and the training data (fit(DataTrain)) to find optimal parameters for the βs:

```
WFModelNN=workflow() |>
         add_model(ModelDesignNN) |>
         add_recipe(RecipeDiamonds) |>
         fit(DataTrain)
```

Since the *workflow* WFModelNN is now a fitted *workflow*, we can use it for predicting diamond prices.

We start with generating predictions for the training dataset and evaluating how well the predictions approximate the true prices in the training dataset. Again, we use the augment() command to create the predictions. These predictions are then augmented to the training dataset by creating an extra column named *.pred*. The resulting data frame is saved as DataTrainWithPred.

The metrics() command then compares for each observation the prediction (*.pred*) with the true value for the diamond price (*Price*) and calculates the root of the *mean squared error* $\sqrt{MSE}$, r^2 and the mean absolute error (*mae*) for the training data:

```
DataTrainWithPredNN=augment(WFModelNN, new_data=DataTrain)
metrics(DataTrainWithPredNN, truth=Price, estimate=.pred)
```

```
## # A tibble: 3 x 3
##    .metric .estimator .estimate
##    <chr>   <chr>          <dbl>
## 1 rmse     standard       198.
## 2 rsq      standard       0.996
## 3 mae      standard       111.
```

As you can see, the *Neural Network* approximates the training data extremely well. For example, $r^2 = 0.996$.

How such a (suspiciously) good approximation is possible, is illustrated in Figures 9.4 and 9.5. In Figure 9.4, you can see a 3D scatter plot of the training data. The two axes on the bottom of the 3D cube reflect *Carat* and *Clarity*

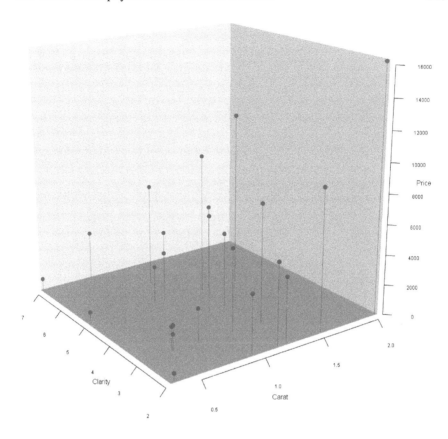

FIGURE 9.4 3D Scatter Plot for the Diamonds Data

for each diamond. The height of each data point (visualized by the red line) depicts the *Price* for each diamond.

The prediction goal for the *Neural Network* is to find a surface that approximates these points as well as possible.

Because of the high number of iterations (`epochs=10000`) and the high degree of non-linearity of the *Neural Network* (50 hidden neurons with non-linear logistic functions and 201 parameters), the *Neural Network* can produce a very flexible prediction surface.

Figure 9.5 shows that the fitted *Neural Network workflow model* generates a prediction surface that almost perfectly approximates the training data. This prediction surface bends in many ways to make the close approximation possible. This high flexibility of the prediction surface (i.e., the underlying prediction function) was made possible by the high number of hidden neurons leading to a total of 201 β parameters.

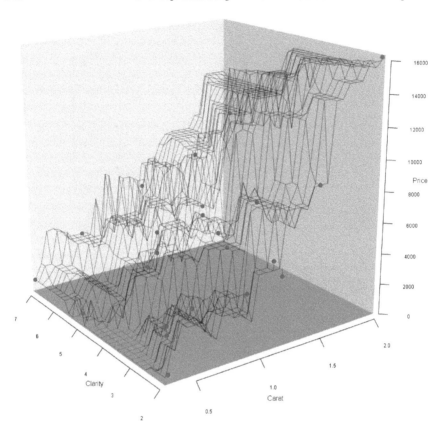

FIGURE 9.5 Diamond Data and Prediction Surface

A *Neural Network* with a sufficiently large number of hidden neurons can take the form of a highly non-linear surface to approximate training data almost perfectly. In fact, a "(...) standard multilayer feedforward network architecture using arbitrary squashing functions can approximate virtually any function of interest to any desired degree of accuracy, provided sufficiently many hidden units are available" (Hornik et al. (1989)).

To intuitively understand the outstanding approximation ability of a *Neural Network*, consider that a *Neural Network* consists of many hidden neurons and thus of many *Sigmoid* functions. *Sigmoid* functions are squashing functions because they squash all input values between two output values (0 and 1 in the case of the *Logistic* function). As Figure 9.3 shows, each *Sigmoid* function forms a step similar to a step in a staircase. Although smoother than a staircase step, a *Sigmoid* function, like a staircase step, is flat first, then upward (or possibly downwards), and finally flat again.

Changing the β values that impact the *effective input j* ($I_{j,i}^{eff}$) of a specific *Sigmoid* activation function and changing the β value that weighs the resulting activity ($\beta_j A_{j,i}^{ct}$), can move a step (*Sigmoid* function) horizontally, increase or decrease the step size, change the steepness, and also convert a step from an upward to a downward step.

Since a *Neural Network* consists of many hidden neurons, many *Sigmoid* (steps) functions can be combined to a staircase-like structure with smaller and bigger steps as well as upwards and downward steps — depending on the β parameter values. This staircase-like structure — if it has enough steps — can approximate a function in any given range to any degree.

The mathematical formula behind this staircase-like structure is the *Neural Network* prediction function. It combines the *Sigmoid* (steps) functions to approximate whatever continuous function needs to be approximated (in a given range) with various up- and downward steps.

Consequently, with this procedure, a *Neural Network* can approximate a given function to any degree of smoothness in a given range by increasing the number of hidden neurons.

Figure 9.6 shows an example of the arguments outlined above. The goal is to approximate a sine function (see the orange dots in the upper diagram in Figure 9.6) in an input range between 0 and 9 with a *Neural Network*. The sine function to be approximated is:

$$y_i = \sin(x_i + 5) + 1$$

We use a *Neural Network* with one input (x_i), three hidden neurons with *Logistic* activation functions, and one output $\widehat{y_i}$.

When all β values are appropriately chosen,[11] the three β weighted activation functions of the three hidden neurons form three steps (see the lower three diagrams in Figure 9.6). When these steps are combined (added up) together with the bias for the output neuron ($\beta_{10} = 2$) they form the *Neural Network* prediction function (see the blue line in the upper diagram of Figure 9.6). As you can see, we get a good approximation of the sine function. The *Neural Network* prediction function forms a staircase-like structure with one step up, one step down, and one step up (see the blue line in the upper diagram of Figure 9.6). If we want to increase the smoothness of the approximation, we could work with six hidden neurons (six steps). With appropriate values for the β parameters, we could form a staircase-like structure with two (smaller) steps up, two (smaller) steps down, and two (smaller) steps up.

---

[11]The underlying β values are not the result of an *Optimizer* process. They have been chosen manually by *trial-and-error* to generate a good approximation.

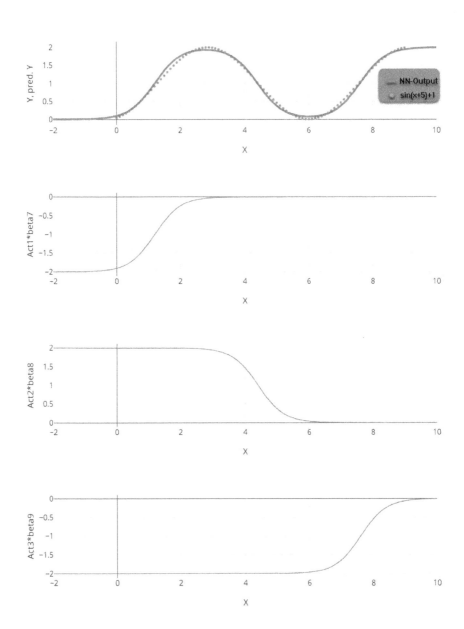

FIGURE 9.6 Three Sigmoid Functions Approximate a Sine Function

You can find a link to a related blog post and a simulation app that allows you to interactively adjust the β values for the *Neural Network* from Figure 9.6 in the *Digital Resource* Section 9.9.

It is important to mention that the procedure above is more like a proof of concept rather than a real proof. The procedure shows only one way a *Neural Network* can possibly approximate a function. It is not likely that the β parameters determined by the *Optimizer* will actually form a staircase-like structure. Also, the mathematical proof from Hornik et al. (1989) is different and more advanced.

Now that we know that *Neural Networks* with enough hidden neurons can approximate any training dataset to a very high degree, the crucial question is, how well our fitted *Neural Network* can predict the testing data — *data the Neural Network has never seen before*.

In the code block below, we use the `augment()` and the `metrics()` commands as above when evaluating training data performance, except that we now evaluate the testing data (`DataTest`):

```
DataTestWithPredNN=augment(WFModelNN, new_data=DataTest)
metrics(DataTestWithPredNN, truth=Price, estimate=.pred)
```

```
## # A tibble: 3 x 3
##    .metric .estimator .estimate
##    <chr>   <chr>          <dbl>
## 1 rmse     standard       2202.
## 2 rsq      standard        0.709
## 3 mae      standard       1273.
```

The prediction result is not good. For instance, for the testing data, the *mae*, the amount our model on average over/underestimates a diamond's price, is $1,273. This is a typical case of *overfitting*; the training data approximation is good (*mae* = 110.94), but the prediction quality based on the testing data is poor.

Neural Networks with a large number of parameters are prone to *overfitting*, especially when the training dataset is relatively small.

Section 9.7 will guide you through an interactive project where you can tune a *Neural Network* to avoid *overfitting*. You will use the `diamonds` dataset and utilize all four diamond appraisal Cs (*Carat*, *Clarity*, *Cut*, and *Color*) as predictor variables. You will also use *PyTorch* with the `brulee` package instead of `nnet`.

9.6   NNet vs. PyTorch (brulee)

PyTorch is a machine learning framework initially developed by *Facebook* (now *Meta AI*). Since 2022, it is curated by the *Linux Foundation*. *PyTorch* was for a long time only accessible through *Python*, but in 2021, the developers of tidymodels created the *R* package brulee (Kuhn and Falbel (2022)), which makes some of the functionality from *PyTorch* available to tidymodels. This includes an *MLP* network implementation.

In this section, we will discuss some of the differences between a *Neural Network* created with the nnet package and a *Neural Network* created by *PyTorch* (via the brulee package).

The nnet package (Venables and Ripley (2002)) was one of the earliest *R* packages to support *Neural Networks*. It is well suited for educational purposes, especially to demonstrate how *Neural Networks* can be used for predictions and to display *Neural Networks* as graphs.[12]

In contrast, *PyTorch* is an advanced data science toolkit, and its *Neural Network* functionality is more up-to-date. Some of *PyTorch's* functionality, including support for *MLP* networks was recently included in *R* through the brulee package.

There are quite a few differences between *MLP* networks supported by nnet and by *PyTorch*. In this section, we will focus on two aspects:

Hyper-Parameters: In *PyTorch*, you can set and tune numerous *hyperparameters* that are either unavailable in nnet or are available, but not as advanced. For example, in nnet, you can tune the number of hidden neurons for one hidden layer. In *PyTorch*, you can set and tune the number of hidden neurons for multiple hidden layers.

Activation Functions: *PyTorch* allows us to use the *Rectified Linear Unit (ReLU)* activation function, while nnet does not support *ReLU* activation function. In what follows, we will introduce how *ReLU* functions work and why they are superior to classical *Sigmoid* activation functions, which are supported in nnet.

9.6.1   Hyper-Parameters

Below is a selective list of *hyper-parameters* that *PyTorch* supports. The list is limited to the *hyper-parameters* that we will later use in the interactive Section 9.7.

---

[12]Using the nnet package in combination with the NeuralNetTools package (Beck (2018)) allows us to convert any nnet *Neural Network* into a graph and save it as a png-file.

epochs= Determines the maximum number of *epochs* used by the *Optimizer* for training. Internally *PyTorch* generates a validation dataset and if the prediction error does not improve for five consecutive *epochs*, it stops the training even if the maximum number of *epochs* set by epochs= has not been reached.

hidden_neurons= This *hyper-parameter* determines the number of hidden neurons and, at the same time, the number of hidden layers. When working with only one hidden layer like here, you can assign a number to hidden_neurons=, which determines the number of neurons for the only hidden layer (e.g., hidden_neurons=50 for 50 neurons in the only hidden layer).

Suppose you would like to work with more than one layer. In that case, you must assign a vector to hidden_neurons= where each element determines the number of hidden neurons for consecutive hidden layers (e.g., hidden_neurons=c(25,30,20) for a *Neural Network* with three layers where the first layer consists of 25 neurons, the second layer of 30 neurons, and the third of 20 neurons).

dropout= *PyTorch* allows randomly switching off a predefined percentage of hidden neurons for each iteration of the *Optimizer* process. The value assigned to dropout determines the proportion of hidden neurons randomly switched off at each iteration. For example, dropout=0.25 indicates that the *Optimizer* randomly switches off 25% of the hidden layer's neurons at each iteration of the training process.

penalty= Determines the weight of the penalty term compared to the MSE in the target function when *regularization* is used (see Chapter 7 for details). By default *Ridge regularization* is used with penalty=0.001.

9.6.2 ReLU Activation Functions

Unlike the nnet package, *PyTorch* supports *ReLU* activation functions. In this section, we will discuss *ReLU* activation functions and focus on:

1. Introducing the *ReLU* activation function.

2. Demonstrating that *Neural Networks* with *ReLU* activation functions has the same outstanding approximation properties as a *Neural Networks* with *Sigmoid* activation functions.

3. Discussing the problem of the *Vanishing Gradient* in context of classical *Sigmoid* vs. *ReLU* activation functions. A *Vanishing Gradient* can lead to a situation where the *Optimizer* cannot change the β parameters anymore, although they are still far from optimal.

Let us start with how a *ReLU* activation function determines the activity of a hidden neuron:

$$Act_{j,i} \;\; = \;\; max\left(0, I_{j,i}^{eff}\right) \tag{9.10}$$

with $j :=$ hidden neuron number and $i :=$ observation number

Equation (9.10) shows the algebraic form of a *ReLU* activation function. If the *effective input* is greater than 0, the *ReLU* function returns the *effective input* as activity ($Act_{j,i} = I_{j,i}^{eff}$). If the *effective input* is smaller than 0, the *ReLU* function returns 0 ($Act_{j,i} = 0$). You also can see this in Figure 9.7 below. For all positive *effective inputs*, we get the *Linear-Parent-Function* graph (y=x-graph). For all negative values we get a straight line with $y = 0$.

Figure 9.7 shows, that the graph of the *ReLU* activation function is limited to depicting only half of a step. In contrast, the graph of a *Sigmoid* activation function depicts a full step. Therefore the question arises if *Neural Networks* with *ReLU* activation functions have the same outstanding approximation properties as *Neural Networks* with *Sigmoid* activation functions?[13]

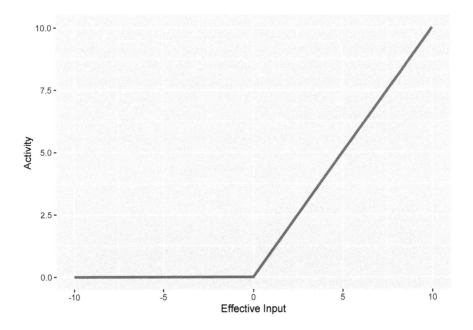

FIGURE 9.7 The ReLU Activation Function

The answer is that *ReLU* activation functions do have the same outstanding approximation properties. This is because we can combine two *ReLU* functions into a complete step, and then they have the same approximation properties as classical *Sigmoid* (full-step) functions.

---

[13]See Section 9.5 for the approximation properties of *Neural Networks* with *Sigmoid* activation functions.

We can show this with an example by using a *Neural Network* with one predictor variable (x), one hidden layer, and multiple hidden neurons.

Let us look at the first hidden neuron. Before its activity is transmitted to the output neuron it is weighted with β_3. Therefore we consider ($\beta_3 Act_{1,i}$) rather than its activity ($Act_{1,i}$) alone:

$$\beta_3 Act_{1,i} = \beta_3 \cdot max\left(0, I_{1,i}^{eff}\right) \tag{9.11}$$

Since we have only one predictor variable x, substituting the resulting *effective input* $I_{1,i}^{eff} = \beta_1 + \beta_2 x_i$ into Equation (9.11) leads to:

$$\beta_3 Act_i \;\; = \;\; \beta_3 max\left(0, \beta_1 + \beta_2 x_i\right) \tag{9.12}$$

with: β_1: parameter for bias neuron $B1$ and

                       β_2: parameter for the only predictor variable x

Equation (9.12) can be plotted and for $\beta_1 = 0$, $\beta_2 = 1$, and $\beta_3 = 1$, the plot resembles the *ReLU* from Figure 9.7.

By changing the β parameters β_1, β_2, and β_3 the graph of the augmented *ReLU* function in Figure 9.7 can be transformed:

- horizontally shifted (by changing β_1)

- the slope can be changed (by changing β_3)

- the graph can be turned upside down (by changing β_3 to a negative value)

- the graph can be mirrored horizontally (by changing the sign of $\beta 2$)

When using the transformations above on two different augmented *ReLU* functions (two hidden neurons) they can jointly form a step function similar to a *Sigmoid* function, except that the step based on the two *ReLU* function has two kinks and the slope between the two kinks is constant.

In Section 9.9, we provide a link to an Internet app and a related blog post where you can transform and combine two *ReLU* functions to form a complete step function.

In summary: If we can combine two hidden neurons with *ReLU* activation functions into a complete step function, we can expect the same approximation properties from a *Neural Network* with *ReLU* activation functions that we derived in Section 9.5 for *Neural Networks* with *Sigmoid* functions.

The constant slope of a *ReLU* activation function is a major advantage over a *Sigmoid* function. Let us compare the slope of the *Logistic* activation function in Figure 9.3 with the slope of the *ReLU* activation function in Figure 9.7. The *ReLU* activation function has a constant slope of one for all positive *effective inputs*. In contrast, the slope of the *Logistic* activation function is always smaller than one, and it becomes very small when the *effective input* gets greater in absolute terms (when approaching the red and blue lines in Figure 9.3).

While the small slope of *Logistic* activation functions is not a problem for *Neural Networks* with one layer, it is a problem for *Neural Networks* with many layers.

When the *Optimizer* adjusts individual β values in a multi-layer *Neural Network* and calculates by how much they change from iteration to iteration, the weighted slopes of the activation functions in different layers are multiplied.[14] If these weighted slopes are smaller than one, each multiplication makes the change of the related β smaller. With enough layers, the calculated change might get close to zero. Consequently, the β parameters will not change anymore, and the optimization process gets stuck. This problem is called the **Vanishing Gradient**.[15]

Since *ReLU* activation functions have a constant slope of one for positive *effective inputs*, the *Vanishing Gradient* problem is mostly mitigated when using *ReLU* activation functions.

In the following interactive Section 9.7, you will work with a *Neural Network* with *ReLU* activation functions. You will tune a *Neural Network* and estimate diamond prices.

9.7 ⊘ Using PyTorch to Predict Diamond Prices

Interactive Section

In this section, you will find content together with *R* code to execute, change, and rerun in RStudio.

The best way to read and to work with this section is to open it with *RStudio*. Then you can interactively work on *R* code exercises and *R* projects within a web browser. This way you can apply what you have learned so far and extend your knowledge. You can also choose to continue reading either in the book or online, but you will not benefit from the interactive learning experience.

---

[14]In terms of calculus: The partial derivative for the related β parameters contain (weighted) products of the *activities* from multiple layers.

[15]The detailed explanation of the *Vanishing Gradient* problem exceeds this book's scope. You can find more detailed information in Wang (2019).

To work with this section in *RStudio* in an interactive environment, follow
these steps:

1. Ensure that both the `learnR` and the `shiny` package are installed. If not,
   install them from RStudio's main menu (Tools -> Install Packages ...).

2. Download the `Rmd` file for the interactive session and save it in your `project`
   folder. You will find the link for the download below.

3. Open the downloaded file in RStudio and click the `Run Document` button,
   located in the editing window's top-middle area.

For detailed help for running the exercises including videos for Windows and Mac users
we refer to: https://blog.lange-analytics.com/2024/01/interactsessions.html

Do not skip this interactive section because besides providing applications of
already covered concepts, it will also extend what you have learned so far.

Below is the link to download the interactive section:

https://ai.lange-analytics.com/exc/?file=10-DeepLearnExerc100.Rmd

In this section, you will use *PyTorch* to run and tune a *Neural Network* model
predicting diamond prices. By default, *PyTorch* uses *ReLU* activation functions.

Tuning a *Neural Network* requires more computer resources than the machine
learning models from the previous chapters. We implemented some restrictions to allow you to run and tune the model in a browser. Instead of using
all 53,940 observations from the `diamonds` dataset, we will choose only 500
randomly selected observations, and we will tune only two *hyper-parameters*
(`hidden_neurons=` and `dropout=`). In the initial setup, three values are tried
out for `hidden_neurons` and two values for `dropout`.

You can change the values from the initial setup or add more values for each
hyper-parameter. However, increasing the values that are tried out for each
of the *hyper-parameters*, will also increase the execution time for the tuning
process (the maximum computing time available in a browser is currently
set to 30 minutes). Please consider, with such a long execution time and *R*
running in a browser, the tuning process might become unstable, and the
browser might crash.

If you need more computing time to tune more *hyper-parameters* with more
values or you plan to use all 53,940 observations from the `diamonds` dataset,
we provide an alternative. You can download an *R* script with similar code as
here without computing time restrictions. The *R* script runs in *RStudio* and
you can run the tuning for several hours overnight. You find a link and a short
description for this *R* script in the *Digital Resource* Section 9.9.

By default, the *R* script utilizes the complete diamonds dataset. Since computing time is only limited by your patience, you can try out more values for the pre-set *hyper-parameters* (hidden_neurons= and dropout=), and you can add different *hyper-parameters* such as penalty=tune() to try out various degrees of *regularization*.

Let us now go to the *Neural Network* that you will run in a browser. You will estimate the price of diamonds with a *Neural Network* under real-world conditions:

1. You will use all big *C* variables *Carat*, *Clarity*, *Cut*, and *Color* as predictor variables. We used *Carat* and *Clarity* already in Section 9.5. Here, the variables *Cut* and *Color* are added to the analysis. *Cut* describes the quality of the cut of a diamond and is rated from 1 (lowest) to 6 (highest). *Color* rates the color of a diamond from 1 (highest) to 7 (lowest); note the opposite direction of the rating scale.

2. As already explained in Section 9.6, you will use the more advanced *PyTorch Neural Network* from the brulee package instead of the *Neural Network* from the nnet package.

3. You will tune the *Neural Network's hyper-parameters* (hidden_units and dropout) by using *Cross-Validation*.

Keep in mind that you have to install the brulee package before you can execute the code. After the brulee package is installed, the *PyTorch* software must also be installed. This is straightforward: When the package is used for the first time (i.e., with library(brulee)) a popup window asks to download and install the required software. After confirming with "Yes", the *PyTorch* software will be installed.

We again use the *10-Step Template* introduced in Section 6.6. Steps 1 – 4 are already prepared for you.

Step 1 - Generate Training and Testing Data:

```
library(tidymodels); library(janitor); library(brulee)
set.seed(888)
DataDiamonds=sample_n(diamonds, 500) |>
            clean_names("upper_camel") |>
            select(Price, Carat, Cut, Color, Clarity) |>
            mutate(Cut=as.integer(Cut), Color=as.integer(Color),
                Clarity=as.integer(Clarity))
set.seed(888)
Split70=initial_split(DataDiamonds, prop=0.7, strata=Price, breaks=5)
```

```
DataTrain=training(Split70)
DataTest=testing(Split70)
```

In the code block above, we load the data and choose randomly 500 observations. Then we select the outcome variable (*Price*) and the predictor variables *Carat*, *Clarity*, *Cut*, and *Color* transforming the factor-levels of the last three variables to numerical integer values. Finally, we split the data into training and testing data.

Step 2 - Create a Recipe:

We use the same `recipe()` command as in Section 9.5:

```
RecipeDiamonds=recipe(Price~., data=DataTrain) |>
              step_normalize(all_predictors())
```

Again, we use `step_normalize()` for *Z-score Normalization*[16] of all predictors. As explained in Section 9.5, the predictor variables for a *Neural Network* need to be scaled. Otherwise, the *Optimizer* likely will not generate suitable β values.[17]

Step 3 - Create a Model Design:

In the code block below, we create a *model design*. Like in Section 9.5, we use the `mlp()` command to create an *MLP* network model. However, we utilize the `brulee` package and therefore *PyTorch* rather than the `nnet` package (see `set_engine("brulee")`):

```
ModelDesignNN=mlp(hidden_units=tune(), dropout=tune(),
              epochs=100, penalty=0) |>
          set_engine("brulee") |>
          set_mode("regression")
```

The *hyper-parameters* `hidden_units` and `dropout` are prepared for tuning (see `hidden_units=tune()` and `dropout=tune()`). The *hyper-parameter* `penalty` is set to zero (no *regularization*) and `epochs` is set to 100 (the default).

When you use the provided *R* script from the *Digital Resource* Section 9.9 to run the code in *RStudio* rather than in a browser, you can increase the value for `epochs` (e.g., `epochs=1000`), and you can tune other *hyper-parameters*. For example, you can set `penalty=tune()` to introduce different degrees of

---

[16]If you would like to review scaling procedures like *Z-score Normalization*, we recommend reading Section 4.6 again.

[17]Internally, `mlp()` normalizes the predictor variables. So, omitting `step_normalize()` would not have created any damage. However, we used `step_normalize()` in the *recipe* to make the process more explicit.

regularization. Remember that you have to provide the values you would like to try out for each *hyper-parameter* in Step 5 (*Create a Hyper-Parameter Grid*).

Step 4 - Add the Recipe and the Model Design to a Workflow:

Below, we add the *recipe* and the *model design* to a workflow, which will be tuned in Step 7:

```
TuneWFModelNN=workflow() |>
            add_model(ModelDesignNN) |>
            add_recipe(RecipeDiamonds)
```

Steps 5 – 10 in the code block below are the steps you will execute (and potentially modify).

It is recommended to execute the code below unchanged in a first attempt. Then, you can start modifying the code and see what happens. Make small changes first to see how the computing time responds on your machine. To use different values for the *hyper-parameters*, modify the *Hyper-Parameter Grid* in Step 5.

```
# Step 5 - Create a Hyper-Parameter Grid:
#          To try out different hyper-parameter values, change the
#          values that are assigned to the respective hyper-parameters
#          below.
ParGridNN=expand.grid(hidden_units=c(10, 20, 50), dropout=c(0, 0.25))

# Step 6: - Create Resamples for Cross-Validation:
#          You can change v= to consider a different
#          number of folds (e.g. v=10). Note, computing
#          time will change proportionately.
set.seed(888)
FoldsForTuningNN=vfold_cv(DataTrain, v=7, strata=Price)

# Step 7 - Tune the Workflow and Train All Models:
#   (this step requires patience; run time 5-30 minutes)
set.seed(888)
TuneResultsNN=tune_grid(TuneWFModelNN, resamples=FoldsForTuningNN,
                  grid=ParGridNN, metrics=metric_set(rmse, rsq, mae))

# Step 8 - Extract the Best Hyper-Parameter(s)
BestHyperParNN=select_best(TuneResultsNN, "rmse")
print("Best Hyper-Parameters:")
print(BestHyperParNN)
```

```
# Step 9 - Finalize and Train the Best Workflow Model:
# (this step requires a little patience; run time 1-10 minutes)
set.seed(888)
BestWFModelNN=TuneWFModelNN |>
             finalize_workflow(BestHyperParNN) |>
             fit(DataTrain)

# Step 10: Assess Prediction Quality Based on the Testing Data:
DataTestWithPredBestModelNN=augment(BestWFModelNN,DataTest)
metrics(DataTestWithPredBestModelNN, truth=Price,
        estimate=.pred)

# Plot Validation Performance of Hyper-Parameters
autoplot(TuneResultsNN)
```

When you execute the code block above, the tuning process starts. It can take a while until you get a result. Depending on your computer, it can take between 5 and 30 minutes. To accommodate longer computing time in the browser, we extended the maximum computing time available to 30 minutes.

If you use the initial settings, when you execute the code above in a browser, the command `autoplot(TuneResultsNN)` (at the end of the code block) will create a plot similar to the one in Figure 9.8.

You can see in Figure 9.8 that more hidden neurons lead to a lower *mean average error*, lower *root mean squared error*, and higher r^2. Figure 9.8 also shows that a higher `dropout` rate leads to a higher *mean average error*, higher *root mean squared error*, and lower r^2. This suggests trying more hidden neurons and lower `dropout` rates.

For your information, we also calculated the metrics based on the testing data in Step 10 of the template. Please keep in mind that metrics based on testing data should only be used to assess the last model and not for tuning adjustments because this could lead to *overfitting*.

9.8 When and When Not to Use Neural Networks

- *Neural Networks* shine when they consist of many layers and many hidden neurons (some *Neural Networks* like *Natural Language Processing* networks, often have millions or even billions of parameters). These networks are well suited to model highly complex non-linear relationships.

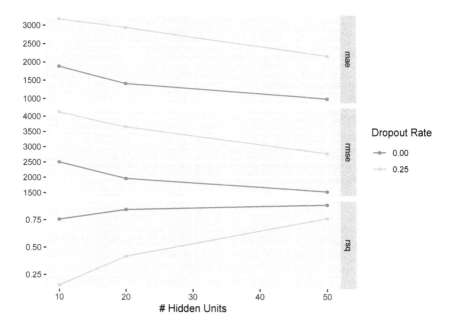

FIGURE 9.8 Plot and Predictions

- *Neural Networks* with many layers and hidden neurons are also prone to *overfitting* if not accompanied by large datasets (see Section 9.5 for details). Even datasets with hundreds or thousands of observations might not be big enough to avoid *overfitting* when using large(r) *Neural Networks*.

  There is no rule on how many layers and how many hidden neurons a *Neural Network* should have. You can start with a reasonable architecture (number of hidden layers and hidden neurons) given the size of your dataset and then use tuning to find the best performing *Neural Network* based on *Cross-Validation*.

- *Neural Networks* with one hidden layer like in this chapter, perform well to predict relationships between multiple predictor variables and one outcome variable. However, other machine learning algorithms such as *Random Forest* (see Chapter 10) should also be considered since they often perform similar or better.

- *Neural Networks* can also predict linear relationships. However, since the β parameters cannot be interpreted as in linear *OLS* models, *OLS* is better suited to predict linear relationships. It is good practice to first develop a linear model as a benchmark and then evaluate if a *Neural Network* (or other machine learning model) can outperform it.

9.9 Digital Resources

Below you will find a few digital resources related to this chapter such as:

- Videos
- Short articles
- Tutorials
- *R* scripts

These resources are recommended if you would like to review the chapter from a different angle or to go beyond what was covered in the chapter.

Here we show only a few of the digital resourses. At the end of the list you will find a link to additonal digital resources for this chapter that are maintained on the Internet.

You can find a complete list of digital resources for all book chapters on the companion website: https://ai.lange-analytics.com/digitalresources.html

Neural Network Video from StatQuest

A video from *StatQuest* by Josh Starmer. This video is Part 1 from a series of eight videos about Neural Networks. While most of the videos exceed the scope of this book, Part 1 complements topics in the book.

Link: https://ai.lange-analytics.com/dr?a=343

How Two ReLU Functions Can Form a Complete Step Function

This is a blog post by Carsten Lange that shows how two Rectified Linear Unit (*ReLU*) activation functions can be combined into a complete step function (squashing function). The post includes a simulation that allows for changing the beta values of two *ReLU* functions with the goal of creating a complete step function.

Link: https://ai.lange-analytics.com/dr?a=352

R Script for Tuning and Training a Neural Network to Predict Diamond Prices

Here you can download an *R* script to tune and train a neural network to predict diamond prices. The R script contains similar code as the related interactive section of the book. In contrast to the interactive section, the code runs in *RStudio* instead of a browser, and the maximum runtime is not restricted.

The *R* script loads the complete set of observations from the diamonds dataset, and all *hyper-parameters* can be tuned, The maximum number of epochs is set to 1000 and can be changed.

It is recommended that you experiment with tuning settings in the R script (see Step 5) and try to improve the cross-validation results. At the very end of the R script, you find sample tuning settings that produce relatively good results but require between one to several hours of computing time, depending on your computer. Use the sample tuning setting only after you have experimented with the tuning, and then see if your results can beat the sample tuning results.

Link: https://ai.lange-analytics.com/dr?a=354

More Digital Resources

Only a subset of digital resources is listed in this section. The link below points to additional, concurrently updated resources for this chapter.

Link: https://ai.lange-analytics.com/dr/deeplearn.html

10

Tree-Based Models — Bootstrapping Explained

Tree-based models are a type of machine learning technique that uses a tree-like structures to make predictions. The most basic type of a *tree-based* model is a *Decision Tree*. A *Decision Tree* guides observation through a tree-like structure with many branches. The location where a specific observation ends up determines the prediction (more about *Decision Trees* in Section 10.3).

Other *tree-based* models are based on a combination of *Decision Trees*. Because they combine an ensemble of machine learning models (i.e., *Decision Trees*), they fall in the category of *ensemble* models. *Tree-based* models can be used for classification and regression tasks.

Since *tree-based* models are built based on *Decision Trees*, you will learn about *Decision Trees* in Section 10.3. Section 10.3.1 introduces the idea behind *Decision Trees*, and in the interactive Section 10.3.2, you can create your own *Decision Tree* model for a classification task. In that section, you will use a *Decision Tree* model to predict the survival of passengers on the *Titanic*.

How an *ensemble* of *Decision Trees* can be combined into a Random Forest will be covered in Section 10.4. While the idea behind a *Random Forest* model is introduced in Section 10.4.1, we will show a real-world application in Section 10.4.2. There, we will use a *Random Forest* model together with tidymodels to estimate the *COVID-19* vaccination rate for each county in the continental U.S.

In Section 10.5, we will introduce several Boosting Trees algorithms, which are also *ensemble* models because they combine multiple *Decision Trees*. *Boosting Trees* are more advanced and more recent algorithms based on *Decision Trees*. We will briefly introduce the ideas behind some *Boosting Trees* algorithms such as *AdaBoost*, *LightGBM*, and *CATBoost* in Section 10.5. Later, in Section 10.5.1, the idea behind another *Boosting Trees* algorithm called *Gradient Boosting* will be explained in more detail, and in the interactive Section 10.5.2 you will use *XGBoost*, which is a computational advanced version of *Gradient Boosting* for a real-world application. You will again estimate the *COVID-19* vaccination rate for the continental U.S. counties.

10.1   Learning Outcomes

This section outlines what you can expect to learn in this chapter. In addition, the corresponding section number is included for each learning outcome to help you to navigate the content, especially when you return to the chapter for review.

In this chapter, you will learn:

- How you can guide an observation through a Decision Tree (see Section 10.3.1).

- How to use decision rules when observations are guided through a *Decision Tree* (see Section 10.3.1).

- How you can use a training dataset to train a Decision Tree (see Section 10.3.1).

- How to use a trained Decision Tree to make predictions for new observations (see Section 10.3.1).

- How to interpret the structure of a trained Decision Tree to gain insight into the underlying causality implications (see Section 10.3.1).

- How sensitive the structure of a Decision Tree can react to small changes in the data or the *hyper-parameters* (see Section 10.3.2).

- How several *Decision Trees* can be combined into an *ensemble* model like a Random Forest (see Section 10.4.1).

- How you can use the Subspace Method and Bagging to create slightly different *Decision Trees* for a *Random Forest* (see Section 10.4.1).

- How you can use Bootstrapping to create multiple *Bootstrap* samples and *Out of Bag* samples from one training dataset (see Section 10.4.1).

- How to use a Random Forest model to predict vaccination behavior for the continental U.S. counties (see Section 10.4.2).

- How you can use Gradient Boosting to combine *Decison Trees* into an *ensemble* where each *Decision Tree* adjusts for the errors of the previous *Decision Tree* (see Section 10.5).

- How you use an interactive project to predict vaccination behavior with the **XGBoost* algorithm for the continental U.S. counties (see Section 10.5.2).

10.2 R Packages Required for the Chapter

This section lists the *R* packages that you need when you load and execute code in the interactive sections in *RStudio*. Please install the following packages using `Tools` -> `Install Packages` ... from the *RStudio* menu bar (you can find more information about installing and loading packages in Section 3.4):

- The `rio` package (Chan et al. (2021)) to enable the loading of various data formats with one `import()` command. Files can be loaded from the user's hard drive or the Internet.

- The `janitor` package (Firke (2023)) to rename variable names to *Upper-Camel* and to substitute spaces and special characters in variable names.

- The `tidymodels` package (Kuhn and Wickham (2020)) to streamline data engineering and machine learning tasks.

- The `kableExtra` (Zhu (2021)) package to support the rendering of tables.

- The `learnr` package (Aden-Buie et al. (2022)), which is needed together with the `shiny` package (Chang et al. (2022)) for the interactive exercises in this book.

- The `shiny` package (Chang et al. (2022)), which is needed together with the `learnr` package (Aden-Buie et al. (2022)) for the interactive exercises in this book.

- The `rpart` package (Therneau and Atkinson (2022)) to create *Decision Trees*.

- The `rpart.plot` package (Milborrow (2022)) to plot *Decision Trees*.

- The `ranger` package (Wright and Ziegler (2017)) to create a *Random Forest*.

- The `xgboost` package (Chen et al. (2023)) to perform *Extreme Gradient Boosting (XGBoost)*.

- The `parallel` package (R Core Team (2022)) for parallel processing the *Random Forest* algorithm.

- The `doParallel` package (Corporation and Weston (2022)) for parallel processing the *XGBoost* algorithm.

10.3 Decision Trees

As mentioned above, a *Decision Tree* machine learning model can be used for classification and regression tasks.

In the following Section 10.3.1, the idea behind *Decision Trees* will be introduced in an intuitive way using a *classification* task.

10.3.1 The Idea Behind a Decision Tree

The best way to introduce the idea behind *Decision Trees* is to see the algorithm in action. We will use the *Titanic* dataset[1] in *R* to generate a *Decision Tree* and discuss the resulting graph.

In the code block below, we download the data, rename the variables into *UpperCamel* form, and `select()` the variables *Survived*, *Sex*, *Class* (renamed from *Pclass*), *Age*, and *Fare* (renamed from *FareInPounds*) for the analysis. For better readability, we use `mutate()` to convert *Survived* to data type `logic` (*Survived = TRUE* for a passenger that survived and *Survived = FALSE* otherwise). Since we perform a *classification* task, the outcome variable *Survived* also has to be converted into a `factor` variable:

```
library(rio); library(tidymodels); library(janitor)
DataTitanic=import("https://ai.lange-analytics.com/data/Titanic.csv") |>
          clean_names("upper_camel") |>
          select(Survived, Sex, Class=Pclass, Age,
                Fare=FareInPounds) |>
           mutate(Survived=as.logical(Survived)) |>
           mutate(Survived=as.factor(Survived))
```

Afterward, as usual, we create a training and a testing dataset:

```
set.seed(777)
Split7525=initial_split(DataTitanic, strata=Survived)
DataTrain=training(Split7525)
DataTest=testing(Split7525)
head(DataTrain)
```

```
##     Survived    Sex Class Age    Fare
## 1     FALSE   male     3  35   8.050
## 2     FALSE   male     1  54  51.862
## 3     FALSE   male     3   2  21.075
## 4     FALSE   male     3  20   8.050
## 5     FALSE   male     3  39  31.275
## 6     FALSE female     3  14   7.854
```

In the code block below, we create a *recipe* and a *model design*:

---

[1]See Section 3.5.2 for more details about the *Titanic* dataset.

```
RecipeTitanic=recipe(Survived~., data=DataTrain)

ModelDesignDecTree=decision_tree(tree_depth=3) |>
                    set_engine("rpart") |>
                    set_mode("classification")
```

The *recipe* stored in `RecipeTitanic` does not scale the data because this is not required for *Decision Trees* and other *tree-based* machine learning models.

For the *model design*, we use the command `decision_tree()` from the *R* package `rpart` (`set_engine("rpart")`), and set the analysis mode to classification (`set_mode("classification")`). The argument `tree_depth=3` determines that our *Decision Tree* has three levels (see Figure 10.1).

In a real-world application the `tree_depth` might be greater than three, but it should not be too high as this can cause *overfitting*.

To create a fitted *workflow* model, we add the *model design* and the *recipe* to a *workflow* and then use `fit(DataTrain)` to fit the model to the training data:

```
WfModelTitanic=workflow() |>
                add_model(ModelDesignDecTree) |>
                add_recipe(RecipeTitanic) |>
                fit(DataTrain)
```

The resulting *R* object `WfModelTitanic` can be used for predictions and to generate a graphical representation of the fitted *Decision Tree*:

```
library(rpart.plot)
rpart.plot(extract_fit_engine(WfModelTitanic),
            yes.text="YES", no.text="NO",roundint=FALSE)
```

The command `extract_fit_engine(WfModelTitanic)` extracts the model from the *workflow* `WfModelTitanic` and the `rpart.plot()` command plots the graphical representation of the fitted *Decision Tree* (see Figure 10.1).

We will later explain how the *Decision Tree* in Figure 10.1 was generated. For now, let us focus on how the tree can be used for predicting survival on the *Titanic*.

A *Decision Tree* like the one in Figure 10.1 consists of hierarchically organized nodes (the blue and green rectangles). It can be compared to an *ancestry tree*. The *root node* on top of the tree has no ancestors but is a *parent* to two *children*. Each of these *children* is a *parent* to two other *children*. This process continues until it stops at the bottom of the tree. The *terminal nodes* at the bottom have *parents* but no *children*.

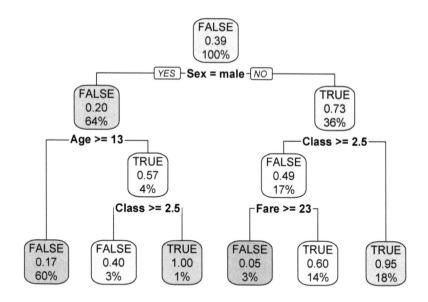

FIGURE 10.1 Decision Tree for Titanic Survival

In contrast to an *ancestry tree*, a *Decision Tree* is not used to display any ancestry. Instead, it guides observations from a dataset starting at the *root node* to one of the *terminal nodes*. *Decision rules* are used after each *parent node* to determine to which of the following two *child nodes* an observation is moved on its way towards the *terminal nodes*.

Decision Rules

A *decision rule* determines if an observation is moved to the left child or to the right child of a *parent node*. A *decision rule* states a condition such as Sex=male (see the first *decision rule* between the *root node* and its two children in Figure 10.1). The condition is either fulfilled *(YES)* or not fulfilled *(NO)*:

If the condition is fulfilled, the observation moves to the left child node. Otherwise, it moves to the right child node.

Now you know how an observation descends down from the *root node* to one of the *terminal nodes*. But how are the three labels inside each node interpreted, and how are they determined?

Let us begin at the *root node* and in our mind process the complete training dataset with all of its 664 observations at once through the *Decision Tree*:

- The *root node* contains the complete training dataset, which is indicated by the label "100%" in the third row of the *root node*. The second label indicates that, sadly, the survival rate was only *0.39* (39%). Since the survival rate is less than 0.5, we would predict that a random passenger (observation) does not survive ($\widehat{Survived} = FALSE$; see the first label in the *root node*).

- Next, all observations are moved from the *root node* to one of its two *child nodes* depending if the *decision rule* `Sex=male` is fulfilled (left child) or not (right child).

  Consequently, male observations (passengers) are moved to the left *child node* and female observations to the right *child node*. When reading the three labels from the left *child node*, we can see that 64% of the training data observations ended up in this node (64% of passengers in the training dataset are male). The survival rate among these passengers was only 0.2 (see second label), and therefore, we would predict that an individual male passenger does not survive ($\widehat{Survived} = FALSE$; $0.2 < 0.5$).

  The right *child node* contains only female observations. From the training data observations, 36% are female. For these female passengers, the survival rate was 0.73. Thus, for an individual female passenger, we would predict that she survives ($\widehat{Survived} = TRUE$; $0.73 > 0.5$).

  In summary: After the first split by *Sex*, we can conclude that men's survival chances were 20%, while the survival chances of women were 73%.

- The process does not stop after the split for *Sex*. When you look at the left *child node* below the *root node*, you can see that the male passengers are further split into older males (13 years and older; moved to the left *child node*) and younger males (moved to the right *child node*).

  Checking the labels in the left *child node* (a *terminal node*), you can see that 60% of the training observations were male and older than 13 years. The survival rate among those was only 0.17. Therefore, we would predict for an older male that he does not survive ($\widehat{Survived} = FALSE$; $0.17 < 0.5$).

  Checking the labels of the right *child node* (not a *terminal node*) below the *Age >= 13 decision rule* shows that 4% of the training observations were young males, and their survival rate was 0.57. Thus, for an individual young male (if we do not know in which class he traveled), we would predict that he survives ($\widehat{Survived} = TRUE$) because $(0.57 > 0.5)$.

- After all observations from the training dataset descend through the *Decision Tree*, they will end up in one of the six *terminal nodes*. Note that the percentages of training data in the six *terminal nodes* add up to 100% $(60\% + 3\% + 1\% + 3\% + 14\% + 18\% \approx 100\%)$.

  We know the survival rate for each *terminal node* based on the training observations that ended up in that node. Therefore, we can predict

($\widehat{Survived} = FALSE$ or $\widehat{Survived} = TRUE$) for each *terminal node* (see the first labels of the six *terminal nodes*).

Decision Tree Predictions for Binary vs. Continuous Variables

The prediction for a specific node for a binary variable like *Survived* (TRUE or FALSE) can be derived as follows:

Using all observations from the training dataset that end up in a specific node, find the proportion for the label TRUE. If this proportion is greater than 50%, predict TRUE for any observation that also ends up in this node. Otherwise, predict FALSE.

The prediction for a specific node for a continuous variable can be derived as follows:

Calculate the mean for the outcome variable from all training data observations that ended up in a specific node. This is the prediction for an observation's outcome that later also ends up in that node.

Now that you know how the training data were guided through the tree to one of the *terminal nodes*, you should be able to interpret the *Decision Tree* as a whole. Try to confirm the following five statements with the *Decision Tree* in Figure 10.1:

1. Adult male passengers 13 years or older, regardless of the class they traveled in and the fare they paid, had only a survival rate of 0.17.

2. Young male passengers (younger than 13 years), regardless of which class they traveled and the fare they paid, had a survival rate of 0.57.

3. Young male passengers (younger than 13 years) traveling in *Third Class* had only a survival rate of 0.4 regardless of the fare they paid.

4. Female passengers, regardless of age and not considering the class they traveled in or the fare they paid, had a survival rate of 0.73.

5. When considering the class female passengers traveled in, we can see female passengers, regardless of age, had a survival rate of 0.95 when they traveled in *First* or *Second Class* regardless of the fare they paid.

Note that not all *decision rules* and nodes from the *Decision Tree* in Figure 10.1 make sense — a major weakness of *Decision Trees*.

For example, if you look at the *decision rule* that created the fourth and fifth *terminal nodes* in Figure 10.1 and the related *parent node*, you can see that females traveling in *Third Class* had a lower survival rate when the fare they paid was more than 23 British pounds as compared to otherwise (5% vs. 60%). It makes little sense that a higher ticket price in the same class would lower somebody's survival chances.

TABLE 10.1 9-Year Old Boy on the Titanic

Survived	Sex	Class	Age	Fare
TRUE	male	3	9	15.9

We will discuss more problems related to the interpretability of *Decision Trees* in Section 10.3.2. For now, let us focus on predicting the observations from the testing dataset.

We start with taking a random observation from the testing dataset related to a nine year-old boy traveling in *Third Class* and see how to predict his survival:

From the testing data observation, we know already that the boy did survive ($Survived = TRUE$). However, we are interested in the *Decision Tree's* prediction ($\widehat{Survived}$).

Given that the passenger is male, younger than 13 years, and that he travels in *Third Class*, we can follow the observations through the *Decision Tree*. Starting at the *root node*, it moves to the left (male), then to the right (younger than 13 years), and then to the left (traveling in *Third Class*). The observation ends up in the second *terminal node* from the left and is predicted not to survive ($\widehat{Survived} = FALSE$).

However, if you look at the observation above, you can see that the passenger actually did survive. So, we count this testing observation as a *False Negative*.[2]

If we guide all testing observations through the *Decision Tree*, we can generate predictions for all testing observations and augment the predictions to the testing data frame `DataTest`:

```
DataTestWithPred=augment(WfModelTitanic, new_data=DataTest)
head(DataTestWithPred)
```

```
## # A tibble: 6 x 8
##    Survived Sex     Class   Age  Fare .pred_class
##    <fct>    <chr>   <int> <dbl> <dbl> <fct>
## 1 FALSE    male        3    22  7.25 FALSE
## 2 TRUE     female      1    35 53.1  TRUE
## 3 FALSE    male        3    27  8.46 FALSE
## 4 TRUE     female      3    27 11.1  TRUE
## 5 FALSE    female      3    31 18    TRUE
## 6 FALSE    male        2    35 26    FALSE
## # i 2 more variables: .pred_FALSE <dbl>,
## #    .pred_TRUE <dbl>
```

---

[2]Note, `tidymodels` treats `TRUE` (*survived*) as the positive class.

Since we know for each passenger (observation of the testing dataset) if they survived or not, and also what the *Decision Tree* predicted (see the .pred_class column), we can generate a *confusion matrix* and also use the metric_set() command to calculate the metrics *accuracy*, *sensitivity*, and *specificity* for the testing data:

```
conf_mat(DataTestWithPred, truth=Survived, estimate=.pred_class)
```

```
##              Truth
## Prediction TRUE  FALSE
##       TRUE    63    14
##      FALSE    23   123
```

```
metricSetTitanic=metric_set(accuracy, sensitivity, specificity)
metricSetTitanic(DataTestWithPred, truth=Survived, estimate=.pred_class)
```

```
## # A tibble: 3 x 3
##    .metric     .estimator .estimate
##    <chr>       <chr>          <dbl>
## 1 accuracy    binary         0.834
## 2 sensitivity binary         0.733
## 3 specificity binary         0.898
```

With an overall *accuracy* of 83%, the prediction results are not bad. The model worked particularly well in predicting passengers that did not survive (negative class; *specificity*). As you can see, *specificity* is higher than *sensitivity*. However, the difference is not big enough to consider the dataset as *unbalanced*.

This leaves us with one topic that we have not touched on so far:

How does the *Optimizer* determine the decision rules?

Decision rules are determined from the top of the *Decision Tree* down to the bottom. The *Optimizer* starts with finding the best *decision rule* for the *root node*, then moves down to the *child nodes* and finds the *decision rule* for each of the *child nodes* and then for the *child nodes* of the *child nodes*.[3] The process stops when either the maximum level set with the *hyper-parameter* level is reached (level=3 in our case) or when splitting a node further no longer increases the predictive quality.

Decision rules consist of two components:

1) The splitting variable. That is, the variable used to split the

---

[3] *Decision rules* of the previous level are never reversed, even if this would allow for a better *decision rule* on the current level. There is no turning back to reverse a *decision rule* on a previous level. This type of algorithm is called a *greedy algorithm*.

observations from the *parent node* into the two *child nodes*. For example, *Sex*, *Age*, or *Fare*.

2) The splitting value. The *splitting value* is relevant for continuous variables. For example, when the *splitting variable* is *Age*, we have to decide on the passenger's age that determines if an observation is moved to the left or the right *child node* (13 years or older for *YES* in our case; see Figure 10.1).

To find the best *splitting variable* with the best *splitting value*, the *Optimizer* compares all combinations of *splitting variables* and *splitting values*.[4]

What criterion determines if a splitting variable/value combination is good?

The *Decision Tree* algorithm from the `rpart` package uses *Gini Impurity* as a criterion for classification problems. Other measures that can be set include *Information Gain* and *Chi-Square*.[5] Here we focus on *Gini Impurity*.[6]

The *Titanic* passengers were different in many ways. Some of their differences (e.g., their *Sex*) were crucial for survival, while others were less important. When we split a *parent node* (for instance, the *root node*) into two *child nodes*, we want the two *child nodes* to be as different as possible regarding survival proportions. Ideally, we would like to get one *child node* with a survival proportion of 100% and the other with 0%. This would give us very good predictive quality. In that case, the two nodes would be perfectly pure, one containing a pure group of survivors and the other a pure group of non-survivors. *Gini Impurity* would be consequently at the lowest level for both *child nodes*.

Let us follow this admittedly unrealistic path by assuming that all men on the *Titanic* died and all women survived. A *decision rule* of `Sex=male` would create two pure *child nodes* with one containing only non-survivors and the other containing only survivors. *GiniImpurity* should be 0 for both pure *child nodes*.

Gini Impurity for an individual *child node* is defined by the product of the proportions for the observation for the two different classes ($P_{Surv.}$ and $P_{NonSurv.}$) multiplied by two. In our case:[7]

$$G^{Imp} = 2P_{Surv.}.P_{NonSurv.} \qquad (10.1)$$

In our example that creates two pure *child nodes*, Equation (10.1) shows the

---

[4]There are a few shortcuts that avoid considering all values of a variable as *splitting values*, but this exceeds the scope of this book.

[5]See Sharma (2020) for an intuitive description of the different standards.

[6]Singh (2021) provides an intuitive introduction about *Gini Impurity*.

[7]*Gini Impurity* is calculated for an individual node and estimates "(...) the probability that two entities taken at random from the dataset of interest (with replacement) represent (...) different types" (Wikipedia contributors (2023b)).

Gini Impurity for the female *child node* would indeed be 0 ($P_{Surv.} = 1$ and $P_{NonSurv.} = 0$) and the same would be true for the male *child node* with only non-survivors ($P_{Surv.} = 0$ and $P_{NonSurv.} = 1$).

Let us use another extreme example for a *decision rule* on the top level of the *Decision Tree* in Figure 10.1 and see how *Gini Impurity* changes from the *root node* to the two *child nodes*. We use `Blood Type = O` instead of `Sex = male`. Obviously, this *decision rule* makes little sense, since blood type will not influence the survival chance on the *Titanic*. The proportions of survivors in both *child nodes* would be approximately the same as in the *parent node* (the *root node*): $P_{Surv.} = 0.39$ and $P_{NonSurv.} = 0.61$ (see Figure 10.1).

Equation (10.1) shows that the resulting *Gini Impurities* would be the same for the *parent node* and the two *child nodes*:

$$G^{Imp}_{Parent} = G^{Imp}_{LeftChild} = G^{Imp}_{RightChild} = 2 \cdot 0.39 \cdot 0.61 = 0.48$$

The value of the *Gini Impurity* is not so crucial here. What is crucial is that the *decision rule* is unable to lower the *Gini Impurity* from the *parent node* to the *child nodes*. *Gini Impurity* was 0.48 in the parent node and the (weighted) average from the two *child nodes* is still 0.48. The *decision rule* is useless!

Finally, let us leave the extreme examples and take a look at the *decision rule* `Sex = male` from the *Decision Tree* in Figure 10.1. By how much could this *decision rule* lower *Gini Impurity*? We know already from the last example that the *root node* has a *Gini Impurity* of $G^{Imp}_{Parent} = 0.48$. According to Equation (10.1), the *Gini Impurity* for the left *child node* is (see Figure 10.1):

$$G^{Imp}_{male} = 2 \cdot 0.2 \cdot 0.8 = 0.32$$

The *Gini Impurity* for the right *child node* is:

$$G^{Imp}_{female} = 2 \cdot 0.73 \cdot 0.27 = 0.39$$

The *Gini Impurity* for a *decision rule* is the average of the two *child nodes* weighted by the proportion of the observations that ended up in the two *child nodes*:

$$G^{Imp}_{male/female} = 0.64 \cdot 0.32 + 0.36 \cdot 0.39 = 0.35$$

Consequently, the *decision rule* `Sex=male` decreased the *Gini Impurity* by 0.13 from $G^{Imp}_{Parent} = 0.48$ to $G^{Imp}_{male/female} = 0.35$.

We know that the *Optimizer* calculated the *Gini Impurity* decrease for all possible *splitting variable/value* combinations. Therefore, a *Gini Impurity* decrease of 0.13 must have been the largest. Otherwise, `Sex=male` would not have been chosen as the *decision rule*.

10.3.2   The Instability of Decision Trees

You saw already one drawback of *Decision Trees* in the previous section — not all *decision rules* make sense.

This section will show another drawback of *Decision Trees*. They react very sensitively to small changes. For example, in the code block below, the *Titanic* dataset is split into testing and training data:

```
set.seed(888)
Split7525=initial_split(DataTitanic, strata=Survived)
DataTrain=training(Split7525)
DataTest=testing(Split7525)
```

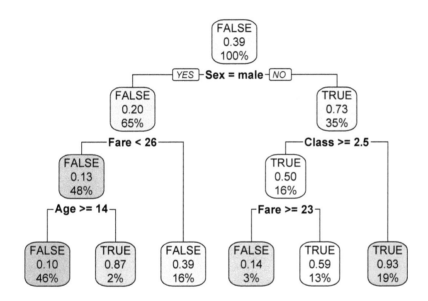

FIGURE 10.2 Decision Tree for Titanic Survival with set.seed(888)

The code is identical to the code from the previous section, except that the `set.seed()` command is changed from `set.seed(777)` to `set.seed(888)`, resulting in a change in the composition of the testing and training data.

Afterward, we processed the slightly changed training data with the same *R* code as in the previous section and created a *Decision Tree*. When assessing the new *Decision Tree* based on the testing data by calculating a *confusion matrix* and the related metrics, you can see below that the results did not change very much.

```
##           Truth
## Prediction TRUE FALSE
##      TRUE   64    14
##      FALSE  22   123

## # A tibble: 3 x 3
##   .metric    .estimator .estimate
##   <chr>      <chr>          <dbl>
## 1 accuracy   binary         0.839
## 2 sensitivity binary        0.744
## 3 specificity binary        0.898
```

However, when you compare the structure of the *Decision Tree* from Figure 10.1 from the previous section to the structure of the *Decision Tree* in Figure 10.2, which was created using `set.seed(888)` instead of `set.seed(777)`, you can see that different *decision rules* are used. A small change in the data led to a major change in the structure of the resulting *Decision Tree*, making interpretation questionable.

10.3.3 ◎ Project: Test the Instability of Decision Trees

In the following interactive project, you can research if what you observed in this section is an exception or if *Decision Trees* are generally reacting sensitively to small changes.

Interactive Section

In this section, you will find content together with *R* code to execute, change, and rerun in RStudio.

The best way to read and to work with this section is to open it with *RStudio*. Then you can interactively work on *R* code exercises and *R* projects within a web browser. This way you can apply what you have learned so far and extend your knowledge. You can also choose to continue reading either in the book or online, but you will not benefit from the interactive learning experience.

To work with this section in *RStudio* in an interactive environment, follow these steps:

1. Ensure that both the `learnR` and the `shiny` package are installed. If not, install them from RStudio's main menu (Tools -> Install Packages ...).

2. Download the `Rmd` file for the interactive session and save it in your `project` folder. You will find the link for the download below.

3. Open the downloaded file in RStudio and click the `Run Document` button, located in the editing window's top-middle area.

For detailed help for running the exercises including videos for Windows and Mac users we refer to: https://blog.lange-analytics.com/2024/01/interactsessions.html

Do not skip this interactive section because besides providing applications of already covered concepts, it will also extend what you have learned so far.

Below is the link to download the interactive section:

https://ai.lange-analytics.com/exc/?file=15-TreeBasedExerc100.Rmd

In the interactive project below, you can change the argument in the `set.seed()` to create different training and testing data and observe how the *confusion matrix* based on the testing data and the related metrics changes. You can also observe how the *Decision Tree* structure changes because, with the code block below, you will generate a graphical representation for the *Decision Trees* you generate.

To create new *Decision Trees*, you only need to change the argument in the `set.seed()` command and execute the code. We recommend the following procedure:

Step 1: Leave the `set.seed(777)` as it is and execute the code.

Step 2: Take a screenshot or use your phone to take a photo of the *confusion matrix*, the metrics for the testing data, and the graphical representation of the structure of the *Desision Tree*.

Step 3: Change the value for `set.seed()` to whatever value you like and go to Step 2.

Repeat **Step 2** and **Step 3** as often as you wish and save the results. When done, compare the results saved as screenshots or photos. You will likely find that the confusion matrices and the metrics did not change much, while the structure of the *Decision Trees* changed considerably.

```
set.seed(777)
Split7525=initial_split(DataTitanic, strata=Survived)
DataTrain=training(Split7525)
DataTest=testing(Split7525)

RecipeTitanic=recipe(Survived~., data=DataTrain)

ModelDesignDecTree=decision_tree(tree_depth=3) |>
                   set_engine("rpart") |>
                   set_mode("classification")

WfModelTitanic=workflow() |>
```

```
                    add_model(ModelDesignDecTree) |>
                    add_recipe(RecipeTitanic) |>
                    fit(DataTrain)

DataTestWithPred=augment(WfModelTitanic, new_data=DataTest)

# For better readability, we exchange the positive and
# negative classes, making TRUE the positive class.
library(tidyverse)
DataTestWithPred=mutate(DataTestWithPred,
                Survived=fct_relevel(Survived,"TRUE","FALSE"),
                .pred_class=fct_relevel(.pred_class,"TRUE","FALSE"))

library(rpart.plot)
rpart.plot(extract_fit_engine(WfModelTitanic),
           yes.text="YES", no.text="NO",roundint=FALSE)

conf_mat(DataTestWithPred, truth=Survived, estimate=.pred_class)
metricSetTitanic=metric_set(accuracy, sensitivity, specificity)
metricSetTitanic(DataTestWithPred, truth=Survived, estimate=.pred_class)
```

To summarize, interpreting *Decision Trees* is easy and straightforward. However, the fact that the structure of *Decision Trees* reacts so sensitively to small changes is a major obstacle to use *Decision Trees* for solving real-world problems. Imagine an irresponsible researcher who changes the set.seed() value until the structure of the *Decision Tree* reflects what they would like to see.

Why did we cover *Decision Trees* in this chapter if their interpretability is flawed and their predictive quality, although not bad, can be exceeded by other machine learning models?

The reason is that combining several *Decision Trees* gives us a very strong predictive quality. The combination of machine learning models of the same or different types is called an *ensemble*.

Combining many *Decision Trees* into one *ensemble* is what *Random Forest* and *Boosting Trees* models do. We will cover these *ensemble models* in the following sections.

10.4   Random Forest

A Random Forest is an *ensemble model* that can be used for classification and regression tasks. A *Random Forest* consists of many (sometimes hundreds or thousands) of slightly different *Decision Trees*. When these *Decision Trees* are created some *randomness* is involved. Thus the name *Random Forest*.

Since the *Decision Trees* in a *Random Forest* are all slightly different, they produce slightly different predictions. The prediction of a *Random Forest* model is calculated as the aggregation of all the predictions from the various *Decision Trees*:

- In the case of regression, the prediction from a *Random Forest* is calculated from the mean predictions of its *Decision Trees*.

- In the case of binary classification, the class that is predicted by the majority of *Decision Trees* will be the predicted class of the *Random Forest*. Sometimes, this is called "the vote of the *Decision Trees*" for a specific class.

10.4.1   The Idea Behind Random Forest

Although each individual *Decision Tree* inside the *Random Forest* is not well suited for prediction (*weak learners*), the idea is that the aggregation of *Decision Trees* leads to good predictive quality.

The idea that a combination of *weak learners* can lead to a strong prediction is analogous to the *Wisdom of Crowds* phenomenon described in Galton (1907):

Visitors at a stock and poultry exhibition in England submitted guesses about the weight of an ox. Although most of the visitors were off with their predictions, surprisingly, the mean of all predictions was very close to the actual weight of the ox.

In order to generate different predictions the *Decision Trees* in a *Random Forest* must be diverse — similar to the diverse visitors of Galton's stock and poultry exhibition. The question is:

How do Random Forest models ensure their Decision Trees are all (slightly) different?

Two strategies are employed by the *Random Forest* model that ensure a diverse set of *Decision Trees*:

Random Subspace Method: Every time a new *Decision Tree* is created (i.e., the *decision rules* for the tree), the *Random Forest* model does not consider all predictor variables. Instead, it uses only a random subset of predictor variables. So, for example, if we have seven predictor variables, two predictor variables are randomly selected as candidates for the best splitting rules for a specific *Decision Tree*. This limits the predictive quality of individual trees but increases diversity among trees.

The number of predictor variables considered for each tree in `tidymodels` is by default $\sqrt{M}$ (rounded down if needed), where M denotes the number of predictors in the model. So, for example, in a case where we have seven predictors, each *Decision Tree* will only consider two randomly chosen predictors ($\sqrt{7} = 2.65$; rounded down to 2). M is a *hyper-parameter* and can be either set or tuned.

Bagging: Every time a new *Decision Tree* is created, the *Random Forest* model uses a different training dataset. These different training datasets are derived from the original dataset by drawing observations from the original dataset with replacement(!!!) until the new training dataset contains the same number of observations as the original dataset. This procedure is called *Bootstrapping*.

Bootstrapping and Out-of-Bag Data

The three tables below show a training dataset and two *Bootstrap* samples derived from it:

Training Data					Bootstrap Sample 1					Bootstrap Sample 2			
ID	Name	Sex	Age		ID	Name	Sex	Age		ID	Name	Sex	Age
1	Adam	m	22		7	Gert	m	18		6	Fiola	f	87
2	Bertha	f	54		7	Gert	m	18		3	Carlos	m	32
3	Carlos	m	32		3	Carlos	m	32		5	Ernst	m	32
4	Dora	f	21		6	Fiola	f	87		4	Dora	f	21
5	Ernst	m	32		3	Carlos	m	32		6	Fiola	f	87
6	Fiola	f	87		2	Bertha	f	54		6	Fiola	f	87
7	Gert	m	18		2	Bertha	f	54		1	Adam	m	22

Suppose the two *Bootstrap* samples are used to build *Decision Tree 1* and a *Decision Tree 2*, respectively. You can see that *Bootstrap Sample 1* contains the observations for Bertha, Carlos, and Gert twice. At the same time, the observations for Adam, Dora, and Ernst are not included in this dataset. The observations for Adam, Dora, and Ernst are consequently not used to train *Decision Tree 1*. Since these observations are not in the *bag of the training data* for *Decision Tree 1*, they are called *Out-of-Bag* data.

Out-of-Bag (OOB) data are very useful because they can be used for validation purposes. After all, they were never used to train the related *Decision Tree*. The number of *OOB* observations is also reasonably large because the expected value for the number of observations falling in the *OOB* dataset is about 1/3 of the training dataset.

As an exercise try to find the *OOB* data for *Decision Tree 2*.[a]

---

[a]The *OOB* sample for *Decision Tree 2* consists of Bertha and Gert.

10.4.2 Predicting Vaccination Behavior with Random Forest

Now it is time to showcase an application for *Random Forest*. In this section, we will use a *Random Forest* model to predict the U.S. vaccination rates during the *COVID-19* pandemic. The analysis is based on research conducted by the author and his co-author, published in October 2022.[8]

The data are from September 2021 and the outcome variable is the proportion of fully vaccinated (two shots) residents in 2,630 continental U.S. counties (*PercVacFull*).[9]

The following predictor variables were used:

Race/Ethnicity: Proportion of African Americans (*PercBlack*), Asian Americans (*PercAsian*), and Hispanics (*PercHisp*) for the county.[10]

Political Affiliation: The proportion of voters who voted for the *Republican* presidential candidate (*PercRep*).[11] Since only *Republican* and *Democratic* votes were considered, the proportion of voters who voted for the *Democratic* presidential candidate equals $(1 - PercRep)$.

Age Groups: Proportion of young adults (20 – 25 years; *PercYoung25*) and proportion of older adults (65 years and older; (*PercOld65*)).[12]

Income-related: To control for income effects, we used the county's proportion of households receiving food stamps (*PercFoodSt*).[13]

In the code block below, we load the data, select the variables to use, and split the observations into training and testing data:

```
DataVax=import("https://ai.lange-analytics.com/data/DataVax.rds") |>
        select(PercVacFull, PercRep,
               PercAsian, PercBlack, PercHisp,
               PercYoung25, PercOld65,
               PercFoodSt, Population) |>
        mutate(Population=frequency_weights(Population))
set.seed(2021)
Split85=initial_split(DataVax, prop=0.85, strata=PercVacFull, breaks=3)
```

---

[8]See Lange and Lange (2022).

[9]Source: Centers for Disease Control and Prevention (CDC) (2021a).

[10]Source: Centers for Disease Control and Prevention (CDC) (2021b).

[11]Source for the raw data: Park, A. et al. (2021). The authors of Lange and Lange (2022) calculated the proportions.

[12]Source: Centers for Disease Control and Prevention (CDC) (2021b).

[13]Source: Esri (Environmental Systems Research Institute) (2023). The author thanks *ESRI* for the permission to use their proprietary data for the interactive sections of this book.

```
DataTrain=training(Split85)
DataTest=testing(Split85)
```

Above, you can see that *Population* (i.e., the population of the related U.S. county)[14] was selected as one of the variables, although *Population* is neither an outcome nor a predictor variable for this research. *Population* will be used later in the *workflow model* to weigh the observations. To mark the variable *Population* as being neither outcome nor predictor variable, we used the command `frequency_weights()`.

The `recipe()` in the code block below is the same as in Section 10.3.2 except that now *PercVacFull* is chosen as the outcome variable.

```
RecipeVax=recipe(PercVacFull~., data=DataTrain)
```

The dot in the argument `PercVacFull~.` indicates that all variables in `Data-Train` except the outcome, *PercVacFull*, should be used as predictor variables. However, the variable *Population* is also excluded because we marked it as *frequency weight* when we loaded the data and selected the variables.

In the code block below, we define the *model design* and use the `rand_forest()` command to choose a *Random Forest* model from the *R* ranger package (see `set_engine()`). To keep things simple, we set the *hyper-parameters* rather than tuning them:

```
library(parallel)
ModelDesignRandFor=rand_forest(min_n=5, mtry=2, trees=2000) |>
                   set_engine("ranger",  num.threads=detectCores()) |>
                   set_mode("regression")
```

We set `min_n=5`, which means that at least five observations are required in a node of a *Decision Tree* to allow a split and to create two new *child nodes*. The *hyper-parameter* `mtry` determines the number of randomly chosen variables as candidates for a split in the *Decision Trees*. It is set to `mtry=2`. Both settings coincide with the defaults for *Random Forest*.[15]

We increased the number of *Decision Trees* used for the *Random Forest* from the default (`trees=500`) to `trees=2000`. In contrast to the *hyper-parameters* `min_n` and `mtry`, a high number of trees in a *Random Forest* cannot cause *overfitting*.

The last argument we provide in the code block above is determined in

---

[14] Source: Centers for Disease Control and Prevention (CDC) (2021b).

[15] `min_n=5` is the default for regression problems, and the default for `mtry` is calculated as $\sqrt{Number of Predictors} = \sqrt{7} \approx 2$ (rounded down), as we have seven predictor variables.

the set_engine() command. The *Random Forest* implementation in tidy-models allows us to execute R code parallel on multiple computer cores to speed up computing time. *Random Forest* is well suited for parallel computing because the various *Decision Trees* can be developed independently from each other in any order and afterward combined into a *Random Forest*. We set the argument num.threads (the number of processes that run in parallel) to be equal to the number of computer cores of the executing computer (num.threads=detectCores()). This worked well on a computer with 16 logical cores.

In the code block below, we create the *workflow* and add the *recipe*, the *model design*, and we add the variable *Population* with add_case_weights(Population) to weigh the observations with their respective county's population:

```
set.seed(2021)
WfModelVax=workflow() |>
            add_recipe(RecipeVax) |>
            add_model(ModelDesignRandFor) |>
            add_case_weights(Population) |>
            fit(DataTrain)
```

Weighting the county observations with their population is needed because the U.S. counties have very different population sizes. Using unweighted observations would implicitly assign the same weight to counties with a few hundred residents as counties with millions of residents, which would not be reasonable.

When printing WfModelVax, you can see the setup of the fitted *workflow* and, in addition, how it performed on the *OOB* dataset.

```
## == Workflow [trained] =======================
## Preprocessor: Recipe
## Model: rand_forest()
##
## -- Preprocessor ---------------------------
## 0 Recipe Steps
##
## -- Case Weights ---------------------------
## Population
##
## -- Model ----------------------------------
## Ranger result
##
## Call:
##   ranger::ranger(x = maybe_data_frame(x), y = y, mtry = min_cols(~2,
##
```

```
## Type:                             Regression
## Number of trees:                  2000
## Sample size:                      2234
## Number of independent variables:  7
## Mtry:                             2
## Target node size:                 5
## Variable importance mode:         none
## Splitrule:                        variance
## OOB prediction error (MSE):       0.01218
## R squared (OOB):                  0.4281
```

The performance on the *OOB* validation data is pretty good, but the real challenge is the testing data. To see how the model performs on the testing data, we have to augment the testing data with the predictions and then use the `metrics()` command to generate and print the performance metrics:

```
DataTestWithPred=augment(WfModelVax, new_data=DataTest)
metrics(DataTestWithPred, truth=PercVacFull, estimate=.pred)
```

```
## # A tibble: 3 x 3
##    .metric .estimator .estimate
##    <chr>   <chr>          <dbl>
## 1 rmse     standard       0.109
## 2 rsq      standard       0.458
## 3 mae      standard       0.0753
```

The *Random Forest* model over/underestimates the counties' vaccination rates by about eight percentage points ($mae = 0.0753$).

In the next section, 10.5, we will introduce some *Boosting Trees* algorithms. *Boosting Trees* algorithms are more advanced than *Random Forest*. They run faster, and their predictive performance is similar and sometimes better than the performance of *Random Forest*.

10.5 Boosting Trees Algorithms

As mentioned above, *Boosting Trees* algorithms are an improvement of *Random Forest*. They are based on many *Decision Trees* like *Random Forest*. However, the underlying *Decision Trees* are not randomly modified as in *Random Forest*. Instead, they are *boosted* by weighing the training data used for each *Decision Tree* or by changing how the *Decision Trees* are created and combined. Examples for *Boosting Trees* algorithms are:

- **AdaBoost:** *AdaBoost* is an *ensemble* algorithm like *Random Forest*. The *AdaBoost* algorithm uses only *tree stumps* (*Decisision Trees* with one level tree depth) for its trees. It starts by using the outcome and predictor variables from the training dataset to create the first tree.[16] Then, for the second and following *Decision Trees*, the errors of the previous *Decision Tree* are used as outcome variables. When these *Decision Trees* are combined to generate a prediction, they are weighted according to their predictive quality. Higher weight is assigned to trees with better predictive quality. This weighting of the trees is in contrast to a *Random Forest*, which uses an unweighted average for combining the predictions from its *Decision Trees*.

  We mention **AdaBoost** here because it was one of the earliest *Boosting Trees* algorithms. However, we will not go into more detail because, meanwhile, more powerful *Boosting Trees* algorithms have been developed.[17]

- **Gradient Boosting:** This is a very powerful algorithm. *Gradient Boosting* starts with creating a first prediction based on the mean of the training dataset's outcome variable. To create the first tree, it uses the errors from the first prediction as the outcome variable and the variables from the training data as predictor variables. Afterward, it combines the initial prediction and the prediction from the first *Decision Tree*. Then, based on the resulting new prediction errors, it creates a second *Decision Tree*. Afterward, based on the errors from this prediction, it creates a third tree. This process continues until a predefined number of trees is created, or another stopping criteria is reached.

  We will cover *Gradient Boosting* in more detail in Section 10.5.1.[18]

- **XGBoost:** The *XGBoost* algorithm[19] is a variation of *Gradient Boosting*. The major difference is that it is optimized for performance as it supports parallelization to use multiple computer cores, and it supports *distributed computing* to run the algorithm simultaneously on a cluster of computers. This makes *XGBoost* significantly faster than regular *Gradient Boosting* especially for large datasets. In addition, *XGBoost* penalizes complex models, which helps to avoid *overfitting*.

  You will use the `tidymodels` implementation of *XGBoost* in the interactive Section 10.5.2 to predict vaccination behavior with the same dataset that was used in the previous section with *Random Forest*.[20]

- **LightGBM and CATBoost:** These two algorithms are mentioned here because they are improvements of *XGBoost* in terms of computer processing

---

[16] *AdaBoost* is based on a paper by Freund and Schapire (1996).
[17] See Kurama (2018) for more details about *AdaBoost*.
[18] See Yıldırım (2020) for an introduction to *Gradient Boosting*.
[19] See Chen and Guestrin (2016).
[20] See Morde (2019) for an introduction to *XGBoost*.

time and the data volume the algorithms can handle, but they will not be covered further in this book.[21]

Both algorithms are currently not directly available through `tidymodels`, but they can be used in connection with the `treesnip` package.

10.5.1   The Idea Behind Gradient Boosting

As mentioned above *Gradient Boosting* builds *Decision Trees* based on prediction errors. Since no prediction errors are available at the starting point when building the *Gradient Boosting ensemble*, an initial prediction is needed. *Gradient Boosting* starts with the mean of the outcome variable as prediction for all observations. Afterward, it uses the errors from previous predictions to build new trees to enrich the *ensemble*.

To explain the process in more detail, let us see step-by-step how *Gradient Boosting* works. To keep it simple, we limit the *ensemble* to only three *Decision Trees*. In reality *Gradient Boosting* works with many more *Decision Trees*.[22]

Let us assume we want to create an *ensemble* with *Decision Trees* D_1^{ecTree}, D_2^{ecTree}, and D_3^{ecTree}. The goal is to predict an outcome variable Y_i.

As mentioned above, the initial prediction is only based on the mean of the outcome variable from the training dataset:

$$\widehat{Y}_i = \overline{Y} := \frac{1}{N} \sum_{i=1}^{N} Y_i \qquad (10.2)$$

Note that Equation (10.2) implies that the predictions for all observations are the same because the mean of the outcome variable is a single number. This is reasonable, but Equation (10.2) represents a very weak learner, and thus we have to expect large prediction errors ($u_{0,i}$). We can calculate these errors for all training observations because we know the true outcome for each training observation:

$$u_{0,i} = Y_i - \overline{Y} \qquad (10.3)$$

Note that the index 0 in $u_{0,i}$ indicates that the errors for the i observations are related to the starting prediction in the *ensemble*. Equation (10.3) can also be written as Equation (10.4), which states that at the initial stage, the known outcomes from the training dataset Y_i consist of the predicted outcome ($\overline{Y}$) and the related errors ($u_{0,i}$):

---

[21] See Pramoditha (2021) for and introduction to *LightGBM* and Delgado (2022) for *Cat-Boost*.

[22] For example, the default for the *XGBoost* algorithm we use in this section is 15 and can be tuned. Using 100 or more trees is not uncommon.

$$Y_i = \overline{Y} + u_{0,i} \tag{10.4}$$

Because we used a *weak learner*, the errors, $u_{0,i}$, most likely contain systematic impacts on the outcome. To integrate these systematic impacts, we can create a *Decision Tree* ($D_1^{ecTree}(Obs_i)$) that uses the known errors (see Equation (10.3)) as values for the outcome variable and variables from the training dataset as predictor variables (Obs_i). Predicting errors seems to be a little odd, but please bear with us. It will make perfect sense very soon.

Below is the prediction equation for the initial errors based on the first *Decision Tree*:

$$\hat{u}_{0,i} = D_1^{ecTree}(Obs_i) \tag{10.5}$$

Since the *Decision Tree* in Equation (10.5) does not predict the initial errors ($u_{0,i}$) perfectly, it will also create its own prediction errors ($u_{1,i}$). Consequently, the true initial errors consist of the predictions from the first *Decision Tree* and the errors related to these predictions:

$$u_{0,i} = \underbrace{D_1^{ecTree}(Obs_i)}_{\hat{u}_{0,i}} + u_{1,i} \tag{10.6}$$

Substituting Equation (10.6) into Equation (10.4) gives us:

$$Y_i = \underbrace{\overline{Y} + D_1^{ecTree}(Obs_i)}_{\widehat{Y}_i} + u_{1,i} \tag{10.7}$$

Now, you can see why predicting errors makes sense. Equation (10.7) shows that the predictions $\widehat{Y}_i$ improved. It is not only based on the mean of the outcome ($\overline{Y}$) but also on the first *Decision Tree's* prediction ($D_1^{ecTree}(Obs_i)$).

Gradient Boosting uses a slight modification from the prediction in Equation (10.7). *Gradient Boosting* predicts the outcome at the stage of the first *Decision Tree* as:

$$Y_i = \underbrace{\overline{Y} + \gamma D_1^{ecTree}(Obs_i)}_{\widehat{Y}_i} + u_{1,i} \quad \text{with: } 0 < \gamma < 1 \tag{10.8}$$

Equation (10.8) is identical to Equation (10.7), except that the influence of the *Decision Tree* on the prediction is weakened by multiplying with the learning rate γ. The learning rate γ is a tuneable *hyper-parameter*. It is usually set to values considerably smaller than one. For example, the *Gradient Boosting* algorithm *XGBoost* in tidymodels uses $\gamma = 0.3$ as the default learning rate.

Since in Equation (10.8) γ weakens the influence of the first and only *Decision*

Tree, it is reasonable to assume that the related errors $(u_{1,i})$ still contain some systematic impacts on the outcome variable Y. Therefore, we create a second *Decision Tree* $(D_2^{ecTree}(Obs_i))$ based on the predictor variables in the training dataset and the known errors from the first *Decision Tree*. These errors are known because we can calculate them as the difference between the known outcome values from the training dataset and the predictions from Equation (10.8):

$$u_{1,i} = Y_i - \underbrace{\overline{Y} + \gamma D_1^{ecTree}(Obs_i)}_{\widehat{Y}_i} \quad \text{with: } 0 < \gamma < 1$$

After creating the second *Decision Tree* $(D_2^{ecTree}(Obs_i))$ to predict the errors from the first *Decision Tree* $(u_{1,i})$, the prediction equation for the outcome Y improves to:

$$Y_i = \underbrace{\overline{Y} + \gamma D_1^{ecTree}(Obs_i) + \gamma D_2^{ecTree}(Obs_i)}_{\widehat{Y}_i} + u_{2,i} \quad \text{with: } 0 < \gamma < 1$$

The errors from the prediction by the second *Decision Tree* $(u_{2,i})$ may still contain some systematic information, and since their values are known, we can use a third *Decision Tree* to integrate the systematic impacts from these errors, which leads to:

$$Y_i \;\; = \;\; \underbrace{\overline{Y} + \gamma D_1^{ecTree}(Obs_i) + \gamma D_2^{ecTree}(Obs_i) + \gamma D_3^{ecTree}(Obs_i)}_{\widehat{Y}_i} + u_{3,i}$$
$$\text{with: } 0 < \gamma < 1$$

$$\widehat{Y}_i \;\; = \;\; \overline{Y} + \gamma D_1^{ecTree}(Obs_i) + \gamma D_2^{ecTree}(Obs_i) + \gamma D_3^{ecTree}(Obs_i) \quad (10.9)$$
$$\text{with: } 0 < \gamma < 1$$

We stop here since we decided to use only three *Decision Trees*. In real-world applications, many more trees would be added. In fact, the number of *Decision Trees* to be added is a tuneable *hyper-parameter* for *Gradient Boosting* models.

Equation (10.9) can be used to predict the outcome Y_i for any observation i as long as the values for the predictor variables (Obs_i) are known. For example, we could use the observations from a testing dataset to assess how well a *Gradient Boosting* model performs.

Equation (10.9) also allows us to explain why weakening the influence of the *Decision Trees* through the *learning rate* γ makes sense. Assume we would have a prediction equation such as Equation (10.9) without a learning rate γ but with many more *Decision Trees*. The errors of each *Decision Tree* would be corrected by the following *Decision Tree*, and this correction would not be artificially weakened. Such an ongoing unregulated correction could lead to a severe *overfitting* problem because the prediction equation could possibly approximate the training data almost perfectly.

10.5.2 ⊘ Using XGBoost to Predict Vaccination Rates

Interactive Section

In this section, you will find content together with R code to execute, change, and rerun in RStudio.

The best way to read and to work with this section is to open it with *RStudio*. Then you can interactively work on R code exercises and R projects within a web browser. This way you can apply what you have learned so far and extend your knowledge. You can also choose to continue reading either in the book or online, but you will not benefit from the interactive learning experience.

To work with this section in *RStudio* in an interactive environment, follow these steps:

1. Ensure that both the learnR and the shiny package are installed. If not, install them from RStudio's main menu (Tools -> Install Packages ...).

2. Download the Rmd file for the interactive session and save it in your project folder. You will find the link for the download below.

3. Open the downloaded file in RStudio and click the Run Document button, located in the editing window's top-middle area.

For detailed help for running the exercises including videos for Windows and Mac users we refer to: https://blog.lange-analytics.com/2024/01/interactsessions.html

Do not skip this interactive section because besides providing applications of already covered concepts, it will also extend what you have learned so far.

Below is the link to download the interactive section:

https://ai.lange-analytics.com/exc/?file=15-TreeBasedExerc200.Rmd

In this section, you will use a *Gradient Boosting* algorithm to predict vaccination rates in U.S. counties based on socioeconomic predictor variables. We will use the same data and predictor variables that we used in Section 10.4 (see Section 10.4.2 for details about the data).

To be precise, we will use *XGBoost*, which is available in the tidymodels package. *XGBoost* is based on *Gradient Boosting*, but it is a more advanced and a more effective type of *Gradient Boosting*. This is because *XGBoost* is optimized for parallel processing and thus can run simultaneously on different *CPUs* on your computer. Optionally, it can run in a distributed environment. That is, it can run on different computers at the same time. You will see how fast the *XGBoost* algorithm is when you run and tune an *XGBoost* machine learning model on your computer, but first, let us prepare the tuning.

We start with downloading the data, selecting the outcome, the predictor variables, and the variable we will use later to weigh our observations.

```
library(rio); library(tidymodels); library(xgboost)
DataVax=import("https://ai.lange-analytics.com/data/DataVax.rds") |>
        select(PercVacFull, PercRep,
               PercAsian, PercBlack, PercHisp,
               PercYoung25, PercOld65,
               PercFoodSt, Population) |>
          mutate(Population=frequency_weights(Population))
```

Since we will tune some of the *hyper-parameters* of the *XGBoost* algorithm, we again use the *10-Step Tuning Template* from Section 6.6:

Step 1 - Generate Training and Testing Data: The training and testing data are generated as follows:

```
set.seed(2021)
Split85=initial_split(DataVax, prop=0.85, strata=PercVacFull,
                      breaks=3)

DataTrain=training(Split85)
DataTest=testing(Split85)
```

Step 2 - Create a Recipe: The *recipe* below determines the outcome variable (*PercVacFull*) and chooses all other variables as predictor variables, which excludes *Population* because this variable was set to `frequency_weights()` when the data were loaded and the variables were selected:

```
RecipeVax=recipe(PercVacFull~., data=DataTrain)
```

Step 3 - Create a Model Design: The *model design* below uses the `boost_tree()` command to choose a *Gradient Boosting* machine learning model. The algorithm *XGBoost* is selected in the `set_engine()` command with the argument `xgboost`. Since we predict a continuous variable (the vaccination rate), `set_mode()` is set to `regression`:

```
ModelDesignBoostTrees=boost_tree(trees=tune(), tree_depth=tune())|>
                      set_engine("xgboost") |>
                      set_mode("regression")
```

For the `boost_tree()` command, we set two *hyper-parameters* up for tuning. The *hyper-parameter* `trees` determines the number of *Decision Trees*, and the *hyper-parameter* `tree_depth` specifies how many levels each of these *Decision Trees* has.

Step 4 - Add the Recipe and the Model Design to a Workflow: As before, we add the *recipe* and the *model design* to a *workflow*:

```
WfModelVax=workflow() |>
           add_model(ModelDesignBoostTrees) |>
           add_recipe(RecipeVax) |>
           add_case_weights(Population)
```

Note the command `add_case_weights(Population)` at the end of the *workflow model*. It ensures that the observations (the U.S. counties) are weighted according to their population.

Steps 1 – 4 are already prepared for you and executed in the background. Below, you can execute the code block for **Steps 5 – 10** from the *10-Step Tuning template*.

In **Step 5**, the *hyper-parameter* values that are tried out are determined in the *parameter grid*. We encourage you to experiment with these values.

In **Step 6**, ten folds are chosen for *Cross-Validation*. You may change `v=10` to a lower value to speed up the tuning process.

Step 7 tunes the *workflow model*. Note that the command `doParallel::registerDoParallel()` prepares the tuning for parallelization. It is essential to install the `doParallel` package before you tune. Otherwise, *R* will throw an error. After tuning is completed, the `autoplot` command will visualize the *Cross-Validation* performance for all chosen *hyper-parameter* combinations.

In **Step 8**, the *hyper-parameters* that performed best with the *Cross-Validation* folds are chosen to use them in a final model in **Step 9**.

This best model is then evaluated based on the testing data in **Step 10**.

After you load the code below into *RStudio* (see the info box at the beginning of this section), we recommend to Run the Document in a browser without any changes. Afterward, evaluate the diagram generated by `autoplot()`, change the *hyper-parameter* values in Step 5 accordingly, and execute the code block again.

```
# Step 5 - Create a Hyper-Parameter Grid
set.seed(2021)
ParGridVax=expand.grid(tree_depth=c(1, 2, 5, 10, 15),
                       trees=c(5, 10, 15, 50, 100))

# Step 6 - Create Resamples for Cross-Validation:
FoldsVax=DataTrain |>
         vfold_cv(v=10, strata=PercVacFull, breaks=5)
```

```r
# Step 7 - Tune the Workflow and Train All Models:
# Make sure the doParallel package is installed!!!
doParallel::registerDoParallel()


set.seed(2021)
StartTime=Sys.time()
TuneResultsVax=tune_grid(WfModelVax,
                         resamples=FoldsVax,
                         grid=ParGridVax,
                         metrics=metric_set(mae))
RunTime=Sys.time()- StartTime

# Visualize tuning results
print("TUNING RESULTS:")
autoplot(TuneResultsVax)

# Step 8 - Extract the Best Hyper-Parameter(s):
BestParVax=select_best(TuneResultsVax, metric="mae")



# Step 9 - Finalize and Train the Best Workflow Model:
set.seed(2021)
BestWFModelVax=finalize_workflow(WfModelVax, BestParVax) |>
               fit(DataTrain)

# Step 10 - Assess Prediction Quality Based on the Testing Data:
DataTestWithPred=augment(BestWFModelVax, new_data=DataTest)
MetricsBestModel=metrics(DataTestWithPred, truth=PercVacFull,
                         estimate=.pred)

# Print computation time
print("TUNING TIME:")
print(RunTime)

# Best parameters from tuning
print("BEST PARAMETERS:")
print(BestParVax)

# Print metrics for best model
print("TESTING DATA METRICS BEST MODEL:")
print(MetricsBestModel)
```

When you execute the code block above unchanged in *RStudio*, your results should be similar to the ones below.

Figure 10.3 shows a visualization for the predictive performance for all tried out *hyper-parameter* values based on *Cross-Validation*.

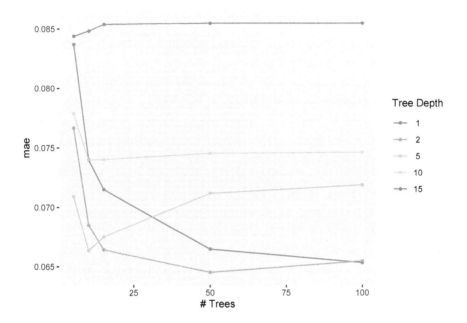

FIGURE 10.3 Tuning the Tree Depth and the Number of Trees

You can see that the `mae` (*mean absolute error*) was lowest for a `tree_depth` value of two in combination with 50 *Decision Trees*. This makes sense. A *Decison Tree* with only two levels is a very *weak learner*. Therefore, even after processing the errors through many trees, some systematic information was left over so that even *Decision Tree* number 50 had something to contribute.

You can see that `tree_depth` values of 10 and 15 did not perform very well. Maybe you should try a few `tree_depth` values below or slightly above five.

The situation is not as clear for the number of trees. It looks like that significantly more than 50 trees cannot considerably lower the error. However, for a *Decision Tree* with only one level (also called a *tree stump*), it might make sense to increase the number of trees used to more than 100. This might lower the `mae` even beyond the current minimum because the red line in Figure 10.3 indicates a falling `mae` for `tree_depth=1`.

10.6   When and When Not to Use Tree-Based Models

- *Decision Trees* have a high educational value because the graphical representation provides an intuitive way to see which variables influenced the predictions.

- As a standalone model *Decision Trees* should not be used for solving *real-world* problems. The reasons are:

  - Although most *decision rules* are reasonably interpretable, some *decision rules* might not make sense. This is a serious drawback from the otherwise good interpretability of *Decision Trees*.

  - The structure of *Decision Trees* responds very sensitively to a change in *hyper-parameters* such as the tree depth or minor changes in the data. With an unstable tree structure, interpretation becomes challenging and is not credible.

  - *Decision Trees* are *weak learners* in the sense that other machine learning models often perform better.

- Although *Decision Trees* are *weak learners*, combining many *Decision Trees* into an *ensemble model* such as *Random Forest* or *Boosting Trees* models often leads to excellent predictive results.

- *Random Forest* models are a good choice for regression and classification tasks. This is especially true when non-linearity or predictor variable interactions are suspected in the underlying data. Generally, using a linear *OLS* model as a benchmark is always a good idea to evaluate if the data present a linear process that can be addressed with *OLS*.

- For very complex models with many predictor variables, *Deep Learning* models such as *Neural Networks* may be a better choice, and these models should be run in addition to *Random Forest* as an alternative to evaluate, if they perform better.

- If computing time is an issue when running a *Random Forest* model, *Boosting Trees* algorithms such as *XGBoost* might be the better choice. For example, *XGBoost* performs faster than *Random Forest*, and its predictive quality is similar and often better than *Random Forest*.

10.7 Digital Resources

Below you will find a few digital resources related to this chapter such as:

- Videos
- Short articles
- Tutorials
- *R* scripts

These resources are recommended if you would like to review the chapter from a different angle or to go beyond what was covered in the chapter.

Here we show only a few of the digital resourses. At the end of the list you will find a link to additonal digital resources for this chapter that are maintained on the Internet.

You can find a complete list of digital resources for all book chapters on the companion website: https://ai.lange-analytics.com/digitalresources.html

10.7.1 Decision Trees

Decision and Classification Trees, Clearly Explained!!! from StatQuest by Josh Starmer

The video introduces the basics of Decision Trees for classification. It is a good video to start learning about Decision Trees.

Link: https://ai.lange-analytics.com/dr?a=407

Regression Trees, Clearly Explained!!! from StatQuest by Josh Starmer

The video introduces the basics of Decision Trees used for regression. We recommend watching the StatQuest video about Decision Trees for classification first.

Link: https://ai.lange-analytics.com/dr?a=403

Decision Trees in Machine Learning Using R from DataCamp by James Le and Arunn Thevapalan

This is a free tutorial from *DataCamp* about *Decision Trees*. The provided *R* code shows how to build a Decision Tree model using *tidymodels*.

Link: https://ai.lange-analytics.com/dr?a=408

More Digital Resources

Only a subset of digital resources is listed in this section. The link below points to additional, concurrently updated resources for this chapter.

Link: https://ai.lange-analytics.com/dr/dectrees.html

10.7.2   Random Forest

Random Forests Part 1 - Building, Using and Evaluating from StatQuest by Josh Starmer

This video is Part 1 of a video series about Random Forest. The video explains the basics of Random Forest, including an introduction to Bootstrapping.

Link: https://ai.lange-analytics.com/dr?a=409

Tuning Hyper Parameters in a Random Forest Model

This blog post by Carsten Lange shows how the *hyper-parameters* of a *Random Forest* model that estimates *COVID-19* vaccination rates in 2021 can be tuned using the *10-Step Tuning* template.

Link: https://ai.lange-analytics.com/dr?a=353

More Digital Resources

Only a subset of digital resources is listed in this section. The link below points to additional, concurrently updated resources for this chapter.

Link: https://ai.lange-analytics.com/dr/randforest.html

10.7.3   Boosting Trees Algorithms

Gradient Boosting Video from StatQuest

A video from *StatQuest* by Josh Starmer. The video is the first part of four videos about *Gradient Boosting*. This video focuses on the main ideas behind using *Gradient Boosting* to predict a continuous variable.

Link: https://ai.lange-analytics.com/dr?a=404

Tuning XGBoost with tidymodels

This blog post from *tidyTuesday* by Julia Silge describes how to use *tidymodels* to build and tune an *XGBoost* model. The goal is to predict the outcome of volleyball games. The blog post also provides a video and an *R* tutorial.

Link: https://ai.lange-analytics.com/dr?a=406

More Digital Resources

Only a subset of digital resources is listed in this section. The link below points to additional, concurrently updated resources for this chapter.

Link: https://ai.lange-analytics.com/dr/boosttrees.html

11

Interpreting Machine Learning Results

In the previous chapters, you learned about different machine learning algorithms and applied machine learning models to predict continuous and categorical outcomes based on a set of predictor variables. We have also touched upon how to analyze the prediction errors to evaluate the performance of a machine learning model.

This chapter examines how a model's predictor variables impact the predictions of an outcome. In other words, what factors are most important for the model's outcome prediction, and how much do they contribute.

Being able to interpret machine learning results is crucial for many applications. For example, mortgage lenders can use machine learning models to estimate default risk scores for loan applications.

If a loan applicant is not approved, the bank must be able to explain the factors influencing the model's prediction to ensure that the decision is fair and unbiased.

Not that long ago, many machine learning models, especially *Deep Learning* models, would be considered *black box* models, meaning that although they generate excellent prediction results, they fail to provide insights on how the predictions are derived, which variables are the most important ones, and how much each variable contributed to the predicted outcome. The *black box* problem turned some analysts to linear *OLS* models because their results are much more interpretable.[1] However, this caused a dilemma. Although the prediction results from linear *OLS* models are more interpretable, they often do not produce a predictive quality comparable to non-linear machine learning models such as *Random Forest* or *Neural Network*.

The good news is that researchers made significant progress in recent years in machine learning interpretability. There are so many techniques to interpret

---

[1]The coefficients for the predictive variables show how a change of a variable will impact the prediction, the *P-values* indicate the significance of the prediction, and the overall contribution of the predictor variables is additive separable. You can find more about the interpretation of *OLS* and its limits in Wooldridge (2020).

machine learning models that we can only cover a few selected algorithms in this book.[2]

In this chapter, we will introduce interpretation techniques to answer the following three questions for specific machine learning models, such as *tree-based* models, but also for machine learning models in general:

Impacts of Predictor Variable Change

Question 1: If the value of a predictor variable changes, how will this impact the predicted outcome?

In Section 11.5, we analyze how the prediction for a specific observation would change if one of the values for one of the predictor variables changes. We will visualize the result with a so-called *Ceteris Paribus Plot*.

As an example, think about the loan applicant case. How would the predicted risk score change if the applicant's yearly salary were higher or lower?

We also use *Partial Dependence Plots* in Section 11.5 to quantify and visualize the impact on model predictions overall when the value for a predictor variable changes. *Partial Dependence Plots* are a summary of *Ceteris Paribus Plots* for all observations and thus explain the overall impact of a predictor variable's change.

Predictor Variable Importance

Question 2: Which variables are more or less important for the prediction, and which variables can potentially be dropped?

Section 11.6 focuses on *tree-based* models, and we quantify how important each predictor variable is for the model's outcome prediction. We will visualize the results in a *Variable Importance Plot (VIP)* that shows a list of all predictor variables and their importance for the model prediction.

We quantify *Variable importance* in two ways:

1) In Section 11.6.1, we use an *impurity* reduction measure to analyze how much each predictor variable reduces *impurity* when splitting the observations in the *Decision Trees* from parent nodes to the related two *child nodes*.

2) In Section 11.6.2, we estimate *Variable Importance* by the damage to the model's predictive quality (the increase of MSE) when the influence of a specific predictor variable is removed. The greater the damage, the higher the importance of that particular variable.

---

[2] A good overview about the interpretability of machine learning models and the related algorithms is provided in the book by Molnar (2020).

Predictor Variable Contribution

> Question 3: *What is a predictor variable's contribution to the predicted*
> *outcome of an observation?*

We will introduce two techniques quantifying the contribution of predictor variables to a specific prediction: *SHAP* (*SHapley Additive exPlanations*) values and the *LIME* (*Local Interpretable Model-agnostic Explanations*) approach.

Section 11.7 introduces *SHAP* values. *SHAP* values measure how much each predictor variable contributes to the prediction result for an observation.

Section 11.8 introduces *LIME*. In contrast to *SHAP values*, *LIME* does not interpret machine learning models directly. Instead, *LIME* approximates a machine learning model with a simpler interpretable model (e.g., a linear *OLS*) in the neighborhood of an observation. The simpler model is then used for interpretation.

In the case of our example with the loan applicant, *SHAP values* and *LIME* values could provide the following kind of information: Because of the applicant's young age, the risk score is higher by 17 units, because of the applicant's low income, the risk score is higher by 5 units, and because the applicant never defaulted on a loan their, risk score is lower by 12 units.

11.1 Learning Outcomes

This section outlines what you can expect to learn in this chapter. In addition, the corresponding section number is included for each learning outcome to help you to navigate the content, especially when you return to the chapter for review.

In this chapter, you will learn:

- How machine learning interpretation methodologies can be categorized into model-agnostic and model-specific methods (see Section 11.3).

- How machine learning interpretation methodologies can be categorized into local methods (i.e., related to a specific observation) and global methods (i.e., related to the complete model; see Section 11.3).

- How you can generate and interpret Ceteris Paribus Plots to analyze the impact of changing predictor variables related to a specific observation (see Section 11.5.1).

- How you can generate and interpret Partial Dependence Plots to analyze the impact of changing predictor variables for a machine learning model (see Section 11.5.2).

- How you can use **Variable Importance Plots (VIP)** to identify predictor variables that are more or less important for the prediction. The less important variables are potential candidates to be dropped from the analysis (see Section 11.6).

- How you can use **SHAP** values to quantify the contribution of each predictor variable to the prediction of a specific observation of interest (see Section 11.7).

- How you can use the **Local Interpretable Model-agnostic Explanations (LIME)** methodology to approximate a non-linear machine learning model with a linear *OLS* model. The latter can then be used to interpret the related impacts of the predictor variables (see Section 11.8).

11.2   R Packages Required for the Chapter

This section lists the *R* packages that you need when you load and execute code in the interactive sections in *RStudio*. Please install the following packages using `Tools -> Install Packages ...` from the *RStudio* menu bar (you can find more information about installing and loading packages in Section 3.4):

- The `rio` package (Chan et al. (2021)) to enable the loading of various data formats with one `import()` command. Files can be loaded from the user's hard drive or the Internet.

- The `janitor` package (Firke (2023)) to rename variable names to *Upper-Camel* and to substitute spaces and special characters in variable names.

- The `tidymodels` package (Kuhn and Wickham (2020)) to streamline data engineering and machine learning tasks.

- The `kableExtra` (Zhu (2021)) package to support the rendering of tables.

- The `learnr` package (Aden-Buie et al. (2022)), which is needed together with the `shiny` package (Chang et al. (2022)) for the interactive exercises in this book.

- The `shiny` package (Chang et al. (2022)), which is needed together with the `learnr` package (Aden-Buie et al. (2022)) for the interactive exercises in this book.

- The `wooldridge` package (Shea (2023)) to provide the wage data that will be used throughout this chapter.

- The `ranger` package (Wright and Ziegler (2017)) to create a *Random Forest*.

- The `parallel` package (R Core Team (2022)) to perform parallel processing.

- The `DALEX` package (Biecek (2018)) to use various techniques, including *SHAP* values, to interpret machine learning results.

- The `DALEXtra` package (Maksymiuk et al. (2020)) extends the `DALEX` package. Extra functionality provided by `DALEXtra` includes working directly with `tidymodels` trained *workflows*.

- The `vip` package (Greenwell and Boehmke (2020)) to generate *Variable Importance Plots*.

- The `lime` package (Hvitfeldt et al. (2022)) to use the *LIME* approach to interpret machine learning models.

11.3 Categorizing Interpretation Methods

In what follows, we will introduce several interpretation methodologies. Not every methodology can be applied to all models. To help you decide which methodology to use for which interpretation task, we categorize them by tasks in this section.

For example, some methods are only appropriate for explaining a prediction result for a specific observation (local interpretation methods). In contrast, others are only appropriate to help us understand a model in general and how it makes predictions overall (global interpretation methods).

Going back to the previous example of lenders making a loan decision, you have to decide if you want to analyze why a specific applicant (observation) is not approved for a loan (local interpretation methods) or how, in general, the model predicts loan risk related to one particular predictor variable (global interpretation methods).

Local vs. Global Interpretation

Local Interpretation: To analyze the prediction of a specific observation and to interpret the impact of predictor variables on that specific observation, we use *local* interpretation methodologies.

Global Interpretation: To analyze the predictions of a machine learning model in general and to interpret the impact of predictor variables regardless of specific observations, we use *global* interpretation methodologies.

Another property of interpretation methodologies you need to consider is whether the interpretation methodology is *model-specific* or *model-agnostic*. Some methodologies are developed for specific machine learning models (*model-specific*), and while others can be applied to interpret almost every machine learning model (*model-agnostic*). For example, an *impurity-based Variable Importance Plot* (see Section 11.6.1), which is related to *decision rules* in a *Decision Tree*, can be applied to *tree-based* models like *Random Forest* but cannot be applied to *Neural Networks*.

In contrast, a *Ceteris Paribus Plot* or a *Partial Dependence Plot* can be applied to any machine learning model as long as it generates predictions (*model-agnostic*).

Model-Specific vs. Model-Agnostic Interpretation

Model-Specific: Interpretation methodologies that can only be applied to a specific model type are called *model-specific*.

Model-Agnostic: Interpretation methodologies that can be applied regardless of which model was used to generate the predictions are called *model-agnostic*.

11.4   Data, Model Design, and Workflow-Model

For all interpretation methodologies that we introduce in the following sections, except for the interactive Section 11.7.3,[3] we use the same dataset and the same *workflow* model. The objective is to predict hourly wages based on several predictor variables such as education, tenure, and sex.

In this section, we will briefly introduce the data and the workflow for the wage predicting example.

For the data, we use the `wage1` dataset from the `wooldridge` package.[4] The `wage1` dataset contains hourly wage data for 526 observations together with several predictor variables. To keep it simple, we use only the predictor variables for a person's years of education (*Educ*), their tenure at their current job (*Tenure*), and a dummy variable, *Female* (with 1 for *female*) that indicates if the person is female or not:

---

[3]Later in the interactive Section 11.7.3, you will work with an up-to-date real-world model to predict vaccination rates during the *COVID-19* pandemic.

[4]The `wooldridge` package (Shea (2023)) provides various datasets related to an econometrics textbook (Wooldridge (2020)). It is published on CRAN under a *GLT3* license.

```
library(rio)
library(janitor)
library(tidymodels)
library(wooldridge)
DataWage=wage1 |>
        clean_names("upper_camel") |>
        select(Wage, Educ, Tenure, Female) |>
        mutate(Female=as.factor(Female))
```

Adding more predictor variables would likely improve the predictive quality, but again, we try to keep things simple for this example.

As usual, we divide the data into *training* (DataTrain) and *testing* (DataTest) data:

```
set.seed(777)
Split7525=initial_split(DataWage, prop=0.75, strata=Wage)
DataTrain=training(Split7525)
DataTest=testing(Split7525)
```

We will use a *Random Forest* model to predict the wage, and as before, for better performance, we set the number of threads to run parallel to num.threads=detectCores(). This determines that we run as many threads in parallel as the computer has processing cores:

```
library(parallel)
ModelDesignRF=rand_forest() |>
            set_engine("ranger", num.threads=detectCores(),
                    importance="impurity") |>
            set_mode("regression")

RecipeWage=recipe(Wage~., data=DataTrain)

set.seed(777)
WfModelWageRF=workflow() |>
            add_model(ModelDesignRF)|>
            add_recipe(RecipeWage) |>
            fit(DataTrain)
```

In the code block above, the *model design* and the *recipe* are defined, and both are added to the *workflow* WfModelWageRF, which is then fitted to the training data. Later in Section 11.6.1, we will create an *impurity-based Variable Importance Plot*, which requires us to generate the underlying data during the *workflow's* fitting stage. Therefore, we set `importance="impurity"` in the *model design*.

In the following sections, we will interpret the *workflow* model `WfModelWageRF` as a whole (*global interpretation*), and we will interpret a specific observation of interest (*local interpretation*). The observation of interest is the observation of a woman (*Female* = 1) with 17 years of education (*Educ* = 17) and 18 years of tenure in her current job (*Tenure* = 18). She has an hourly wage of $8.90:[5]

```
ObsHelga=tibble(Wage=8.9, Educ=17, Tenure=18,
                Female=factor(1, levels=c(0,1)))
print(ObsHelga)
```

```
## # A tibble: 1 x 4
##    Wage  Educ Tenure Female
##   <dbl> <dbl>  <dbl> <fct>
## 1   8.9    17     18 1
```

To make it easier to address this observation of interest later on, we call the women Helga and the related observation `ObsHelga`.

It is essential to distinguish between Helga's actual hourly wage ($8.90) and her *predicted* hourly wage — the wage predicted by the *Random Forest* model. In the following sections, we can only explain Helga's *predicted* hourly wage (*.pred*) but not her true wage. Consequently, we have to use the data frame with Helga's predictor variable values (`ObsHelga`) and augment it with the predicted wage:

```
ObsHelga=augment(WfModelWageRF, new_data=ObsHelga)
print(ObsHelga)
```

```
## # A tibble: 1 x 5
##    Wage  Educ Tenure Female .pred
##   <dbl> <dbl>  <dbl> <fct>  <dbl>
## 1   8.9    17     18 1       9.24
```

You can see see that Helga's true hourly wage is $8.90, while the *Random Forest* model predicted a wage of $9.24 (*.pred* = 9.24).

---

[5]This wage seems to be very low, but consider that the wage data are from 1976 (see Shea (2023)).

11.5 Visualizing the Impact of Changing Predictor Variables

In this section, we will use *Ceteris Paribus Plots* and *Partial Dependence Plots* to visualize how a change in a single predictor variable impacts the predictions for the outcome variable.

We will analyze changes of the variable *Tenure*, but the methodology is also valid for changes of other predictor variables.

11.5.1 Ceteris Paribus Plots

A *Ceteris Paribus Plot* visualizes how changing the values for a predictor variable impacts the prediction for a single observation of interest (*local interpretation*). The observation of interest here is the observation for Helga:

```
## # A tibble: 1 x 5
##     Wage  Educ Tenure Female .pred
##    <dbl> <dbl>  <dbl>  <fct> <dbl>
## 1    8.9    17     18 1       9.24
```

In the previous section, we predicted a wage of $9.24 for Helga. But how would Helga's predicted wage change if her *Tenure* was greater or smaller and all other predictor variable values would remain the same?

To find the answer, we need to leave $Educ = 17$ and $Female = 1$ as they are. Then, we use the *Random Forest workflow* WfModelWageRF to generate wage predictions for various values of *Tenure*.[6] The graphical representation of the result leads to the *Ceteris Paribus Plot* in Figure 11.1.

In the *Ceteris Paribus Plot*, the *Tenure* values are plotted against the related wage predictions from the *Random Forest* model. The plot in Figure 11.1 was generated with the following *R* code:

```
library(DALEX)
ExplainerRF=DALEX::explain(extract_fit_engine(WfModelWageRF),
                      data=DataTrain, y=DataTrain$Wage)

CPPlot=predict_profile(explainer=ExplainerRF,
                    new_observation=ObsHelga,
                    variables="Tenure")
plot(CPPlot, variables="Tenure")
```

---

[6]In general, allowing only one variable to change and leaving all other variables constant is called *ceteris paribus* (Latin for: *everything else the same*). Thus, the name of the plot.

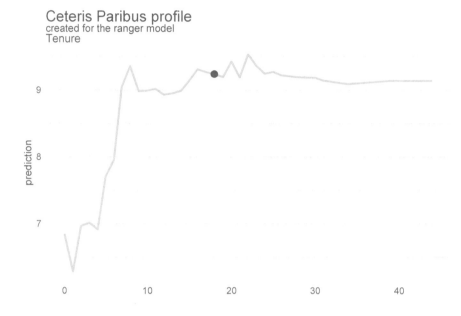

FIGURE 11.1 Ceteris Paribus Plot for the Variable Tenure

Most interpretation algorithms work in two steps. First, an *explainer* object (here *ExplainerRF*) is created, which is a container that stores the training data, the *model design*, and some other information but does not perform any interpretation tasks. In the second step, the interpretation is performed with another command based on the information from the *explainer* object.

Note, when we create the *explainer* object with the command `explain()`, the command is prefixed with DALEX::. This ensures that the `explain()` command from the DALEX package is used. It is necessary because both the tidyverse package and the lime package that we use later in Section 11.8 contain a command `explain()`.

The *Ceteris Paribus plot* is created with the command `predict_profile()`. Arguments are the *explainer* (`explainer=ExplainerRF`), the observation used for the plot (`new_observation=ObsHelga`), and the variable that is analyzed (`variables="Tenure"`).

In the *Ceteris Paribus plot* in Figure 11.1, Helga's $Tenure/\widehat{Wage}$ combination is marked with a blue dot. You can see that Helga's predicted wage would mostly stay the same if she had some more or less tenure. However, if Helga had much less tenure ($Tenure < 8$), her predicted wage would be much smaller. All this makes perfect sense for somebody with a high tenure and education.

A *Ceteris Paribus* plot interprets only the prediction for a specific observation (*local interpretation*). What if we want to get a *global interpretation* of the whole prediction model? The following section provides a tool for this purpose.

11.5.2 Partial Dependence Plot

The idea behind *Partial Dependence Plots* is first to create a *Ceteris Paribus plot* for every or at least many observations from the training dataset and then create an average of these individual plots.

You can see the individual *Ceteris Paribus plots* in Figure 11.2 as the light grey lines. Each line represents a *Ceteris Paribus plot* for one of the training observations. The ensemble of grey lines in Figure 11.2 is called an *Individual Conditional Expectation (ICE)* plot.

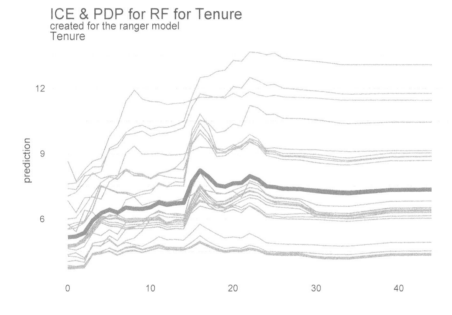

FIGURE 11.2 ICE Plot Combined with a Partial Dependence Plot

If we calculate for each *Tenure* value the average from the related values of the light grey lines (the *Ceteris Paribus plots*), we get the bold blue line, which is called a **Partial Dependence Plot (PDP)**.

The code to generate the *ICE* plot and the *PDP* plot is shown below:

```
library(DALEX)
ICEPDPPlot=model_profile(explainer=ExplainerRF, variables="Tenure",
```

```
                              N=NULL)
plot(ICEPDPPlot,geom="profiles")+ggtitle("ICE & PDP for Tenure")
```

The `model_profile()` command generates the plot based on the explainer object defined above (`explainer=ExplainerRF`), and selects the predictor variable to be analyzed (`variables="Tenure"`). The argument `N=NULL` determines that all training observations are used for the *ICE* plot. Alternatively, `N` random observations from the training dataset can be used.

The *PDP* plot (bold blue line) in Figure 11.2 shows how *Tenure* determines the predicted wage for the *Random Forest* model.

In the first 17 years, higher *Tenure* values increase the predicted wage with a sharp increase in years 16 and 17. Afterward, a longer tenure does not lead to a significant increase in predicted wage. This result is what one would expect. Companies value tenure up to a certain degree. Afterward, an increasing tenure neither helps nor hurts.

11.6 Variable Importance for Tree-Based Models

In the previous section, we used *Ceteris Paribus plots* and *Partial Dependence Plots* to analyze the quantitative impact of predictor variable changes. In contrast, *Variable Importance Plots (VIP)* focus on the relevance of a predictor variable for a model rather than its quantitative impact on the outcome. As the name suggests, *VIPs* focus on predictor variable *importance*.

VIPs can help you decide if a specific predictor variable is important enough to be kept in a model or if it should be dropped.

11.6.1 Impurity-Based Variable Importance Plot

When we covered *Decision Trees* in Section 10.3, the task was to predict survival on the *Titanic* — a classification task. For a classification task, every split that is used in a tree reduces the *impurity* from the parent node (before the split) to the two resulting *child nodes* (after the split). In Section 10.3, we used the *Gini* coefficient to measure *impurity* reduction.

When using a *Decision Tree* to predict a *continuous* outcome, every split also reduces the *impurity* from the parent node (before the split) to the two resulting *child nodes* (after the split). However, we can no longer use the *Gini* coefficient to measure *impurity* reduction because the *Gini* coefficient is a specific measure for classification only. An alternative for a continuous outcome variable to measure *impurity* reduction is to use the variance of the outcome variable before and after the split.

Let us use the wage prediction example to show how this works. Assume in a *Decision Tree*, we have already corrected for tenure and education at a higher level of the tree. Now we reach a decision rule that splits for Sex=male. Assuming sex discrimination is present, this parent node would contain men with high salaries (positive deviation from the mean) and women with low salaries (negative deviation from the mean), leading to a high variance. Now, if we split by Sex=male, the left *child node* would only contain men. Since the new mean for this *child node* would be higher, the deviation of the higher-paid male observations from the new mean would be relatively low. The same is true in a mirrored way for the female node. The new mean in this node would be lower; thus, the deviation from this mean for the lower-paid female workers would also be relatively low. The *decision rule* Sex=male reduced the variance and thus the *impurity* in the two *child nodes* compared to the *parent* node.

Regardless, if we measure *impurity* with the *Gini* coefficient or through variance, in both cases, the more a splitting rule can reduce the *impurity* from the parent node to the two *child nodes*, the more effective the related predictor variable.

The importance of a variable in an impurity-based Variable Importance Plot is measured as the average impurity reduction for all splits, where the variable was the splitting variable.[7]

Since all *tree-based* models consist of one or more *Decision Trees* and each *Decision Tree* consists of several splits, *impurity-based Variable Importance* can be measured for all *tree-based* models. However, since it cannot be used for models that are not *tree-based*, it is a model-specific interpretation method.

Since *impurity-based Variable Importance* is calculated for a whole model and not for a specific observation, it is a global interpretation method.

Instead of using the training data to calculate the reduction of *impurity* for the predictor variables, the *VIP* package uses the *Out-of-Bag* data (see Section 10.4.1) to calculate the *Variable Importance*. Using *Out-of-Bag* data rather than training data improves the generality of *Variable Importance* plots.

The *impurity* reduction is calculated at the time when the *Decision Trees* are created. Therefore, to trigger the calculation of *impurity* reduction for every split, the argument importance="impurity" is required in the workflow command.[8] If we want to use a different *importance* measure like importance="permutation" in the following section, we have to set the argument importance= differently before the *workflow* is fit to the training data, or we have to repeat the fitting.

---

[7]See Molnar (2020), Section 5.4.

[8]We did this in Section 11.4.

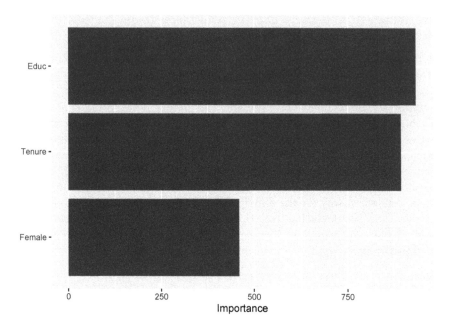

FIGURE 11.3 Impurity-Based Variable Importance Plot for Wage Model

The *R* code to generate the *impurity-based Variable Importance* plot is shown below:

```
library(vip)
vip(extract_fit_engine(WfModelWageRF))
```

After loading the library `vip`, the `vip()` command creates the *Variable Importance* plot. The command's major argument is the fitted prediction model. It is extracted from the *workflow* `WfModelWageRF` with the `extract_fit_engine()` command.

The bar plot in Figure 11.3 suggests that education (*Educ*) carries the greatest importance for the model, followed by the *Tenure*, and then the variable *Female*. The variable *Female* has a lower importance than the other two variables, but it is still important.

11.6.2 Permutation-Based Variable Importance Plot

An alternative to using *impurity* reduction as a criteria for *Variable Importance* is *permutation-based Variable Importance*.[9]

---

[9]See Molnar (2020), Section 8.5.

The basic idea is to switch off a specific predictor variable and see how much damage this creates in terms of an increased error. Afterward, the procedure is repeated for all other predictor variables. The greater the damage caused by switching off a specific predictor variable, the greater the importance of this predictor variable.

This raises the question, how can we switch off a predictor variable? Setting all values to zero is not an option because it would introduce bias. Setting the values to the mean or median of the predictor variable's values would be an option, but it would wipe out information about the variable's distribution.

The way *permutation-based Variable Importance* methodology approaches the problem is to scramble the values for the switched-off variable over all observations, thus maintaining mean, median, and the distribution of the switched-off variable. Afterward, the scrambled (switched-off) predictor variable and the other predictor variables are used to predict the outcome. The difference between the now bigger prediction error and the original prediction error measures the damage done by scrambling and thus measures the *Variable Importance*.

The procedure is repeated for all other predictor variables, and the damage, i.e., the *Variable Importance*, is compared in the *Variable Importance* plot.

Since *permutation-based Variable Importance* is calculated overall for a model, regardless of a specific observation, it is a global interpretation method.

Permutation-based Variable Importance uses the *Out-of-Bag* data from each *Decision Tree* rather than the training data. This improves the generality of the methodology but also ties it to *tree-based* models. Therefore, it is a model-specific interpretation method. However, *model-agnostic* approaches for *permutation* also exist. They usually use a validation dataset instead of the *Out-of-Bag* dataset.

Since the *Out-of-Bag* data for each *Decision Tree* are used to calculate *permutation-based Variable Importance*, the required data are calculated when the *Decision Trees* are developed — when the *Random Forest workflow* model is fitted to the data. To trigger this calculation the argument `importance="permutation"` has to be set during *model design*.

Remember, we set `importance="impurity"` in Section 11.4, when we created the *workflow*. Therefore, we have to create the *workflow* again with the changed argument and again fit it to the training data:

```
ModelDesignRF=rand_forest() |>
  set_engine("ranger", num.threads=detectCores(),
  importance="permutation") |>
  set_mode("regression")
```

```
set.seed(777)
WfModelWageRF=workflow() |>
        add_model(ModelDesignRF)|>
        add_recipe(RecipeWage) |>
        fit(DataTrain)
```

The command to create *permutation-based Variable Importance* is the same as the one for *impurity-based Variable Importance* (see Section 11.6.1), except it requires us to set the metric for the error via the metric= argument:

```
library(vip)
vip(extract_fit_engine(WfModelWageRF), metric="rmse")
```

Options for the error metric include metric="rmse" (*root mean squared error*), metric="mae" (*mean absolute error*), and metric="rsq" (r^2). It is recommended to use the metric that was used for the underlying machine learning model.

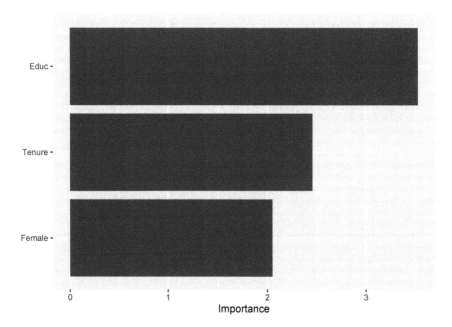

FIGURE 11.4 Permutation-Based Variable Importance Plot for Wage Model

The *permutation-based Variable Importance Plot* in Figure 11.4 is similar to the *impurity-based Variable Importance Plot* in Figure 11.3, except that the variable *Female* now shows a greater importance.

This reminds us to be careful when working with interpretation algorithms and look at the bigger picture and not so much at the details when interpreting the results.

11.7 SHAP Contribution of Predictor Variables

An interpretation methodology that can quantify the contributions of each predictor variable's value to the outcome prediction of a specific observation is the *SHAP* values methodology.

The **SHAP** values methodology is a recent approach to interpreting machine learning predictions (see Lundberg and Lee (2017)). However, the basic idea for the *SHAP* values methodology is based on a game theory approach called **SHAPLEY** values after its original author Shapley (1953).

In this section, we first introduce *SHAPLEY* values in Section 11.7.1. Then, in Section 11.7.2, we transfer the concept of *SHAPLEY* values to the concept of *SHAP* values.

11.7.1 SHAPLEY Values

SHAPLEY values were developed by Shapley (1953). It is a game theory approach to divide a gain from a project among the individuals who contributed to the project. The idea is to use the marginal contribution to distribute the gain. The marginal contribution of an individual can be calculated when comparing the gain with and without the contribution of that individual. The challenge is that marginal contributions for the same individual can differ depending on which level of a project an individual starts contributing, but this can be better explained with an example.

Suppose, as an example, a business hires three economists: The three economists, Angela, Bruce, and Carsten, contribute to the company with their economic advice. Before any of the three economists were hired, the business made a profit of $7 million (measured in thousands of dollars and displayed as 7,000 at the top of the flow chart in Figure 11.5).

We call a group of contributors to a project a *coalition,* and because *none* of the economists contributed in the scenario at the beginning of the flow chart in Figure 11.5, this scenario is labeled as *Coalition: none.*

In contrast, the scenario at the bottom of the flow chart in Figure 11.5 *Coalition: ABC* indicates that all three economists contribute, which leads to a profit of 7,107. Comparing the profit from *Coalition: none* to *Coalition: ABC* shows that all economists' contribution is 107.

Given that the three economists have slightly different talents (Angela specializes in financial economics, Bruce specializes in health economics, and Carsten
specializes in machine learning), we cannot equally divide the profit of 107
among the three economists. We have to find out the individual marginal contribution of each economist. The marginal contribution is calculated as the
difference between a coalition where an individual contributed and a coalition
where the same individual did not contribute. There is a problem: The contribution varies for each individual economist depending on which stage they
joined the project.

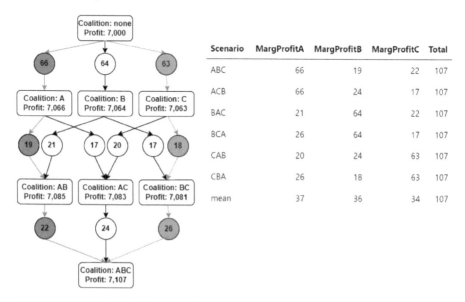

Scenario	MargProfitA	MargProfitB	MargProfitC	Total
ABC	66	19	22	107
ACB	66	24	17	107
BAC	21	64	22	107
BCA	26	64	17	107
CAB	20	24	63	107
CBA	26	18	63	107
mean	37	36	34	107

FIGURE 11.5 The Shapley Graph

For example, when we follow the red path in the flow chart in Figure 11.5, we
can see that Angela joins first, then Bruce, and lastly, Carsten. When Angela
joins, the profit increases from *Coalition: none* by 66 to *Coalition A*, where
Angela is the only contributor (from 7,000 to 7,066). When Bruce joins, the
profit increases by 19, and finally, when Carsten joins, the profit increases
by 22. Therefore, Angela's marginal contribution is 66, Bruce's is 19, and
Carsten's is 22. Should Angela get 66 of the total contribution of 107? This is
more than half and does not sound reasonable.

Why this is not reasonable becomes more clear when we look at the blue path
in the flow chart in Figure 11.5. Following that path, we see that Angela joins
last and contributes only 26.

The different results make sense: In the initial coalition, the company did
not have an economist, so when Angela joins, she contributes all of the economics expertise. However, following the blue path, Angela joins last. Before

she joined, the company had already hired two economists, contributing their economics knowledge and their specialties. When Angela joins, the profit still goes up because she adds financial economics expertise, but economics, in general, was already well covered by Bruce and Carsten.

The order in which coalition members join should not influence their estimated overall contribution. Therefore, we could look at every possible scenario where Angela can join, calculate her marginal contribution for each scenario, and then calculate the average as an estimate of Angela's overall contribution.

This is exactly the idea behind *SHAPLEY* values, and you can see how it works in the table displayed in Figure 11.5. Since we have three economists, there are precisely six ($3! = 1 \cdot 2 \cdot 3$) different scenarios for the order in which they can join the project, and these six scenarios are displayed in the rows of the table. When Angela joins first (Scenarios *ABC* and *ACB*), her contribution is 66. When she joins second (Scenarios *BAC* and *CAB*), her contribution is 21 and 20, receptively. When she joins last (Scenarios *BCA* and *CBA*) her contribution is 26. The average for all six scenarios is 37, which is Angela's estimated overall contribution — her *SHAPLEY* value.

We can follow a similar procedure for Bruce and Carsten, and we get *SHAPLEY* values of 36 and 34, respectively. They are displayed in the last row of the table in Figure 11.5 and add up to the overall contribution of the three economists of 107.

SHAPLEY values always ensure that their sum adds up to the total contribution (107 in our case).

11.7.2 From SHAPLEY to SHAP Values

Now that you understand how *SHAPLEY* values are calculated, it is a small step to understand *SHAP* values.

The underlying idea of the *SHAP* values approach is to apply the *SHAPLEY* logic to the *SHAP* approach.[10] This is reflected in the definition of *SHAP* values:

SHAP values quantify the contributions of all predictor variables' values to the prediction for a specific observation.

Since the *SHAP* values approach is based on an individual observation, the *SHAP* algorithm is considered local.

Since *SHAP* can be applied to any machine learning model that can generate predictions, the algorithm is considered model-agnostic.

---

[10]O'Sullivan (2022a) compares the *SHAPLEY* and the *SHAP* approaches and provides mathematical foundation for both approaches. He also briefly discusses how *SHAP* values can be computationally approximated.

To explain the transition from the *SHAPLEY* to the *SHAP* approach, let us work with the same wage prediction example as in the previous sections. Again, our goal is to explain the wage prediction of the *Random Forest* model from Section 11.4. In detail, we want to estimate the contributions of the predictor variable values $Educ = 17$, $Tenure = 18$, and $Female = 1$ to the predicted wage (*.pred*) for the observation Helga:

```
print(ObsHelga)
```

```
## # A tibble: 1 x 5
##     Wage  Educ Tenure Female .pred
##    <dbl> <dbl>  <dbl> <fct>  <dbl>
## 1   8.9    17     18 1       9.24
```

When we discussed *SHAPLEY* values in Section 11.7.1, we considered six scenarios where three economists joined a project in a different order. Similarly here, the values for the predictor variables ($E := Educ = 17$, $T := Tenure = 18$, and $F := Female = 1$) are added step-wise, in different order to predict Helga's wage (see Figure 11.6).

Because three predictor variables can be ordered in six different ways ($3! = 1 \cdot 2 \cdot 3$) there are six different paths through the flow chart in Figure 11.6. Each path reflects one possible order of adding the predictor variable values to the prediction. The six different paths are also listed in the rows of the table next to the flow chart (for example, Row 1 and Row 6 represent the red and blue paths, respectively).

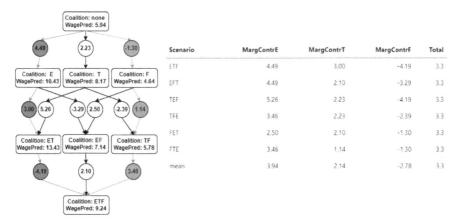

Scenario	MargContrE	MargContrT	MargContrF	Total
ETF	4.49	3.00	-4.19	3.3
EFT	4.49	2.10	-3.29	3.3
TEF	5.26	2.23	-4.19	3.3
TFE	3.46	2.23	-2.39	3.3
FET	2.50	2.10	-1.30	3.3
FTE	3.46	1.14	-1.30	3.3
mean	3.94	2.14	-2.78	3.3

FIGURE 11.6 Deriving SHAP Values for Observation Helga

The entries of each row in the table show the marginal contributions of the related predictor variable for the scenario. Each marginal contribution is the difference between two coalitions — one before the related predictor variable was added and one afterward.

For example, the sixth row in the table in Figure 11.6 represents the blue path through the flow chart. The marginal contribution of $Educ = 17$ is 3.46. The predictor value for $Educ$ was added at the end of the blue path leading to *Coalition: ETF*. The coalition without $Educ = 17$ (*Coalition: TF*), contained only the predictors *Tenure* and *Female*.

The *Coalition: TF* without *Education* leads to a predicted wage of 5.78. The *Coalition: TEF* that includes *Education* leads to a predicted wage of 9.24. Therefore, including $Educ = 17$ in the wage prediction increased the predicted wage by \$3.46 ($9.24-5.78$) — which is the marginal contribution of $Educ = 17$ for the blue path (*Scenario TEF*).

The marginal contribution of *Tenure* for the scenario in the sixth row in the table can be calculated in a similar way. *Tenure* was added second along the blue path, and the difference between the wage prediction from the *Coalition: TF* (including $Tenure = 18$) and *Coalition: F* (without *Tenure*) is 1.14 ($5.78-4.64$).

The third value in the sixth row of the table represents the marginal contribution of $Female = 1$. The predictor value $Female = 1$ was considered first for the step-wise wage prediction along the blue path. The marginal contribution of $Female = 1$ is the difference between *Coalition: F* and *Coalition: none* ($4.64 - 5.94 = -1.3$).

Marginal contributions for other paths through the flow chart in Figure 11.6 can be calculated in a similar way. You find them in the table to the right of the flow chart.

To summarize, the marginal contribution of $Educ = 17$, $Tenure = 18$, and $Female = 1$ for the scenario, where the step-wise prediction was performed in the order F, TF, and ETF, are:

$$\underbrace{3.46}_{MargContrE} + \underbrace{1.14}_{MargContrT} + \underbrace{(-1.30)}_{MargContrF} = \underbrace{3.3}_{MargContrAll}$$

You can see that the marginal contributions add up to 3.3, which is the same for all orderings (all rows). This value represents the cumulative contribution from all three predictor variables to the predicted wage. We can show this by calculating the difference between *Coalition: ETF*, where all predictor variable values are considered, and *Coalition: none*, where no predictor variable is considered:

$$\underbrace{9.24}_{\text{Coalition: ETF}} - \underbrace{5.94}_{\text{Coalition: none}} = \underbrace{3.3}_{\text{MargContrAll}}$$

How to predict the wage for the coalitions in Figure 11.6?

We mentioned before that the wage prediction for Helga's wage based on all three predictor variable values could be calculated based on the fitted *Random Forest* model from Section 11.4:

```
CoalitionETF=predict(WfModelWageRF, new_data=ObsHelga)
cat("Helga's predicted wage from Coalition ETF is:",
    round(CoalitionETF[[1]],2))
```

```
## Helga's predicted wage from Coalition ETF is: 9.24
```

To predict the wage for *Coalition: none* at the top of the flow chart in Figure 11.6, we have to consider that no information about Helga can be used for this coalition. In the absence of any information, the mean is often a reasonable way to predict a variable. Therefore, we use the mean of the training data for the wage prediction from *Coalition: none*:

```
CoalitionNone=mean(DataTrain$Wage)
cat("Helga's predicted wage for Coalition `none` is:",
    round(CoalitionNone,2))
```

```
## Helga's predicted wage for Coalition `none` is: 5.94
```

Generating the predictions for Helga's wage for the remaining six coalitions is a bit more tricky, and we will talk about it a little later.

Instead, we use the table in Figure 11.6 to calculate *SHAP* values for the predictor variables. Because all possible predictor orders have been considered in the rows of the table, we can calculate the overall contribution of $Educ = 17$, $Tenure = 18$, and $Female = 1$ to the wage prediction as the mean of the columns *MargContrE*, *MargContrT* and *MargContrF*. You can find the resulting *SHAP values* in the "*mean*" row of the table in Figure 11.6.

It is a very useful property of the *SHAP* methodology that the *SHAP values* always add up to the cumulative contribution of all predictor variables:

$$
\underbrace{3.94}_{\text{SHAP Educ=17}} + \underbrace{2.14}_{\text{SHAP Tenure=18}} + \underbrace{(-2.78)}_{\text{SHAP Female=1}} = \underbrace{3.3}_{\text{SHAP Cummalitiv}}
$$

We can use the *SHAP values* from the equation above to interpret the results from the *SHAP* approach: The fact that Helga has a high education ($Educ = 18$) contributes \$3.94 to her predicted wage, the fact that she has a long tenure ($Tenure = 18$) contributes \$2.14, and the fact that she is female ($Female = 1$)

contributes negative \$2.78 to her predicted wage.[11] All these contributions add up to 3.3 and explain why Helga's wage is \$3.30 higher than the wage of an average worker.

Predicting wage for the remaining six coalitions in Figure 11.6:

We have already explained that the predicted wage for *Coalition: none* is calculated as the mean wage from the observations in the training dataset. We also showed that the wage prediction that uses all predictor variables (*Coalition: ETF*) could be calculated as the prediction from the analyzed machine learning model (the *Random Forest Model* from Section 11.4 in our case).

To calculate the predictions for the six remaining coalitions in the flow chart in Figure 11.6, we used a very simplified approach.

To create the predictions for *Coalition: E*, *Coalition: T*, and *Coalition: F*, we created three new *Random Forest* models designed for one predictor variable each. Then we fitted each of the three *Random Forest* models to the training data for the predictor variables *Educ*, *Tenure*, and *Female*, respectively. Afterward, we used the three fitted *Random Forest* models to create the three predictions for Helga's wage based on $Educ = 17$ (*Coalition: E*), $Tenure = 18$ (*Coalition: T*), and $Female = 1$ (*Coalition: F*).

For the wage predictions for *Coalition: ET*, *Coalition: EF*, and *Coalition: TF*, we proceeded in a similar fashion: We created three new *Random Forest Models* designed for two predictors each and then fitted each model with the related two predictor variables from the training dataset (*ET*, *EF*, and *TF*). As before, we used the corresponding predictor values from the observation Helga to generate the wage predictions for the three coalitions.

The advantage of this simplified approach is that it is possible to showcase the approach in an *R* script (see the Digital Resource Section 11.10 for a link to a blog article that describes the approach in detail and provides the related *R* script.). The disadvantage is that this simplified approach has a conceptual and a computational drawback:

The Conceptual Drawback: Our goal is to generate *SHAP* values to explain the *Random Forest* model from Section 11.4 — the one that was used for *Coalition: ETF* in Figure 11.6. However, for the six coalitions that use only one or two predictor variables, we used similar but still different *Random Forest* models because these *Random Forest* models were designed for one and two predictor variables. This is conceptually problematic.

The Computational Drawback: The simplified approach is not scalable.

---

[11]The fact that Helga's sex reduces her wage by almost \$3 should not come as a surprise. The data are from 1976 and reflect sex discrimination during that time. To analyze sex discrimination in present times, we could use a similar methodology based on most recent data.

Using three predictor variables led to eight coalitions to consider. One was based on the *Random Forest* model we wanted to explain (Coalition: ETF), and for another one, we used the mean of the outcome variable from the training dataset as the predicted wage. That left six models for which we had to design and train six new *Random Forest* models. Creating six new *Random Forest* models is not a significant computational problem. However, the number of coalitions ($NCoalitions$) grows exponentially with the number of predictor variables ($NPredVar$):

$$NCoalitions = 2^{NPredVar} \tag{11.1}$$

For three predictor variables, we need eight coalitions ($2^3 = 8$), but for 20 predictor variables, we need to design and fit more than 1 million *Random Forest* models ($2^{20} = 1,048.576$). The computational cost of this is excessively high.

Fortunately, many highly effective computer algorithms exist to estimate *SHAP* values to explain the predictions of machine learning models. For example, *KernelSHAP*, a kernel based *SHAP* values model, was developed by Lundberg and Lee (2017). Later, Lundberg et al. (2019) developed *TreeSHAP*, a very effective *model-specific* algorithm limited to *tree-based* models. Both algorithms are beyond the scope of this book, but an introduction and a comparison of both models can be found in O'Sullivan (2022b).

In the following section, you will use the `DALEX` and the `DalexExtra` *R* packages to estimate *SHAP* values to interpret the results from the vaccination project that you used in the interactive Section 10.4.2. Below, we present the basic ideas of the `DALEX` algorithm.

`DALEX`, like our simplified approach, uses the mean of the outcome variable for the first coalition (*Coalition: none*) and the final model to predict the outcome for the last coalition (*Coalition: ETF*). For all other coalitions, `DALEX` also uses the final machine learning model, which avoids designing and fitting new machine learning models for every coalition.

However, using a model that is designed to use all predictor variables for a coalition that considers less than all predictors raises the question of which values to use for the variable(s) not covered by this coalition. For example, if we want to predict *Coalition: TF* from Figure 11.6, we would use the $Tenure = 18$ and $Female = 1$ values from observation Helga, but what do we use for $Educ$?

The `DALEX` solution is to substitute all *Tenure* and *Female* values in the training dataset observations with Helga's values $Tenure = 18$ and $Female = 1$, but leave all values for $Educ$ untouched. Then, based on the new dataset, the *Random Forest* model creates predictions for all observations. This way, the values from observation Helga ($Tenure = 18$ and $Female = 1$) are utilized to predict, and the distribution of the missing variable ($Educ$) is preserved.

After all predictions for the new dataset have been created, the prediction for the *Coalition: TF* is the mean of the predictions from the newly created dataset. The predictions for other coalitions are calculated in a similar way.

This algorithm works well when there are not too many predictor variables, and it does not use extra computing time to fit extra *Random Forest* models. However, it needs to predict as many observation as in the training dataset for each coalition. Given that the number of coalitions exponentially grows with the number of predictor variables (see Equation (11.1)), this can turn into a computational problem.

To address this problem, DALEX allows you to limit the number of paths through a flow chart like the one shown in Figure 11.6. Since a path through the flowchart is the same as a row in the table next to it, DALEX chooses a limited number of random rows from the table and then only calculates predictions for the required coalitions. The number of rows (paths) can be set with an argument.

In the next interactive section, you can use DALEX to interpret the predictions for the vaccination project that you used before in the interactive Section 10.4.2 to predict U.S. counties' vaccination rates with a *Random Forest* model.

11.7.3 ◎ Project: Apply the SHAP Algorithms in a Project

At the end of the previous section, we explained how DALEX approximates *SHAP* values. Here, you will work with a real-world application that uses the same *Random Forest* model and the same data used in Section 10.4.2 predicting the U.S. continental counties' vaccination rates during the *COVID-19* pandemic.

We will show how you can use tidymodels with the DALEX and DALEXtra packages to generate *SHAP values* to interpret the prediction results for a specific U.S. county.

Afterward, in the interactive Section 10.4.2 you can use the provided *R* code to create *SHAP values* for any county and interpret the results.

We start by reviewing the data processing for the *Random Forest workflow* used in Section 10.4.2.

Below, the libraries and data are loaded, and the data are split into training and testing data:

```
library(rio); library(janitor); library(tidymodels)
library(DALEX); library(DALEXtra)
DataVax=import("https://ai.lange-analytics.com/data/DataVax.rds")  |>
             select(PercVacFull, PercRep,
                    PercAsian, PercBlack, PercHisp,
```

```
                     PercYoung25, PercOld65,
                     PercFoodSt, Population) |>
            mutate(Population=frequency_weights(Population))
set.seed(2021)
Split85=DataVax |> initial_split(prop=0.85,
                                 strata=PercVacFull,
                                 breaks=3)

DataTrain=training(Split85)
DataTest=testing(Split85)
```

Recall from Section 10.4.2 that *Population* is not a predictor variable. Instead, we use the population of each U.S. county to weigh the county's observations. This is why the variable *Population* is marked as `frequency_weights`.

In the *R* code below, we create the *recipe*, the *model design*, add both to the *workflow*, and fit the *workflow* with the training data:

```
set.seed(2021)
RecipeVax=recipe(PercVacFull~., data=DataTrain)

library(parallel)
ModelDesignRandFor=rand_forest(min_n=5, mtry=2, trees=2000) |>
               set_engine("ranger", num.threads=detectCores()) |>
               set_mode("regression")

WfModelVax=workflow() |>
           add_model(ModelDesignRandFor) |>
           add_recipe(RecipeVax) |>
           fit(DataTrain)
```

Above, we use parallel processing to speed up the process to create a fitted *Random Forest workflow*. We set the number of threads to run parallel to `num.threads=detectCores()`, which determines that we run as many threads in parallel as the computer has processing cores.

Next, we build the *explainer* object for the *SHAP* values methodology. As explained in Section 11.5, the DALEX package, like many other *R* interpretation packages, stores information about the model to be analyzed, the training dataset, and additional information for the respective methodology in a so-called *explainer* object. This *explainer* object is then used as an input for the actual analysis command, which performs the analysis.

```
DataTrainPredOnly=select(DataTrain, -PercVacFull, -Population)

ExplainerRandForest=explain_tidymodels(WfModelVax,
                    data=DataTrainPredOnly,y=DataTrain$PercVacFull,
                    verbose=FALSE)
```

In the R code above, we use the command `explain_tidymodels()` from the `DALEXtra` package, which allows us to create the *explainer* object directly from the `tidymodels` *workflow* `WfModelVax`. The command `explain_tidymodels()` requires that the training data assigned to the `data=` argument contain exclusively the prediction variables. This is why we first used `select()` to create a data frame containing only the predictor variables before creating the *explainer* object. The outcome variable *PercVacFull* (a county's rate of fully vaccinated adults) is provided through the `y=` argument, and `verbose=FALSE` suppresses message output.

Now, everything is ready to calculate the *SHAP* values for one of the observations with the `predict_parts()` command. In the interactive part of this section further below, you can create and interpret *SHAP* values for almost any continental U.S. county, but for now, we keep it simple and choose *Los Angeles County*, CA.

In the `DataVax` data frame, *Los Angeles* has a `CountyID=133`, which means that the *Los Angeles* observation is in the $133rd$ row of the dataset.

The plot in Figure 11.7 was created with the `predict_parts()` command. In Figure 11.7, the bars indicate the *SHAP values* for the respective predictor variables, with the label at the vertical axis indicating the value of the respective predictor variable in *Los Angeles County*. The box plots overlaying each bar indicate the distribution of the *SHAP values* for the 25 randomly chosen scenarios (orderings of predictor variables). You find the R code that generates Figure 11.7 below:

```
set.seed(2021)
CountyID=133
SHAPObject=predict_parts(
    explainer=ExplainerRandForest,
    new_observation=DataVax[CountyID,],
    type="shap", B=25)

plot(SHAPObject)
```

We use the argument `new_observations=DataVax[CountyID,]` to create *SHAP values* for the observation Los Angeles. Also, the *explainer* object that we created above is assigned to the argument `explainer=` and the argument `B=25`

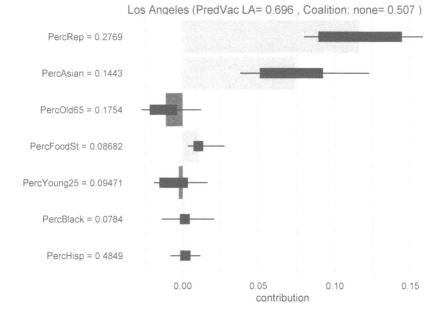

FIGURE 11.7 SHAP Values for Los Angeles County, CA

determines that we want to use only 25 scenarios (different orderings of the seven predictor variables) out of $2^7 = 128$ possible orderings.[12]

The *SHAP values* and the values of the predictor variables for *Los Angeles County* that are visualized in Figure 11.7, are displayed in Table 11.1 in columns *SHAP* and *County*.[13] We also added the U.S. values for the predictor variables in column *Nation*. These values were not used in any way to create the *SHAP values*, but they will help later to interpret the *SHAP values*.

As shown in Section 11.7.2 the difference between the prediction from the *Random Forest* model for *Los Angeles County* ($PredVac_{LA} = 0.696$)[14] and *Coalition: none* ($CoalNone = 0.507$)[15] equals the sum of all *SHAP values*:

---

[12]See Kuhn and Silge (2022), Section 18.5. for details.

[13]The related values were extracted from the SHAP Object: `SHAPObject |> as_tibble() |> filter(B==0) |> select( SHAP=contribution, County=variable_value)`.

[14]The value was extracted from the *SHAP* object `SHAPObject` with: `round(attr(SHAPObject, "prediction"),3)`.

[15]The value was extracted from the *SHAP* object `SHAPObject` with: `round(attr(SHAPObject, "intercept"),3)`. Note that this value is not equal to the national vaccination rate because `Coalition: none` is calculated from the average of the training data and not all data. In addition, the average the *SHAP* algorithm calculates is not weighted with the counties' population.

TABLE 11.1 Los Angeles (PredVac LA= 0.696 , Coalition: none= 0.507)

Variable	SHAP	County	Nation
PercAsian	0.074	0.144	0.063
PercBlack	0.001	0.078	0.136
PercFoodSt	0.011	0.087	0.115
PercHisp	0.001	0.485	0.191
PercOld65	-0.011	0.175	0.173
PercRep	0.116	0.277	0.478
PercYoung25	-0.002	0.095	0.310

Sources: column SHAP, column County,
predicted U.S. Vac. Rate, and Coalition
'none' are extracted from the SHAP
object.
Source PercRep Nation: Cook Political
Report,
https://www.cookpolitical.com/2020-national-popular-vote-tracker.
Biden=0.513, Trump=0.469 was transformed
to PercRep=0.469/(0.513+0.469) to account
for the fact that we considered only two
parties.
Sources column Nation: Census, United
States Population, estimates base, July
1, 2022, (V2022),
https://www.census.gov/quickfacts/fact/table/US.

$$\underbrace{0.696}_{PredVac_{LA}} - \underbrace{0.507}_{CoalNone} = 0.189$$

$$\underbrace{0.074}_{ShapAsian} + \underbrace{0.001}_{ShapBlack} + \underbrace{0.011}_{ShapFoodSt} + \underbrace{0.001}_{ShapHisp} +$$

$$\underbrace{-0.011}_{ShapRep} + \underbrace{0.116}_{ShapOld65} + \underbrace{-0.002}_{ShapYoung25} = 0.19$$

Since *CoalNone* (*Coalition: none*) does not consider the impact of any predictor variable and since the prediction from the *Random Forest* model considers all predictor variables, the difference between $PredVac_{LA}$ and *CoalNone* reflects the cumulative contribution from all predictor variables on the prediction. The individual *SHAP values* assign shares of this cumulative contribution to the individual predictor variables.

With this knowledge, we can explain the *SHAP values* in Figure 11.7. However, we will only explain the largest *SHAP values*. This is good practice because *SHAP values* vary depending on which scenarios (predictor variable orderings) are randomly selected by the algorithm. Thus, for small *SHAP values*, a variation in value can lead to a change of sign of the *SHAP* value and, therefore, change the direction of how the related variable impacts the prediction.

Below we interpret the *SHAP values* for *PercRep*, *PercAsians*, and *PercFoodSt* and *PercOld*65:

- The Republican vote (*PercRep*) in *Los Angeles County* is lower than in the nation (see Table 11.1). This leads to a positive *SHAP* value, increasing the vaccination rate by 11.6%.

- The proportion of Asians (*PercAsian*) in *Los Angeles County* is greater than in the nation (see Table 11.1). This leads to a positive *SHAP* value, increasing the vaccination rate by 7.4%.

- The proportion of food stamp recipients (*PercFoodSt*) in *Los Angeles County* is smaller than in the nation (see Table 11.1). This leads to a positive *SHAP* value, increasing the vaccination rate by 1.1%.

- The interpretation of *PercOld*65 is unclear. Los Angeles has about the same proportion of older people as the nation (see Table 11.1). Because of a higher *COVID-19* hospitalization and death risk, we know that older people tend to have a lower vaccination hesitancy.[16] However, in Figure 11.7, the *SHAP* value indicates that the predicted vaccination rate decreased by 1.1%. In addition, the whiskers from the box plot for *PercOld*65[17] in Figure 11.7 overlap positive and negative values, making it difficult to decide in which direction this variable influences the true vaccination rate.

The interpretation of the variables *PercRep*, *PercAsian*, and *PercFoodSt* makes sense because we know that Republican voters are more vaccination hesitant, Asians are less vaccination hesitant, and lower income (i.e., more food stamp recipients) is believed to lead to higher vaccination hesitancy.[18]

Now that you know how to interpret the *SHAP* diagram for *Los Angeles County*, you should look at other U.S. counties.

The interactive application below allows you to choose a continental U.S. County and then display the *SHAP* diagram with the table we used for *Los Angeles County*. This is an excellent exercise to learn how to interpret *SHAP* values and the related diagrams.

---

[16] See Lange and Lange (2022) for details.

[17] The box plot shows the distribution of the *SHAP values* for *PercOld*65 for the randomly selected scenarios. We chose 25 scenarios (B=25).

[18] See Lange and Lange (2022) for more details.

Interactive Section

In this section, you will find content together with *R* code to execute, change, and rerun in RStudio.

The best way to read and to work with this section is to open it with *RStudio*. Then you can interactively work on *R* code exercises and *R* projects within a web browser. This way you can apply what you have learned so far and extend your knowledge. You can also choose to continue reading either in the book or online, but you will not benefit from the interactive learning experience.

To work with this section in *RStudio* in an interactive environment, follow these steps:

1. Ensure that both the `learnR` and the `shiny` package are installed. If not, install them from RStudio's main menu (Tools -> Install Packages ...).

2. Download the `Rmd` file for the interactive session and save it in your `project` folder. You will find the link for the download below.

3. Open the downloaded file in RStudio and click the `Run Document` button, located in the editing window's top-middle area.

For detailed help for running the exercises including videos for Windows and Mac users we refer to: https://blog.lange-analytics.com/2024/01/interactsessions.html

Do not skip this interactive section because besides providing applications of already covered concepts, it will also extend what you have learned so far.

Below is the link to download the interactive section:

https://ai.lange-analytics.com/exc/?file=17-InterpretExerc100.Rmd

To generate a *SHAP* diagram for a continental U.S. county of your choice, you have to proceed in two steps:

Step 1:

The code chunk below helps you to find the *CountyID* for the county you are interested in. You need the *CountyID* for the next step below to create the *SHAP* diagram.

To find the *CountyID*, substitute the ... in the code block below with the name or part of the name of the county you are interested in (do not include the word "county"!):

```
CountySearchStr="..."


######## Do not change code below this line ##################
VecMatchingCountyNames=grep(CountySearchStr, DataCountyInfo$County,
                            ignore.case=TRUE)
VecMatchingFIPS=grep(CountySearchStr, as.character(DataCountyInfo$Fips),
                     ignore.case=TRUE)
```

```
VecMatching=sort(c(VecMatchingCountyNames, VecMatchingFIPS))
unique(DataCountyInfo[VecMatching,])
DataMatchingCounties=DataCountyInfo[VecMatching,]
print(DataMatchingCounties)
```

Step 2:

Here you can create the *SHAP* diagram and the related table with some extra info. All you have to do is substitute the ... in the code block below with the *CountyID* that you got in Step 1 (the number only; no quotes).

Executing the code takes a while (depending on your computer between 1 – 8 minutes). You can change the B= argument (the number of scenarios to be calculated) to a lower value to speed things up, but the trade-off is a lower precision.

After you get the results, take a moment to interpret the *SHAP* values and decide which *SHAP* values should not be interpreted (hint: take the value of the *SHAP* value and the box plot into account).

```
CountyID= ...

set.seed(2021)

SHAPObject=predict_parts(
           explainer=ExplainerRandForest,
           new_observation=DataVax[CountyID,],
           type="shap", B=25)

### Do not change code below this line ##########

CountyPred=round(attr(SHAPObject, "prediction"), 3)
VacRateCoalNone=round(attr(SHAPObject, "intercept"), 3)
TitleShap=paste(substr(DataCountyInfo[[CountyID, 3]], 1, 15),
                "(PredVac=", CountyPred,
                "Coalition: none =", VacRateCoalNone,")")

SHAPObject$label=TitleShap
plot(SHAPObject)

ShapTable=SHAPObject |>
          as_tibble() |>
          filter(B==0) |>
          select(Variable=variable_name, SHAP=contribution,
                 County=variable_value) |>
```

```
      mutate(Nation=c(0.063, 0.136, 0.115, 0.191, 0.173,
                      0.478, 0.310)) |>
      mutate(County=round(as.numeric(County), 3))|>
      mutate(SHAP=round(SHAP, 3))

kable(ShapTable, caption=TitleShap) |>
kable_styling(bootstrap_options=c("striped", "hover"),
              position="center", full_width=T)
```

11.8 Local Interpretable Model-agnostic Explanations (LIME)

LIME (Local Interpretable Model-agnostic Explanations) is, as the name suggests, a local and model-agnostic interpretation algorithm. It was developed in 2016 by Ribeiro et al. (2016).

Because *LIME* is a local interpretation method, the goal is to explain the prediction for a specific observation from a complex model such as *Neural Network* or *Random Forest* model. However, instead of interpreting the complex model directly, *LIME* uses a simpler but interpretable model such as linear *OLS* to interpret the observation of interest.

The underlying assumption is that the complex model (e.g., *Random Forest*) can be approximated by the simpler model (e.g., *OLS*) in the neighborhood of the observation of interest. Neighborhood means, in this context, similar values for the predictor variables as the observation of interest. In short:

LIME uses an interpretable machine learning model (e.g., OLS) to approximate a complex machine learning model in the neighborhood of the observation of interest.

The three steps below will give you an idea how *LIME* accomplishes this task in *R*.[19]

Step 1: Because not enough observations might be available in the neighborhood of the observation of interest, *LIME* creates artificial predictor variable values with similar values as the observation of interest (5,000 observations by default).

For each continuous predictor variable *LIME* analyzes the distribution of

---

[19]The *R* implementation is explained in detail in Hvitfeldt et al. (2022).

the training data using quartile bins.[20] Then, for each continuous predictor variable, random values are generated that match the distribution of the training data. However, only the values that fall in the same quartile bin as the observation of interest are used to create the artificial observations. This ensures that no values are used that differ too much from the observation of interest.

For categorical variables such as *Female*, only the category that coincides with the the the one of the observation of interest (*Female* = 1 in our example) is used when artificial observations are created.

Step 2: Since we want to *explain* the predictions of the complex model (e.g., *Random Forest*) in the neighborhood of the observation of interest, we need to create these predictions with the *Random Forest* model (the complex model) from the artificial observations.

Step 3: Finally, the dataset created in Step 2 is used with *OLS* (or another interpretable model) to analyze the impact of the predictor variables on the predictions from the *Random Forest* (the complex model). The artificial observations are weighted based on their similarity to the observation of interest. Similar observations receive a high weight, while dissimilar observations get a low weight.[21] This ensures that the *OLS* model focuses more on observations closer to the observation of interest.

The result from the *OLS* model provides an estimate of how much each predictor variable value from the observation of interest contributes to the related prediction.

Now, let us see *LIME* in action. We again use the results from the *Random Forest* model to predict wages (the fitted *workflow*; WfModelWageRF) that was introduced in Section 11.4 together with the observation for Helga, which is the observation of interest:

```
print(ObsHelga)
```

```
## # A tibble: 1 x 5
##     Wage  Educ Tenure Female .pred
##    <dbl> <dbl>  <dbl>  <fct> <dbl>
## 1   8.9    17     18      1  9.24
```

In the code block below, the lime() command creates an *explainer* object, which only includes the *Random Forest* model (extracted from the fitted

---

[20] Quartiles are the default, but other quantiles can be set with the n_bins= argument in the lime() command.

[21] To measure the similarity a metric akin to *Euclidean Distance* is used (see Section 4.5.1 for *Euclidean Distance*). By default, *LIME* uses *Gower Distance*, which, compared to *Euclidean Distance*, provides a better measure of dissimilarity between data points with mixed types of predictor variables.

workflow model by `extract_fit_engine()`), the training data, and statistics calculated from the training data.

```
library(lime)
set.seed(777)
ExplainerLime=lime(DataTrainPredOnly,
                model=extract_fit_engine(WfModelWageRF))
```

Again, the *explainer* object `ExplainerLime` is only a container that contains the prediction model together with statistics about the training data.

In the code block below this *explainer* object is entered as an argument into the `lime::explain()` command which executes the *LIME* interpretation.[22]

```
library(lime)
set.seed(777)
ObsHelgaPredOnly=select(ObsHelga, Educ,Tenure,Female)
LimeResults=lime::explain(ObsHelgaPredOnly, explainer=ExplainerLime,
                    n_features=3)
```

Note that before executing `lime::explain()`, we used `select()` to create a data frame that exclusively contains the predictor variables. This is needed because the `lime::explain()` command expects that type of data frame. We also set the argument `n_features=3` because we want to consider all three predictor variables. For an analysis with many predictor variables, using only a subset of predictors is reasonable.

The *OLS* prediction results are saved in the *R* object `LimeResults`. To visualize the results in Figure 11.8 we use:

```
plot_features(LimeResults)
```

The bar diagram in Figure 11.8 shows the results of the *LIME* analysis. Each bar quantifies the contribution from Helga's predictor variable values $Educ = 17$, $Tenure = 18$, and $Female = 1$ to the predicted wage from the linear *OLS* model. The latter can be retrieved from the *LIME* object:

```
cat("Helga's predicted wage from the OLS model is:",
    round(LimeResults$model_prediction[1],2))
```

```
## Helga's predicted wage from the OLS model is: 7.82
```

---

[22]We prefixed the `explain()` command with `lime::` to determine that we would like to use the `explain()` command from the `lime` package and not from another package such as the `tidyverse` package or the `DALEX` package.

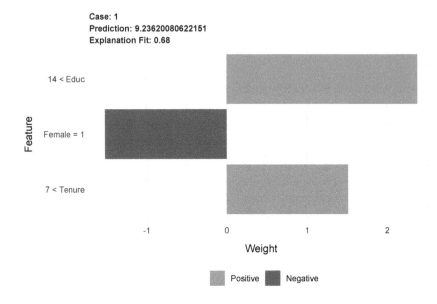

FIGURE 11.8 LIME Results for Observation Helga from the Wage Model

In the upper-left corner of the *LIME* plot in Figure 11.8, you find the r^2 for the linear *OLS* model ($r^2 = 0.68$) and the predicted wage for Helga from the original *Random Forest* model ($.pred = 9.24$).

The bars in the diagram of Figure 11.8, together with the vertical axis labels, can be interpreted as follows:

- The fact that Helga has a high education ($Educ = 17$) puts her in the upper quartile ($Educ > 14$), and it contributes about \$2.50 (exact value is 2.38) to her predicted wage.

- The fact that Helga has a high tenure ($Tenure = 18$) puts her in the upper quartile ($Tenure > 7$), and it contributes \$1.50 (exact value is 1.51) to her predicted wage.

- The fact that Helga is female, deducts about \$1.50 (exact value is 1.53) from her predicted wage.

If we retrieve the intercept from the linear *OLS* prediction from the *LIME* object

```
cat("The Intercept from the linear OLS model is:",
    LimeResults$model_intercept)
```

```
## The Intercept from the linear OLS model is: 5.463 5.463 5.463
```

we can show that the *Intercept*, together with the quantitative impacts from Helga's predictor variables values, add up to the prediction of the linear *OLS* model (*.predOLS*):

$$\underbrace{5.46}_{Intercept} \; + \; \underbrace{2.38}_{ContrEduc} \; + \; \underbrace{1.51}_{ContrTenure} \; + \; \underbrace{-1.53}_{ContrFem} \; = \; \underbrace{7.82}_{.predOLS}$$

11.9 When and When Not to Use Interpretation

We should always use interpretation algorithms to better understand why our model predicts certain outcomes and quantify the impact of individual and cumulative predictions. It is also a good practice to use various interpretation methodologies together to check if the results are similar.

For choosing an appropriate interpretation methodology, it is important to consider which type of questions we can answer with which methodology. Below is a list that gives some pointers:[23]

- Ceteris Paribus Plots:
    - Can be used to quantify the impact of variable change for a specific observation.
    - *Model-agnostic* and *local*.
- Partial Dependence Plots:
    - Can be used to quantify the impact of variable change for a complete model, but they are not specific to individual observations.
    - *Model-agnostic* and *global*.
- Variable Importance Plots (VIP)
    - Analyze the importance of variables but not the quantitative impact on the predictions.
    - *VIPs* are well suited for deciding which predictor variables should stay in a model and which ones should be dropped.
    - *Model-specific* (*model-agnostic* versions also exist) and *local*.
- SHAP Values
    - Quantify the impact of predictor variable values on a specific prediction.
    - *Model-agnostic* and *global*.
- LIME:

---

[23]See Molnar (2020) for a detailed overview of interpretation methodologies.

- Uses an interpretation proxy model like linear *OLS* to quantify the impact of predictor variable values on a specific prediction.
- Can be used together with *SHAP values* to verify if the results from both methodologies match.
- Can be used as an alternative method to *SHAP values* when estimating *SHAP values* is computationally too expensive.
- *Model-agnostic* and *local*.

11.10   Digital Resources

Below you will find a few digital resources related to this chapter such as:

- Videos
- Short articles
- Tutorials
- *R* scripts

These resources are recommended if you would like to review the chapter from a different angle or to go beyond what was covered in the chapter.

Here we show only a few of the digital resourses. At the end of the list you will find a link to additonal digital resources for this chapter that are maintained on the Internet.

You can find a complete list of digital resources for all book chapters on the companion website: https://ai.lange-analytics.com/digitalresources.html

The Ultimate Guide to PDPs and ICE Plots

A comprehensive tutorial by Conor O'Sullivan in Towards Data Science. It describes the intuition and maths behind *Partial Dependence Plots (PDP)* and Individual Conditional Expectation (ICE) plots.

Link: https://ai.lange-analytics.com/dr?a=432

Machine Learning Made Simple: Permutation Based Feature Importance

A YouTube video by Davnsh Senthi. In the video, he explains the underlying idea of *Permutation Based Feature Importance* with an example step by step.

Link: https://ai.lange-analytics.com/dr?a=435

How to Create Your Own SHAP Algorithm in R

This blog post from the AI blog of Carsten Lange shows how you can create a simplified *SHAP* value approximation in *R*.

The post explains the code, talks about drawbacks, and provides alternatives that are available as *R* packages. The related *R* script is also provided.

Link: https://ai.lange-analytics.com/dr?a=412

LIME: Explain Machine Learning Predictions: Intuition and Geometrical Interpretation

An article in *T*owards Data Science by Giorgio Visani. The article explains visually and intuitively how *LIME* works.

Link: https://ai.lange-analytics.com/dr?a=434

More Digital Resources

Only a subset of digital resources is listed in this section. The link below points to additional, concurrently updated resources for this chapter.

Link: https://ai.lange-analytics.com/dr/interpret.html

12

Concluding Remarks

I hope the previous chapters gave you a basic but sound foundation about how to use machine learning models for research or applications in your industry. Especially, I hope that the book sparked your interest in exploring machine learning further.

This leads to the question, where to go next? What is a good strategy to further extend your machine learning knowledge? There are many answers to this question. We will focus on six strategies:

1) Extend your knowledge about the mathematical foundations of machine learning models. One of the standard machine learning books that gives you a sound mathematical introduction is *Introduction to Statistical Learning* by James et al. (2023).

2) Extend your machine learning toolkit. We used the `tidymodels` package as a toolkit in the previous chapters of this book. The `tidymodels` package offers two distinctive strengths: i) It standardizes the data and modeling *workflow*, and ii) it provides many strong machine learning tools. We focused on the standardization aspect of machine learning that `tidymodels` provides. If you would like to take advantage of the analytical strength of `tidymodels`, then *Tidy Modeling with R* by Kuhn and Silge (2022) is the right place to start your journey.

3) Apply machine learning directly to your field of research or a use case in your industry, such as finance or marketing. For the latter fields, we recommend *Tidy Finance with R* by Voigt et al. (2023) and *Hands-On Data Science for Marketing* by Hwang (2019), respectively.

4) At some point in time, you might need to review topics from this book. The best way to find a topic you are interested in is to go to the *Learning Outcomes* section of the related chapter. There, you can review the learning outcomes and then go to the section(s) you would like to read again.

5) Take online classes. Although this can be expensive in some cases, free or less costly high-quality options are also available. For

example, *EdX* provides excellent online courses authored by faculty from Harvard, UC San Diego, and other top universities. One course we especially recommend is Machine Learning Fundamentals[1]. It introduces machine learning in a more formal way than this book, but the course is still intuitive. *EdX* courses are free as long as you do not require a certificate.

Another good source for online courses is *DataCamp*. The *DataCamp* learning platform provides a wide range of data science and *AI* online courses with readings, videos, and exercises. Some courses are free, and the first chapters of all other courses are free to read. This way you can find out if *DataCamp* is for you and if you want to subscribe for $25/month.

6) Extend your machine learning skills with a more random strategy. As you know from machine learning (see *Bootstrapping* in Chapter 10), *randomization* can be a solid tool to reach a goal.

For a more random learning strategy, signing up to *Medium*[2] might be a good option. Depending on your preferences and reading history, you get a daily email with recommendations for articles to read. If you think that you do not have the time, you could read in the evening in bed, and this way, carve the needed time out of your busy schedule.

Read the articles without pressure but with enjoyment. If you are tired after a few pages, stop reading and sleep. Otherwise, read the complete article and sleep a little later. In any case, you win either by falling asleep smoothly or improving your skills. Signing up to *Medium* is free, and many articles are free to read. In addition, you can read up to three "members only" articles for free. If you would like to read more, you can consider a subscription for $50/year.

Whatever strategy you use to extend your knowledge in machine learning, I wish you an enjoyable journey.

Happy Analytics!

---

[1]https://www.edx.org/learn/machine-learning/the-university-of-california-san-diego-machine-learning-fundamentals
[2]https://medium.com/

Bibliography

Aden-Buie, G., Schloerke, B., and Allaire, J. (2022). *Learnr: Interactive Tutorials for R*. R package version 0.11.2.

Asaithambi, S. (2017). Why, how and when to scale your features. *GreyAtom*. https://medium.com/greyatom/why-how-and-when-to-scale-your-features-4b30ab09db5e (last accessed: 12/14/2023).

Bank of England (2022). Bank of England inflation calculator. *Online*. https://www.bankofengland.co.uk/monetary-policy/inflation/inflation-calculator (last accessed: 12/14/2023).

Beck, M. W. (2018). NeuralNetTools: Visualization and analysis tools for neural networks. *Journal of Statistical Software*, 85(11):1–20.

Biecek, P. (2018). Dalex: Explainers for complex predictive models in R. *Journal of Machine Learning Research*, 19(84):1–5.

Centers for Disease Control and Prevention (CDC) (2021a). COVID-19 vaccinations in the United States, county. *Online*. https://data.cdc.gov/Vaccinations/COVID-19-Vaccinations-in-the-United-States-County/8xkx-amqh/data.

Centers for Disease Control and Prevention (CDC) (2021b). Vaccine hesitancy for COVID-19: County and local estimate. *Online*. https://data.cdc.gov/Vaccinations/Vaccine-Hesitancy-for-COVID-19-County-and-local-es/q9mh-h2tw.

Chan, C.-H., Chan, G. C., Leeper, T. J., and Becker, J. (2021). *Rio: A Swiss-Army Knife for Data File I/o*. R package version 0.5.29.

Chang, W., Cheng, J., Allaire, J., Sievert, C., Schloerke, B., Xie, Y., Allen, J., McPherson, J., Dipert, A., and Borges, B. (2022). *Shiny: Web Application Framework for R*. R package version 1.7.4.

Chawla, N. V., Bowyer, K. W., Hall, L. O., and Kegelmeyer, W. P. (2002). SMOTE: Synthetic minority over-sampling technique. *Journal of Artificial Intelligence Research*, 16.

Chen, T. and Guestrin, C. (2016). XGBoost a scalable tree boosting system. In Krishnapuram, B., editor, *Proceedings of the 22nd ACM SIGKDD International Conference on Knowledge Discovery and Data Mining*, pages 321–357.

ACM, New York, NY. https://api.semanticscholar.org/CorpusID:4650265 (last accessed: 12/28/2023).

Chen, T., He, T., Benesty, M., Khotilovich, V., Tang, Y., Cho, H., Chen, K., Mitchell, R., Cano, I., Zhou, T., Li, M., Xie, J., Lin, M., Geng, Y., Li, Y., and Yuan, J. (2023). *XGBoost: Extreme Gradient Boosting*. R package version 1.7.5.1.

Corporation, M. and Weston, S. (2022). *Doparallel: Foreach Parallel Adaptor for the 'parallel' Package*. R package version 1.0.17.

Cortez, P., Cerdeira, A., Almeida, F., Matos, T., and Reis, J. (2009). Modeling wine preferences by data mining from physicochemical properties. *Decision Support Systems*, 47(4):547–553.

Delgado, F. (2022). A beginner's guide to CatBoost with Python. *MLearning.ai*. https://medium.com/mlearning-ai/a-beginners-guide-to-catboost-with-python-763d7e7ac199 (last accessed: 12/28/2023).

Delua, J. (2021). Supervised vs. unsupervised learning: What's the difference? *IBM Blog*. https://www.ibm.com/cloud/blog/supervised-vs-unsupervised-learning (last accessed: 12/28/2023).

Esri (Environmental Systems Research Institute) (2023). Geoenrichment. *Online*. https://www.esri.com/en-us/arcgis/products/location-services/services/geoenrichment (last accessed: 12/28/2023).

Federal Reserve Bank of St. Louis (2023). Economic research resources. *Online*. https://fred.stlouisfed.org/ (last accessed: 12/28/2023).

Firke, S. (2023). *Janitor: Simple Tools for Examining and Cleaning Dirty Data*. R package version 2.2.0.

Freund, Y. and Schapire, R. E. (1996). Experiments with a new boosting algorithm. In *Proceedings of the Thirteenth International Conference on International Conference on Machine Learning*, ICML'96, pages 148–156, San Francisco, CA, USA. Morgan Kaufmann Publishers Inc.

Friedman, J., Tibshirani, R., and Hastie, T. (2010). Regularization paths for generalized linear models via coordinate descent. *Journal of Statistical Software*, 33(1):1–22.

Galton, F. (1907). Vox populi. *Nature*, 75(1949):450–451.

Greenwell, B. M. and Boehmke, B. C. (2020). Variable importance plots—an introduction to the vip package. *The R Journal*, 12(1):343–366.

Gujarati, D. and Porter, D. (2009). *Basic Econometrics*. Economics series. McGraw-Hill, New York, NY.

Hanck, C., Arnoldand, M., Gerber, A., and Schmelzer, M. (2023). *Introduction to Econometrics with R*. Online. https://www.econometrics-with-r.org/index.html (last accessed: 12/28/2023).

Haykin, S. (1999). *Neural Networks*. Prentice Hall, Upper Saddle River, NJ.

Hechenbichler, K. and Schliep, K. (2004). Weighted k-Nearest-Neighbor techniques and ordinal classification. Technical report, Institut für Statistik, Ludwig-Maximilians-Universität München. https://epub.ub.uni-muenchen.de/1769/1/paper_399.pdf (last accessed: 12/28/2023).

Hendricks, P. (2015). *Titanic: Titanic Passenger Survival Data Set*. R package version 0.1.0.

Hennig, C. M., Murtagh, F., and Rocci, R. (2016). *Handbook of Cluster Analysis*. Chapman and Hall/CRC, Boca Raton, FL.

History.com (2023). Titanic. *Online*. https://www.history.com/topics/early-20th-century-us/titanic (last accessed: 12/28/2023).

Hornik, K., Stinchcombe, M., and White, H. (1989). Multilayer feedforward networks are universal approximators. *Neural Networks*, 2(5):359–366.

Hvitfeldt, E. (2023). *Themis: Extra Recipes Steps for Dealing with Unbalanced Data*. R package version 1.0.2.

Hvitfeldt, E., Pedersen, T. L., and Benesty, M. (2022). *Lime: Local Interpretable Model-Agnostic Explanations. Vignette: Understanding Lime*. R package version 0.5.3.

Hwang, Y. H. (2019). *Hands-On Data Science for Marketing*. Packt, Birmingham, United Kingdom.

IBM (2021). Telco customer churn. *Online*. https://www.ibm.com/docs/en/cognos-analytics/12.0.0?topic=samples-telco-customer-churn (last accessed: 12/28/2023).

James, G., Witten, D., Hastie, T., Tibshirani, R., and Taylor, J. (2023). *An Introduction to Statistical Learning*. Springer, New York, NY.

Jensen, J. D., Thurman, J., and Vincent, A. L. (2021). *Lightning Injuries*. Statpearls, Treasure Island, FL. https://www.ncbi.nlm.nih.gov/books/NBK441920 (last accessed: 12/28/2023).

Kaggle (2015). House sales in King County, USA. *Online*. https://www.kaggle.com/datasets/harlfoxem/housesalesprediction (last accessed: 12/28/2023).

Kaggle (2018). Telco customer churn. *Online*. https://www.kaggle.com/datasets/blastchar/telco-customer-churn (last accessed: 12/28/2023).

Kuhn, M. (2008). Building predictive models in R using the caret package. *Journal of Statistical Software*, 28(5):1–26.

Kuhn, M. and Falbel, D. (2022). *Brulee: High-Level Modeling Functions with 'torch'.* R package version 0.2.0.

Kuhn, M. and Silge, J. (2022). *Tidy Modeling with R. A Framework for Modeling in the Tidyverse.* O'Reilly, Sebastopol, CA.

Kuhn, M. and Wickham, H. (2020). *Tidymodels: A Collection of Packages for Modeling and Machine Learning Using Tidyverse Principles.* R package version 1.1.1.

Kurama, V. (2018). A guide to AdaBoost: Boosting to save the day. *Paperspace Blog, Series: Ensemble Methods.* https://blog.paperspace.com/adaboost-optimizer/ (last accessed: 12/28/2023).

Lange, C. (2003). *Neuronale Netze in der Wirtschaftswissenschaftlichen Prognose und Modellgenerierung (Neural Networks in Economic Modeling).* Physica, Heidelberg, Germany.

Lange, C. and Lange, J. (2022). Applying machine learning and AI explanations to analyze vaccine hesitancy. *arXiv.* https://arxiv.org/pdf/2201.05070.pdf (last accessed: 12/28/2023).

LeCun, Y., Cortes, C., and Burges, C. J. C. (2005). The MNIST database of handwritten digits. *Online.* http://yann.lecun.com/exdb/mnist/ (last accessed: 12/28/2023).

Lundberg, S. and Lee, S.-I. (2017). A unified approach to interpreting model predictions. *arXiv.* https://arxiv.org/abs/1705.07874 (last accessed: 12/28/2023).

Lundberg, S. M., Erion, G. G., and Lee, S.-I. (2019). Consistent individualized feature attribution for tree ensembles. *arXiv.* https://arxiv.org/abs/1802.03888 (last accessed: 12/28/2023).

Lyer, V. (2021). Behold: The confusion matrix. not a confusing matrix anymore. *Medium.* https://vijayasriiyer.medium.com/behold-the-confusion-matrix-10afd3feb603 (last accessed: 12/28/2023).

Maksymiuk, S., Gosiewska, A., and Biecek, P. (2020). Landscape of R packages for explainable artificial intelligence. *arXiv.* https://arxiv.org/abs/2009.13248 (last accessed: 12/28/2023).

Manassa, I. (2021). Mathematics behind gradient descent. *Geek Culture.* https://medium.com/geekculture/mathematics-behind-gradient-descent-f2a49a0b714f (last accessed: 12/28/2023).

McCulloch, W. S. and Pitts, W. (1943). A logical calculus of the ideas immanent in nervous activity. *The Bulletin of Mathematical Biophysics*, 5(4):115–133.

McDonald, J. F. and Moffitt, R. A. (1980). The uses of tobit analysis. *The Review of Economics and Statistics*, 62(2):318.

Milborrow, S. (2022). *Rpart.plot: Plot 'rpart' Models: An Enhanced Version of 'plot.rpart'*. R package version 3.1.1.

Mohajon, J. (2020). Confusion matrix for your multi-class machine learning model. *Towards Data Science*. https://towardsdatascience.com/confusion-matrix-for-your-multi-class-machine-learning-model-ff9aa3bf7826 (last accessed: 12/28/2023).

Molnar, C. (2020). *Interpretable Machine Learning. A Guide for Making Black Box Models Explainable*. Independently published, second edition. https://christophm.github.io/interpretable-ml-book/ (last accessed: 12/28/2023).

Morde, V. (2019). XGBoost algorithm: Long may she reign! *Towards Data Science*. https://towardsdatascience.com/https-medium-com-vishalmorde-xgboost-algorithm-long-she-may-rein-edd9f99be63d (last accessed: 12/28/2023).

Narula, S. C. (1979). Orthogonal polynomial regression. *International Statistical Review/Revue Internationale de Statistique*, 47(1):31–36.

O'Sullivan, C. (2022a). From Shapley to SHAP — understanding the math. *Towards Data Science*. https://towardsdatascience.com/from-shapley-to-shap-understanding-the-math-e7155414213b (last accessed: 12/28/2023).

O'Sullivan, C. (2022b). KernelSHAP vs TreeSHAP. *Towards Data Science*. https://towardsdatascience.com/kernelshap-vs-treeshap-e00f3b3a27db (last accessed: 12/28/2023).

Park, A. et al. (2021). Presidential precinct data for the 2020 general election. *New York Times*. https://github.com/TheUpshot/presidential-precinct-map-2020 (last accessed: 12/28/2023).

Pramoditha, R. (2021). Can LightGBM outperform XGBoost? Boosting algorithms in machine learning — Part 5. *Towards Data Science*. https://towardsdatascience.com/can-lightgbm-outperform-xgboost-d05a94102a55 (last accessed: 12/28/2023).

R Core Team (2022). *R: A Language and Environment for Statistical Computing*. R Foundation for Statistical Computing, Vienna, Austria.

Ribeiro, M. T., Singh, S., and Guestrin, C. (2016). "Why Should I Trust You?": Explaining the predictions of any classifier. *arXiv*. https://arxiv.org/abs/1602.04938 (last accessed: 12/28/2023).

RStudio Team (2022). *RStudio: Integrated Development Environment for R*. RStudio, Inc., Boston, MA.

Sanchez, G. (2021). *Handling Strings with R*. Leanpub, Victoria, Canada.

Schliep, K. and Hechenbichler, K. (2016). *Kknn: Weighted K-Nearest Neighbors*. R package version 1.3.1.

Shapley, L. S. (1953). A value for n-person games. In *Contributions to the Theory of Games (AM-28), Volume II*, pages 307–318. Princeton University Press, Princeton, NJ.

Sharma, A. (2020). 4 simple ways to split a decision tree in machine learning. *Analytics Vidhya*. https://www.analyticsvidhya.com/blog/2020/06/4-ways-split-decision-tree/ (last accessed: 12/28/2023).

Shea, J. M. (2023). *Wooldridge: 115 Data Sets from "Introductory Econometrics: A Modern Approach, 7e" by Jeffrey M. Wooldridge*. R package version 1.4.3.

Singh, H. (2021). How to select best split in decision trees using Gini impurity. *Analytics Vidhye*. https://www.analyticsvidhya.com/blog/2021/03/how-to-select-best-split-in-decision-trees-gini-impurity (last accessed: 12/28/2023).

Tay, J. K., Narasimhan, B., and Hastie, T. (2023). Elastic Net regularization paths for all generalized linear models. *Journal of Statistical Software*, 106(1):1–31.

Therneau, T. and Atkinson, B. (2022). *Rpart: Recursive Partitioning and Regression Trees*. R package version 4.1.19.

Vaughan, D. (2022). Multiclass averaging. *Online*. https://yardstick.tidymodels.org/articles/multiclass.html (last accessed: 12/28/2023).

Venables, W. N. and Ripley, B. D. (2002). *Modern Applied Statistics with S*. Springer, New York, NY, fourth edition.

Verhulst, P.-F. (1845). Recherches Mathématiques Sur La Loi D'accroissement De La Population. 18:2013–2015.

Voigt, S., Weiss, P., and Scheuch, C. (2023). *Tidy Finance with R*. Chapman and Hall/CRC, Boca Raton, FL.

Wang, C.-F. (2019). The vanishing gradient problem. its causes, its significance, and its solutions. *Towards Data Science*. https://towardsdatascience.com/the-vanishing-gradient-problem-69bf08b15484 (last accessed: 12/28/2023).

Wickham, H. (2016). *Ggplot2: Elegant Graphics for Data Analysis*. Springer, New York, NY.

Wickham, H. (2019). *Advanced R*. Chapman and Hall/CRC, Boca Raton, FL.

Wickham, H., Averick, M., Bryan, J., Chang, W., McGowan, L. D., Francois, R., Grolemund, G., Hayes, A., Henry, L., Hester, J., Kuhn, M., Pedersen,

T. L., Miller, E., Bache, S. M., Müller, K., Ooms, J., Robinson, D., Seidel, D. P., Spinu, V., Takahashi, K., Vaughan, D., Wilke, C., Woo, K., and Yutani, H. (2019). Welcome to the tidyverse. *Journal of Open Source Software*, 4(43):1686.

Wickham, H. and Grolemund, G. (2017). *R for Data Science: Import, Tidy, Transform, Visualize, and Model Data*. O'Reilly, Sebastopol, CA.

Wikipedia contributors (2023a). Camel case. *Wikipedia, the Free Encyclopedia*. https://en.wikipedia.org/w/index.php?title=Camel_case&oldid=1188598129 (last accessed: 12/28/2023).

Wikipedia contributors (2023b). Diversity index. *Wikipedia, the Free Encyclopedia*. https://en.wikipedia.org/w/index.php?title=Diversity_index&oldid=1189901595 (last accessed: 12/28/2023).

Wikipedia contributors (2023c). Feature scaling. *Wikipedia, the Free Encyclopedia*. https://en.wikipedia.org/w/index.php?title=Feature_scaling&oldid=1191906790 (last accessed: 12/28/2023).

Wikipedia contributors (2023d). Sigmoid function. *Wikipedia, the Free Encyclopedia*. https://en.wikipedia.org/w/index.php?title=Sigmoid_function&oldid=1187110185 (last accessed: 12/28/2023).

Wong, K. J. (2023). 6 types of clustering methods — an overview. *Towards Data Science*. https://towardsdatascience.com/6-types-of-clustering-methods-an-overview-7522dba026ca (last accessed: 12/28/2023).

Wooldridge, J. M. (2020). *Introductory Econometrics: A Modern Approach*. Cengage Learning, Boston, MA, seventh edition.

Wright, M. N. and Ziegler, A. (2017). ranger: A fast implementation of random forests for high dimensional data in C++ and R. *Journal of Statistical Software*, 77(1):1–17.

Yıldırım, S. (2020). Gradient Boosted Decision Trees-Explained. *Towards Data Science*. https://towardsdatascience.com/gradient-boosted-decision-trees-explained-9259bd8205af (last accessed: 12/28/2023).

Zhu, H. (2021). *kableExtra: Construct Complex Table with 'kable' and Pipe Syntax*. R package version 1.3.4.

Index

Milton Keynes UK
Ingram Content Group UK Ltd.
UKHW051535141024
449569UK00001B/39

9 781032 434056